Presented pursuant to the GRA Act 2000 c.20, s.6

CW00734728

Ministry of Defence
Annual Report and Accounts

including the Annual Performance Report and
Consolidated Departmental Resource Accounts

2006-07

(For the year ended 31 March 2007)

Laid in accordance with the Government Resources and Accounts Act 2000

Ordered by the House of Commons to be printed
23 July 2007

London: The Stationery Office
HC 697

23 July 2007
£40.00

Introduction

i. The Ministry of Defence's Annual Report and Accounts is a comprehensive overview of Defence and how the Department has used the resources authorised by Parliament from April 2006 to March 2007. It has two main sections: the first comprises the Department's Annual performance Report for 2006-07, including performance against our Public Service Agreement (PSA) targets. The second comprises the Departmental Resource Accounts for 2006-07. There are also a number of Annexes containing background information on the Department, its organisation and administration. Further information is published in parallel on the Department's website at www.mod.uk.

Section One: Annual Performance Report

ii. Since 2000 the Defence Management Board has used a Balanced Scorecard to assist in the assessment, reporting and management of Defence performance. The scorecard for 2006-07 (Figure 10 at Annex D) encapsulates the Government's key objectives as set out in the Department's Public Service Agreement and the Board's wider supporting objectives and priorities, as set out in the *Departmental Plan 2005-2009*. A more detailed explanation of how the Defence Balanced Scorecard works is at Annex D. The Annual Performance Report is set out on the same basis as the Departmental Plan, with four main sections on Purpose, Future Capabilities, Enabling Processes and Resources, and it reports performance against the targets set out therein. Each section contains separate chapters on the individual high level scorecard objectives, supplemented by an essay providing additional background on some relevant aspect of Defence business during the year. At the highest level the Ministry of Defence's objectives are set out in the Public Service Agreement. The Annual Performance Report therefore starts with a summary of performance as of 31 March 2007 against the targets set in the 2004 Spending Review, including the separate Efficiency Target. Supporting detail is provided throughout the report. A full description of these targets and the way in which performance against them is measured, together with quarterly performance reports, can be found on the MoD website at www.mod.uk.

Section Two: Departmental Resource Accounts 2006-07

iii. The Department is required to prepare resource accounts for each financial year detailing the resources acquired, held, or disposed of during the year and the way in which it has used them. The Resource Accounts are prepared on an accruals basis in accordance with Treasury guidelines. They must give a true and fair view of the state of affairs of the Department, the net resource outturn, resources applied to objectives, recognised gains and losses, and cash flows for the financial year. The Accounts are audited by the Comptroller and Auditor General supported by the national Audit Office to ensure that they are true and fair and that they have been properly prepared. The Departmental Resource Accounts for 2006-07 together with the Comptroller and Auditor General's certification comprise Section Two of the Annual Report and Accounts.

Further Information

iv. The Annexes to the Annual Report and Accounts contain background information, mainly in regard to the administration of the Ministry of Defence. These include information on accounting to Parliament; the higher organisation of the Department; detailed conflict prevention assessments; a description of the Department's performance management system; summary performance of Defence Agencies, Trading Funds and Non Departmental Public Bodies; performance against Government standards for efficient administration; and a summary of the major Defence equipment projects and international collaborative activity. Further information, including the Department's annual Corporate Governance report and the annual report on the work of the Defence Audit Committee are published in parallel on the MoD website and www.mod.uk. Other sources of more detailed information on specific aspects of defence performance and activity are identified throughout the report at the end of every chapter.

Contents

Ministerial Responsibilities

Secretary of State for Defence Rt. Hon. Des Browne MP

The Right Honourable Des Browne MP was appointed Secretary of State for Defence on the 6th May 2006. The Secretary of State for Defence is the Cabinet Minister charged with making and executing Defence policy and with providing the means by which it is executed, the Armed Forces. As Chairman of the Defence Council and of its three Service Boards (the Admiralty Board, the Army Board and the Air Force Board) he is responsible for the command, administration and discipline of the Armed Forces on behalf of the Crown. Although ultimately responsible for all elements of defence, The Secretary of State is supported by three subordinate Ministers: The Minister of State for the Armed Forces, the Minister of State for Defence Equipment and Support and the Under-Secretary of State for Defence and Minister for Veterans. The Secretary of State assigns responsibility to them for specific aspects of the Armed Forces and the Ministry of Defence's business but retains specific responsibility for: policy, (including nuclear issues and European defence); operations; personnel; finance and efficiency; oversight of major acquisition decisions and Defence industrial issues; and media and communications.

Minister of State for the Armed Forces Rt. Hon. Bob Ainsworth MP

Responsibilities

Defence policy and planning, including:
- Arms control and disarmament; export licensing
- International organisations
- US visiting forces
- Size and shape of the Armed Forces
- Intelligence and security, including counter terrorism
- Defence diplomacy

Operations, including:
- Overseas commitments and garrisons
- Northern Ireland
- Military Aid to the Civil Authorities
- Nuclear accident response
- Military assistance overseas

The Armed Forces (Regular and Reserves), including:
- Readiness
- Sustainability
- Personnel issues
- Performance
- Training
- Reputation
- Inquiries, Boards of inquiry, Inquest

Regional issues and the Devolved Administration

Defence Estates Committee

Defence Equipment and Support business in the House of Commons

Minister of State for Defence Equipment and Support Lord Drayson

Responsibilities

Defence Equipment Programme and through life Defence logistics support, including:
- ABRO
- Defence Aviation Repair Agency (DARA)

Defence Industrial Strategy

Defence science and technology, including:
- Defence Science and Technology Laboratory (Dstl)
- QinetiQ
- Commercial policy throughout the Department

Defence exports

International aspects of defence equipment and support

Defence business in the House of Lords

Under-Secretary of State for Defence and Minister for Veterans Derek Twigg MP

Responsibilities

Service personnel issues, including:
- Recruitment, basic training, and education
- Pay
- Equal opportunities
- Service families and Service Children's Education
- Defence Medical Services
- Cadets
- Compensation and claims casework

Veterans affairs, including:
- Legacy veterans' health issues
- War graves
- Medals and memorials
- Commemorative events
- Prisoners of War

Defence estates, including:
- Defence estate acquisition and disposal
- Service housing
- Heritage and Historic buildings

Other issues, including:
- United Kingdom Hydrographic Office (UKHO)
- Met Office
- Non-Departmental Public Bodies
- MoD Police
- Health and safety
- Low flying
- Civilian personnel policy and casework
- Visits by Peers and MPs/Armed Forces Parliamentary Scheme

Foreword
by the Secretary of State

Defending the UK and its interests is a huge responsibility. In today's inter-dependent world it means helping to bring peace and stability to many countries across the world. Increasingly, our security is tied up with the security of others.

The success of that effort is down to the men and women who make defence happen. I have the utmost respect for the men and women of our Armed Forces, both Regular and Reservist, who have risen to these challenges so magnificently over the past year. I also acknowledge the vital work done by the many civilians who support them.

I have been pleased to oversee the introduction of better support and welfare packages, which go some way to demonstrate the Government's gratitude to our Armed Forces. In the last twelve months we have introduced a number of new measures including: an enhanced operational welfare package, a dedicated Service Life Insurance Scheme, an above inflation pay rise and an operational tax free bonus. Accommodation is a key priority. Whilst much of it is of a good standard, the legacy of having a previously neglected estate means that bringing it all up to standard is going to take time. Last year we spent £700M on housing and accommodation and we expect to spend £5Bn in the next decade. The result will be vastly improved accommodation for all Service families and personnel.

Operational tempo continues to be high and our forces are fighting difficult and dangerous campaigns in Iraq and Afghanistan. Campaigns in which lives have been lost and many personnel have been wounded. These operations represent a huge commitment for our personnel and their families. The entire nation is in your debt.

Our forces in Afghanistan take a leading role as part of an international effort to support the democratically elected Afghan Government. We are working in partnership with the Foreign and Commonwealth Office and the Department for International Development to bring sustainable security, governance and reconstruction to that country. We are making progress on all three objectives.

The situation in Iraq remains difficult. We are determined to support Iraq in its drive to be able to govern itself as a democratic country with a functioning economy and capable security forces.

Right Honourable Des Browne MP
Secretary of State for Defence

Our aim is to develop the capacity of the Iraqi security Forces as part of that self-determination process. We have continued to make good progress in the crucial task of building up the Iraqi Security Forces, enabling us to reduce our force levels. Concentrating our forces on fewer bases will allow more of them to drive forward the crucial task of building up the Iraqi Security Forces. We remain committed to Iraq for as long as Iraq needs us.

The pace of both operations makes it more important than ever that our forces have the equipment they need when they need it and at the right price for the taxpayer. The Defence Industrial Strategy is now firmly embedded in our equipment programme and continues to transform our relationships with industry. The principles set out in that Strategy underpin the new Defence Equipment and Support organisation. Defence Equipment and Support was launched in April 2007 taking responsibility for every stage in the life of our equipment – boosting efficiency, reducing costs and speeding up the acquisition process.

Defence does not stand still. We are a dynamic and complex organisation meeting the security challenges of today whilst preparing for an uncertain future. We will achieve this through our people, the world class men and women who serve this country so well.

Preface

This has been a very busy year for Defence. Overseas the Armed Forces continued successfully to prosecute operations in the Balkans, Iraq and Afghanistan in support of wider international efforts to bring peace and security to those regions. Not for decades have they sustained over such an extended period an operational tempo matching the current scale and intensity. At home, at the same time as sustaining and supporting these operations, the Department continued to make progress with a series of major initiatives to improve the way we work, particularly in but by no means confined to acquisition and support. This includes a continuing programme of major organisational change.

This report sets out in detail what we are doing and how we are doing it, with a short top level summary and report against our Public Service Agreement targets at the front. We continued broadly to meet these targets, albeit with some risk. In particular we have continued to achieve our highest priority: success on operations. We have only been able to do this by taking risk against other, lower priority goals. In particular the need to continue to operate above the overall level of concurrent operations which the Armed Forces are structured and resourced to sustain over the long term has constrained their ability to prepare for the full range of operations envisaged in security and defence planning.

But there has been visible progress and there are several respects in which demands are easing. Force levels in Northern Ireland have now effectively reduced to those comparable to any other part of the United Kingdom for the first time since 1969. We have been able to withdraw UK combat forces from the Balkans, where they were first deployed in 1992. Of the four provinces in Iraq for whose security we were responsible at the beginning of the year, we have been able to return three to the Iraqi Government and Security Forces, and to reduce UK forces deployed in their support. In Afghanistan we have helped the elected Government extend its authority into the south of the country and supported effective reconstruction and stabilisation work for the first time in several decades.

We are very alive to the issues raised by the operational tempo the Armed Forces are sustaining. With Ministers and Defence Management Board colleagues, we have worked to alleviate and manage the pressures. With Treasury agreement we increased the resources provided to support operations during the year.

This enabled the procurement of new protected vehicles, the introduction of a new operational allowance, and further improvements in the already high level of medical support. We have continued with our long-term programme to improve the living accommodation provided for Service personnel and their families. We have also implemented in full the recommendations of the Armed Forces Pay Review Body for a pay rise for most Service personnel, especially the lowest paid, larger than anywhere else in the public sector. It is vital, especially at times like these, that we give members of the Armed Forces the support they deserve.

But while conducting, supporting and sustaining military operations is our highest priority, it is far from all that the Department has to do, or has done. Perhaps most significantly, the programme of acquisition change to implement the 2005 Defence Industrial Strategy made major progress, with the establishment of the Defence Acquisition Change Programme last summer and the implementation of many of its recommendations. The establishment of the new Defence Equipment and Support organisation on 2 April 2007 will help improve the effectiveness and through life management of acquisition. For the second year running we met all elements of our PSA target, despite these being progressively more challenging year-by-year. We also completed a major externally peer-reviewed assessment of our research programme – which gave us high marks – and published the new Defence Technology Strategy. Further work continues in all these areas with a particular focus on ensuring that our people have the skills they need.

We are taking forward a series of major programmes to improve the efficiency and effectiveness of the Department. Changes to our top level structures and organisation in light of the conclusions of the Capability Review, the significant simplification of service personnel management processes underpinned by the Joint Personnel Administration system and the continuing rationalisation and harmonisation of Defence information systems are affecting everyone in Defence from top to bottom.

We are improving coordination with other Departments over the work we do on their behalf, and the contribution Defence makes to their objectives. As this report makes clear, the MoD is closely involved and affected by aspects of the work of almost every other department, extending well beyond the traditional security agenda. This includes the significant contribution we make to the Government's sustainability goals. Our performance will be key to whether the Government achieves the objectives it has set itself. Our work with the youth and veterans communities and our contribution to skills, and to science and innovation, also contribute to the Government's wider domestic goals. But the Capability Review that reported in March shows that we have to work harder to get over what we do, how we can contribute, and the implications of the work of other Departments on defence. We are determined to rise to this challenge.

We do not underestimate the difficulties we face. We are asking a great deal of our people, military and civilian. During the year covered by this report 76 Service personnel were killed and 85 seriously injured on operations in support of our country and the people of Iraq and Afghanistan. The Army and the Royal Air Force continue to fail to meet harmony guidelines. Readiness levels for contingent operations have fallen from the peak reached last year, where the continuing shortfall in the high level collective training we are able to conduct is having a longer term impact. The reductions in the size of the Armed Forces, in parallel with the very high level of commitment of our people to what they do, are keeping our staff turnover levels well below the private sector average and relatively steady over time. Delivering the continuing programme of major organisational and cultural change across defence while supporting our operational commitments will be a major challenge. That our people, military and civilian, have delivered and continued to deliver all that they have is a tribute to their courage, their professionalism and their commitment to our country's defence and security.

Bill Jeffrey CB
Permanent Under Secretary of State

Air Chief Marshall Sir Jock Stirrup
GCB AFC ADC DSc FRAeS FCMI RAF
Chief of the Defence Staff

Summary Assessment

Current Operations

Over the year the Armed Forces remained broadly on course to deliver their policy and military objectives, albeit with some risk. This required taking greater risk against other defence objectives, in particular readiness for contingent operations and achievement of single Service harmony guidelines. The proportion of regular forces deployed on operations and other military tasks increased from just under 20% to 21.4% over the year, and the Armed Forces continued to operate above the overall level of concurrent operations which they are resourced and structured to deliver for the fifth successive year. The number of personnel deployed to Afghanistan rose substantially, but numbers fell in Iraq, Northern Ireland and the Balkans. There was a substantial increase in the number of Urgent Operational Requirements, reflecting the tempo of operations and the increase in the number of personnel deployed to Afghanistan during the year.

Future Operations

In order to support and sustain current operations the Department has taken deliberate risk against achieving the Public Service Agreement readiness target to undertake future contingent operations. It has not been possible to maintain the high level of readiness achieved in 2005-06, and it is uncertain whether readiness will recover to the target level by April 2008. This does not mean that the Armed Forces cannot support their current operational commitments, but their ability to take on additional operations that are more than additional operations other than on a minor scale is now limited.

Policy

There was continuing progress in developing complementary NATO and EU political and military capabilities, and the Department remained on course to meet the European Security Public Service Agreement target. But there is a need for fairer sharing of collective commitments, and for investment in expeditionary capabilities. The Department also remained broadly on course to achieve the Conflict Prevention PSA target, with some slippage.

Wider Government

Sustainability issues and their implications for security and defence are being incorporated in defence planning and management. Good progress was made in taking forward sustainable operations across the defence estate, but there is more to do to meet targets. The Department is strongly committed to social issues. Service personnel gained over 17,500 accredited qualifications in 2006-07, and the Department provided over 33,000 learning credit grants. Youth and veterans programmes also contributed to the Government's sustainable community goals.

Future Effects

All three Services continued to take forward their modernisation programmes, with significant new capabilities being introduced into service during the year and further efficiencies achieved. Roll out of enhanced command, control and communication systems continued alongside work to improve the Department's and the Armed Forces' capability to manage and use information.

Future Capabilities and Infrastructure

The Department invested about £5.3Bn in equipment for the Armed Forces over the year, and over £2Bn in supporting infrastructure. Equipment acquisition performance continued to improve. For the second year running the Department met or exceeded its Public Service Agreement targets for equipment procurement, despite these being more demanding than those for 2005-06. The Department continued to invest heavily in strategic infrastructure. Significant changes to improve acquisition were made under the Acquisition Reform programme, including the establishment of the new Defence Equipment and Support organisation in April 2007.

Efficiency and Change

The Department remained on course to deliver the efficiency gains and the personnel reductions and relocations agreed in the 2004 Spending Review. By 31 March 2007 over £2Bn of efficiencies had been delivered, civilian staff numbers had fallen by over 11,000, military posts by some 10,000, and 1,885 posts had been relocated out of London and the South East.

Future Personnel Plans

There was considerable progress in delivering the Service Personnel Plan. The Joint Personnel Administration system was rolled out successfully across all three Services, although there were significant temporary accounting problems during the year. Service personnel terms and conditions continued to improve, including a good pay settlement and introduction of the operational allowance. The Armed Forces Act simplifying and harmonising military law received the Royal Assent. The civilian People Programme also continued to make progress, with a particular focus on support to operations and improving acquisition skills, and the new People Pay and Pensions Agency was successfully launched.

Science, Innovation and Technology

The defence science and technology community provided essential support to help counter the increasing threat from improvised explosive devices on operations, and to counter terrorism. In addition to a continuing peer-reviewed, high quality and well managed research programme of some £500M a year, a considerable programme of work was taken forward to implement the science and technology aspects of the Defence Industrial Strategy, including the launch of programmes to stimulate innovation in defence research.

Personnel Management

The continuing high operational tempo has meant that the Army and the Royal Air Force did not meet individual separated service or unit harmony guidelines. There were further improvements in providing for the welfare of young recruits, a continuing effort to improve Basic Skills, and significant progress with major military training rationalisation. Service personnel career satisfaction remained broadly constant. Work continued to improve Civil Servants' management and leadership skills. Civilian staff satisfaction levels fell over the year, but remained high overall.

Health and Safety

Further improvements were made to military medical support during the year. The number of patients assessed by Regional Rehabilitation Units and the proportion of Service personnel medically downgraded nevertheless continued to increase, and the Department did not meet its target of 90% 'fit for task' by April 2007. The civilian sickness absence rate continued to fall, remaining comparable with private sector performance. Defence safety management systems were judged to be generally robust, the number of deaths attributable to health and safety failures fell during the year, and the Department remained on course to meet Government targets for improved Health and Safety performance by 2010.

Logistic Support

The logistic support required to sustain the high tempo of operations was successfully provided against a growing requirement over the year as forces deployed to Afghanistan increased in number. The logistic transformation programme continued to deliver improved support arrangements and financial efficiencies. But the continuing impact of reduced levels of support for the Royal Navy and the impact of operations on RAF aircraft meant that the level of routine logistic support provided to the Services continued to fall slightly below the target level.

Business Management

The Department was assessed as one of the stronger departments in the Capability Review. There were significant developments in the Department's systems, process and structures. These included a new system for managing strategic risk, major changes to improve acquisition performance leading up to the establishment of Defence Equipment and Support, and the launch of a further study into streamlining the Head Office in light of the Capability Review.

Finance

Total Defence expenditure during the year was some £34Bn, including a near cash requirement of some £31.4Bn. The additional cost of operations was just under £1.8Bn. The Department remained firmly in command of its finances. Overall defence expenditure remained well within the total resources voted by Parliament, and the Department met all its Treasury Control totals, but the non-capital cost of Operations exceed the resources voted to cover them by some £21M (1.4%).

Manpower

The programmes to transform and restructure the Armed Forces meant that during 2006-07 military trained strength fell by 3% from just over 183,000 to just under 178,000. At the end of the year all three Services were outside Manning Balance, and there is some risk that they may not return to balance by 1 April 2008. Pinch points remained in all three Services. Recruiting increased in a challenging environment, and Voluntary Outflow rates remained broadly stable. Service diversity continued to improve, although not yet to target levels. The Reserve Forces continued to provide the support to operations required. Civilian staff numbers continued to fall, reducing by 5.6% from 104,000 to 98,000 during the year, and the Department remained on course to achieve the Spending Review efficiency target for civilian reductions by 1 April 2008. As a result of the continuing reduction programme civilian recruitment, turnover and progression remained low, significantly constraining the Department's ability to meet civilian diversity targets.

Estate

The quality of the estate – including single living and family accommodation – continued to improve, but there is a long way yet to go to achieve target standards for single living accommodation across the estate. New estate management arrangements began to bed down, albeit with some teething problems. A substantial rationalisation and relocation programme continued with several major announcements during the year. There was good progress with environmental stewardship and conservation.

Reputation

Considerable work went into external and internal communications and accountability during the year. The overall reputation of the Armed Forces and MoD rose among the public and remained very high among military and civilian personnel. But the favourability ratings on how well the Forces are equipped and their personnel are looked after are a cause for concern.

Performance against SR2004
Public Service Agreement Objectives and Targets

This section shows current performance against 2004 Spending Review (SR2004) Public Service Agreement (PSA) and Efficiency Targets (April 2005 to March 2008).

2004 Spending Review Public Service Agreement

The Ministry of Defence Vision is reflected in the three objectives and six targets of the Department's Public Service Agreement. The Agreement represents a contract between the Department and the taxpayer as to what we will, as a Department, deliver. The SR2004 PSA is shown below.

MoD Public Service Agreement 2005-06 to 2007-08

Aim: to deliver security for the people of the United Kingdom and the overseas Territories by defending them, including against terrorism, and act as a force for good by strengthening international peace and security.

Objective I: Achieve success in the Military Tasks we undertake at home and abroad.

1. Achieve the objectives established by Ministers for Operations and Military Tasks in which the United Kingdom's Armed Forces are involved, including those providing support to our civil communities.

2. By 2008, deliver improved effectiveness of UK and international support for conflict prevention by addressing long-term structural cases of conflict, managing regional and national tension and violence, and supporting post-conflict reconstruction, where the UK can make a significant contribution, in particular Africa, Asia, Balkans and the Middle East. (*Joint target with the Foreign and Commonwealth Office and the Department for International Development*).

Objective II: Be ready to respond to the tasks that might arise.

3. Generate forces which can be deployed, sustained and received at the scales of effort required to meet the Government's strategic objectives.

4. Play a timely role in the development of the European Security Agenda, and enhance capabilities to undertake timely and effective security operations, by successfully encouraging a more efficient and effective ANTO, a more coherent and effective European Security and Defence Policy (ESDP) operating in strategic partnership with NATO, and enhanced European defence capabilities. (*Joint target with the Foreign and Commonwealth Office*).

5. Recruit, train, motivate and retain sufficient military personnel to provide the military capability necessary to meet the Government's strategic objectives.

Objective III: Build for the future.

6. Deliver the equipment programme to cost and time.

Target 1

Achieve the objectives established by Ministers for Operations and Military Tasks in which the United Kingdom's Armed Forces are involved, including those providing support to our civil authorities.

ON COURSE WITH SOME RISK

Over the year the Armed Forces remained broadly on course to deliver their policy and military objectives, albeit with some risk. This required taking greater risk against other defence objectives, in particular readiness for contingent operations and achievement of single Service harmony guidelines. The proportion of regular forces deployed on operations and other military tasks increased from just under 20% to 21.4% over the year, and the Armed Forces continued to operate above the overall level of concurrent operations for which they are resourced and structured to deliver.

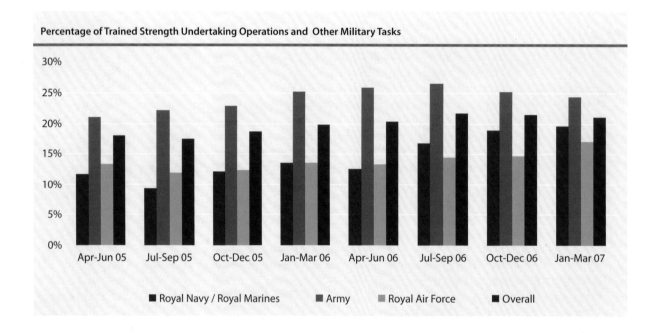

Percentage of Trained Strength Undertaking Operations and Other Military Tasks

■ Royal Navy / Royal Marines   ■ Army   ■ Royal Air Force   ■ Overall

Target 2

Improve effectiveness of the UK contribution to conflict prevention and management as demonstrated by a reduction in the number of people whose lives are affected by violent conflict and a reduction in potential sources of future conflict, where the UK can make a significant contribution. (*Joint target with Foreign and Commonwealth Office and Department for International Development*).

BROADLY ON COURSE WITH MINOR SLIPPAGE

The Department remained broadly on course to achieve the Conflict Prevention PSA target, with some slippage. Of the twelve detailed indicators underpinning the target, nine were broadly on course at the end of the year, one (increasing the number of military personnel across the world available for UN Peacekeeping) had already been met, and two (the Middle East Peace Process and Iraq) were not on course. Detailed assessments against the performance indicators are at Annex C.

Overall Progress

A – Afghanistan	E – Middle East Peace Process	I – Sudan
B – Balkans	F – Nepal	J–UN Peacekeeping
C – DRC	G – Nigeria	K – UN Peacekeeping
D – Iraq	H– Sierra Leone	L – African Peacekeeping

Key

| Met | Broadly on course with minor slippage | Not on course, major slippage |

Target 3

Generate forces, which can be deployed, sustained and recovered at the scales of effort required to meet the government's strategic objectives.

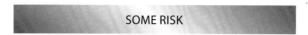

SOME RISK

In order to support and sustain current operations the Department has taken deliberate risk against achieving the Public Service Agreement readiness target to undertake future contingent operations. It has not been possible to maintain the high level of readiness achieved in 2005-06, and it is uncertain whether readiness will recover to the target level by April 2008. This does not mean that the Armed Forces cannot support their current operational commitments, but their ability to take on additional operations that are more than Small Scale Focused Intervention is now limited.

Assessment against Performance Indicators

a. By 2008, ensure more than 73% of force elements show no serious or critical weakness against their required peacetime readiness levels

Readiness levels dropped steadily from 77% in the fourth quarter of 2005-06 to 67% in the fourth quarter of 2006-07. Further information is set out in paragraph 48.

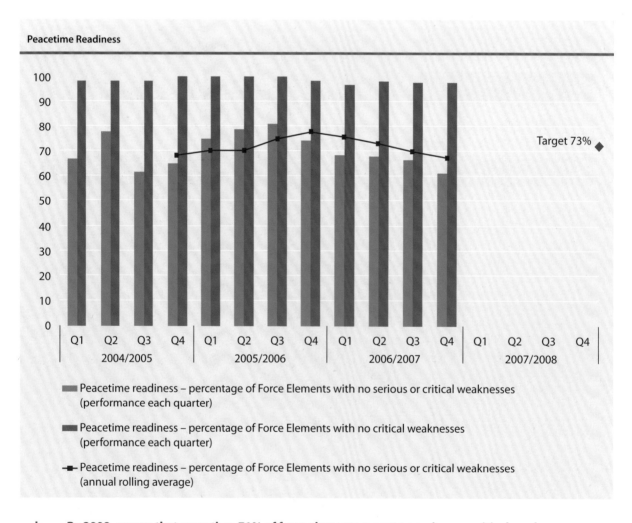

b.   By 2008, ensure that more than 71% of force elements report no serious or critical weaknesses against the ability to generate from peacetime readiness to immediate readiness for deployment on operations.

Over the year performance fell from an average of 70% in the fourth quarter of 2005-06 to an average of 55% in the fourth quarter of 2006-07. Further information is at paragraph 49.

Assessed ability to generate Force Elements from peacetime to immediate readiness

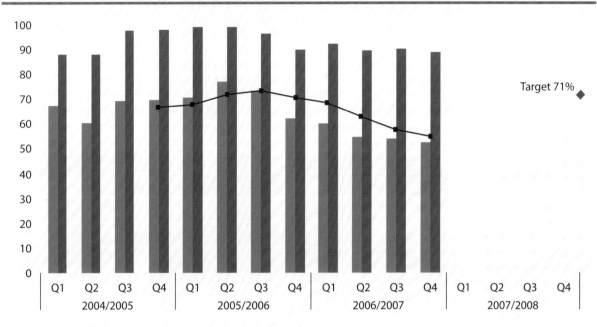

■ Ability to generate from peacetime readiness to immediate readiness –
percentage of Force Elements with no serious or critical weaknesses (performance each quarter)

■ Ability to generate from peacetime readiness to immediate readiness –
percentage of Force Elements with no critical weaknesses (performance each quarter)

━■━ Ability to generate from peacetime readiness to immediate readiness –
percentage of Force Elements with no serious or critical weaknesses (annual rolling average)

**c. By 2008, ensure that the assessed ability of the Department physically to deploy its Force Elements,
sustain them in theatre and thereafter recover them to their home basis shows a 5% improvement in the
numbers of serious or critical weakness compared with the average reported in 2004-05.**

Over the year capability improved from an average of 78.7% in the fourth quarter of 2005-06 to an average of 79.6%
in the fourth quarter of 2006-07. Further information is at paragraph 50.

Assessed ability to deploy, sustain and recover Force Elements for contingent operations

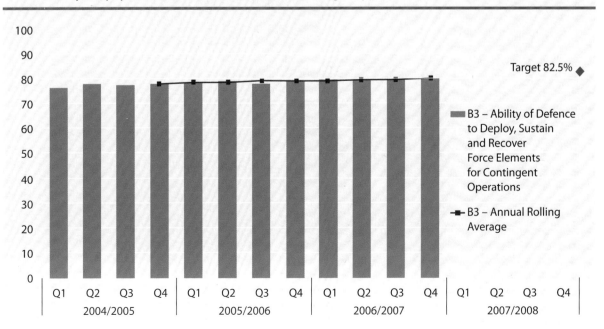

Target 4

Play a leading role in the development of the European Security Agenda, and enhance capabilities to undertake timely and effective security operations by successfully encouraging a more efficient and effective NATO, a more coherent and effective ESDP operating in strategic partnership with NATO, and enhanced European defence capabilities. (*Joint target with FCO*).

There was continuing progress in developing complementary NATO and EU political and military capabilities. Detailed information is set out in paragraphs 64-69.

Assessment against Performance Indicators

a. A more efficient and effective NATO

- Continuing effective NATO-led operations and missions;

- NATO Response Force fully operational;

- Comprehensive Political Guidance endorsed.

b. A more coherent and effective ESDP operating in strategic partnership with NATO

- Continuing effective EU civil and military missions;

- Reform of Secretariat structures and new facilities for generating the EU operations Centre provided stronger capability to plan and run civilian and civil-military operations.

c. Enhanced European defence capabilities

- EU military requirements catalogue agreed in support of Headline Goal 2010;

- EU Battlegroups concept achieved Full Operational Capability.

Target 5

Recruit, train, motivate and retain sufficient military personnel to provide the military capability necessary to meet the Government's strategic objectives.

ON COURSE WITH SOME RISK

At the end of the year all three Services were outside Manning Balance, and there is some risk that they may not return to within Manning Balance by 1 April 2008. Pinch points remained in all three Services. Recruiting increased in a challenging environment, and Voluntary Outflow rates remained broadly stable.

Assessment against Performance Indicators

a. Manning Balance

Manning Balance is defined as between -2% and +1% of the requirement, and is measured against the target prevailing at the time. Since the total requirement of Service manning is dynamic, this target will fluctuate over the PSA period. At 1 April 2007:

- The Royal Navy (including the Royal Marines) trained strength is 5.1% below the requirement – 3.1% below manning balance.

- The Army's total trained strength is 2.5% below the requirement – 0.5% below the manning balance target range.

- The Royal Air Force's total trained strength is 3.2% below the requirement – 1.2% below the manning balance target range.

- There are continuing shortages within some specialist groups in all three Armed Services. Further information is set out in paragraphs 320 – 322.

Service manning surplus/deficit over the last year (source: DASA)

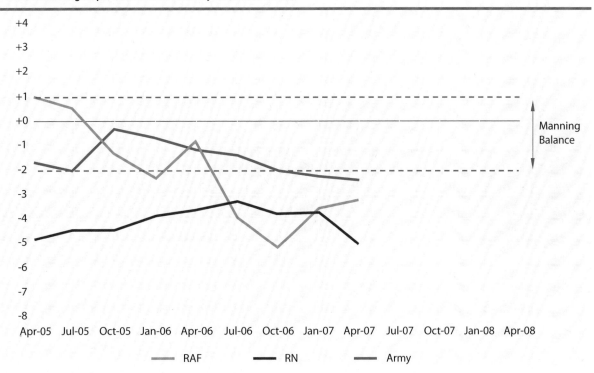

b. Gains to Trained Strength (trained recruits provided to the front line)

Further information is at paragraph 324.

Gains to trained strength

	2006-07			2005-06		
	Target	Achieved		Target	Achieved	
Naval Service Officers	410	450[P]	110%	410	370	90%
Naval Service Other Ranks	2,960	2,320[P]	79%	2,700	2,330	86%
Army Officers	1,020	960	95%	810	750	93%
Army Other Ranks	9,050	7,640	84%	9,230	7,770	84%
Royal Air Force Officers	500	400[P]	81%	370	380[r]	103%[r]
Royal Air Force Other Ranks	1,200	1,010[P]	84%	1,800	1,860[r]	103%[r]

Notes:
1. Naval Service and RAF Data from DASA. Army Figures come from the Adjutant General TLB.
2. Army numbers and target show officers completing the Royal Military Academy Sandhurst and soldiers completing Phase 2 training. This metric is used for internal management and does not match the figures produced by DASA and published in Tri Service Publication 4.
3. 'P' denotes provisional. Following the introduction of a new Personnel Administration System, all Naval Service and RAF data from 1 November 2006 are provisional and subject to review
4. r denotes revised.

c. Medically Fit For Task

The target is for at least 90% of Service personnel to be medically fit for task by 1 April 2007, an increase of 1% from the performance at 31 March 2005. The proportion of Service personnel medically downgraded continued to increase during 2006-07, and the Department did not meet its target of 90% 'fit for task' by April 2007. At 31 March 2007 85.9% of the overall Armed Forces personnel were reported as fit for task. The vast majority of personnel unfit for task are working normally but their deployability is limited. Further information is at paragraph 264.

d. Voluntary Outflow Exits

The Voluntary Outflow exits for 2006-07 are shown in the table below. Further information is at paragraph 325.

Voluntary Outflow Rates

	Stable long term Voluntary Outflow	Year ending 31 March 2007	Year ending 31 March 2006	October 1999 to October 2006
Naval Service Officers	2.0%	3.0%[P]	3.0%	2.5%
Naval Service Other Ranks	5.0%	6.0%[P]	6.0%	6.4%
Army Officers	4.1%	4.3%[3]	4.3%	3.9%
Army Other Ranks	6.2%	5.8%[3]	5.5%	5.7%
RAF Officers	2.5%	3.0%[P]	2.5%	2.4%
RAF Other Ranks	4.0%	4.9%[P]	4.8%	3.8%
Tri-Service Officers	N/A	3.6%[P]	3.4%	3.2%
Tri-Service Other Ranks	N/A	5.6%[P]	5.4%	5.4%

Notes:

1. Data from DASA

2. 'P' denotes provisional. Following the introduction of a new Personnel Administration System, all Naval Service and RAF data from 1 November 2006 are provisional and subject to review

3. Army data at 1 April 2007 are not available. Consequently Army data shown are for the latest 12 months available, comprising data from 1 March 2006 to 28 February 2007.

4. Voluntary Outflow Goals as set out in the Departmental Plan 2005-2009

e. Performance against Harmony Guidelines

Performance against individual separated service and unit tour interval harmony guidelines is shown below. The continuing high operational tempo meant that the Army and the Royal Air Force did not meet individual or unit harmony guidelines in 2006-07. Further information is at paragraphs 227-229.

	Guidelines	Performance
Levels of Individual Separated Service		
Royal Navy/ Royal Marines	In any 36 month period, no one to exceed 660 days separated service	At 31 March 2007 fewer than 1% of the Royal Navy had exceeded the guidelines
Army	In any 30 month period, no one to exceed 415 days separated service	At 31 March 2007, 13.4% of the Army personnel on current trained strength had exceeded the guidelines
Air Force	Not greater than 2.5% of personnel exceeding more that 140 days of detached duty in 12 months	At 31 March 2007, 6.2% of the RAF had exceeded the guidelines
Unit Tour Intervals		
Royal Navy	Fleet Units to spend maximum of 60% deployed in a 3 year cycle.	The Royal Navy continues broadly to meet its Unit Tour Interval Harmony guidelines.
Army	24 month average interval between unit tours.	Infantry average tour interval of 21.0 months; Royal Artillery 20.7 months; Royal Engineers 21.2 months; Royal Signals 18.4 months; Royal Logistic Corps 23.3 months.
Royal Air Force	Unit tour intervals to be no less than 16 months.	Unit Tour Intervals are not easily measured for the Royal Air Force. However RAF Regiment Field Squadrons average tour intervals around 10.5 months; Air Combat and Service Support units also breaching guidelines; Nimrod, Air Transport and Air-to-Air Refuelling squadrons heavily tasked

Target 6

Deliver the Equipment Programme to time and cost.

ON COURSE

Performance against the PSA is measured against all Category A to C projects that have passed Main Gate and are yet to achieve In Service Dates (ISD) at the start of the financial year. For the second year running the Department met or exceeded its Public Service Agreement targets for equipment procurement, despite them being more demanding than those for 2005-06. Further information is at paragraphs 161 – 162.

Assessment against Performance Indicators

a. Achieve at least 97% of Key User Requirements for all Category A to C Projects that have passed Main Gate approval, to be achieved throughout the PSA period.

99% of Key User Requirements achieved (97% 2005-06).

b. Average In-Year variation of forecast ISD, for all Category A to C Projects that have passed Main Gate Approval, to be no more than 0.5 months in 2006-07 and 0.4 months in 2007-08.

Average In-Year variation of forecast ISD of 0.5 months (0.7 months 2005-06).

c. Average In-Year variation of forecast costs for Design and Manufacture phase, for all Category A to C projects that have passed Main gate approval, of less than 0.3% in 2006-07 and 0.2% in 2007-08.

Average In-Year cost increase of 0.0% (0.2% 2005-06).

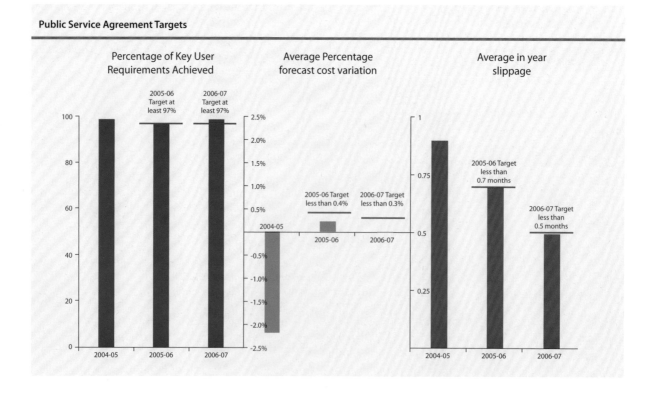

2004 Spending Review Efficiency Target

As part of Spending Review 2004, the Department agreed that it would realise total annual efficiency gains of at least £2.8Bn by 2007-08, of which three quarters will be cash releasing. As part of this programme the MoD will by 31 March 2008:

- Reduce its civilian staff by at least 10,000
- Reduce the number of military posts in administrative and support functions by at least 5,000
- Be on course to have relocated 3,900 posts out of London and the South East by 2010

ON COURSE

Performance Assessment

The Department remained on course to deliver the efficiency gains and the personnel reductions and relocations agreed in the 2004 Spending Review. By 31 March 2007 over £2Bn efficiencies had been delivered, civilian staff numbers had fallen by over 11,000, military posts by some 10,000, and 1,885 posts had been relocated out of London and the South East. Detailed information is set out in paragraphs 142-150.

Programme	Achievement by 31 March 2006 (£M) [1]	Achievement by 31 March 2007 (£M) [1]	Planned Efficiency Gains by 31 March 2008 (£M) [1] [2]
Force Structure changes	**106**	**298**	**388**
Corporate Services	**343**	**296**	**253**
Military Personnel Management	16	38	85
Civilian Personnel Management*	24	30	48
Finance Function	2	16	11
Information Services*	301	212	109
Procurement and Logistics	**836**	**1169-1219**	**1681**
Equipment Procurement *	54	206	374
Defence Logistics Transformation	662	780-830	1002
Whole Fleet Management*	54	55	116
Estates Modernisation*	31	62	95
Other Procurement	35	66	92
Productive Time*	**105**	**139**	**88**
Organisational changes	**0**	**2**	**8**
Relocation	**18**	**18**	**18**
Manpower	**86**	**344**	**557**
RN	15	32	32
Army	18	64	88
RAF	51	143	203
Civilian	2	105	234
Adjustment[3]	**-9**	**-68**	**-106**
Total	**1,485**[4]	**2198-2248**	**2887**

Notes:
1. Planned and Achieved Efficiencies include efficiencies during 2004-05, 2005-06, 2006-07 and 2007-08. Because of the size of the Defence Logistics Transformation Programme, the validation process takes some time and this is the reason why a range is given in the table above.
2. The targets reflect a number of revisions since the publication of the Efficiency Technical Note in December 2005 and the 2006/07 Spring Performance Report.
3. Adjustment to avoid double counting of manpower savings.
4. This has increased from £1107M reported last year following a final validation of Defence Logistics Transformation Programme. The figure has been confirmed as higher after audit.
* Efficiency gains marked with an asterisk include an element of non-cashable gains.

Purpose

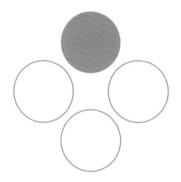

Current Operations

Objective: to succeed in Operations and Military Tasks Today

Public Service Agreement Target (SR2004 MoD Target 1)
Achieve the objectives established by Ministers for Operations and Military Tasks in which the United Kingdom's Armed Forces are involved, including those providing support to our civil communities.

Assessment and Performance Measures

Assessment: Over the year the Armed Forces remained broadly on course to deliver their policy and military objectives, albeit with some risk. This required taking greater risk against other defence objectives, in particular readiness for contingent operations and achievement of single Service harmony guidelines. The proportion of regular forces deployed on operations and other military tasks increased from just under 20% to 21.4% over the year, and the Armed Forces continued to operate above the overall level of concurrent operations which they are resourced and structured to deliver for the fifth successive year. The number of personnel deployed to Afghanistan rose substantially, but numbers fell in Iraq, Northern Ireland and the Balkans. There was a substantial increase in the number of Urgent Operational Requirements, reflecting the tempo of operations and the increase in the number of personnel deployed to Afghanistan during the year.

Achieve the objectives established by ministers for Operations and military basics:

- The Armed Forces remained broadly on course, with some risk, to achieve success against the policy and military objectives set for Operations overseas, including in Iraq, Afghanistan and the Balkans and in response to the deteriorating security situation in Lebanon;
- The Armed Forces contributed to seven UN Peacekeeping Missions, in Cyprus, Democratic Republic of Congo, Georgia, Liberia, Sierra Leone, Sudan and Nepal;
- A minimum nuclear deterrent capability was maintained throughout the year;
- The integrity of UK waters and airspace was maintained throughout the year;
- The security of the UK's Overseas Territories, including the Falkland Islands, Gibraltar and the Sovereign Base Areas in Cyprus, was maintained;
- Continuing support was provided to the civil authorities at home, including in Northern Ireland, provision of Search and Rescue and Fisheries Protection Services, and the investigation and disposal of suspected explosive devices.

Monitor the proportion of the Armed Forces deployed in support of Operations and Military Tasks:

- The proportion of regular forces deployed on operations and other military tasks increased from just under 20% in the last quarter of 2005-06 (including about 25% of the Army) to 21.4% in the last quarter of 2006-07 (including about 24% of the Army);
- The Armed Forces continued to operate above the overall level of concurrent operations for which they are resourced and structured to deliver for the fifth successive year;
- UK military personnel deployed in support of operations in Iraq (including reserves) reduced from some 9,200 in April 2006 to some 8,100 in March 2007;
- UK military personnel deployed to Afghanistan (including reserves) rose from some 2,500 in April 2006 to 6,300 in March 2007;
- UK military personnel deployed to the Balkans (including reserves) reduced from about 900 in April 2006 to about 400 on withdrawal of the UK battle group in Bosnia-Herzegovina in March 2007;
- UK military personnel deployed to or stationed in Northern Ireland reduced from about 9,000 in April 2006 to 7,000 in March 2007. The Royal Irish (Home Service) battalions were declared non-operational in September 2006;
- About 317 civilians were deployed outside the UK on, or in support of, operations or other Government objectives during the year.

Fig. 1 Principal Deployments of the Armed Forces on 1st April 2007

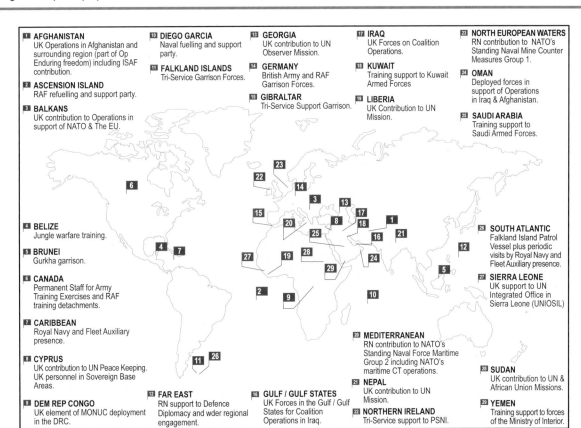

1 AFGHANISTAN
UK Operations in Afghanistan and surrounding region (part of Op Enduring freedom) including ISAF contribution.

2 ASCENSION ISLAND
RAF refuelling and support party.

3 BALKANS
UK contribution to Operations in support of NATO & The EU.

4 BELIZE
Jungle warfare training.

5 BRUNEI
Gurkha garrison.

6 CANADA
Permanent Staff for Army Training Exercises and RAF training detachments.

7 CARIBBEAN
Royal Navy and Fleet Auxiliary presence.

8 CYPRUS
UK contribution to UN Peace Keeping. UK personnel in Sovereign Base Areas.

9 DEM REP CONGO
UK element of MONUC deployment in the DRC.

10 DIEGO GARCIA
Naval fuelling and support party.

11 FALKLAND ISLANDS
Tri-Service Garrison Forces.

12 FAR EAST
RN support to Defence Diplomacy and wder regional engagement.

13 GEORGIA
UK contribution to UN Observer Mission.

14 GERMANY
British Army and RAF Garrison Forces.

15 GIBRALTAR
Tri-Service Support Garrison.

16 GULF / GULF STATES
UK Forces in the Gulf / Gulf States for Coalition Operations in Iraq.

17 IRAQ
UK Forces on Coalition Operations.

18 KUWAIT
Training support to Kuwait Armed Forces

19 LIBERIA
UK Contribution to UN Mission.

20 MEDITERRANEAN
RN contribution to NATO's Standing Naval Force Maritime Group 2 including NATO's maritime CT operations.

21 NEPAL
UK contribution to UN Mission.

22 NORTHERN IRELAND
Tri-Service support to PSNI.

23 NORTH EUROPEAN WATERS
RN contribution to NATO's Standing Naval Mine Counter Measures Group 1.

24 OMAN
Deployed forces in support of Operations in Iraq & Afghanistan.

25 SAUDI ARABIA
Training support to Saudi Armed Forces.

26 SOUTH ATLANTIC
Falkland Island Patrol Vessel plus periodic visits by Royal Navy and Fleet Auxiliary presence.

27 SIERRA LEONE
UK support to UN Integrated Office in Sierra Leone (UNIOSIL)

28 SUDAN
UK contribution to UN & African Union Missions.

29 YEMEN
Training support to forces of the Ministry of Interior.

© Crown copyright 2007

1. The Ministry of Defence and the Armed Forces exist to defend the United Kingdom and its interests and strengthen international peace and stability. Their principal effort over the year, in conjunction with other Government Departments and the international community, was to support the Government in achieving strategic success in current operations. Throughout the year the Armed Forces, supported by their civilian colleagues, worked successfully towards this goal at home and overseas, remaining broadly on course to deliver the policy and military objectives set by Ministers, albeit with some risk. This required them consistently to operate above the level of concurrent operations, as set out in the December 2003 Defence White Paper, which our force structures assume (see paragraphs 38 to 43). Achieving this required taking greater risk against other defence objectives, in particular readiness for contingent operations and achievement of single Service harmony guidelines (see paragraphs 45-52 under *Future Operations* and 217-219 under *Personnel Management*). The MoD has made it very clear that in balancing between objectives the overriding priority is operational success.

2. In particular, during 2006-07, UK forces continued to be engaged in two highly demanding Medium Scale peace enforcement missions in high risk environments, in Iraq (Operation TELIC) and in Afghanistan (Operation HERRICK). These involved overcoming significant armed opposition from insurgents fighting hard to frustrate the international community's and the elected Iraqi and Afghan Governments' objectives. The level of violence in both theatres was the highest since full-scale warfighting ended in 2003 and 2001 respectively, and sadly during the year 76 Service personnel were killed and 85 seriously injured on these operations in the service of our country and of the people of Iraq and Afghanistan. Those who died were brought home swiftly and with fitting ceremony recognising their sacrifice; in June 2007 the MoD and Ministry of Justice announced improvements in the support provided to their families. Those seriously injured were evacuated promptly back to the United Kingdom, where since December 2006 a Military Managed Ward Unit at the University Hospital Birmingham NHS Foundation Trust has enabled military patients to recover alongside their comrades (see paragraph 241 under *Health and Safety*). Nevertheless, there was real progress in the two critical areas of building the capacity of Iraq's and Afghanistan's own national security forces (known as security sector reform); and in providing sufficient security for reconstruction and development

work (principally by the Department for International Development) to proceed (see the essay on the Comprehensive Approach in Afghanistan on page 40. This required great efforts from all defence personnel, both those in the front line and those preparing for or supporting operations.

3. The MoD worked with the Foreign and Commonwealth Office (FCO), the Department for International Development (DfID), the United States Government, and with other allies and partners throughout the year to review collective strategic objectives, and agree the best ways and means to integrate and achieve them. It also continued to identify operational lessons, and to make adjustments as necessary. In Iraq and Afghanistan the threat to UK forces continued to evolve, and the clear articulation of operational risk helped the Department focus on key matters that required action at the highest level during the year. In particular this resulted in the deployment of additional forces to Afghanistan (see paragraph 20), the acquisition and deployment to Iraq and Afghanistan of protected patrol vehicles to improve the protection of UK personnel and a range of Defence Aids Suites and survivability enhancements to helicopters and fixed wing aircraft. Additionally, the development of Operational Intelligence Support Groups has greatly enhanced the operational success through the provision of strategic level intelligence to commanders on the ground. The Armed Forces continued to exploit the latest technologies to maintain the initiative and keep losses to a minimum. They also introduced innovations, in particular through security measures for force protection, surveillance, and action against the infrastructure and forces facing them.

Protected Patrol Vehicle recently deployed to Iraq and Afghanistan

4. The Armed Forces were also deployed on other, smaller operations around the world, particularly in the Balkans and Africa. Figure 1 shows the wide range of their deployments as of 1 April 2007. They also continued to discharge a number of standing tasks, including wide-ranging assistance to a number of Departments in the United Kingdom in support of the Government's domestic objectives. Political progress

in the Balkans and in Northern Ireland enabled a draw-down in force levels in these theatres, which has slightly relieved the pressure of operations.

Urgent operational Requirements

5. The Department has procured new equipment and enhanced existing equipment for operations in Iraq and Afghanistan through its Urgent Operational Requirements (UORs) process. Between late 2001 and March 2007 some 610 UORs were approved, for a total expenditure of £1.9Bn. The process has been very successful: 98% of UORs delivered to Iraq during the warfighting phase of the operation, and reported upon, were found to be either effective or highly effective; and 100% of UORs delivered to Afghanistan since the British move to the South, and reported upon, have been rated by troops in theatre as either effective or highly effective. 229 UORs were approved in 2006-07 (134 for Afghanistan and 95 for Iraq) for £763M. This was a substantial increase over 2005-06, reflecting the tempo of operations and the large increase in the number of personnel deployed to Afghanistan during the year (see paragraph 20 below). Enhancements to existing capabilities have included provision of protection upgrades to vehicles on operations, new Protected Patrol Vehicles to supplement the vehicles already in theatre, a range of Defensive Aids Suites and survivability enhancements to helicopters and fixed wing aircraft, electronic counter measures, communications and surveillance equipment, base security, and deployable accommodation. Further information on the cost of UORs can be found in Note 2 to the Departmental Resource Accounts on page 236.

Operational Allowance

6. Recognising the increased and enduring nature of danger in Iraq, Afghanistan and the Balkans, in October 2006 the Government introduced a non-taxable Operational Allowance funded by the Treasury, backdated to 1 April 2006. The amount was based on the tax and National Insurance paid by a Private Soldier within five years service deployed on operations for six months to ensure that it was targeted at the majority of personnel who are currently deployed on operations. For a six month deployment, the allowance is currently worth some £2,240. For 2006-07 it was paid at a daily rate of £12.75 to take into account those personnel who deploy for periods that are greater or less than six months. The first payments were made by Christmas 2006 and as at 31 March 2007 some £40M had been paid to about 36,000 personnel. In June 2007 the Government announced a 3.6% increase, backdated to 1 April 2007. Reflecting the increased security and stability in the Balkans (see paragraph 84 under *Policy*), it also announced the allowance would no longer be payable to personnel serving in that area from 1 September 2007.

Iraq

Iraq

Base map derived from Defence Geographic Centre series GSGS 11157 Iraq Governates Edition 12
Maps produced are not to be taken as necessarily representing the views of the UK Government on boundaries or political status.

© Collins Bartholomew Limited 2007
© Crown copyright 2007

7. The United Kingdom's Armed Forces continued their deployment in Iraq under the mandate of United Nations Security Council Resolution 1723. As one of 26 nations contributing to the Multi-National Forces Iraq, UK forces were the second largest contributor of international military assistance behind the United States. UK military and civilian personnel have made a significant contribution towards creating the conditions required to transfer security responsibility to the Iraqi authorities by helping to train and mentor the Iraqi Security Forces (ISF), providing security, conducting joint security and counter-terrorist operations with the ISF and capacity building of national institutions. During 2006, in a process backed by the UN, the first fully elected Government of Iraq – the Iraqi National Unity Government – was formed of representatives from across all the main elements of Iraqi society. Responsibility for security in three provinces also transferred to the Iraqi authorities.

A soldier carrying out patrols in Basra City

8. The UK's area of responsibility comprises the four southern-most provinces in Iraq – Al Basrah, Al Muthanna, Dhi Qar and Maysan – and is known as Multinational Division (South East) (MND(SE)). In 2006-07 the number of UK personnel deployed in the Gulf region on, or in support of, Operation TELIC reduced slightly from some 9,200 at the beginning of the year to about 8,100 by its end. This included approximately 7,100 personnel based in Iraq itself, mainly in the

MND(SE) area. The net additional cost of operations in Iraq during 2006-07 was £965M. Troop reductions were also made during the year by our MND(SE) partners, with Japan and Italy both ending their contributions to military ground operations, leaving around 1,500 personnel from Australia, Romania, Denmark, the Czech Republic and Lithuania and UK command.

New Body Armour

9. The Reserve Forces continued to make a valuable contribution to military operations. In Iraq they performed a wide range of tasks including force protection duties, logistics, medical support and reinforcing Regular units. In addition, up to 20 members of the Sponsored Reserves were also deployed in theatre at any one time providing meteorological information, aircraft maintenance and heavy equipment transporter drivers.

10. Around 170 defence civil servants were also deployed in Iraq during the year, filling posts providing policy and financial advice to deployed UK forces and coalition headquarters, specialised scientific support, fire services, and Ministry of Defence Police. They also worked as advisors and mentors helping develop the Iraqi Ministry of Defence in Baghdad.

11. Although violence in southern Iraq was much lower than elsewhere in the country, Basra continued to suffer from violence mainly between Shia groups, with the remainder of other attacks aimed at coalition forces in MND(SE). In response to increasing attacks, all aspects of the protection of personnel were enhanced by continuous improvements in tactics and training, supported by the development of improved body armour, new armoured vehicles, modern surveillance technologies such as Unmand Aerial Vehicles (UAVs) and the building of enhanced base protection to reduce the risks to UK personnel. 31 soldiers, sailors and airmen were nevertheless killed in Iraq during the year, bringing the total since the start of Operation TELIC to 31 March 2007 to 134, of whom 103 were as a result of hostile action. 51 military personnel also sustained very serious, or serious, injuries.

12. During the year, UK forces operating in MND(SE) provided military support to security operations and training the Iraq Security Forces, thereby helping to create the security conditions to enable economic development and reconstruction and a democratic political process, to move the country towards security self reliance. Key activities included:

● training and mentoring the 10th Division of the Iraqi Army (which is based in southern Iraq), including using Global Conflict Prevention Pool funding to build a parade square and assault course at the Iraqi Military Academy at Tallil. The Division proved its professionalism during Operation SINBAD and is now planning and leading security operations in Basrah City with minimal Coalition support. Two 10th Division battalions also performed well in Baghdad supporting the joint Iraqi/coalition operation Fardh al Qanoon. The Iraqi Ground Forces Command in Baghdad assumed operational command of 10th Division in January 2007;

● working with the Iraqi Government, Provincial Authorities and Security Forces in Operation SINBAD to make Basra a more secure and prosperous environment in which to live and work through a range of security operations, reconstruction projects and security mentoring (see paragraphs 15 below and 89 under *Policy*);

● maintaining the sovereignty and integrity of Iraqi territorial waters, in particular protecting Iraq's offshore oil infrastructure and the security of merchant vessels;

- developing the Iraqi Navy by providing around 30 UK personnel located at Umm Qasr Naval Base south of Basra to train and mentor Iraqi naval and marine personnel. In addition, twelve Iraqi naval officers were trained in the UK at the Britannia Royal Naval College Dartmouth and HMS Collingwood;

- training and mentoring the Department of Border Enforcement (DBE) to help them ensure the integrity of Iraq's southern borders and prevent smuggling, including supporting the DBE during an operation at two border points in MND(SE) to make procedures more efficient, improve equipment and improve infrastructure;

- improving the Iraqi Police Service is at the heart of HMG's current work and with the assistance of over 50 FCO-led International Police Advisors, the MoD is helping to develop specific niche training programmes in leadership, intelligence and internal affairs that help build long-term capacity; and

- providing an additional £39M for infrastructure projects and equipment such as radios and police vehicles to help build the capability of the Iraqi Security Forces.

13. Nationally, UK military personnel supported training at the Iraqi Military Academy and elsewhere, as part of the NATO Training Mission-Iraq, contributing to the commissioning of a total of 571 officers in four groups between January and December 2006.

14. Reflecting the growing capability of Iraqi security forces and national and provincial government, Iraqi authorities officially took over responsibility for security in Al Muthanna province in July 2006 – the first province in Iraq to achieve this – and in Dhi Qar province in September, both within the UK's area of responsibility. These were followed by An-Najaf province, bordering the Multi-National Division (South East) area, where the Iraqi authorities took over responsibility for security in December 2006 and in Maysan province in April 2007. On behalf of the coalition, UK forces in MND(SE) managed many projects that helped improve the lives of local people. These included, in Maysan, refurbishing four schools, building new and improving existing sewerage mains and the development of a refuse collection scheme. New stands for water tanks were built, new water networks were created and existing ones improved, and improvements were made to electricity distribution and the road system in Dhi Qar. In Al Muthanna, a province-wide project to spray the date crop was undertaken as well as improvements made to electricity supply.

Operation SINBAD

SINBAD – Iraqi Security Forces and Multi-National forces working together.

15. To improve the deteriorating security situation and economic environment in Basra City, in September 2006 Operation SINBAD, a joint Iraqi/Coalition operation, was launched to improve security and deliver a small number of short-term infrastructure projects. It covered each of the 16 districts of Basra City in turn and ran until January 2007. Over $77M was invested in reconstruction projects and over 24,000 short-term jobs were created. Lasting improvements included 212 kilometres of new water pipe laid, 70,000 date palm offshoots planted (providing about 1,000 new jobs, stimulating local agriculture and helping restore the marsh-land ecosystem), 249 schools refurbished and 20 Primary Health Centres refurbished and stocked. While SINBAD was initially led by the Coalition, the Iraqi Security Forces grew in capability throughout the operation and took the lead for the latter phases without overt Coalition support. Local politicians were engaged and happy with the work conducted, and levels of support and positive feedback from the local population increased during the operation. Overall, Operation SINBAD delivered promising results that should help towards achieving the conditions for transition to Provincial Iraqi Control in Al Basrah province.

Operation SINBAD

Afghanistan

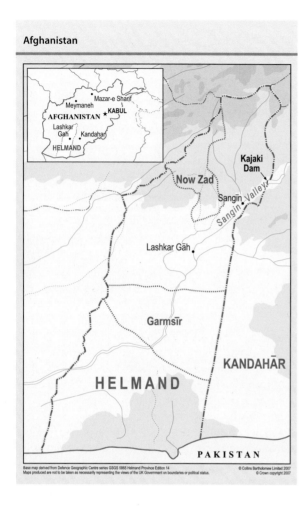

16. The UK continued to play a leading role within the NATO led International Security Assistance Force (ISAF) in Afghanistan. The net additional cost of UK operations in Afghanistan during 2006-07 was £742M. ISAF represents NATO's largest ever mission, with 37 nations contributing over 35,000 troops in March 2007, in addition to 8,000 US personnel under Coalition command, 30,000 personnel of the Afghan National Army (ANA) and some 60,000 Afghan National Police (ANP). The ISAF is in Afghanistan at the invitation of the elected Afghan Government and with UN authorisation, to provide the secure environment necessary for reconstruction and development to take place. NATO Foreign Ministers reaffirmed the long-term commitment of their countries to this goal when they met in Brussels in January 2007. The Afghan people have enthusiastically embraced the opportunity to shape their country's future with 70% of registered voters participating in the 2004 Presidential elections, and 51.5% in the 2005 Parliamentary and Provincial Council elections. The Afghan Government is working hard to strengthen its institutions and to extend its remit across the entire country. The United Kingdom and the international community, have an important role

to play in ensuring that more is done in the year ahead to build on this progress.

17. During the year the UK Armed Forces:

● led ISAF for nine months from May 2006, using the headquarters of the Allied Rapid Reaction Corps (for which the UK is the framework nation and provides 60% of the manpower) under the command of Lieutenant General David Richards, supported by elements of 1 Signal Brigade. In February 2007 command was handed over to a composite headquarters under US leadership;

● successfully prosecuted extensive, intense and demanding operations against the Taleban in Helmand Province in the south of Afghanistan;

● provided direct assistance to reconstruction in a security environment which is not safe for civilian personnel from the Department for International Development or Non Government Organisations to work; and

● continued to train and mentor elements of the Afghan National Army and Police.

18. Despite initiatives aimed at improving security, insurgent attacks increased significantly during the year. In order to minimise the risks to UK personnel, new, enhanced armoured vehicles were procured and deployed. Nevertheless, 45 soldiers, sailors and airmen were killed in Afghanistan during the year, bringing the total from the start of Operation HERRICK to 31 March 2007 to 52. A further 34 were seriously injured.

19. With ISAF support, Provincial Reconstruction Teams (PRTs), across Afghanistan (including a UK-led force in Mazar-e Sharif in the early part of the year), have brought real benefits to the people in northern and western Afghanistan, paving the way for reconstruction and helping extend the authority of the elected Afghan Government. At the beginning of the year the security situation in these areas was broadly stable, with neither the Taliban nor other illegal armed groups posing a credible threat to the Government, but control of the south was disputed. ISAF therefore expanded into the south and east of Afghanistan in 2006, extending its operations across the whole of Afghanistan. This was critical to stabilisation, extending the authority of the Government of Afghanistan across the whole country and facilitating reconstruction. Following the handover of the UK's previous area of operations in the north of Afghanistan to other NATO Allies in the spring, the main focus of UK operations during the year was therefore Helmand Province in the south of Afghanistan, to support the UK-led PRT in the province as part of the comprehensive

cross-Government strategy to establish the security conditions for improved governance, reconstruction and development to take place (see the essay on the Comprehensive Approach on page 40).

Operation Herrick

20. Over the year, the number of UK forces in theatre grew from around 2,500 service personnel in April 2006 to some 6,300 in March 2007. In April 2006, elements of 16 Air Assault Brigade, (including UK Apache attack helicopters on their first operation) deployed to Helmand to create the security conditions needed to enable reconstruction and development. It saw intense fighting in Garmsir (in the south of the province), around Now Zad and in the Sangin valley (in the north and east) over the summer. Additional UK forces also provided a regional manoeuvre capability based in Kandahar, and RAF and Fleet Air Arm aircraft from Joint Force Harrier based at Kandahar provided close air support to operations throughout the year. In June, a squadron from the RAF Regiment was deployed to provide additional force protection at Kandahar Airfield. In July the Government announced the deployment to Helmand of a further 1,000 UK troops and additional Chinook helicopters, reflecting the challenging operational environment. 16 Air Assault Brigade was replaced by 3 Commando Brigade in October (including the first operational deployment of the Royal Marines' new Viking armoured vehicle). Supported by increasingly capable Afghan National Army and Police units, UK forces continued to undertake operations against those unwilling to see an extension of the authority of the elected Afghan Government. Over the winter these forces inflicted a series of tactical defeats in successful operations in Garmsir, around Lashkar Gah in the centre, and in the Sangin valley and the Kajaki Dam. In its turn 3 Commando Brigade was replaced by 12 Mechanised Brigade in April 2007. In February 2007 the Government announced that the UK would deploy a further 1,400 personnel over the summer (see paragraph 63 under *Policy*) to provide a manoeuvre reserve for Regional Command (South), together with

additional reconnaissance and surveillance, close air support, support helicopters and air transport, bringing the eventual total number of UK personnel deployed to some 7,700. Personnel from the United States, Canada, Denmark and Estonia, fought alongside and supported UK troops in Helmand during the year.

Chinook bringing an underslung load to the base at Sangin.

21. This military activity was coordinated with the establishment of a UK-led cross-government Provincial Reconstruction Team (PRT) in Lashkar Gah. This enabled improved mentoring of local Afghan institutions and governance, working with the Helmand authorities to strengthen provincial level democracy and with the Provincial Development Committee to help prioritise its efforts in line with Afghan national plans to enable sustained Afghan-led reconstruction efforts to get off the ground. It also took forward over 100 Quick Impact Projects across Helmand Province during the year that improved the lives of ordinary Afghans, including a number of reconstruction and development projects such as building windmill-powered wells and schools, water infrastructure works and providing emergency food distribution (also see paragraph 89 under *Policy*). The $180M Kajaki Dam project will, once completed, provide irrigation and electricity across the region. Since 2001, the UK has spent over £500M on reconstruction and development in Afghanistan, making the UK Afghanistan's second largest bilateral donor after the US. The UK's long-term commitment to

the reconstruction and development of Afghanistan is underpinned by the Afghanistan Compact and the ten-year UK-Afghanistan Development Partnership Arrangement, which supports the Afghan Government's interim National Development Strategy. The Arrangement, signed in February 2006 by the Prime Minister and the elected President of Afghanistan, commited £330M of development assistance to Afghanistan over three years (2006-09). £102M of this assistance was disbursed in 2006-07 and £115M will be 2008-09.

Supply Convoy – Helmand.

22. The Afghan Security Forces made an increasing contribution to the security of their own country during the year, although more still needs to be done to help them achieve this. The Afghan National Army (ANA) has been reformed and is now more professional, accountable and ethnically balanced. Approximately 30,000 ANA soldiers and close to 60,000 Afghan National Police (ANP) officers have been recruited, trained and equipped. Work is underway to ensure greater co-ordination of the army and police, with the development of command centres at provincial and regional levels. The UK continued to provide trainers and mentors to the ANA and ANP, in particular through Operational Mentoring and Liaison Teams which have trained ANA personnel in military and security aspects from very basic soldiering skills and weapon handling to dealing with suicide attacks and more advanced operations. For example, following work with 3 Commando Brigade, 3/205 Brigade of the ANA based around Kandahar developed from a partially complete unit with limited combat capabilities and support and a crippling absence rate into a stable Brigade with growing self confidence, able to work in bigger and better units and with a fully trained pool of drivers, mechanics, storemen and medics providing real and effective support. Five ANA personnel attended the Commissioning Course at Sandhurst and the Advanced Command Staff Course at Shrivenham.

23. Increasing numbers of the Reserve Forces continue to contribute across the full range of our operations in Afghanistan. They contributed to the efforts of all three Services, providing force protection units, individual augmentees, logisticians and specialists. A small number of Sponsored Reserves were deployed to provide meteorological information.

24. There were some 62 MoD civil servants working in Afghanistan, in 2006-07, providing support to the Helmand Taskforce, ISAF HQs and the Government of Afghanistan. Among these was the Senior Political Advisor to COMISAF, General Richards and two advisors working within the Afghan Ministry of Defence to advise the Afghan Defence Minister and assist in the civilianisation of the previously solely military organisation.

The Balkans

25. During 2006-07, the UK contributed approximately 600 troops to operations in Bosnia-Herzegovina (a reduction of about 90 since 2005-06) and commanded the Multinational Task Force North West. Using home-based troops on standby the UK also provided one third of the Operational Reserve Force capability able to deploy to Bosnia-Herzegovina and Kosovo. The total net additional cost of operations in the Balkans during the year was £57M. UK support for security sector reform in Bosnia continued. The Government provided some £1M Global Conflict Prevention Pool funds for post-conflict reconstruction through the UK-founded Peace Support Operations Training Centre in Bosnia. Over 100 trained officers have graduated from the centre, with some already engaged in humanitarian operations in Ethiopia and Eritrea, in conflict prevention in Iraq and the Democratic Republic of Congo, and in peace support operations closer to home. The UK also provided training to former soldiers made redundant and returning to civilian life, and contributed to the provision of a small arms and light weapons destruction facility in Northern Bosnia-Herzegovina, with some 250,000 weapons destroyed over the year. The international community continued its pursuit of persons indicted for war crimes but Radovan Karadzic, the former Bosnian Serb leader, and Ratko Mladic, his chief of the Bosnian Serb army, remained at large.

26. The security situation in Bosnia-Herzegovina continued to improve during the year. Fair and democratic elections in Bosnia passed off smoothly in October 2006; in December Bosnia-Herzegovina joined the NATO Partnership for Peace programme, together with Serbia and Montenegro, and in January 2007 a single, multi-ethnic military force compatible with NATO was established. In December 2006 the EU therefore decided to restructure the European Force in the region and in February 2007 it announced a significant reduction of forces from 6,000 to 2,500 and the UK battle group in Bosnia-Herzegovina was consequently withdrawn at the end of March 2007, 15 years after UK combat troops were first deployed in 1992. The UK will continue to provide a small number of staff officers in the Sarajevo HQ and at the Peace Support Operations Training Centre in Sarajevo (less than 20 personnel in all), contribute to the EU Police Mission in Bosnia (the UK is contributing 16 civilian police officers to the 170 strong mission), and in rotation with Germany and Italy provide a UK-based battalion on standby for the NATO-EU Reserve force dedicated to the Balkans area. Approximately 85 civilians were deployed in the Balkans in 2006-07.

27. The UK continued to provide a small valuable specialist capability to the NATO Kosovo Force of some 175 military personnel able to deploy across the province, together with around 100 UK Police Officers, including around 60 from the Ministry of Defence Police. The process to determine the future status of Kosovo, begun in 2005, continued throughout 2006-07 and is now in its final stages. Numerous discussions were held with Prisitina and Belgrade, led by the UN Special Envoy, Martti Ahtisaari. Draft proposals were presented to both parties in February 2007 and to UN Security Council delegations in March. Formal discussions began in April. The MoD continued to support UN work to transform and professionalise the Kosovo Protection Corps and the successful Train the Trainer de-mining programme.

Crisis Response Operations

28. In July 2006 the Armed Forces successfully evacuated over 4,500 British and other nationals from Lebanon to Cyprus during the fighting between Israel and Hezbollah. The operation involved some 2,500 personnel from all three Services. A naval task group commanded by HMS Illustrious, supplemented by RAF CH-47 Chinook helicopters, picked up the evacuees, with Operational Liaison and Reconnaissance teams deployed to help the UK Ambassador in Lebanon and plan the evacuations. The operation was successful and demonstrated the ability of UK Forces in the region to respond to a complex and sensitive situation at short notice.

HMS Gloucester, tasked with getting the young and the old away from conflict zone of Lebanon. .

United Nations (UN) Peackeeping Operations

29. The UK continued to support a number of United Nations Operations. During 2006-07 the Armed Forces provided some 320 UK military personnel to seven UN Peacekeeping Missions, in Cyprus; the Democratic Republic of Congo; Georgia; Liberia; Sierra Leone; Sudan; and Nepal. This included staff officers, whose specialist skills and experience are highly valued, in a range of UN Mission HQ staff appointments. Five Ministry of Defence Police have been deployed to Sudan as part of the EU's support package to the African Union Mission in Sudan. The UN Mission in Cyprus remains the UK's largest commitment, with about 280 members of an overall force of some 860.

Other Military Tasks

Independent Nuclear Deterrent

30. The UK's Trident submarine force continued to provide a constant and independent nuclear deterrent capability at sea, in support of NATO and as the ultimate guarantee of our national security. The MoD continues to make the necessary investment at the Atomic Weapons Establishment Aldermaston to ensure that it has the requisite facilities and skills to maintain a safe and reliable Trident warhead stockpile and to prepare for decisions, likely to be necessary in the next Parliament, on the possible refurbishment or replacement of the existing warhead.

Defence of UK Airspace and Waters

31. The UK's Air Defence and Maritime Patrol forces continued to protect national rights and interests by ensuring the integrity of the UK's airspace and territorial waters. The Royal Navy maintained a naval presence in UK waters, and RAF Air Defence units

provided the ability to respond rapidly to suspicious activity by aircraft, and to engage any that are a proven threat to life.

Security of UK Overseas Territories

32. Some 4,500 UK military personnel, supported by UK defence civil servants and locally employed civilians, continued to be stationed or deployed in support of the security and defence of the UK's Overseas Territories. In Cyprus the MoD maintained important military facilities within the Eastern and Western Sovereign Base Areas, which provided vital support to the evacuation of civilians from Lebanon in July 2006. UK Forces in the Falkland Islands continued to demonstrate the Government's commitment to the security of the UK Territories in the South Atlantic. HMS Endurance both maintained British interests in the South Atlantic and Antarctica and helped to police the Antarctic Treaty to preserve the pristine nature of Antarctica. Gibraltar continued to provide a Forward Mounting Base with Gibraltar-based UK Armed Forces providing valuable security, logistic, communications and training facilities in support of operations. The Trilateral process started in October 2004 between the UK, Spain and the Government of Gibraltar concluded successfully in September 2006 with the Cordoba agreement. This was the first agreement from the Trilateral process, and covered non-military issues on telecoms, borders, civilian air travel and pensions for Spaniards who used to work in Gibraltar.

Military Aid to The Civil Authorities

33. The Home Office and Police lead on security within the UK but the MoD and Armed Forces provide specialist support when requested, drawing on defence capabilities. Explosive Ordnance Disposal teams respond to hundreds of calls from the police each year, though fortunately only a minority require disposal action. We also provided specialist defence scientific, technical and military capabilities to police criminal investigations and protection of the public on more than 60 occasions in 2006.

Northern Ireland

34. The year saw further progress towards an enduring political settlement in Northern Ireland. Following the cessation of the Provisional IRA's armed campaign in July 2005, security normalisation began on 1 August 2005. Since then the military presence in Northern Ireland has been scaled down significantly, reducing during the year from nearly 9,000 in April 2006 to 7,000 in March 2007 (of whom nearly 200 were serving overseas). By 1 August 2007 there will be no more than 5,000 military personnel in ten core sites in Northern Ireland, stationed there on the same basis as military

units based anywhere else in the United Kingdom and potentially available for world-wide operations. The Independent Monitoring Commission noted in March 2007 that the Armed Forces continued to meet this timetable. However, although the security situation in Northern Ireland continues to improve there are still threats from dissident paramilitary groups and of organised public disorder. There is therefore a continuing requirement for some residual military support to the police in Northern Ireland. However, since there is no further need for routine military support to the police, the three Royal Irish (Home Service) battalions, having successfully completed the task for which they were raised, were declared non-operational in September 2006. Their contribution to creating the environment for normalisation to begin, and their sacrifice, fortitude and commitment was recognised by the presentation of the Conspicuous Gallantry Cross to the Royal Irish Regiment by Her Majesty the Queen at a commemorative parade on 6 October 2006.

Fisheries Protection

35. In 2006-07 the Fishery Protection Squadron, based in Portsmouth, delivered 845 Fishery Patrol Days (855 in 2005-06) to the Marine Fisheries Agency of the Department for Environment, Food and Rural Affairs, policing fishing grounds for which the UK has responsibility. Of these, 73% were delivered by the three River Class Offshore Patrol Vessels, which continued to demonstrate extremely high levels of availability through the Contractor Logistic Support arrangement with Vosper Thorneycroft. 5,230 fishing vessels were identified (5,025 in 2005/06), 1312 were boarded (1258 in 2005-06), and 21 were detained at a UK port for further investigation and prosecution (19 in 2005-06). Overall the Squadron detected 221 fishing infringements demonstrating the success of intelligence-led operations. The UK is committed to the development of Joint Operations with EU partners to increase the efficiency and effectiveness of patrols.

Search and Rescue

36. The defence Search and Rescue (SAR) service exists to help military aircrew in difficulty. RN and RAF helicopters were deployed at eight bases around the UK, and in the Falkland Islands and Cyprus. Four RAF Mountain Rescue Teams, expert in dealing with aircraft crashes were based in remote areas in the Northern half of the UK. The RAF also maintained a Nimrod Maritime Patrol Aircraft on standby for SAR duties. These provided about two-thirds of the UK's integrated National Search and Rescue Framework for the Department for Transport's Maritime Coastguard Agency (MCA). The RAF also maintained the UK Aeronautical Rescue Coordination Centre at RAF Kinloss in Scotland, which coordinates the response

of all UK SAR aircraft and Mountain Rescue Teams and contains the UK Mission Control Centre for the global satellite based distress beacon detection system. Defence Search and Rescue services were called out 1,867 times in 2006-07 (1,833 in 2005-06), helping 1,457 people (1,466 in 2005-06) including some 1,430 civilians. In May 2006 the Government announced plans for the MoD and MCA to launch a joint Private Finance Initiative (PFI) competition to provide the MoD/MCA helicopter capability when the MCA service contract expires in 2012 and the MoD Sea Kings reach the end of their useful lives in 2017. The Competitive Dialogue stage of the competition began in February 2007, and selection of a preferred bidder is planned for early 2009. On the introduction of the new contract military involvement in UK based SAR will reduce to a minimum military aircrew manning level of 66 RN and RAF personnel compared to about 210 today.

Search and rescue

Drugs

37. The Armed Forces worked closely with the Serious Organised Crime Agency and other international agencies to combat the trafficking of drugs. In particular, Royal Naval vessels deployed to the Atlantic and the Caribbean contributed to a number of successful joint operations with our international partners and were directly involved in the destruction or seizure of about 17 tonnes of cocaine which, if it had reached the UK, represents a street value approaching £700M.

Activity and Concurrency Levels

38. The proportion of regular forces undertaking operations and other military tasks increased from just under 20% in the last quarter of 2005-06 to 21.4% in the last quarter of 2006-07 (see Table 1). Figure 2 sets out activity levels overall and by Service since 2001.

39. During the year the **Royal Navy** maintained the continuous at sea deterrent and the integrity of UK territorial waters and economic zones. It contributed to wider UK security through supporting UK commitments in Iraq, the Gulf, the North and South Atlantic, and to the NATO Response Force Maritime Component, and sustained the national strategic deterrent. During the deployment of 3 Commando Brigade in the second half of the year the Naval Service provided the bulk of personnel in Afghanistan. Aircraft from the Fleet Air Arm supported coalition activity in the Gulf and ISAF operations in Afghanistan. The Royal Navy maintained a presence in the Far East under the Five Powers Defence Agreement; HMS Westminster undertook an extended deployment. The Navy also carried out a large scale civilian evacuation from Lebanon. In the Antarctic HMS Endurance successfully completed an extended deployment in support of the Government's security and environmental goals.

Table 1: Percentage of Regular Armed Forces undertaking Operations or other Military Tasks during 2006-07

	January to March 2007	October to December 2006	July to September 2006	April to June 2006
Naval Service	19.7%	18.9%	16.6%	12.6%
Army	24.0%	25.2%	26.4%	25.9%
RAF	16.8%	14.6%	14.5%	13.4%
Overall	21.4%	21.4%	21.6%	20.2%

Notes:
1. Percentages are quarterly averages and reflect the burden of activity imposed by the operations and other military tasks undertaken by each service. Figures are based on man-day equivalents.
2. A list of Military Tasks can be found on the Department's website (www.mod.uk).

The overall percentage of Naval Service personnel undertaking operations and other military tasks rose from 13.5% in the last quarter of 2005-06 to 19.7% in the last quarter of 2006-07. The substantial increase largely reflects the deployment of 3 Commando Brigade and elements of the Fleet Air Arm to Afghanistan for 6 months from October 2006.

40. The **Army** deployed troops on operations in Iraq, Afghanistan, Northern Ireland, Bosnia, Kosovo, Ivory Coast and Sierra Leone and supported a variety of worldwide UN operations (including Cyprus). Both Iraq and Afghanistan were medium scale operations sustained throughout the year. Reflecting the normalisation process, force levels in Northern Ireland reduced. The percentage of Army personnel undertaking operations and other military tasks was much the same at the end of the year (24.0% in the last quarter of 2006-07) as at the beginning (25.1% in the last quarter of 2005-06), although it rose to 26.4% in the second quarter of the year prior to the replacement of 16 Air Assault Brigade by 3 Commando Brigade in Afghanistan (see paragraph 20).

41. The main areas of overseas commitment for the **Royal Air Force** continued to be the Gulf, Afghanistan and the Balkans. The Harrier, Nimrod, Support Helicopter and Air Transport fleets in particular were heavily committed to supporting operations in Iraq and Afghanistan throughout the year. The RAF also contributed to the permanent commitments in Northern Ireland, the Falkland Islands and Cyprus, and a range of other Military Tasks. Reflecting the increasing pressure of operations, the percentage of Royal Air Force personnel undertaking operations and other military tasks rose from 13.4% in the last quarter of 2005-06 to 16.8% in the last quarter of 2006-07.

42. The level of concurrent operations the MoD plans to be able to conduct and which it is resourced to have the capacity to deliver, was set out in the December 2003 Defence White Paper *Delivering Security in a Changing World*. This stated that the Armed Forces should be able to:

- mount an enduring Medium Scale peace support operation simultaneously with an enduring Small Scale peace support operation and a one-off Small Scale intervention operation;

- reconfigure forces rapidly to carry out the enduring Medium Scale peace support operation and a Small Scale peace support operation simultaneously with a limited duration Medium Scale intervention operation; and

- given time to prepare, undertake a demanding one-off Large Scale operation while still maintaining a commitment to a simple Small Scale peace support operation.

43. Figure 3 sets out in broad terms the level of concurrent operations the MoD and Armed Forces have in fact sustained since 2001. We have operated at the limits of, or above, the level that we are resourced and structured to deliver for seven of the last eight years, and every year since 2002. This is having an unavoidable impact on Service personnel (see paragraphs 216-218 under *Personnel Management*), and on the readiness of the Armed Forces to undertake contingent operations, in particular their ability to conduct higher level collective training (see paragraphs 55-58 under *Future Operations*).

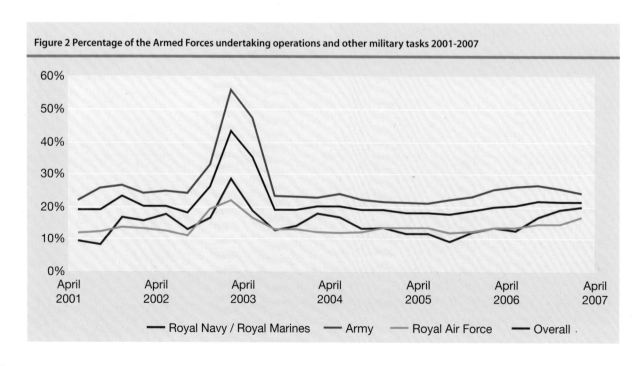

Figure 2 Percentage of the Armed Forces undertaking operations and other military tasks 2001-2007

Figure 3 Concurrency 2001-2006

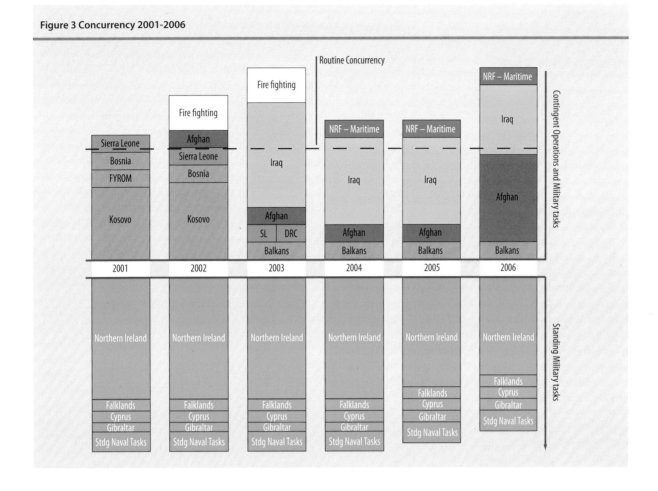

Further sources of information

44. Additional information on Current Operations is available from the following sources;

– Quarterly PSA reports to HM Treasury at www.mod.uk;

– *UK Defence Statistics 2007* available at www.dasa.mod.uk (from September 2006);

– Detailed information on current operations at www.mod.uk;

– Defence White Paper *Delivering Security in a Changing World,* (Cm 6041-I in December 2003) available at www.mod.uk;

– NAO Report Ministry of Defence Reserve Forces HC 964 dated 28 March 06 available at www.nao.org.uk;

– Cost of Operations at paragraph 260 and the analysis of Conflict Prevention costs at Note 2 to the accounts on page 200.

– The Defence Committee Sixth Report of Session 2004–05 on Iraq: An Initial Assessment of Post Conflict Operations (HC 65-I on 24 March 2005) available at www.parliament.the-stationery-office.co.uk;

– The Government's response to The Defence Committee Sixth Report of Session 2004–05 on Iraq: An Initial Assessment of Post Conflict Operations(HC436 on 20 July 05) available at www.mod.uk;

– Information on the Afghanistan Compact at www.fco.gov.uk;

– The Defence Committee Fourth Report of Session 2005-06 on Costs of peace-keeping in Iraq and Afghanistan:

– Spring Supplementary Estimates 2005-06(HC 980 on 16 March 2006) available at www.parliament.the-stationeryoffice.co.uk;

– The Government's response to The Defence Committee Fourth Report of Session 2005-06 on Costs of peacekeeping in Iraq and Afghanistan: Spring Supplementary Estimates 2005-06(HC1136);

– The Defence Committee Fifth Report of Session 2005-06 on The UK Deployment to Afghanistan (HC558 on 6 April 2006);

– Defence White Paper Delivering Security in a Changing World, (Cm 6041-I in December 2003) available at www.mod.uk;

– NAO *Third Validation Compendium Report* on PSA Data systems (HC127 dated 19 December 2006);

– House of Commons Defence Committee report on MoD Annual Report and Accounts 2005-06 (HC57 dated 28 November 2006), and the Government response (HC376 dated 9 March 2007).

– 14th Report of the Independent Monitoring Commission, March 2007 available from www.independentmonitoringcommission.org.

Essay: The Comprehensive Approach in Afghanistan

The Armed Forces are deployed in Afghanistan at the request of the Afghan Government as part of the United Nations mandated NATO-led International Security Assistance Force. Its purpose is to create a secure environment on the ground that enables national reconstruction and the creation over time by the people of Afghanistan of a stable country governed in their interests, with their consent, and by their own representatives. This is a long term mission. Achieving it requires joint and coordinated civil and military action, often described as a comprehensive approach. Without a military presence to provide a secure environment the international organisations, donor nations and Non-Government Organisations cannot do their work and help in reconstruction. But without the national development facilitated by this civil assistance there cannot over time be a long term settlement. So while the role played by the Armed Forces is essential, it is not enough in itself to deliver strategic success.

A successful stabilisation strategy therefore requires the linking up of civilian and military efforts, and an understanding of what policies will effectively contribute to stabilisation in a particular region. Afghanistan Provincial Reconstruction Teams embody this joint military and civilian approach on the ground. They are locally-based teams of international military and civilian personnel. Their core tasks are to support the extension of the authority of the Afghan Central Government, to support reform of the security sector, and to facilitate development and reconstruction. Each is tailored to the prevailing local security situation, socio-economic conditions, terrain, and reach of the Central Government. Every Team has a lead nation responsible, but they often contain military and civilian personnel from several nations. They work within the framework of the Afghanistan National Development strategy to build local confidence in the Afghan Government by engaging directly with local communities to prioritise quick impact projects, providing local political liaison and outreach with isolated communities, building the capacity of key institutions (including the Afghan National Army and Police) and supporting the delivery of essential services. The United Kingdom has spent some £20M on Microfinance Investment and Support Facility throughout Afghanistan. This has helped up to 170,000 people to set up small businesses. But the people of Afghanistan can only run businesses when they are secure, which is why supporting security sector reform has remained a key task for UK Armed Forces.

Within a Provincial Reconstruction Team the primary military role is to provide an enabling security environment in which the authority of the Afghan Government can be extended, security sector reform can be undertaken as well as development and reconstruction work. Military resources are divided between teams undertaking liaison with the local population, providing force protection, and providing support functions (such as overseeing locally-engaged guards or translators). In the first stages of the international effort to support the Afghan Government the UK led two Provincial Reconstruction Teams in the north of Afghanistan, at Mazar-e-Sharif (from 2003 to early 2006) and Meyanmeh (from 2003 to September 2005). These were instrumental in brokering peaceful resolutions to tribal disputes, overseeing the disarmament of militia forces, and providing effective police training. Development advisers within the Teams were able to manage projects including civil service training, refurbishment of government buildings and provision of equipment. There was also a good relationship with the various Non Governmental Organisations providing local reconstruction and assistance.

By the beginning of 2006 the security situation in these areas was broadly stable. ISAF therefore extended its operations into the south and east of Afghanistan, expanding the authority of the Government of Afghanistan across the whole country and facilitating reconstruction. This was critical to stabilisation. Clearly, however, the security environment in the south has been much less permissive, and required a significantly greater military effort to enable wider stabilisation, reconstruction and development work to proceed. This has been reflected in the increased number of UK military personnel deployed to the south of Afghanistan, where they have been conducting and supporting a sustained series of operations to counter insurgents.

As part of this wider effort, in May 2006 the UK deployed a fully integrated multi-disciplinary military/civilian mission to Helmand province, supported by funding channelled both through national programmes, and directly through Quick Impact Projects to give people access to alternative livelihoods. Other international agencies and a small number of Non Government Organisations have also supported reconstruction projects in Helmand. Using the model successfully applied in northern Afghanistan, the UK-led Provincial Reconstruction Team in Lashkar Gah includes advisors on development, governance, police reform and the justice sector. Local joint working is based on an integrated plan, supported by the structure of the Helmand executive group. This brings together the military commander with local representatives of the Foreign Office, the Department for International Development and the British Embassy Drugs Team, who are also the individuals within the Provincial Reconstruction Team responsible for delivering the various work strands of the plan. The group is directed by the UK Regional Coordinator (who has primacy for civilian issues) and the UK task force commander (who has primacy for military issues), ensuring that the vital Civil-Military link is maintained at all levels and that projects support each other.

There is still a long way to go, but much has already been achieved. Following decades of conflict, national Afghan institutions have been established from scratch. There have been successful national elections for the President and Parliament. Afghanistan is now educating over five million children, more than a third of whom are girls. Women, excluded from society by the Taliban, hold a quarter of the seats in the national Parliament. Nearly 30,000 Afghan National Army soldiers and more than 60,000 Afghan National Police officers have been recruited, trained and equipped. Getting to this point has required sustained and coordinated military and civil effort, both of which the UK has made, and continues to make, an important contribution.

Future Operations

Objective: Be ready for the tasks of tomorrow.

Public Service Agreement Target (SR2004 MoD Target 3)
Generate forces which can be deployed, sustained and recovered at the scales of effort required to meet the Government's strategic objectives.

Assessment and Performance Measures

Assessment: In order to support and sustain current operations the Department has taken deliberate risk against achieving the Public Service Agreement readiness target to undertake future contingent operations. It has not been possible to maintain the high level of readiness achieved in 2005-06, and it is uncertain whether readiness will recover to the target level by April 2008. This does not mean that the Armed Forces cannot support their current operational commitments, but their ability to take on additional operations that are more than Small Scale Focused Intervention is now limited.

Military Capability – by April 2008 achieve an average of 73% in the numbers of Force Elements reporting no serious or critical weakness against peacetime readiness targets:

- An average of 67% of Force Elements reported no critical or serious weaknesses in 2006-07 (77% in 2005-06);
- 2% of Force Elements reported critical weaknesses throughout the year;
- The proportion of Force Elements reporting serious or critical weaknesses increased from 26% in the last quarter of 2005-06 to 39% in the last quarter of 2006-07.

Force Generation – by April 2008 achieve 71% of Force Elements reporting no serious or critical weakness against the assessed ability to move from peacetime to immediate readiness:

- An average of 55% of Force Elements reported no critical or serious weaknesses in 2006-07 (70% in 2005-06);
- The proportion of Force Elements reporting critical weaknesses increased from 11% in the last quarter of 2005-06 to 12% in the last quarter of 2006-07;
- The proportion of Force Elements reporting serious or critical weaknesses increased from 39% in the last quarter of 2005-06 to 48% in the last quarter of 2006-07.

Force Sustainability – by April 2008 achieve 5% improvement in the ability to Deploy, Sustain and Recover forces for Contingent Military Tasks against the most demanding concurrency assumptions in Defence Planning Assumptions:

- Average performance in 2004-05 was 77.5%. This makes the target, as defined above, 82.5% by April 2008. Average performance during 2006-07 was 79.6%.

Readiness

45. The Ministry of Defence has a graduated readiness system in place to ensure that the right Force Elements (such as an Aircraft Carrier, an Army Brigade or an aircraft) are ready to deploy to conduct the range of missions that may be needed. The MoD sets requirements for the three Services in terms of the Force Elements required and the readiness at which they need to be held. Underpinning this are specific parameters for manning levels, equipment and logistic support, and collective training (that is the training units do together to ensure they can fight effectively as part of a larger force). Measuring and aggregating readiness is complex, not least because it is based on a judgment of what is required to enable the Armed Forces to respond to a wide range of potential challenges. How this is done is set out in the essay on *Measuring and Reporting Readiness* in the Department's Annual Report and Accounts 2004-05, and in greater detail in the National Audit Office Report *Assessing and Reporting Military Readiness* (see *Further Sources of Information* at the end of the chapter).

46. The overriding defence priority is success on current operations. Successfully prosecuting the military campaigns in Iraq and Afghanistan since 2002 has required the Armed Forces to operate significantly beyond the level that they are resourced and structured to sustain over the medium to long term. In order to support and sustain the increased actual operational tempo the Department has of necessity been unable to produce forces which meet the PSA readiness targets for contingent operations. This has been scrutinised by the National Audit Office, the Public Accounts Committee and the House of Commons Defence Committee. The readiness of certain Naval Force Elements continued to reflect the effects of the decision in 2005 to reduce the resources for support of Maritime contingent operations. Moreover, military personnel, particularly in the Army, have been engaged to such an extent on supporting and sustaining current operations that they have not had the time available to conduct the level of collective training needed to prepare fully for other contingent operations (paragraph 55 below). The Bowman conversion programme in the Army (paragraph 51) and the personnel drawdown programme in the Royal Air Force (paragraph 52) also had an impact. These factors are reflected in the fact that, as last year's *Annual Report and Accounts* suggested might be the case, it has not been possible to maintain the high level of readiness achieved in 2005-06. It is uncertain whether readiness will recover by April 2008 to the level required to meet the PSA target. This does not mean that the Armed Forces cannot support their current operational commitments, but their ability, particularly in the land environment, to take on new operations is more limited that it otherwise would be.

Performance against PSA Targets

47. 'Peacetime' readiness levels require the Armed Forces to be ready to respond to events in line with the levels envisaged in the Department's planning assumptions, from humanitarian support to war-fighting (see paragraph 1 under *Current Operations*). While these can be exceeded for limited periods without a significant impact on longer term readiness for contingent operations, the Armed Forces have now been engaged on operations at or above these levels for long enough that peacetime readiness levels dropped significantly during 2006-07. The 2004 Spending Review Public Service Agreement set a target of an average of 73% of Force Elements reporting no critical or serious weaknesses in achieving their funded peacetime readiness, representing a 5% improvement over the average quarterly performance in 2004-05. This level was reached in the third quarter of 2005-06, peaked at 77% in the fourth quarter of that year, and then dropped steadily throughout 2006-07 to 67% in the fourth quarter of the year. The proportion of Force Elements reporting serious weaknesses that would make deploying them within the required timescale difficult but not impossible increased from 26% in the fourth quarter of 2005-06 to 39% in the fourth quarter of 2006-07. The proportion of Force Elements reporting critical weakness that would make deploying them with the required timescale almost impossible remained steady at 2%.

Figure 4 Peacetime Readiness

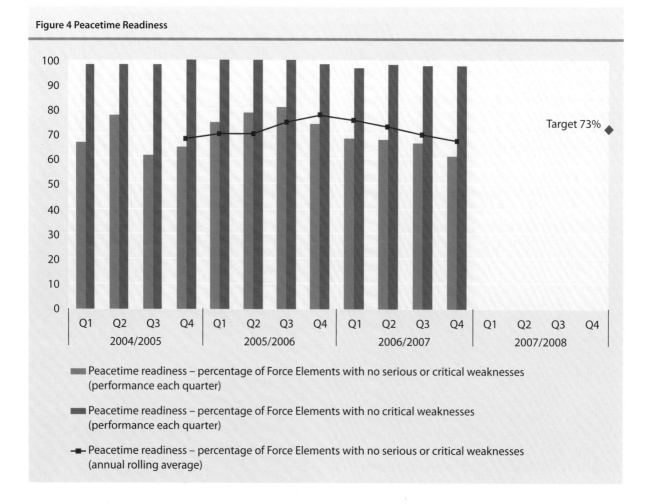

■ Peacetime readiness – percentage of Force Elements with no serious or critical weaknesses (performance each quarter)

■ Peacetime readiness – percentage of Force Elements with no critical weaknesses (performance each quarter)

-■- Peacetime readiness – percentage of Force Elements with no serious or critical weaknesses (annual rolling average)

HMS Iron Duke being replenished in the North Atlantic

48. The PSA Readiness Target also requires the Department to report the Armed Forces' ability to generate Force Elements from peacetime to immediate readiness, with a goal of 71% on average reporting no serious or critical weaknesses by April 2008 (a 5% improvement in the level achieved in 2004-05). Whether or not this is achieved is not taken into account in determining whether or not the PSA target has been met. Over the year performance fell off from an average of 70% in the fourth quarter of 2005-06 to an average of 55% in the fourth quarter of 2006-07, with the proportion of Force Elements reporting critical weaknesses rising slightly from 11% in the last quarter of 2005-06 to 12% in the last quarter of 2006-07, and the proportion reporting serious or critical weaknesses rising from 39% to 48%. This reflected the pressure on the Armed Forces resulting from operating above Defence Planning Assumptions, particularly in the Land environment, and the constraints on conducting collective training over and above that required for current operations until commitments return to the levels within Defence Planning Assumptions (see paragraph 49).

Figure 5 Assessed ability to generate force elements from peacetime to immediate readiness

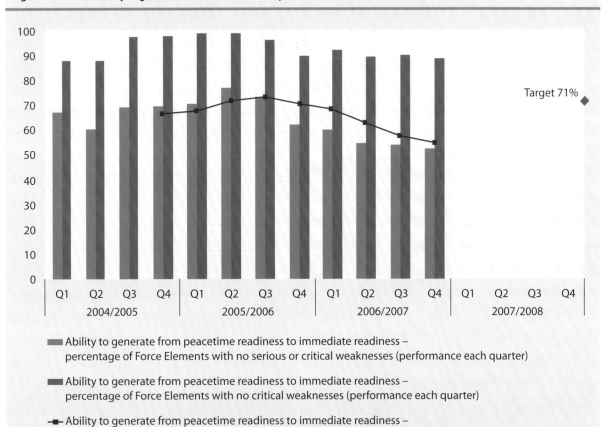

Target 71%

- ▬ Ability to generate from peacetime readiness to immediate readiness – percentage of Force Elements with no serious or critical weaknesses (performance each quarter)

- ▬ Ability to generate from peacetime readiness to immediate readiness – percentage of Force Elements with no critical weaknesses (performance each quarter)

- ▬■ Ability to generate from peacetime readiness to immediate readiness – percentage of Force Elements with no serious or critical weaknesses (annual rolling average)

49. Finally, the PSA Target requires the Department to report the ability to deploy the Armed Forces on operations at the most demanding level assumed by the planning assumptions (two medium and a small scale concurrently), sustain them in theatre and thereafter recover them to their home bases. Again, whether or not this is achieved is not taken into account in determining whether or not the PSA target has been met. Measuring this capability in the same way as the other readiness targets proved significantly more complex than expected at the time of the 2004 Spending Review – but we have now developed a mechanism for doing so, based on the regular qualitative assessments that we have been conducting since 2004-05. The assessment is a summary of defence's ability to deploy, sustain and recover the Force Elements required to conduct the most demanding contingent deployments that we have set out in out planning assumptions. The assessment is, therefore, a theoretical one, based on a generic operational scenario. Over the year our capability has improved very slightly, from an average of 78.7% in the fourth quarter of 2005-06 to an average of 79.6% in the fourth quarter of 2006-07 against a target of 82.5% by April 2008. This reflected some minor underlying improvement in Air transport and Battle Field Helicopter support.

Nimrod MR2 – heavily committed to Current Operations.

Royal Navy Readiness

50. The Royal Navy met all its mandated operational commitments, both at home and overseas, during 2006-07. While the Royal Navy largely continued to meet mandated readiness targets, the combination of a few critical specialist manpower shortages, difficulties with logistic support and industrial challenges had an impact in some areas on overall readiness states. Work is in hand to address these and other support issues. The Reduced Support Period applied to the surface fleet has now ended although the effects continue to have an impact on the availability and readiness of surface units. Based on the current and anticipated levels of funding, recovery of all units to previous levels of readiness and availability will not be achieved for some time. Submarines, aircraft and Royal Marine units were unaffected by the reduced support period.

Army Readiness

51. The Army remained heavily committed to operations throughout 2006-07. It successfully delivered trained and prepared Force Elements for all UK and overseas operations. It also provided completely the Spearhead Land element, but did not deliver the Airborne Task Force to the required readiness over the year for contingent operations. As in 2005-06, the continued high level of commitment to operations in Iraq and Afghanistan and the programme to bring into service the Bowman communications system across the Field Army severely constrained the Army's ability to provide further reaction forces (see paragraph 53). In particular, infantry, artillery, medical and ISTAR force elements were especially affected.

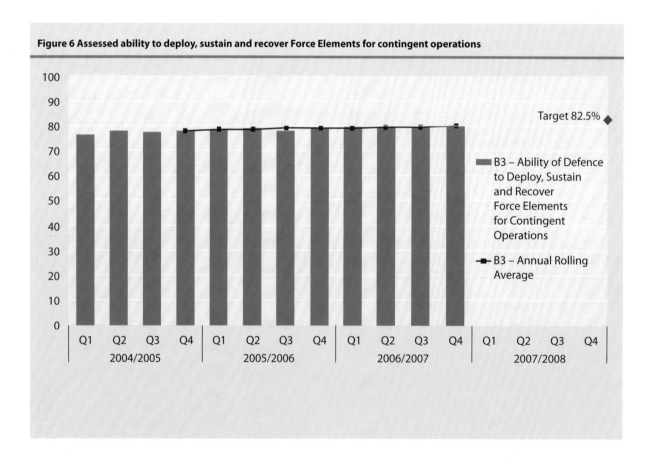

Figure 6 Assessed ability to deploy, sustain and recover Force Elements for contingent operations

Royal Air Force Readiness

52. The Royal Air Force continued successfully to meet its enduring Military Tasks and overseas commitments during 2006-07, successfully contributing forces to UK-based operations and to theatres around the world including the Gulf, Northern Ireland, the South Atlantic, Afghanistan and the Balkans. However, the high operational tempo, constrained training for contingent operations, reduced aircraft availability arising from planned modification and maintenance programmes, and specific manning imbalances arising over the period of the drawdown in Royal Air Force personnel numbers.

Joint Rapid Reaction Forces

53. The Joint Rapid Reaction Force (JRRF) is intended to provide a pool of highly capable, flexible and rapidly deployable Force Elements, trained and available on a graduated scale of readiness to deploy in support of Britain's foreign and security policy objectives. It is designed to be able to mount and sustain for up to six months a non-enduring Focused Intervention operation of up to Medium Scale, so long as operational concurrency remains within the level provided for in the Department's planning assumptions (see paragraph 42 under *Current Operations*). The level of operational commitment significantly exceeded this throughout 2006-07, with major forces deployed in Iraq, Afghanistan and the Balkans. The full JRRF contingent capability therefore could not be provided, reflecting the fact that the Armed Forces ability to support further short notice deployments was significantly constrained, with particular pressures on the Land component (see paragraph 51). Essential standby capabilities, for example for non-combatant Evacuation Operations, were maintained.

54. The Joint Force Headquarters (JFHQ) provides the standing operational headquarters to form the nucleus of a UK response to emerging crises for a range of rapid response operations. It maintained a high tempo of operational and training activity over the year: JFHQ deployed to Cyprus to command Force Elements assisting the non-combatant evacuation operation in Lebanon in support of the Foreign and Commonwealth Office. The Joint Force Logistics Component HQ, which provides rapidly deployable logistic command and control node for contingent operations, deployed to Afghanistan to help provide theatre-level logistic support to UK forces in Helmand. JFHQ also conducted a full scale exercise in Mozambique; ran two Medium Scale force projection and planning exercises drawing on wider expertise from other Government Departments, including

the FCO and the Post Conflict Reconstruction Unit; mentored the Greek Armed Forces in the development of their EU Force Headquarters; deployed specialists to UK and UN operational headquarters in Iraq, Afghanistan, the Democratic Republic of Congo and Sudan; and took forward contingency planning for a number of potential operations. The Permanent Joint Operating Bases in Cyprus, Gibraltar, Diego Garcia and the Falkland Islands were exercised in a variety of scenarios, or reviewed to update existing Joint Contingency Plans.

Collective Training

55. The Department's training priority during the year was to deliver pre-deployment training to a sufficient standard to support current operations. This was achieved, although the pressure of numbers on pre-training resources and infrastructure capacity meant that in some cases it was not as thorough as was desirable. But the Armed Forces, particularly the Army, were engaged to such an extent on supporting and sustaining current operational commitments that they were not able to conduct the level of collective training needed to prepare fully for other potential contingent operations, particularly at medium and large scale; in contrast, the higher level joint headquarters exercise programme described above was able to exercise and sustain the ability to command and control such operations through the use of command post exercises that train the headquarters' staff but not the subordinate force elements. Over time this is unavoidably reducing the readiness of both commanders and the forces they command to conduct the full potential range of contingent operations by limiting the range and depth of their experience. It is not possible to address this shortfall without reducing the standard of training and preparation for current operations.

Training for deployment to Iraq

56. The Department is analysing the qualitative impact of the training shortfall and has developed a new Joint Collective Training and Exercise Strategy (JCT&E) that takes into account current commitments and constraints. This provides strategic guidance for defence training in coming years to ensure that the Armed Forces can continue to conduct enduring operations whilst retaining contingent capabilities at an appropriate level. The strategy will also support restoration of the full capability to conduct all types of military operations as soon as possible after operational commitments return to the levels assumed in the Defence Planning Assumptions. At a management level, defence is seeking to mitigate the effects of the current level of commitments on training for contingent operations through the Defence Exercise Programme (DXP) management process. This identifies opportunities within single service exercise programmes for combining events in order to achieve efficiencies and greater collective synergies.

House-clearing drills to prepare for deployment

57. The changes and synergies achieved by the new JCT&E and DXP processes make year on year comparison of the volume of exercises difficult. On the one hand the overall volume of collective training has fallen because the overall Defence Exercise Programme has comprised a more focused and balanced range of events, including more use of combined training events. These have delivered both efficiencies and improved quality of training. Overseas combined training involving potential coalition partners, such as

Exercise STEPPE EAGLE with Kazakhstan, have been particularly successfull. On the other hand we are now recording more training events on the DXP, where hitherto single services may not have reported or even recorded some exercises. In comparing figures, 680 training events were scheduled for 2006-07, of which 64 (9.4%) had to be cancelled, compared to 533 training events with 58 (10.8%) cancelled in 2005-06 (see table 2 below). Unfortunately this included the planned combined NATO/EU crisis management exercise in February 2007, limiting multi-national exercising at the strategic (i.e. defence ministry) level in the year to a short, national procedural exercise.

Table 2: the number of exercises scheduled and proportion cancelled since 2004-05

Year	Scheduled Training Events	Cancelled Events	Percentage
2006-07	680	64	9.4%
2005-06	533	58	10.8%
2004-05	379	79	20.8%

58. Despite the reduction in overseas training for contingent operations, the increase in pre-deployment training (in particular training for harsh environments) required continued use of overseas training areas. This increased the pressure on strategic lift assets and platforms that were fully focused on operations and had only limited capacity to support exercises. As a result, training events were forced to rely on short notice charter of civilian aircraft. During this audit period, 14 exercises required short notice charters at a cost of nearly £4M.

Sustainability and Deployability

59. The Armed Forces were successfully deployed and sustained on a wide range of military and humanitarian relief operations during the year. The net additional costs incurred to deploy, sustain and subsequently recover forces on operations are met from the central Government reserve. The MoD continues to look for ways to increase the effectiveness of the sustainability and deployability processes, including how better to identify the resources required for sustaining future operations. This process focuses on differentiating between the stock that has to be held and that which can be procured within the warning time for the operation. Given the diverse range of operations being sustained, the UK remained committed to several multinational strategic initiatives to improve the ability to prepare, mount and deploy appropriate personnel and equipment.

60. Air transport provides an important element of deploying and sustaining forces. The Department is making large investments in the future Royal Air Force air transport fleet, in particular through the A400M and Future Strategic Tanker Aircraft projects. The Department has also supported NATO initiatives to increase the strategic airlift available to Allies (see paragraph 64 under *Policy*). In August 2006 it also announced the acquisition of a fifth C-17 transport aircraft, due for delivery in 2008, alongside the purchase of the four C-17 aircraft currently leased from Boeing. While these programmes will provide a robust medium to long-term solution, the Department took forward a range of work to improve the operation of the current airbridge to Iraq and Afghanistan, including an end-to-end review which recommended improvements to facilities at RAF Brize Norton and RAF Akrotiri, and refurbishment of the runway at Kandahar Airfield to enable it to operate large aircraft.

C-17 Globemaster at Kabul International Airport.

Further sources of information

61. Additional information on Future Operations is available from the following sources;

– Defence White Paper *Delivering Security in a Changing World,* (Cm 6041-I in December 2003) available at www.mod.uk;
– Quarterly PSA reports to HM Treasury at www.mod.uk;
– NAO Report *Assessing and Reporting Military Readiness* (HC72 dated 15 June 2005) at www.nao.org.uk;
– MoD Annual Report and Accounts 2004-05 (HC464 dated 28 October 2005), essay on *Measuring and Reporting Readiness* at www.mod.uk;
– Public Accounts Committee Report on *Assessing and reporting military readiness* (HC667 dated 28 February 2006), and the Treasury Minute containing the Government Response (Cm 6775 dated 26 April 2006) at www.official-documents.gov.uk;
– MoD Annual Report and Accounts 2005-06 (HC1394 dated 14 July 2006), essay on *Delivering Readiness at the Front Line* at www.mod.uk;
– NAO *Third Validation Compendium Report* on PSA Data systems (HC127 dated 19 December 2006) at www.nao.org.uk;
– House of Commons Defence Committee report on MoD Annual Report and Accounts 2005-06 (HC57 dated 28 November 2006), and the Government response (HC376 dated 9 March 2007) at www.official-documents.gov.uk.

Essay – Supporting current operations and the impact on readiness

The readiness levels of the Armed Forces are a complex but important measure of the United Kingdom's defence capability. It would be clearly inefficient and expensive to maintain every element of the force structure at the highest levels of readiness at all times. The Armed Forces therefore use a system of graduated readiness, in which individual Force Elements follow a readiness cycle. This is designed to achieve the level of collective readiness and preparation required to enable appropriate Force Elements to deploy on operations, followed by a period of recuperation, development and training for wider roles before potentially deploying again on operations. When followed, such a stable cycle of activity enables personnel and unit harmony (i.e. achieving the proper interval between operational deployments) to be maintained.

Current Operations. In Iraq and Afghanistan the Armed Forces are currently delivering two challenging and enduring Medium Scale Peace Enforcement operations, as well as sustaining both standing military tasks (such as the operation of the nuclear deterrent force) and a number of other smaller contingent operations. The level of effort involved is significantly in excess of that for which defence is routinely structured and resourced. Delivering this has required using Force Elements that would otherwise have been allocated to the Joint Rapid Reaction Force high readiness pool, which comprises the United Kingdom's main strategic reserve. In short, sustaining current operations has required the Department to draw heavily on forces that would otherwise have been held at readiness for contingencies. This is a conscious and measured risk, supported by analysis of the possible consequences and an awareness of the time necessary to restore the ability to generate a Medium Scale contingent force.

The consequences of this approach, and therefore the level of risk involved, are not evenly spread across the force structure. The campaigns in Iraq and Afghanistan require particularly heavy commitment of land forces; associated command and control facilities; intelligence, surveillance, target acquisition and reconnaissance assets; helicopters; strategic air transport; and medical and logistics enabling assets. The force structure in these areas is now fully stretched. For example, the MoD is now deploying four manoeuvre brigades each year from a pool of just nine brigades plus residual assets. The remainder of the force structure is fully involved in supporting this (which includes preparing for operations, manpower augmentation, and training support) while also maintaining the other military commitments worldwide at sea, on the land and in the air.

Readiness for Contingent Operations. As a result of the pressures arising from this level of operational commitment, the available Joint Rapid Reaction Force high readiness reserve has inevitably shrunk from the capacity to conduct a Medium Scale operation to a more limited pool of forces essentially comprising a Small Scale capacity. The Armed Forces remain able to undertake critical non-discretionary operations, including Small Scale Non-combatant Evacuation Operations such as the evacuation of civilians from Lebanon in 2007, and the potential requirement to provide Public Order reinforcements to the Police Service of Northern Ireland. Nor is there any immediate risk to their ability to support the United Kingdom's international reserve commitments (in particular the EU Battle Group and the NATO Response Force), although at the current operational tempo they will need support from NATO allies with Armed Forces less committed to international operations to meet some NATO Response Force obligations.

There are a number of other consequences of the current level of operational commitment:
● Collective training has become increasingly focussed on preparation for operations (training for "the" war) as opposed to covering the range of specialist roles and concepts required for contingent operations at warfighting levels (training for "a" war). In particular the ability to conduct collective training for Large-Scale war-fighting operations in order to maintain 'seed-corn' experience has deteriorated ;
● It has only been possible to support this level of effort through substantial increases in routine activity and erosion of aspects of personnel harmony, with inevitable risks for personnel retention;
● There will inevitably be a medium-term impact on the life of key equipments across defence; and
● The continued generation of Force Elements for current commitments has relied not only on significant internal augmentation of deployed units from other parts of the Armed Forces, but also on considerable and continuing support from the Reserve Forces.

The Armed Forces continue to be able to generate and sustain high quality, properly trained Force Elements for current operations. But when commitments return to the routine levels envisaged in Defence Planning Assumptions, a period of substantially reduced activity and adequate resources will be needed if they are to recuperate and regenerate to the readiness levels required to meet the full range of possible contingent operations for which they plan.

Policy

Objective: Work with Allies, other governments and multilateral institutions to provide a security framework that matches new threats and instabilities

Objective: Public Service Agreement Targets (SR2004 MoD Targets 2 and 4):

By 2008, deliver improved effectiveness of UK and international support for conflict prevention by addressing long-term structural causes of conflict, managing regional and national tension and violence, and supporting post-conflict reconstruction, where the UK can make a significant contribution, in particular Africa, Asia, Balkans and the Middle East. (Joint target with DfID and FCO)

Play a leading role in the development of the European Security Agenda, and enhance capabilities to undertake timely and effective security operations, by successfully encouraging a more efficient and effective NATO, a more coherent and effective European Security and Defence Policy operating in strategic partnership with NATO, and enhanced European defence capabilities. (Joint target with FCO)

Assessment and Performance Measures

Assessment: There was continuing progress in developing complementary NATO and EU political and military capabilities, and the Department remained on course to meet the European Security Public Service Agreement target. But there is a need for fairer sharing of collective commitments, and for investment in expeditionary capabilities. The Department also remained broadly on course to achieve the Conflict Prevention PSA target, with some slippage.

A more efficient and effective NATO:

- Continuing effective NATO-led operations and missions;
- NATO Response Force fully operational;
- Comprehensive Political Guidance endorsed.

A more coherent and effective ESDP operating in strategic partnership with NATO:

- Continuing effective EU civil and military missions;
- Reform of Secretariat structures and new facilities for generating EU Operations Centre provided stronger capability to plan and run civilian and civil-military operations.

Enhanced European defence capabilities:

- EU military requirements catalogue agreed in support of Headline Goal 2010;
- EU Battlegroups concept achieved Full Operational Capability.

Implement Global Counter Terrorism strategy:

- Provision of training to build the counter terrorist capacity of other nations.

Counter the threat from chemical, biological, radiological or nuclear weapons:

- Parliamentary approval of Government's proposals for future UK nuclear deterrent;
- Continuing work to strengthen arms control and export control regimes;
- Continuing progress on destruction of Russian chemical weapons and redirection of former chemical, biological and nuclear weapons scientists.

Effective international and UK conflict prevention initiatives:

- Of twelve indicators, nine broadly on course, one already met, and two not on course;
- Work to reduce proliferation of small arms and light weapons;
- UN resolution on legally binding global treaty in conventional arms.

NATO, European Defence and the United Nations

62. The maintenance of the transatlantic relationship and the security and stability of Europe remains fundamental to the United Kingdom's security and defence policy, and we are a leading contributor to NATO and European Union security and defence arrangements. But our security and prosperity depend also on wider international stability, freedom and stable economic development. As a permanent member of the UN Security Council, the United Kingdom strives internationally to support the rule of law and act as a force for good. We take a comprehensive approach, both diplomatic and military to address the threat posed by international terrorism and to counter the threat from Weapons of Mass Destruction. We are also committed to tackling international conflict and its causes, to mitigate the effects of conflict when it breaks out, and to assist in the task of post-conflict reconstruction.

NATO and European Security

North Atlantic Treaty Organisation (NATO): more efficient and effective

63. The UK continued to make a significant contribution to NATO-led operations and missions in 2006-07, leading the International Security Assistance Force (ISAF) in Afghanistan for most of the year; providing forces to NATO's peacekeeping force in Kosovo, to Operation ACTIVE ENDEAVOUR (a maritime counter-terrorism operation in the Mediterranean), to NATO's Training Mission for Iraqi security personnel, and as part of NATO's support to the African Union's peacekeeping mission in Darfur. UK efforts helped lay the foundations for the successful summit meeting of NATO Heads of State and Government in Riga in November 2006, where all Allies reaffirmed their long-term commitment to Afghanistan and resolve to ensure the success of the ISAF mission, and agreed to review what more they could contribute. Some progress was also made on the lifting of national caveats, and all contributors committed to coming to each other's assistance if needed in an emergency. The UK continued to lobby other NATO and non-NATO members to provide more, and several Allies announced deployments of additional forces at the NATO Ministerial conference in Seville in February 2007. The UK announced at the end of February that it would deploy a further 1,400 UK personnel over the summer (see paragraph 20 under *Current Operations*).

HMS Montrose preparing for Operation ACTIVE ENDEAVOUR

64. Continuing defence transformation is essential for NATO to meet the challenges of the demanding security environment. At the Riga Summit the high-readiness NATO Response Force (NRF) was declared fully operational. The UK made a significant contribution to the NRF 6 rotation of forces (January – June 2006), leading both the Land and Air Component Commands, provided limited Maritime and Air Force Elements to NRF 7 (July – December 2006) and NRF 8 (January – June 2007). Similarly at the Summit, initiatives were agreed to enhance Special Forces' cooperation, and improve multi-national logistics support; and a number of new initiatives were agreed to increase the strategic airlift available to Allies. The Summit endorsed NATO's Comprehensive Political Guidance, which provides the framework to progress this work over the next 10-15 years, in particular to develop modern, rapidly deployable, expeditionary capabilities. Furthermore, recognising that strategic success cannot be achieved by military means alone, and that the international community must work coherently across many other fields (such as reconstruction and development, counter-narcotics, good governance, and law and order), NATO decided to apply this approach throughout an operation, from initial planning to execution, and to enhance its ability to work with relevant international institutions and other organisations. It also decided to develop pragmatic proposals to improve dialogue and cooperation through Partnerships for Peace (in Europe and Central Asia), the Mediterranean Dialogue (in North Africa and the Middle East), the Istanbul Co-operation Initiative (in the Gulf), and with other interested countries such as Japan, Australia and New Zealand.

European Security and Defence Policy: more coherent and effective

65. The UK continued to play a leading role in the development of the European Security and Defence Policy (ESDP), in particular providing a substantial military contingent for the ESDP military mission EUFOR-ALTHEA in Bosnia until March 2007 (see paragraphs 26-27 under *Current Operations*). The Armed Forces also contributed small numbers of personnel to the successful EU military operation in the Democratic Republic of Congo, which supported the UN in maintaining stability over the Congolese election period. The UK also supported the EU's Aceh Monitoring mission in Indonesia, EU Support Action to the African Union's mission in Darfur, missions to support the rule of law in Iraq and Palestine and the rule of law, and security sector reform missions in the Democratic Republic of Congo. The diversity of these operations underlined the EU's unique ability to deploy a range of military and civilian instruments to undertake tasks from security and stabilisation, to monitoring and mentoring of indigenous police forces, to training judiciary, border monitoring and tackling of organised crime.

Primary Health Clinic, Kenya.

66. In 2005 the UK launched a tri-presidency initiative with Austria and Finland on Civil-Military Coordination, to improve internal coherence and external connectivity in the EU's crisis management activities. The UK supported Secretary General Solana's work to reform and improve the Secretariat structures and welcomed the new facilities for generating an EU operations Centre. These give the EU a stronger capability to plan and run civilian and civil-military operations. Experience in Bosnia and in Sudan has demonstrated the importance of the EU and NATO working collaboratively. The UK therefore continued to seek ways to improve EU-NATO relations at the operational and political/strategic levels.

Enhanced European Defence capabilities

67. The UK continued to participate fully in the work of the European Defence Agency, including on the Long Term Vision of the EU's capability needs, evaluation of participating States' investment in defence, and implementation of the Code of Conduct encouraging greater competition in defence procurement. The Headline Goal 2010 sets out the EU Level of Ambition for military crisis management, and the UK continued to work with other Member States and the EU Military Staff on its implementation. In particular, nations agreed the Requirements Catalogue converting the broad level of ambition into specific capability requirements. Work continued to agree the Progress Catalogue in late 2007. This will assess the EU military capabilities needed to meet the Requirements Catalogue and identify shortfalls and associated potential operational risks, to serve as a platform for future capability development.

68. The EU Battlegroups concept achieved Full Operational Capability in January 2007. Two Battlegroups (each about 1,500 personnel) are now on standby for each six-month period, enabling the EU rapidly to launch military response operations. The UK supported this initiative from the outset and continued to work with Partners to develop the idea, in particular to ensure that EU Battlegroups and the NATO Response Force are compatible and mutually supportive (for example, by using NRF standards and criteria for national Battlegroups and harmonising planning timelines). The UK provided a national Battlegroup on standby in 2005, and plans to do so again in 2008 and 2010.

Conventional Arms Control

69. Conventional arms control activities under the Conventional Armed Forces in Europe Treaty, Vienna Document 1999, and Open Skies agreement continued to contribute to conflict prevention and stability across the Organisation for Security and Cooperation in Europe. During this year, under the provision of these agreements, the UK hosted 13 inward visits and participated in 46 outward visits, in addition to various training missions and stand by tasks.

Countering Terrorism

70. The Department continued to make an important contribution to the UK's counter terrorism strategy during 2006-07. While the Armed Forces can play an important role in pursuing terrorists and those who support them, defence concentrated, within the wider government effort, on building the will, understanding and capabilities of other countries to improve their own domestic counter-terrorism capabilities and their ability to cooperate operationally with the UK when necessary. This included military training in a wide range of activities such as combat skills, VIP protection, bomb disposal, coastguard operations, and ensuring an integrated response to crisis management. The Armed Forces' contributions to conflict prevention and peace support operations also helped prevent terrorism by tackling some of its underlying causes.

Countering the threat from chemical, bilolgical, radiological and nuclear weapons

71. The ambitions of a small number of countries of concern, and some terrorists, to acquire chemical, biological, radiological or nuclear weapons, and the imperative of an effective international response, require continuous efforts to safeguard and strengthen international norms. The UK aims to reduce the risk that state or non-state actors will acquire such weapons or use them against the UK, its forces or our interests. The MoD worked closely with other Government Departments to support international export control regimes reducing the threat of proliferation of material, expertise, weapons, and their means of delivery, and to constrain the intent and ability of non states actors and potential proliferating states world-wide to acquire illicit capabilities. In particular it worked with the Foreign and Commonwealth Office and Department for Trade and Industry (now the Department for Business, Enterprise and Regulatory Reform) under the Global Partnership programme to take forward a number of projects to control and reduce existing stockpiles. During the year Ministers agreed new oversight arrangements and a new pooled budget to increase the effectiveness and flexibility of the programme. In close cooperation with the US and Canada the Department also took forward a small programme of work to help redirect former nuclear, biological and chemical weapons scientists from the Former Soviet Union, Iraq and Libya.

Nuclear Arms Control

72. During 2006-07 the International Atomic Energy Agency continued to be unable to confirm the scale or exclusively peaceful intent of Iran's nuclear programme consistent with its obligations under the Nuclear Non Proliferation Treaty (NPT). In October 2006 the Democratic People's Republic of Korea conducted an apparent nuclear explosion. Both issues raised concerns about international nuclear non-proliferation and disarmament, and were referred to the UN Security Council. The UK remains fully committed to all its obligations under the NPT (on non-proliferation, disarmament, and the peaceful use of nuclear energy) and under the Comprehensive Nuclear Test Ban Treaty. We reaffirmed the unequivocal undertaking to accomplish the total elimination of nuclear arsenals leading to nuclear disarmament and continued to press for multilateral negotiations towards mutual, balanced and verifiable reductions in nuclear weapons. In particular in May 2006 the UK supported the tabling by the United States of a draft treaty in the Conference on Disarament to end the production of fissile material for use in nuclear weapons (the Fissile Material Cut-Off Treaty).

Biological Arms Control

73. The Sixth Review Conference of the Biological and Toxin Weapons Convention was held in November/December 2006 and agreed a programme of work for 2007-2010. Defence personnel, particularly experts from the Defence Science and Technology Laboratory, Porton Down, continued to make a key contribution.

Chemical Arms Control

74. In March 2007 the Minister for the Armed Forces announced that the UK had completed destruction at Dstl Porton Down of old UK chemical weapons from the two world wars within the ten year deadline required by the Chemical Weapons Convention. Significant progress was made in the MoD Global Partnership programme to support Russia with destruction of its stockpiles of chemical weapons. Using a project management team at Dstl, the Department took forward projects at the Shchuch'ye Chemical Weapons Destruction facility on behalf of the UK, Canada, Belgium, the Czech Republic, The Netherlands, New Zealand, Norway, Sweden, the EU, and the Nuclear Threat Initiative (a US Non-Government Organisation). In July 2006, the MoD announced that it would provide further assistance, in close partnership with Canada, at a further destruction facility at Kizner.

Export Controls

75. The MoD contributed both specialist and policy advice to the UK's efforts to ensure that the multilateral export control regimes and arrangements (whether dealing with conventional weapons, associated dual use equipment and technology, or equipment and technology that could contribute to a nuclear, biological or chemical weapons programme) continued to evolve to take into account advances in technology and changes in the geopolitical situation. The Department also participated in the preliminary work for the Government's review of the legislation introduced in 2004 under the Export Control Act. Details of licensing decisions and performance achieved in processing export license applications are published in the *Annual Report on United Kingdom Strategic Export Controls*.

Proliferation Security Initiative

76. Defence officials continued to play a leading role in meetings and exercises of the Proliferation Security Initiative Operational Experts Groups. These aim to improve nations' abilities to interdict nuclear, biological and chemical weapons, their precursors and means of delivery. The UK hosted a major maritime industry workshop in October 2006 which brought together representatives of the Governments and the shipping industries of 20 countries.

Deterrence

77. Deterrence aims to convince a potential adversary that the consequence of a particular course of action outweighs the potential gains. All the UK's military capabilities, conventional and nuclear, have a role to play in this. The fundamental principles underpinning nuclear deterrence have not changed since the end of the Cold War. However deterrence in the 21st Century is going to be more complex in a multi-faceted and more fragmented security environment, populated by an array of potential adversaries and presenting less predictable security challenges. The UK's deterrence posture must therefore remain flexible enough to respond to these potential challenges, in whatever form they present themselves. The publication in December 2006 of the Government's White Paper *The Future of the United Kingdom's Nuclear Deterrent* (see essay on page 60), which Parliament approved in March 2007, sets out this position against a particular range of possible future risks and challenges. Nuclear

weapons continue to provide the ultimate guarantee of the UK's security by deterring and preventing nuclear blackmail and acts of aggression against the UK's vital interests that cannot be countered by other means. The UK will retain only the minimum amount of destructive power required to achieve deterrence objectives. The Government deliberately maintains ambiguity about precisely when, how and at what scale the UK would contemplate using nuclear weapons. To do otherwise would simplify the calculations of a potential aggressor by defining more precisely the circumstances in which the Government might consider the use of the UK's nuclear capabilities. However, the Government has made clear many times over many years that the UK would only contemplate using nuclear weapons in extreme circumstances of self-defence and in accordance with the UK's international legal obligations.

Trident missile fired from HMS Vanguard.

Chemical, Biological, Radiological and Nuclear Defence

78. The Armed Forces face a diverse range of potential chemical, biological, radiological and nuclear threats and hazards on operations. The Government's policy is to maintain the UK's political and military freedom of action to pursue the UK's foreign and security policy aims despite the presence, threat or use of such weapons. To achieve this the Department has strategies to counter the threat of these weapons, including a range of capabilities to defend against them, and maintains comprehensive programmes to develop these defensive capabilities further. The UK continues to improve inter-operability with NATO, the EU and, bilaterally, especially with the US, and plays an influential role on NATO's Senior Defence Group on Proliferation, which considers NATO-wide policy on these threats and seeks to develop joint defensive capabilities across the Alliance against these weapons.

Missile Defence

79. The UK has maintained its close relationship with the US in missile defence. In February 2007 the US Government announced its intention to open negotiations with Poland and the Czech Republic over the possible basing of US missile defence system components in those countries. This reflects the US's desire to expand their national missile defence system to provide a more robust defence against an attack from the Middle East, while at the same time offering protection for friends and allies in Europe. The UK is closely engaged in discussion of the implications of these proposals within NATO and with Russia.

UK and International Conflict Prevention

80. While the primary focus of the MoD remains providing the capability to conduct military operations, it is clearly better to prevent the need for them arising. We therefore continued to support the FCO and DfID in work to tackle the underlying causes of conflict and thus minimise the likelihood of a need for UK military intervention. The Government's top level objectives are set out in the joint MoD/FCO/DfID 2004 Spending Review Public Service Agreement target for conflict prevention. The work is primarily taken forward through the Africa and Global Conflict Prevention Pools. The Pools form a tri-departmental programme that ensures a coherent and consistent approach is taken across Government to deliver joined-up UK policy making, action planning and activity to prevent conflict and dispel hostility. The Government has made progress, and remains broadly on course to achieve the PSA target by 2008, albeit with some slippage. Of the twelve detailed indicators underpinning the target, nine were broadly on course at the end of the year, one (increasing the number of military personnel across the world available for UN Peacekeeping) had already been met, and two (the Middle East Peace Process and Iraq) were not on course. During the year there were improvements in the situation in the Balkans (see paragraphs 25-27 under *Current Operations*), with UK efforts focusing on Kosovo's final status process and Bosnia and Herzegovina holding successful elections. The UK made a significant contribution to the success of presidential, parliamentary and provincial elections held in the Democratic Republic of Congo, which were declared credible and transparent by all observers. Detailed reports on progress against the individual Public Service Agreement targets are at Annex C.

81. As set out in the chapter on current operations, the main defence contribution towards this goal during the year was the forces deployed to Iraq, Afghanistan and the Balkans to provide the security on the ground that enable reconstruction and conflict prevention activity to be taken forward. The net cost of these operations in 2006-07 was £1,796M (see Note 2 to the Departmental Resource Accounts). About a further 300 personnel were deployed on UN peacekeeping operations (see paragraph 29 under current operations). The MoD also contributes to the work of the Pools through Defence Relations tools. In particular, the Department provided Security Sector Reform assistance in areas where UK forces were engaged on peace building tasks (see paragraphs 12 and 22 under *Current Operations*), and supported the development of deployable African, Balkans and Central and Eastern European peacekeeping capabilities for regional and international security intervention operations.

Africa Conflict Prevention Pool

82. The MoD continued to work very closely with DfID and FCO on conflict prevention and capacity building in Africa through the Africa Conflict Prevention Pool. Under the Pool's joint strategy, the MoD focused on providing advice, funding and technical support to the African Union for the development of the African Standby Force, which will eventually supply a multi-national pool of African troops held at readiness for service in African-led peace support operations. The development of sub-regional and national capacity to conduct these is an important aspect of this, and the MoD accordingly provided training to the Armed Forces of some 20 African countries over the year in order to improve their ability to take part in peacekeeping missions and to contribute units to the future force. Based on the 'train-the-trainer' principle, much of this work was led by British Military Advisory and Training Teams based in Kenya, South Africa, Ghana and Nigeria. This investment in peace support training yielded significant results over the year; In West Africa, the Department provided training for a Nigerian battalion and company size units from Ghana and Gambia (some 850 troops in all) which deployed with the African Union peacekeeping force in Sudan's Darfur region. In the Republic of South Africa, the Department helped with preparatory training for some 5,300 South African National Defence Force troops deploying on peace support operations in Sudan and with the UN in Burundi and the Democratic Republic of Congo. The Department also continued to support a number of key regional training centres across the continent, including the Kofi Annan International Peacekeeping Training Centre in Ghana, and the Karen Peace Support Training Centre and International Mine Action Training Centre in Kenya. Since the latter opened in 2005 it has

provided de-mining and/or mine awareness training to some 3,800 African and international personnel. As members of the UK-led international Military Advisory and Training Team, some 80 British Service personnel have helped Sierra Leone to build professional, democratically accountable Armed Forces, providing a key pillar of the UK's comprehensive Security Sector Reform effort in the country and eight Ministry of Defence Police deployed in support of election monitoring/security preparations for the elections due in August this year.

Setting up base in Sierra Leone.

Global and African Conflict Prevention Pools

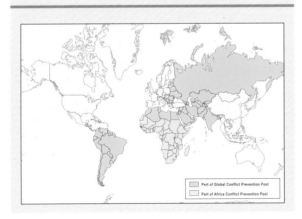

Part of Global Conflict Prevention Pool
Part of Africa Conflict Prevention Pool

Global Conflict Prevention Pool

83. Within the Global Pool the defence contribution is focused on Capacity Building and Security Sector Reform. In particular, through 'train-the trainer' schemes, the Armed Forces transfer their military skills within an accountable and democratic framework to help other countries become self-sufficient and

responsible for their own security, and by extension to enable them to contribute personnel to international Peace Support Operations. The Global Pool's Security Sector Reform strategy continued to work to strengthen the security institutions of partner nations and improve the governance of their security sectors, including the Armed Forces, national intelligence services, and police and justice systems. The British Military Advisory and Training Team based in Vyskov in the Czech Republic continued to play a key role in the delivery of defence reform, and in preparing nations to play a more active part in UN-mandated Peace Support Operations. Amongst many training projects during the year, the Team in Vyskov supported the British Military Advisory and Training Team in Nigeria to train Nigerian troops deploying to Darfur (see paragraph 82). The Department also continued to support the training of members of the new Iraqi and Afghan national armies in professional leadership and military skills (see paragraphs 12 and 22 under *Current Operations*).

Mines awareness lesson in Vyskov.

84. Under the Global Pool MoD, FCO and DfID also worked towards a more coherent response to the reduction of small arms proliferation and armed violence, and in particular pursued a national programme of assistance in stockpile management, security and destruction of small arms and light weapons complementary to the work underway in the UN. The strategy takes a holistic approach to the problem of small arms proliferation, seeking to tackle their supply, demand and availability. This is achieved through support for the implementation of existing regional and national agreements on such weapons; their collection and destruction; the promotion of an initiative to build on regional approaches to agree common global guidelines for controls on transfers of small arms; awareness raising and education programmes. An example of this was the provision of a small arms and light weapons destruction facility in Bosnia-Herzegovina (see paragraph 25 under *Current Operations*).

Steel works in Bosnia used to smelt weapons.

UK and International Conflict Management and Reconstruction

85. But it is not always possible to prevent conflicts. The Government therefore also worked to improve the international community's capability to manage and confine them when they break out, in particular through the United Nations, to develop international humanitarian norms and obligations to minimise the impact of such conflicts on the innocent, and to help with reconstruction and recovery once conflicts are over.

The United Nations

86. Demand for UN peacekeeping continued to grow and the UK worked closely with other nations in the UN Special Committee on Peacekeeping on ways to enhance peacekeeping capacity and capability (see UN peacekeeping targets in Annex C on *Conflict Prevention*). The Global Conflict Prevention Pool UN Strategy (which spends about £7.5M a year) funded work to improve the quantity and quality of peacekeepers. Examples included supporting the development of the UN's best practice guidance, including the development of standard training modules for peacekeepers, especially senior leadership training, and work with a range of current and potential troop contributing countries to improve their capacity for peacekeeping. We continued to implement both the UK National Action Plan on UN Security Council Resolution 1325 on Women, Peace and Security, through audits of the training provided to our Armed Forces to ensure compliance with the UNSCR, as well as our Action Plan on preventing Sexual Exploitation and Abuse.

International Humanitarian Law

87. Work continued with Argentina to address mine clearance issues in the Falkland Islands, and a joint study was conducted over the last austral summer.

The UK continued to take a leading role in ensuring that any use of Cluster Munitions remains firmly within the parameters of international law and international humanitarian law. At the Conference on Certain Conventional Weapons in November 2006, and at the Norwegian Initiative Conference in Oslo in February 2007, the UK led international efforts to reduce the humanitarian impact of cluster munitions. In March 2007 the Secretary of State for Defence announced that the Armed Forces would cease using 'dumb' cluster munitions with no target discrimination capability or no self-destruction, self-neutralisation or self-deactivation capability, making the UK the first major world power to do so. This required the Department to write off some 28 million submunitions worth £112M (see paragraph 292 under *Finance*, and the statement on losses and special payments contained in Note 31 to the Departmental Resource Accounts). The Armed Forces will continue to use 'smart' cluster munitions which have self-destruct mechanisms, reducing the risk of harm to civilians. As with all weapons, their use will be regulated by rules of engagement and internal scrutiny procedures designed to adhere to international law and reflect humanitarian values.

Arms Trade Treaty

88. Defence officials continued to support work towards a legally binding global treaty on the trade in conventional arms. The UK's aim is to ensure that all countries adopt and adhere to high standards in the conduct of the arms trade, with the goal of ensuring that sales are not allowed which will provoke or worsen conflicts; be used by human right abusers or to violate international humanitarian law; destabilise countries or regions; undermine sustainable development; or allow arms to flow from the legitimate to the illicit market. In 2006 the UK set out to secure agreement to a formal UN process to take this work forward. Recognising the growing global support for the initiative from a cross section of countries, in July 2006 the UK co-authored a UN General Assembly Resolution with Argentina, Australia, Costa Rica, Finland, Japan and Kenya, passed with 153 votes in favour. It made clear the importance of human rights and international humanitarian law and called on the UN Secretary General to seek views from countries on the feasibility, scope and draft parameters of a treaty and report back to the UN in 2007. The Secretary General will then convene a Group of Governmental Experts to look at these issues in 2008, and report back to the UN General Assembly later that year.

Post-Conflict Reconstruction

89. The Post Conflict Reconstruction Unit (PCRU) is a tri-departmental (MoD, DfID, FCO) organisation. It works to improve the UK's support for countries emerging from violent conflict to prevent a resurgence of violence and establish the basis for the conditions to enable development. In 2006-07 PCRU advisers in Helmand Province in Afghanistan helped the Provincial Development Council to determine priorities for the province, enhanced co-ordination between the Afghan Army and Police, and managed quick impact projects such as better irrigation, more reliable power supply, and extending reception of the BBC World Service Pashto Service. A PCRU facilitated review led to improvements in integration between the UK military and civilian Departments in implementing the UK Helmand Plan (see paragraph 21 under *Current Operations*). In Iraq, PCRU provided staff for the UK-led Provincial Reconstruction Team in Basra that enabled the Basra Provincial Council to identify and implement priority projects in areas such as water supply and economic development. It also contributed to strengthening integration of military and civilian planning and coordination in Basra (see paragraph 15 under *Current Operations*). PCRU, DfID and FCO also helped the African Union Mission in the Sudan increase awareness of the Darfur Peace Agreement among non signatories and the general public. In Nepal, PCRU supported the Government of Nepal and the UN in establishing priorities for public security reform to strengthen the peace process and plan for the security of key elections later this year. During and immediately following the war in Lebanon, the PCRU helped develop projects to enhance peace building, and improved international coordination of support to the Lebanon Armed Forces to strengthen their ability to bring stability to the south of the country.

Further sources of information

90. Additional information on Defence Policy and related issues is available from the following sources:

– quarterly PSA reports to HM Treasury at www.mod.uk;
– Defence White Paper *Delivering Security in a Changing World,* (Cm 6041-I in December 2003) available at www.mod.uk;
– information on Global and African Conflict Prevention Pools, and Proliferation Security Initiative at www.fco.gov.uk;
– Annual Report on United Kingdom Strategic Export Controls published in July 2006 available at www.fco.gov.uk;
– United Nations Security Council at www.un.org;
– background on NATO Response Force at www.arrc.nato.int/brochure/nrf.htm;
– Zeid Report at www.un.org;
– NATO reference publications and ministerial communiqués, including Comprehensive Political Guidance at www.nato.int;
– NAO Report on PSA target data systems available at www.nao.org.uk;
– UK Global Partnership Fourth Annual Report 2006 available at www.dti.gov.uk;
– Information on Post Conflict Reconstruction Unit at www.postconflict.gov.uk;
– Chatham House Report by Professor Paul Cornish This is available at www.chathamhouse.org.uk/pdf/research/niis/GlobalPartnershipWMD0107.pdf;
– The Future of the United Kingdom's Nuclear Deterrent Cm 6994 available at www.mod.uk;
– EDA background, current initiatives and programmes at www.eda.europa.eu;
– ESDP at www.consilium.europa.eu; and
– Riga Communique at www.nato.int.

Essay – The Future of the UK's Nuclear Deterrent

The United Kingdom's nuclear deterrent has been a central plank of our national security strategy for fifty years. Over this time no country has ever used a nuclear weapon, nor has there been a single significant conflict between the world's major powers. The UK's nuclear deterrent, within NATO, helped make this happen. Following detailed assessment and analysis, the Government set out its plans to maintain the UK's nuclear deterrent capability in a White Paper, *The Future of the United Kingdom's Nuclear Deterrent*, published in December 2006. After three months of extensive public and Parliamentary discussion and debate, the House of Commons voted in March 2007 to endorse the Government's plans.

The timing of these decisions was driven by the life of the Vanguard class submarines and the time it will take to develop replacements. The Department's analysis demonstrated that it was highly unlikely to be technically feasible or cost effective to extend the life of the Vanguard class beyond around 30 years, which already represents a five-year extension to their original design life. Equally, all the Department's experience, and that of industry, France and the US, is that it will take around 17 years to design, build and deploy new ballistic-missile carrying submarines. Given that the second of the Vanguard class is expected to leave service around 2024, this means detailed concept and assessment work needs to begin in 2007 if the UK is to avoid a risk of a gap in deterrence coverage.

The Rationale for retaining a Nuclear Deterrent

The Government believes that the concept of deterrence is just as relevant now as it was during the Cold War. Deterrence is about dissuading a potential adversary from carrying out a particular act because of the consequences of your likely retaliation. This is not an especially complex or unique concept. Nor does it have anything inherently to do with nuclear weapons, or superpower blocs. The United Kingdom's and our Allies' conventional forces are themselves a form of deterrent; they can and do deter various different kinds of states and non-state actors even in today's post-Cold War world.

But nuclear weapons are unique in terms of their destructive power, and as such, only nuclear weapons can deter nuclear threats. No country currently possesses both the capability and intent to threaten the United Kingdom's vital interests with nuclear weapons. But the Government has concluded that it is impossible to be certain that, over the next 20 to 50 years, such a threat may not re-emerge. This is not just a question of uncertainty, although it is important to be realistic about the potential to predict with confidence the strategic developments over these extended periods. There are also identifiable risks and trends of concern. Large nuclear arsenals remain around the world, some of which are being modernised and expanded. Despite international efforts to counter nuclear proliferation, the number of countries with nuclear weapons continues to grow, albeit less quickly than some have predicted. And the Government remains concerned at the implications should international terrorists get access to nuclear weapons.

The Government will redouble its efforts to seek to ensure that these potential future risks and challenges do not develop into threats to the United Kingdom's vital interests. It remains firmly of the view that a world in which there is no place for nuclear weapons would be a safer world. The UK has made significant unilateral reductions in its nuclear capability since the end of the Cold War, and is the only one of the five Nuclear Weapon States to have reduced to a system based on a single platform, a single delivery system and a single warhead design. The UK has also made major reductions in the scale and readiness of that system, halving the number of warheads deployed on deterrent patrol and reducing by more than 70 per cent the explosive power of the warhead stockpile, which now accounts for less than one per cent of the total global stockpile.

The Government will continue to maintain only the minimum capability the United Kingdom requires. But it believes the best way to achieve the goal of a world in which there is no place for nuclear weapons is through a process of international dialogue and negotiation. The next steps in this process should be the early entry into force of the Comprehensive Test Ban Treaty and the beginning of negotiations without preconditions on a Fissile Material Cut Off Treaty which, if successful, would end the production of weapon-useable nuclear material. But this will inevitably take time. And in the interim, the Government has a responsibility to take the steps necessary to ensure our national security and this includes retention of a minimum, independent nuclear deterrent.

Renewing Trident

The White Paper set out three main decisions:

- to extend the lives of the current Vanguard-class submarines from their original design life of at least 25 years to 30 years, and to start work to procure a new class of ballistic-missile submarines to replace the Vanguard-class;

- to participate in the life extension programme for the Trident D5 missile, to enable us to keep that missile in service through to the 2040s; and

- further to reduce the number of operationally available warheads from fewer than 200 to fewer than 160.

Key to the decision to retain a submarine based deterrent was the requirement to ensure the credibility of the United Kingdom's deterrent posture. And fundamental to credibility is the need for the deterrent to be invulnerable to pre-emptive attack, to be able to sustain a high degree of readiness, and to be able to deliver the required destructive power wherever might be required for effective deterrence. There were no credible alternatives to retaining a submarine-based system. All the other options were significantly more vulnerable to pre-emptive attack and all were at least as expensive as the submarine option, some significantly more so. This analysis also led to the conclusion that it was necessary for the foreseeable future for the United Kingdom to continue the existing posture of continuously maintaining a single submarine on deterrent patrol.

The Government's initial estimate is that the cost of procuring a new class of submarines will be in the range £11-14Bn (at 2006-07 prices) for a four submarine solution. This investment will not come at the expense of the conventional capabilities that Armed Forces need. Participation in the Trident D5 life extension programme will cost around £250M and the estimate also includes some £2-3Bn on renewing infrastructure to support the deterrent over the lifetime of the new submarines. The Government will also continue to invest in sustaining capabilities at the Atomic Weapons Establishment. The bulk of these costs are likely to be incurred 2012 to 2027. Once the new submarines come into service, the running costs of the nuclear deterrent are expected to be similar to those of today.

Future Decisions

The Government envisages placing contracts for the detailed design and manufacture of the new submarines in the period 2012-14. It has yet to decide whether the United Kingdom will require a fleet of three or four submarines to meet future deterrent requirements. Four Vanguard-class submarines are needed to sustain continuous deterrent patrols, but work will be undertaken to assess the scope for sufficiently radical design, operating and support changes to enable the MoD to maintain continuous deterrent patrols with a fleet of only three. It is likely to be necessary to decide on any refurbishment or replacement of our existing nuclear warhead in the next Parliament. Such a programme might involve procurement costs of some £2-3Bn. Decisions on any replacement for the Trident D5 missile are unlikely to be necessary until the 2020s. In all this, the Government will continue to work closely with the United States. Details of this collaboration were set out in an exchange of letters between the Prime Minister and the President of the United States, signed in December 2006.

Wider Government

Objective: Contribute to the Government's wider domestic reform agenda, including Sustainable Development

Assessment and Performance Measures

Assessment: Sustainability issues and their implications for security and defence are being incorporated in defence planning and management. Good progress was made in taking forward sustainable operations across defence estate, but there is more to do to meet targets. The Department is strongly committed to social issues. Service personnel gained over 17,500 accredited qualifications in 2006-07, and the Department provided over 33,000 learning credit grants. Youth and veterans programmes also contributed to the Government's sustainable community goals.

Sustainable Procurement, Consumption and Production:

- Sustainable Procurement Interim Delivery Plan completed (with April 2007 targets on sustainable procurement met already);
- Systems established to invest £5 million in 2007-08 for energy efficiency measures;
- All timber and timber products from legal and, where possible, sustainable sources;
- Around 60% of new buildings achieved an 'Excellent' rating, and 72% of refurbishments achieved 'Very Good' rating for sustainability (target 90%);
- 7% of electricity from renewable sources, and 2.5% from Combined Heat and Power (targets of 15% and 10% respectively by 2010);
- Waste management and recycling data systems not in place to measure overall performance, although examples of good practice (target to reduce waste arising by 5% relative to 2004-05 and increase recycling to 40% by 2010).

Climate Change and Energy:

- Work is in hand to assess impact of climate change for new developments and major refurbishment projects;
- Total MoD carbon dioxide emissions for 2006-07 of 5.5 million tonnes;
- Carbon dioxide emissions from Defence buildings fell by 5% in 2005-06, for a total reduction of 6% against the 1999-2000 baseline (target 12.5% reduction in emissions from offices by 2010-11, civil office estate to be carbon neutral by 2012);
- Carbon dioxide emissions of 29,000 tonnes in 2005-06 from administrative vehicle fleet (target 15% reduction by 2010-11);
- 15% energy efficiency built into budgets over the next four years (target 15% by 2010). Energy efficiency programme being developed for 220 largest defence sites.

Sustainable Communities

- Over 17,500 accredited qualifications and 33,000 learning credit grants in 2006-07;
- Expansion of Combined Cadet Forces in state schools;
- Continuing support to mentoring and outreach programmes, including for disadvantaged young people;
- Some 14,300 personnel (about 92%) drew on resettlement support in 2006-07. 94% of those who wished to continue to work secured employment within six months of discharge;
- Major commemorative events, and extension of eligibility for Veterans Badges;
- Continuing research into specialist veterans health issues;
- Improved terms and conditions, including pensions, for Gurkha personnel.

Defence in the wider community

91. In its Sustainable Development Strategy *Securing the Future* the Government set out its goal of a strong, healthy and just society, nationally and internationally, living within environmental limits, to enable all people throughout the world to satisfy their basic needs and enjoy a better quality of life without compromising the quality of life of future generations. Defence's primary contribution to this is through defending the UK and helping to foster international peace and stability, including through providing a range of specialist support to Home Departments in the United Kingdom (see paragraphs 31-33 under *Current Operations*). But the Ministry of Defence and the Armed Forces do a lot more than this. The Department is the third largest landowner in the United Kingdom, making a major contribution to the protection of the environment and preservation of our heritage (see paragraphs 334-338 under *Estates*). The Ministry of Defence provides employment, much of it highly skilled, for around 600,000 people directly or indirectly. Defence spends some £16Bn a year on often high technology goods and services from industry and conducts complex scientific and technological research and development comprising about 30% of the Government's total expenditure in this area (see paragraphs 203-205 under *Science, Innovation and Technology*). The Armed Forces returned about 24,000 personnel to the civilian economy with a wide range of acquired skills and qualifications (see paragraph 200 under *Personnel Management* and the essay on *Defence Training and National Skills* on page 128). The Cadet Forces and MoD sponsored Skill Force make a significant contribution to their local communities and to the development of the young people in them (see paragraphs 109-111). The Department also works to ensure that veterans' contribution to society is recognised, and to provide support to veterans who need it (see paragraphs 118-119 below). Through all this, defence personnel and capabilities, military and civilian, contribute to the goals of almost every other Government Department, and work towards the goal of a sustainable society nationally and internationally, on a daily basis.

Sustainable Development

92. Defence promotes international peace and stability. Without these sustainable development is not possible. But environmental pressures and increased competition for limited natural resources can contribute to tensions and conflict – both within and between states. Climate change is likely to increase these pressures. It follows that the maintenance of international peace and stability will be heavily influenced by sustainability issues around the world. The UK will not be immune from these developments,

and they will have implications for defence. The MoD is therefore working to create a coherent understanding of the interrelationships between sustainability and defence, as these will have significant impacts on what the Armed Forces need to be able to do over time in defence of the UK, its interests and its allies.

Soldier helps to reduce flooding in Iraq

93. The Government's national sustainability goals also have large implications for the management of defence, and the performance of the Ministry of Defence is fundamental to the Government achieving the targets it has set itself. In June 2006 the Prime Minister set out targets for Sustainable Operations on the Government Estate in the areas of climate change and energy, sustainable consumption and production, and natural resource protection and environmental enhancement. In March 2007 the Government issued its *Sustainable Procurement Action Plan* in response to the report of the business-led Sustainable Procurement Task Force. Performance against these targets and objectives is set out immediately below and, for natural resource protection and environmental enhancement, in paragraphs 180 under *Defence Estate*. In March 2007, the National Audit Office also published its report on *Managing the Defence Estate: Quality and Sustainability*. This concluded that the Department faces an unparalleled challenge in managing its estate in a sustainable way, is carrying out much good work both to make it more sustainable and to build effective relationships with external stakeholders, but needs to do more to meet both Government and Departmental targets. Defence performance against central Government targets for sustainable development on the estate is also set out in the Sustainable Development Commission's annual reports on *Sustainable Development in Government*, and more detailed reporting is contained in the MoD's *Sustainable Development Annual Reports*.

Sustainable Consumption and Production: Sustainable Procurement

Leadership and Accountability

94. The 2nd Permanent Under Secretary of the MoD chairs the interdepartmental Sustainable Procurement and Operations Board, and is the Whitehall champion for Sustainable Procurement across central Government Departments. During the year the Department established a Sustainable Procurement Steering Group chaired by the Defence Commercial Director. Defence sustainability data are externally and independently verified by Enviros, an independent environmental consultancy. The MoD Sustainable Procurement Interim Delivery Plan was completed in March 2007, ensuring that by April 2007 the MoD achieved Level one across all five themes of the *Sustainable Procurement Task Force National Action Plan Flexible Framework*. From 1 April 2007 sustainable development has been incorporated in the Defence Plan 2007 as a top level performance target reported to the Defence Management Board. The Department's strong systematic approach towards delivering more sustainable procurement, and its commitment to public reporting and external data verification were commended by the Sustainable Development Commission.

Budgeting and Accounting Practice

95. During the year the Department set aside £5M to support investment in 2007-08 in larger energy efficiency measures such as new site wide heating systems and the Estates Utility Board established a process to identify and prioritise opportunities to fund the up front difference between a 'traditional' and a 'green' solution.

Raising Standards

96. The Department has required that all timber and timber products are procured from legal and, where possible, sustainable sources for several years. Recycled paper is used in all copiers and printers in the MoD Head Office, and all paper used for defence publications comes from sustainable forests.

Market Engagement

97. The Department is working with stakeholders to identify how to take greenhouse gas emissions and other sustainability issues into account more effectively when making procurement, product design and construction decisions. The preliminary focus is on those areas of commodity and estate procurement where there is the greatest scope for sustainable procurement to be integrated into processes.

Building design and construction

98. In March 2006 the Department introduced an in-house environmental performance assessment tool developed to focus on sustainability targets relevant to defence construction, to help integrate sustainability into new build and refurbishment projects. Since then around 60% of new buildings have achieved an 'Excellent' rating for sustainability, and 72% of refurbishments have achieved a rating of 'Very Good', against targets of 90% each. The new, highly energy efficient Wellbeck Defence Sixth Form College was specifically commended in the National Audit Office Report *Building for the future: Sustainable construction and refurbishment on the government estate*, and achieved an Excellent rating under the School Environmental Assessment Method. Green roofs were installed on some of the College buildings to contribute to site biodiversity, demonstrate the MoD's Estates' commitment to sustainability to the public and pupils, and act as an insulating layer. It remains Departmental policy to implement the Department for Environment, Food and Rural Affairs' non-mandatory Minimum Environmental Standards – Quick Wins. Their uptake by contractors will be audited in the near future.

Waste management

99. The Government's target is to reduce its waste by 5% by 2010, and 25% by 2020, relative to 2004-05 levels, and to increase its own recycling to 40% of its waste by 2010, and 75% by 2020. The Department continues to work to improve waste reduction, recovery and recycling rates. There are examples of good practice, such as the single living accommodation programme's use of 20% recycled material. But while reporting continued to improve, with almost 200 key sites (which account for a substantial proportion of waste arisings) now reporting data, data systems are not yet in place across the entire estate to measure performance comprehensively. An independent project, due to report in the summer of 2007, is reviewing how radically to improve waste

management across defence. The Department is working with QinetiQ to develop improved waste management technologies for ships and deployed forces.

19th Century wreck at Stanley home to wildfowl and seabirds

HMS Endurance gathering information on climate change in Antarctica.

Climage Change and Energy

100. The most recent conclusions of the UN's Intergovernmental Panel on Climate Change is that the average global temperature is very likely to rise by at least 2% over the next 50 years. The Hadley Centre in the Met Office – an MoD Trading Fund – is internationally recognised as at the forefront of world climate science, and in translating that science into policy advice. The work of HMS Endurance with the British Antarctic Survey also contributes to measuring the environmental impact of climate change. Defence has a key role in addressing the challenges this will bring. The need to operate in hotter conditions in future will affect the operational capability of both people and military equipment, and adapting in order to continue to deliver success on operations will inevitably cost money. The longevity of much defence infrastructure and equipment means that the Department already needs to take account of the likely future climate over the next 50 years in its procurement decisions. Work is in hand to assess the potential impact and review the scope to build resilience to climate change into new developments and major refurbishment projects (see the essay on Defence and Climate Change on page 73). The MoD also needs to mitigate its own environmental impact as far as possible by ensuring that defence activities are as sustainable as possible. In line with Government policy, the Department intends to use its £16Bn annual procurement budget to drive both low carbon and energy efficient solutions from suppliers. Rising energy costs are a compelling further incentive to minimise energy use, as they divert resources away from the Department's core outputs.

Carbon dioxide emissions

101. Defence produces about 1% of the United Kingdom's total carbon dioxide emissions and about 65% of the Government's total building emissions. The Department entered into a strategic relationship with the Carbon Trust three years ago. Total carbon dioxide emissions for 2006-07 (from aviation, marine and ground fuel use, the estate and business travel) were about 5.5 million tonnes. Over 90% derives from energy use on the estate and consumption of marine and aviation fuel (see essay on Defence and Climate Change on page 73).

102. The Government aims to reduce carbon dioxide emissions from its offices by 12.5 per cent by 2010-11, and by 30 per cent by 2020, relative to 1999-2000 levels, and for the Central Government's Office Estate to be carbon neutral by 2012. The Department is not yet able to measure separately carbon dioxide emissions from office buildings, but defence accounts for about two thirds of the carbon dioxide emissions from buildings on the central Government Estate. In 2005-06, the most recent year for which there is data, carbon dioxide emissions from all defence buildings, fell by 5% over the previous year, and by a total of 6% against the 1999-2000 baseline. The Department is developing a plan to implement carbon neutrality on the non-military buildings that constitute its civil estate. The Government also aims to reduce carbon dioxide emissions from road vehicles used for Government administrative operations by 15% by 2010-11, relative to 2005-06 levels. The Department's administrative fleet comprises 7,000 leased vehicles, representing annual carbon dioxide emissions of 29,000 tonnes, in 2005-06. A more comprehensive picture has been built across the TLBs this year and the figure is some 50,000 tonnes.

65

Energy Efficiency

103. The Government's target is for all Departments to increase their energy efficiency per square metre by 15% by 2010, and by 30% by 2020, relative to 1999-2000 levels. Very small buildings can consume very high amounts of energy and square metre baselines can unavoidably vary annually. The MoD has built a 15% energy efficiency target into internal budgets over the next four years. The Department is working with the Carbon Trust and estate contractors to raise awareness of energy efficiency opportunities. During the year Osnabrück Garrison in Germany and 4th Mechanised Brigade became the first Army and first overseas organisation to receive the Carbon Trust's Energy Efficiency Accreditation following investment of more than £1M over the last five years in energy efficient technologies. At RAF Kinloss a pilot project with the Carbon Trust has generated annual savings of £340,000 from an up-front investment of £100,000, following which a further ten projects have been taken forward across the estate, with potential annual savings of some £2M for an up-front investment of about £2.3M. A similar process is now being rolled out across a further 15 sites. The intention is to follow up in due course across the remainder of the 220 MoD sites that generate about 70% of the energy bill.

Energy Sources

104. By 2010 the Government aims to source at least 10% of electricity from renewable sources, and at least 15% of electricity from Combined Heat and Power. In 2006-07 the Department bought 7% of its electricity from renewable sources, and sourced 2.5% of electricity is from Combined Heat and Power. This is planned to increase by a 2.5% each year until 2010.

Sustainable Communities

105. In its most recent report on *Sustainable Development in Government* the Sustainable Development Commission commended the Department's strong commitment to social issues. The main defence contribution in this area is set out in detail in the paragraphs below on young people (paragraphs 109-111) and veterans (paragraphs 116-127). The training provided to defence personnel, military and civilian also contributes to the Government's education and skills objectives (see paragraph 106 and paragraph 218 under *Personnel Management*). Environmental noise from military flying and tank and artillery ranges is a legitimate concern for communities affected. The Department provides routine advice for the public on Military Low Flying and publishes an annual review of low flying activity. The Department encourages all staff to undertake volunteering work. Civil servants serving as, for example, a Magistrate, Special Constable or School Governor are given Special Paid Leave. Service personnel undertake voluntary work at the discretion of their Unit Commander, taking into account military commitments.

Building Skills

Improving Skills

106. As part of our core business the Department and Armed Forces provide considerable basic, specialist and professional skills training to newly recruited young military and civilian personnel. This contributes directly to the Government's skills development goals (see the essay on pages 128 on *Defence Training and National Skills*). The high quality of the Armed Forces work-based learning provision was acknowledged in the Department for Education and Skill's (DfES)[1] Green Paper *Raising Expectations: staying in education and training post-16*, published in March 2007. During the year the Department strengthened links with the Learning and Skills Council to improve the support to young Service personnel, in particular through defence apprenticeship schemes and help for those with poor literacy and numeracy. The Department also worked with Government Skills (the Sector Skills Council for Central Government), which is aiming to produce a common strategic skills framework across Central Government, to ensure that it reflects the needs of the Armed Forces and to help develop the Professional Skills for Government initiative within the defence Civil Service (see paragraph 224 under *Personnel Management*). Following publication in December 2006 of the Leitch Review *Prosperity for All in the Global Economy* into development of the UK skills base, the Department has been working to address aspects of the key recommendations to inform the overall Government response. In June 2007 the MoD and Armed Forces signed the national 'Skills Pledge' called for in the Leitch Report, to give every employee without a Level 2 qualification[2] the chance to get qualified at that level and offer the support to do so (see paragraph 107), and to support employees in improving basic levels of literacy and numeracy (see paragraph 220 under *Personnel Management*).

---

1 DFES became the Department for children, schools and families; and the Department for Innovation, Universities and Skills, on 28 June 2007
2 Level 2 qualification is the normal educational standard expected to enter into skilled employment and is equivalent to five GCSEs at Grades A-C or an equivalent vocational qualification.

Accreditation & National Qualifications

107. Military training and education are designed to meet the Armed Forces' operational and business needs, but they also support each individual's continuing development, encourage greater professionalism and provide an opportunity to acquire professional and vocational qualifications. Service personnel increasingly pursue a wide range of national qualifications through external accreditation of their Service education, training and experience. Under such schemes in 2006-07, Service personnel earned over 9,400 Level 2or 3[3] qualifications, over 5,300 Apprenticeships, nearly 2,000 Advanced Apprenticeships, and over 500 Foundation Degrees. 351 personnel achieved graduate or postgraduate qualifications on sponsored full-time courses. The Royal Air Force was the runner up in the National Employers' Service "Employer of the Year" Award. 2006-07 was also the first full year for the new Defence Sixth Form College, which operated at almost full capacity, with A level 'graduates' progressing to the five Defence Technical Undergraduate Scheme universities.

The Armed Forces Learning Credits Scheme

108. Under the Learning Credits Scheme the Department also provides financial support to Service personnel for personal learning and development:

- The Standard Learning Credit scheme provides financial support for multiple small-scale learning. Personnel are eligible to claim 80% of course fees from public funds up to a maximum of £175 per financial year. Over the last five years about 15% of the trained strength have taken this up, and in 2006-07 there were 26,500 claims totalling about £2.8M;

- The Enhanced Learning Credit scheme complements the standard scheme by providing larger sums for higher level learning. As well as making a minimum personal contribution of 20% towards the cost of the course to demonstrate their commitment, personnel may make three claims towards the cost of learning leading to academic or vocational qualifications of level 3 or higher, up to a maximum of £1,000 a year for three years (not necessarily consecutive) four years after registration, or (from April 2008) £2,000 a year for three years, eight years after registration and up to ten years after leaving the Service. About 560 approved learning providers are participating in the Scheme, 49% mainly academic and 51% vocational. 227,000 personnel had registered by April 2007, including

a number who have left the Armed Forces. During 2006-07 over 6,500 claims were made, totalling some £5.6M. About 40% were used for personal development by personnel with over two years left to serve, 52% by personnel in their last two years of service preparing for civilian life, and the remainder by veterans.

Young people – raising expectations

Cadet Forces

109. Defence contributes to the Government's youth agenda by supporting a range of projects focussed on the well-being of young people. At the core of this are the MoD sponsored Cadet Forces (the Combined Cadet Force, the Sea Cadet Corps, the Army Cadet Force and the Air Training Corps). With some 130,000 cadets supported by 26,000 adult volunteers, based in more than 3,000 locations in towns and cities throughout the country, the Cadet Forces remain one of the biggest national youth organisations. They make a significant contribution to their local communities and to the personal development of both the cadets and adult volunteers. They provide an opportunity to gain many nationally recognised qualifications. They are the largest operating authority for the Duke of Edinburgh award, EDEXCEL's most successful partner in the delivery of the BTEC first diploma in public services[4] (since 2002 more than 8,000 cadets have gained this vocational qualification). This contribution was recognised by the Treasury's provision of an additional £800,000 to establish new Combined Cadet Forces in state schools in London, Weymouth, Dover, Peterborough and Treorchy. The schools taking part in the pilot will enrol their first cadets in September 2007 following preparation and training of the teachers and other adult volunteers involved.

Social Inclusion and Personal Development

110. The MoD continues to work with other organisations to develop wider youth initiatives. During 2006-07 the Department signed a Memorandum of Understanding with the Prince's Trust and Youth Justice Board which agreed mutually supportive pledges on how to further support young people. The MoD introduced a Regional Coordinator of Cadets and Youth post on a trial basis to bring together the organising of partnerships and create an infrastructure for the efficient regional organisation of defence supported youth activities. The Department supports a growing range of highly valued learning and mentoring programmes within schools and colleges across the UK. The Army Cadet Force provides facilities, instructors, adventurous training

---

3 Level 3 qualifications are equivalent to A-levels.

4 Equivalent to four GCSEs at A to C level

and challenging activities to young people across the UK to support the project Outreach programme. This guides and helps 12-14 year old children who are socially disengaged and at risk of criminality to build confidence and self esteem, realise that there are other options and that with encouragement and determination they can achieve goals they thought unobtainable. In 2006-07 24 Army Cadet Force units were involved, helping 717 young people.

School Children on adventurous training and military skills exercises

111. The MoD co-sponsors Skill Force with the Department for Education and Skills.[5] This uses the experience and talents of former Service personnel and others to deliver a range of inspirational and motivational activities to young people. The core programme is targeted mainly at 14-16 year olds who respond more positively to programmes centred on activity based team building. It offers a wide range of activities, such as problem solving, and raising self-esteem through the initiatives such as the Duke of Edinburgh's Award Scheme. The programme has produced dramatic improvements in individuals' personal development and confidence, with those completing the programme entering further education or joining training courses and achieving credible employment. There have been significant reductions in truancy and exclusions and in petty misdemeanours in the community. It has also enabled the schools involved to provide more focused teaching to other pupils, who in their turn achieve greater success as a result. Within the 5741 students currently involved across 211 schools, attendance has improved year on year by 10%, exclusions have fallen significantly and NEET[6] figures have dropped from 4.1% to 2%.

5 DFES became the Department for children, schools and families; and the Department for Innovation, Universities and Skills, on 28 June 2007
6 Not in Education, Employment or Training

Sport

112. Many of the attributes required by military personnel (such as physical fitness, courage, resilience and esprit de corps) are developed by sporting activities. These also support the Government's wider personal development and social responsibility goals. Service personnel are strongly encouraged to participate in sport, with many representing their country at international level. The Armed Forces provided eight members of the 40-strong British squad for the 2006 Winter Olympics, and 19 members of the home countries' squads at the 2006 Commonwealth Games. The Department has made the Royal Artillery Barracks at Woolwich available for shooting events at the London 2012 Olympic Games.

British Army Alpine Ski Championships

Veterans: Support for former service personnel

Strategy for Veterans

113. The MoD has a responsibility to support Armed Forces veterans, especially those who have suffered physical or mental ill-health due to service. The UK veteran community comprises over 10 million individuals. The MoD set out its approach to veterans' issues and what it aims to achieve, in partnership with other key stakeholders in the 2003 Strategy for Veterans. This has three key pillars: to provide excellent preparation for the transition from Service to civilian life; to ensure that the nation recognises veterans' contribution to society; and to provide support to veterans who need it. As such it contributes directly to the Government's goals for social inclusion and sustainable communities. The new Reserves Mental Health Programme became operational in November 2006 (see paragraph 223 under *Health and Safety*). In April 2007 a number of measures were agreed to address gaps in existing welfare provision. These

included extended welfare monitoring for at least two years after leaving for vulnerable seriously injured veterans; piloting of a mentoring project for vulnerable leavers at risk of social exclusion; and a more coherent approach to case management, with the objective of "whole person" assessments and a single case manager.

Transition from Service to civilian life

114. All Service personnel leaving the Armed Forces are provided with structured assistance on making the transition from military to civilian life. The level of support provided depends on their length of military service and the circumstances of their discharge. All personnel are entitled to attend finance and housing briefings. Those who have served at least four years are entitled to a job finding service provided through the Career Transition Partnership for two years after discharge. Those who have served at least six years (five years if enlisted before 1 September 2002) and all medical discharges, regardless of length of service, are also entitled to access a wider range of Transition Partnership services as part of their resettlement preparation, which include vocational training, coaching in job interview technique and CV writing, and dedicated career consultancy support. Some 14,300 (about 92%) of those entitled to access Partnership services drew on this support in 2006-07: 66% of those who wished to continue to work, secured employment within a month of discharge, rising to 94% within six months. A further 7,500[7] personnel who left under the Early Service Leavers scheme and did not qualify for Career Transition Partnership programmes, received a mandatory resettlement brief and interview prior to discharge that included assessment of their vulnerability to social exclusion, review of their post-discharge accommodation, and direction to agencies and organisations that provide support for employment, accommodation and welfare needs. Exceptional arrangements for additional support are made for those assessed as vulnerable to social exclusion.

115. During the past year, for those Service leavers who want help from charities, the MoD made arrangements (compliant with Data Protection Act) to improve the communication of personal details to key Service and ex-Service organisations. The process of transfer of disabled Service leavers with enduring care needs to new providers was also improved. The Department continued to develop a network of support with ex-Service charities that offer niche services to those about to leave the Services and engaged with Regional Development Agencies to encourage and support Service leavers with entrepreneurial aspirations. An innovative programme of locally-delivered resettlement support tailored to the unique circumstances of the Northern Ireland job market

has been provided for the 3,000 Royal Irish soldiers being discharged on disbandment of the three Home Service battalions. This has so far been very successful, with over 90% of the first tranche securing civilian employment with entrepreneurial aspirations.

Recognition and status of veterans in society

116. The key principle of the recognition pillar is that veterans' contributions, both past and present, should continue to be valued. To this end the Government instituted an annual Veterans Day in 2006. This is a nationwide celebration of the country's veterans, their achievements and their continuing contribution to their community through their transferable skills. By the end of 2006-07 the Department had agreed to provide over £300,000 in grants to support Veterans Day 2007 events across the UK, and throughout the year it supported a range of projects to raise intergenerational awareness, in particular encouraging integration of links with schools and families in regional and local events. A service to mark the 150th anniversary of the institution of the Victoria Cross and the 50th anniversary of the formation of the Victoria Cross and George Cross Association took place at Westminster Abbey in June 2006. National commemoration of the 25th anniversary of the South Atlantic conflict took place in June 2007. Since public fundraising was launched in April 2005 for the Armed Forces Memorial to members of the Armed Forces (Regular and Reserve) killed on duty or as a result of terrorist action since the Second World War some £6M has been raised or pledged, including a special payment of £1.5M from the Ministry of Defence. Less than £1M remains to be raised.

Veterans commemorating Falklands 25 Year Anniversary

7 This figure is based on provisional DASA statistics for FY 06/07.

117. The Veterans Badge promotes recognition of Veterans and their contributions. A modified version has been produced for members of the Merchant Navy who served in vessels facilitating military operations. In March 2007 the Government announced that all those who had served before the end of 1984 were eligible for these badges, along with widows and widowers of those who died of illness or significant injury attributable to their Service. Some 430,000 badges had been issued by 30 April 2007. The Artic Emblem was launched in October 2006 for veterans of the Arctic Convoys, and other service north of the Arctic Circle. Over 8,000 had been issued by the end of the year.

Provision of support to veterans who need it

118. The MoD is moving away from delivering services in line with the structure of our own organisations to a more logically presented service for the user. In line with this in July 2006 it was decided to merge the Armed Forces Personnel and Administration Agency and the Veterans Agency into a single Service Personnel and Veterans Agency (SPVA) from April 2007. This will improve the service provided to both Veterans and serving members of the Armed Forces by providing a single point of contact for the whole range of services, enabling more joined up assessment of entitlements, and facilitating development of integrated business processes. The SPVA now provides pay, pension and personnel services to Service personnel from the moment they join the Armed Forces, through their career and subsequently. A new "Veterans UK" service is also being established to provide a 'one stop' point of advice and contact for all the support services designed specifically for veterans, and thus simplify the service provided to veterans and their families and make help more easily accessible.

119. The Department continued to work with other Government Departments, charities and the private sector to tackle ex-Service homelessness and social exclusion, reflecting the complexity of the often personal problems involved, which require effective joint working to address. Research commissioned by the ex-Service Action Group (ESAG), of which the MoD is a member, moved into the second phase in March 2007, and is due to conclude in early 2008. Initial findings indicate that there has been a significant reduction in the proportion of the homeless population in London who have a Service background from 22% in 1997 to around 6%. Lead responsibility for Project Compass, which helps homeless veterans find employment in London, passed to the Royal British Legion in January 2007. This and other changes are intended to allow Compass to stabilise the training model in London and provide support in other areas of the UK. A new centre in Aldershot is expected to open in the summer of 2007 providing accommodation and training facilities to help Service leavers develop marketable job skills and return to sustained employment and independent living.

Veterans Health Issues

120. The MoD has a continuing duty of care to veterans suffering ill health caused by their military service. The Department therefore supports a wide range of research into veterans' health issues. Since 1948 Government policy has been that health care for veterans should be delivered by the National Health Service (NHS). The Department continued to provide information for veterans on what to expect and where to go for assistance from the NHS, and to work with Chief Medical Officers and the Royal Colleges to raise the awareness of civilian health professionals about specific veterans' matters.

121. Following the Health and Social Care Advisory Service's review of Mental Health care provided by the Ex-Services Mental Welfare Society (Combat Stress) in 2005, officials from the four UK Health Departments, MoD and Combat Stress, advised by national clinical experts have been working to develop a new community based model of mental health services for veterans. Preparations to set up host sites across the UK are well advanced and pilots should begin in mid-2007 and run for two years before full evaluation. Research on delayed-onset Post Traumatic Stress Disorder in veterans continued. Another study is following up newly discharged leavers to determine whether there are abnormal suicide rates. The Department is guided by the independent Medical Research Council on a study designed to help ill veterans of the 1990-91 Gulf Conflict (Operation GRANBY) back into civilian life.

122. The publication of MoD sponsored research in July and October 2006 into the possible adverse health effects of the combination of vaccines and Nerve Agent Pre-treatment tablets offered to UK personnel brought to a close the original research commitments made by the Government in July 1997. The evidence from the research programme is overwhelmingly that the combination of vaccines and nerve agent protection tablets that were offered to UK Forces at the time of Operation GRANBY would not have had adverse health effects. Regular publication of mortality data continues to show that Gulf veterans do not suffer an excess mortality compared with a group of similar Service personnel that did not deploy. During the year the retrospective depleted uranium (DU) testing programme for Operation GRANBY and Balkans veterans was completed and the final report of the DU Oversight Board issued. In total 496 individuals participated in the programme, which found no evidence of DU exposure.

123. Research by The King's Centre for Military Health Research into the physical and psychological health of those involved in current operations in Iraq (Operation TELIC) was extended into a second three-year phase (2006-09). The scope of the study was also broadened to include personnel deployed to Afghanistan. A sub-study involving urinary uranium testing found no evidence for DU exposure in a representative sample of personnel involved in the combat phase of Operation TELIC in 2003.

124. In July 2006 the MoD published a comprehensive historical survey of the Service Volunteer Programme at Porton Down by Professor Sir Ian Kennedy. This concluded that the trials which 'amount to serious departures from what should have been done…are few in number and spread over several decades.' and that 'a very great debt of gratitude is clearly owed to those who volunteered to take part in the research at Porton and to those who carried it out'. The Department continued to fund and provide practical support to the independent epidemiological study into mortality and cancer incidence among veterans who took part in this Programme. Findings will be published during 2007. Compensation was paid to the family of a Serviceman who died taking part in trials at Porton Down in 1953.

War Pensions and Armed Forces Compensation Scheme

125. The Service Personnel and Veterans Agency provides financial compensation via the War Pensions Scheme and since April 2005, the Armed Forces Compensation Scheme (AFCS), to some 174,000 veterans and 38,000 widows for death and disablement arising out of service in the Armed Forces. The number of war pensions paid each year continues to decline by some 5%. The Agency is reviewing its Key Targets to ensure that it provides a high standard of service to veterans and widows in paying pensions and compensation. Direct welfare support is also provided to war pensioners and war widows by the War Pensioners Welfare Service, operating across the UK and the Republic of Ireland. Because the AFCS has not yet been running long enough to establish trends and cannot use the values of other schemes to help estimate the liability, the Department cannot yet provide enough evidence to validate the level of provision required to meet the potential future liabilities. This has meant that the accounts for the Armed Forces Pension Scheme are likely to continue to be subject to a technical qualification until the AFCS has been in existence for a number of years and trends established.

126. In July 2006 the MoD announced that work to identify and correct errors in the payments of Armed Forces pensions had discovered that a number of invalidity awards to Service personnel might not have been consistently up-rated over the years as required, and that Project Collins had been set up to identify and correct any such errors. This involves reviewing over 49,000 cases, and is expected to be completed by August 2007. Some 36,000 had been reviewed by 31 March 2007, of which 235 (0.65%) were identified as incorrect. These have been corrected and arrears amounting to some £880,000 were paid. 18 cases were identified as receiving a higher rate of pension than entitled and are being fully investigated. A further 13,000 cases remained to be reviewed and provision has been made to take account of any arrears that may be due.

Gurkha Pensions

127. In March 2007 the Government announced that all Gurkha Service personnel will be given the same terms and conditions of service as British Army regulars, with certain exceptions to meet the wishes of the Government of Nepal. Part of this package involves pensions, with the 2007 intake joining on Armed Forces Pension Scheme (AFPS 2005). Other serving Gurkhas and those who retired on or after 1 July 1997 will be given the opportunity during 2007 to transfer their pension benefits from the Gurkha Pension Scheme into AFPS 75 or AFPS 05. Eligible Gurkhas will be given information about their pension options to enable them to make an informed decision. A Gurkha Project Team has been formed to implement this.

Further sources of information

128. Additional information is available from the following sources:

- *Securing the Future – UK Government sustainable development strategy* (Cm6467 of March 2005) available at www.sustainable-development.gov.uk;
- *'Procuring the Future' – The Sustainable Procurement Task Force National Action Plan'* , June 2006, available at www.sustainable-development.gov.uk;
- *UK Government Sustainable Procurement Action Plan (incorporating the Government Response to the Sustainable Procurement Task Force),* March 2007 available at www.sustainable-development.gov.uk;
- *Sustainable Development in Government 2006*: Annual Report by the Sustainable Development Commission on central Government performance, March 2007, available at www.sd-commission.org.uk/sdig2006;
- NAO Report on *Managing the Defence Estate: Quality and Sustainability* (HC154 of 23 March 2007) available at www.nao.org.uk;
- NAO Report on *Building for the future: Sustainable construction and refurbishment on the government estate* (HC324 of 20 April 2007) available at www.nao.org.uk;
- Evidence to Public Accounts Committee on *Managing the Defence Estate: Quality and Sustainability* on 14 May 2007, to be published as HC537-I, available at www.parliament.uk;
- Evidence to House of Commons Defence Committee on *The Work of Defence Estates* on 15 May 2007, to be published as HC 535-I, available at www.parliament.uk;
- *Bequests to the Nation: An introduction to the MoD Art Collection* available at www.mod.uk;
- MoD *Sustainable Development Action Plan*s available at www.mod.uk;
- MoD *Sustainable Development Annual Reports* available at www.mod.uk;
- *Stewardship Reports on the Defence Estate* available at www.mod.uk;
- *MoD Sustainable Waste Management Strategy* available at www.mod.uk;
- *MoD Sustainable Development Delivery Strategy for Non-Operational Energy* available at www.mod.uk;
- Met Office *Annual Report and Accounts,* available at www.metoffice.gov.uk;
- *Review of UK Military Helicopter Low Flying in Response to a Rule 43 Letter from the Louth and Spilsby Coroner* available at www.mod.uk;
- Annual Reports on *The Pattern of Military Low Flying across the United Kingdom* at www.mod.uk;
- Information on cadets at www.armycadets.com
- Information on Government Skills at www.government-skills.gov.uk;
- Raising Expectations: staying in education and training post-16, March 2007 at www.dfes.gov.uk;
- Leitch Review Prosperity for All in the Global Economy, December 2006 at www.hm-treasury.gov.uk;
- Commemorative booklets at www.veterans-uk.info;
- *Veterans WORLD* available at www.veterans-uk.info;
- AFPAA Annual Report and Accounts 2006-07 at www.veterans-uk.info
- Veterans Agency Annual Report and Accounts 2006-07 at www.veterans-uk.info (from July 2006);
- Homelessness research *Improving the Delivery of Cross Departmental Support and Services for Veterans* at www.mod.uk;
- UK Gulf Veterans Mortality Data at www.dasa.mod.uk;
- Depleted Uranium Oversight Board at www.duob.org.uk;
- Radiation Protection Division, part of the Health Protection Agency at www.hpa.org.uk;
- *The 1990/1991 Gulf Conflict: Health and Personnel Related Lessons Identified* at www.mod.uk;
- Kings College research papers published in The Lancet *'The Health of UK Military Personnel Who Deployed To The 2003 Iraq War'* and *'Is there an Iraq syndrome?'* available at www.thelancet.com (registration required);
- Report on Service Volunteer Programme at Porton Down at www.mod.uk;
- Armed Forces Pension Scheme Annual Report and Accounts at www.official-documents.gov.uk;
- House of Commons Defence Commitee on *UK Operation in Afghanistan* (HC 408), available at www.parliament.uk

Essay – Defence and Climate Change

"Climate change is the most severe problem that we are facing today – more serious even than the threat of terrorism."

Sir David King, Chief Scientist, 2004

"Warming of the climate system is now unequivocal … Most of the observed increase is very likely due to the observed increase in anthropogenic greenhouse gas emissions"

UN Intergovernmental Panel on Climate Change, 2007

The scientific debate over the existence of climate change is over. Because greenhouse gas emissions have exceeded the levels the planet is able to absorb, climate change over the rest of this century is now inevitable. Temperatures and sea levels will rise, and the frequency and intensity of extreme weather events, such as storms, floods, droughts and heat waves, increase. This may feed political instability in regions where water and food resources are scarce or unequally distributed, exacerbated by the pressures of further population growth. There will be implications for defence for which the MoD needs to be prepared. There may be an increased call on the Armed Forces to respond to conflicts and humanitarian crises, and they may have to operate in more extreme conditions than at present. The MoD is therefore working with the Foreign and Commonwealth Office, the Department for International Development and the US Department of Defense on the security implications of climate change. Underpinning this work is climate modelling by the Hadley Centre in the Met Office, a MoD Trading Fund, to predict future climates and assess their defence implications in strategically important regions.

The implications of climate change already need to be factored into the Department's acquisition planning and the Armed Forces' future operating procedures if they are to continue to perform effectively in the future. Defence equipment can have a life of 40-50 years or more. Equipment currently being designed may need to be able to operate across wider ranges of temperature if the Armed Forces are to continue to be able to operate in theatres, such as the Middle East, where environmental conditions are already extreme. Alternatively, the Armed Forces may not be able in time reliably to provide a fully effective military capability in certain regions of the globe. There will also be consequences for management of defence in the United Kingdom. For example, some low lying sites such the ranges at Lydd in Kent are vulnerable to rising sea levels and flooding. But so long as defence planning factors in the likely changes, the consequences should be manageable, albeit at some cost.

At the same time, the Department has both a moral and practical imperative to do what it can to minimise the environmental impact of defence activities. Defence is a large and complex business where nearly every activity uses energy derived mainly from fossil fuels. The Department and the Armed Forces are therefore a significant source of carbon dioxide CO_2 emissions. Finding ways to minimise these without compromising defence capability is therefore both the right thing to do, and also, in the shape of reduced fuel bills, and potentially increased diversity energy sources, of direct benefit to the defence programme. Moreover, since defence activities and the defence estate account for a preponderant share of the Government's operations, if the MoD does not find ways to do so the Government will not meet the overall sustainability targets it has set itself.

The first essential step is to obtain accurate information. This is easier said than done for an organisation with an estate covering 1% of the United Kingdom, about 40,000 buildings, some 300,000 employees and a large inventory of ships, vehicles and aircraft of all shapes and sizes. It is possible to estimate direct defence CO_2 emissions from the energy utilities supplied to the estate, the fuel for military equipment, and the distance travelled on duty by defence personnel. These amount to nearly 5.5 million tonnes of CO_2 a year, about 1% of the UK's emissions, and about 0.02% of global emissions from human activities. 36% comes from defence buildings (about two thirds of estate emissions from all central government departments), a further 36% from military flying, 25% from ships and vehicles, and the remaining 3% from business travel.

The Department cannot yet estimate the indirect emissions arising from defence activities undertaken on its behalf by others, such as manufacture and maintenance of equipment by industry, or the direct emissions from military operations. It is therefore not yet possible to build a comprehensive picture of the complete Defence carbon footprint. MoD will therefore be working with its industry partners to remedy this.

The MoD has so far focussed much of its effort to reduce its CO_2 emissions on its estate. Improvements in building energy management and energy efficiency have delivered reductions in estate CO_2 emissions. The Prime Minister has set a series of cross-Government targets for *Sustainable Operations on the Government Estate* (SOGE), which require the MoD to deliver a 12.5% reduction in CO_2 emissions from buildings by 2010-11 and 30% by 2020. A number of the Department's office buildings must be carbon neutral by 2012. This will require large improvements in energy efficiency, possibly some generation of on-site renewable energy, and payment to offset any remaining emissions. The Department is also assessing the scope to buy more electricity from renewable sources (currently about 7%), to install renewable energy site-based systems for new construction projects, and to install good quality combined heat and power systems where possible. The Department is working with the Carbon Trust to identify opportunities to reduce emissions further. Studies so far indicate that there is considerable scope for investment in projects that will very quickly pay back the initial investment required and deliver substantial emissions reductions. MoD's industry partners will have an important part to play.

It is nevertheless already clear that reducing Defence greenhouse gas emissions to the extent now thought to be necessary over the longer term will be a greater challenge. The draft Climate Change Bill indicates that the United Kingdom will need to deliver a 60% reduction from 1990 levels by 2050. Improvements to military training, reductions in the size of the Armed Forces, and the introduction of newer, more capable aircraft, ships and vehicles can all continue to deliver reduced CO_2 emissions. But the key to delivering sustained progress lies with working with industry to improve understanding of CO_2 emissions from the equipment supply chain and exploring opportunities for efficiency improvements and lower carbon, alternative technologies and energy sources.

The Government's 2005 Sustainable Development Strategy, *Securing the Future* set a goal for the UK to be a leader in Sustainable Procurement in the EU by 2009. The Government subsequently issued its *Sustainable Procurement Action Plan*, which includes the aim of a low carbon, more resource efficient public sector. In response, the MoD is looking to use its buying power, in partnership with other organisations, and other nations' defence departments, to ensure that energy efficient and lower-carbon equipment, including alternative propulsion methods and energy sources where appropriate, are available from our technology and energy providers. Alternative technologies – such as bio-fuels and hybrid propulsion systems in the nearer term, and electric propulsion, fuel cells and hydrogen-based energy technologies in the longer term – would potentially provide direct defence benefits. It will also be important to adapt with industry as it adopts a lower-carbon approach in response to wider social, political and financial pressures to avoid the risk of relying on obsolete or difficult-to-support technology.

Climate change is the greatest challenge currently facing humanity. It raises major issues for defence. The MoD is working to address these issues. It is not yet doing as well as it must to reduce CO_2 emissions from defence activity and to improve energy efficiency. But it is determined to get this right.

Future Capabilities

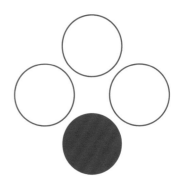

Future Effects

Objective: More flexible Armed Forces to deliver greater effect.

Assessment and Performance Measures

Assessment: All three Services continued to take forward their modernisation programmes, with significant new capabilities being introduced into service during the year and further efficiencies achieved. Roll out of enhanced command, control and communication systems continued alongside work to improve the Department's and the Armed Forces' capability to manage and use information.

Implementation of Force Structure Changes, in particular the Future Army Structure:

- One submarine withdrawn from service;
- Launch of second Type 45 Destroyer;
- Entry into service of three Landing Ship Dock (Auxiliary) vessels, enhancing the capability of the Amphibious Task Force;
- Reformation of 22 Signal Regiment;
- Fourth battalion for 3 Commando Brigade;
- Delivery of Guided Multiple Launch Rocket System;
- Progressive introduction into service of Bowman communications system;
- Introduction into service of range of protected vehicles;
- Enhanced Territorial Army attack helicopter, engineer and logistic capabilities;
- Formation of two Naval Air Squadrons as part of Joint Force Harrier;
- Delivery of further Typhoons, with associated Tornado F3 reductions and withdrawal of Jaguar from service;
- Delivery of first Sentinel airborne stand-off surveillance aircraft.

Enhanced command, control and communications, in particular through Network Enabled Capability:

- Information Management guidance and training introduced;
- Progressive roll out of Defence Information Infrastructure, Bowman, and Cormorant systems and launch of the first Skynet 5 communications satellite;
- Upgrades to the Joint Operational Command System;
- First operational deployment of Defence Information Infrastructure;
- Development of Defence Intelligence Modernisation Programme.

Force Capability Changes

129. In line with the modernisation programme set out in *Delivering Security in a Changing World: Future Capabilities* in July 2004, the Armed Forces continued to adapt to meet future defence and security challenges through significant improvements to force structures, equipment capability and the efficiency and effectiveness with which the Department supports the Armed Forces. These changes include an increased number of deployable infantry battalions through the Future Army Structure programme; the launching of a new generation of powerful, technologically-advanced Royal Navy ships, including amphibious assault ships, Type 45 destroyers and the first of the new generation of nuclear powered submarines; and the entry into service of the first Typhoon fighter aircraft. The programme accounts for about £1.2Bn of the £2.8Bn efficiency savings across defence contained in the 2004 Spending Review (see paragraph 149 under *Efficiency and Change*).

HMS Dauntless

Royal Navy Force Structure and Capabilities

130. The changes to the Royal Navy's force structure set out in the *Future Capabilities* paper were aimed at delivering a versatile maritime force, structured and equipped for rapid deployment anywhere around the world. The changing global threat, together with the benefits of new technology and improved efficiency, means the Royal Navy no longer requires the same number of some types of ship as before. The decommissioning of HMS Sovereign in September 2006 was in line with the objective of reducing the number of attack submarines to eight by 2008. In January 2007 HMS Dauntless, the second of the new and highly capable Type 45 Daring Class air-defence Destroyers, was successfully launched. The new Bay Class Landing Ship Dock (Auxiliary) RFA Mounts Bay entered service in September 2006, followed by RFA Largs Bay in December and RFA Cardigan Bay in March 2007. This will allow the deployment of more people and equipment more quickly to trouble spots around the world and greatly enhanced the capability of the Amphibious Task Force. HMS Astute, the first of the Royal Navy's next generation of nuclear powered attack submarines, was launched in June 2007. Work continued to refine and develop the design of the Future Aircraft Carrier and acquire the Joint Combat Aircraft for use by the Royal Navy and Royal Air Force.

Two Typhoon T1s

Future Army Structure and Capabilities

131. In 2006-07 the Army continued implementation of the measures outlined in December 2004 to reconfigure to its Future Army Structure. Changes during the year included:

- Reformation of 22 Signal Regiment. Based in Stafford as part of the West Midlands Super Garrison, it will provide General Support, communications and enhanced Command and Control to 3(UK) Division, HQ Joint Helicopter Command (JHC) and Headquarters Allied Rapid Reaction Corps (HQ ARRC);

- The provision of a Fourth Manoeuvre unit to 3 Commando Brigade. Formed from the newly named 1 RIFLES, the battalion will be based in Chepstow and will enhance the Commando Brigade's ability to support the Operational Commitments Plot;

- Bringing Armoured Infantry Battalions up to strength by manning their ninth platoons to the full establishment; and

- The further enhancement of Intelligence units.

132. There is a substantial equipment programme to support the Army in future operations, augmented by a programme of equipment procured through the Urgent Operational Requirement process. Deliveries during the year included the Guided Multiple Launch Rocket System; Automatic Lightweight Grenade Launchers; Bulldog, Vector and Mastiff protected vehicles; improved body armour; Titan and Trojan armoured engineering vehicles; over 10,000 Bowman tactical radios; and new fuel and water tankers. The Future Rapid Effect System programme to provide medium weight armoured vehicles made tangible progress, identifying candidate utility vehicles for trials during the summer of 2007.

Future Army Structures (Reserves)

133. In March 2006 the restructuring of the Army's Reserve Forces was announced. This was in line with the Regular Future Army Structures while maintaining an overall establishment of 42,000. The majority of the Territorial Army began implementing this restructuring during the year. New capabilities generated so far include:

- the Regimental Headquarters and first Squadron of the new Territorial Army Air Corps Regiment designed to deliver support to the Apache attack helicopter;

- the Regimental Headquarters and Parachute Engineer Squadron within the new Territorial Royal Engineer Regiment;

- the Regimental Headquarters and first Transport Squadron within one of two new Territorial Logistic Units; and

- a number of smaller new detachments within existing units.

The restructuring has also involved work to rationalise national and regional areas and units and affiliate Territorial units with their Regular counterparts. This has improved training opportunities and support to operations.

Royal Air Force Structure and Capabilities

134. Following the reorganization of RAF Groups and the formation of Expeditionary Air Wings in April 2006, the main restructuring effort in 2006-07 was centred on the collocation of HQ Personnel and Training Command with HQ Strike Command at High Wycombe, which produced a reduction of around 1,000 posts and annual savings of some £23M. The two commands then merged into a single, integrated Air Command on 2 April 2007. Equipment capability improved in a number of areas. Defensive aids were fitted to a wider range of transport aircraft, improving the robustness of the Airbridge to Iraq and Afghanistan. The acquisition of targeting pods for Harrier and Tornado improved targeting accuracy. Two Naval Air Squadrons formed at RAF Cottesmore on 31 March and 1 October 2006 respectively, joining the two existing RAF Harrier Squadrons as a part of Joint Force Harrier. Following their initial formation, RAF Typhoon squadrons continued to take delivery of aircraft and develop towards achieving operational status over the next year. In line with the introduction of Typhoon into service there were reductions to Tornado F3 units, and the Jaguar was withdrawn from service in April 2007. Predator Unmanned Air Vehicles are being acquired to provide a long endurance, unmanned platform for surveillance and reconnaissance missions. Delivery of ASTOR/Sentinel, which will provide an airborne stand-off surveillance radar system is progressing, with one aircraft now being flown by RAF crews and further aircraft due to be delivered over the next year. Work continued on the programmes to acquire the Nimrod MRA4 reconnaissance aircraft, A400M transport aircraft and Future Strategic Tanker aircraft.

Nimrod MRA4 – Trials Aircraft

Information Superiority

135. Getting the right information to the right people at the right time in the right form while denying an adversary the ability to do the same gives the Armed Forces an important advantage. There is a substantial programme of work to achieve this.

Network Enabled Capability

136. Network Enabled Capability (NEC) is about acquiring, connecting, integrating and synchronising the right equipment and technology, and operating to make best use of the information. It is as much about culture as it is about equipment. It both enhances military effect, and plays a part in maintaining the utility of military force in an increasingly complex environment and under ever greater scrutiny. It is therefore a critical enabler of the Comprehensive Approach (see the essay on page 40) which the Department seeks to embrace through integration with other Government Departments, agencies, allies and coalition partners. During 2006-07 progress was made across all three NEC Dimensions of Information, Networks and People.

- **Information**. A Joint Doctrine Note on Information Management, the MoD's Information Management Handbook, and an associated Commanders' Précis were all produced. These publications, together with the establishment of training courses for Senior Information Officers and Information Managers at the Defence Academy, are facilitating the establishment of local Information Management arrangements at all levels of command within broad departmental guidelines. The Department's increasing ability to manage ever greater volumes of operational and non-operational information will allow work to focus on Information Exploitation, including using the Defence Information Infrastructure (see paragraph 138) and other

networks and applications to change operational and non-operational business processes. The Department also continued to improve its ability to protect and secure its electronic data;

- **Networks**. As well a number of specific acquisitions to meet operational requirements, the Department continued to roll out a number of wider information systems. These included the Defence Information Infrastructure (see paragraph 138), roll-out of Bowman (secure tactical communications) and its use on operations, introduction of further Cormorant (theatre communications) systems and the launch of the first Skynet 5 communications satellite in May 2007. Between them these have significantly improved deployed forces' connectivity. Upgrades to the Joint Operational Command System also provided more resilient links between deployed UK forces and headquarters worldwide. Further Information Management and interoperability improvements are planned for the coming year;

- **People**. Realising the full benefits of investment in networks and information requires personnel with the appropriate education and training in how to use them. The NEC Competency Framework continues to be developed for incorporation into defence skills frameworks. Formal Training Needs Analysis studies were launched into developing subject matter experts and the case for broader NEC education across defence to underpin the Department's evolving Information Management, Information Assurance and Battlespace Management capabilities.

Command and Battlespace Management

137. The Command and Battlespace Management programme aims to achieve a winning tempo in the conduct of operations by the development of decision superiority. While elements will only mature over 15 to 20 years it is an integral part of work to enhance military effect by driving forward and managing the development of more integrated command and control of joint military capabilities on operations. The Development, Concepts and Doctrine Centre continued to develop concepts underpinning the ability to change military focus efficiently and effectively in a rapidly changing scenario. This included studies of how command and control and joint battlespace management will be conducted in the future.

Defence Information Infrastructure

138. The Defence Information Infrastructure (Future) (DII(F)) project will provide a standard, consistent platform for defence applications and a more effective environment for the sharing of information, transmission of messages and collaborative working to groups and individuals including those that currently have limited or no connectivity. DII(F) will underpin and act as a catalyst for the Defence Change Programme and will enhance deployed operational capability by being a key enabler of Network Enabled Capability through a single network of information. It will extend into the operational arena, interface with battlespace systems and improve shared information between headquarters, battlefield support and the front line, allowing greater interoperability between MoD and its allies. Work has started to manage the volume of data stored in the system to improve business practices. DII(F) was installed at over 200 sites during the year as roll-out across defence accelerated, including provision to support the Joint Personnel Administration system (see paragraphs 179-184 under *Future Personnel Plans*), and a DII capability was deployed operationally for the first time in Afghanistan. Ultimately it will provide around 300,000 user accounts on approximately 150,000 terminals across about 2,000 MoD sites worldwide.

Defence Intelligence Modernisation Programme

139. The Defence Intelligence Modernisation Programme will deliver a range of new capabilities and benefits including the introduction of IS-enabled business change, an integrated environment for geospatial intelligence, a rationalised fit-for-purpose estate (see paragraph 321 under *Estate*) and new working practices, in order better to meet intelligence users' requirements. The quality of geospatial intelligence and communications within the UK intelligence community were improved during the year, and the Defence Intelligence Command Group moved to Main Building as the first step in the full integration of the Defence Intelligence Staff within the MoD Head Office.

Further sources of information

140. Additional information on Future Effects is available from the following sources:

- 2004 Spending Review: Stability, security and opportunity for all: Investing for Britain's long-term future: New Public Spending Plans 2005-2008(Cm 6237) at www.hm-treasury.gov.uk;
- The Defence Committee Fourth Report of Session 2004-05 Future Capabilities (HC 45-i & ii on 17 March 2005) available on www.parliament.the-stationery-office.co.uk;
- The Government's Response to the Defence Committee Fourth Report of Session 2004-05 Future Capabilities (Cm6616, July 2005) available at www.mod.uk;
- Releasing resources to the front line: Independent Review of Public Sector Efficiency at www.hm-treasury.gov.uk;
- MoD Annual Report and Accounts available at www.mod.uk.

Essay – Royal Air Force Transformation

The December 2003 Defence White Paper *Delivering Security in a Changing World* outlined international terrorism, the proliferation of weapons of mass destruction, and weak and failing states as the key future security challenges. The July 2004 *Future Capabilities* White Paper set out the future shape of the Armed Forces to meet these challenges: smaller, more flexible, agile and adaptable. This was predicated upon 'effects' based operations, combined with development of fully integrated Network Enabled Capability, enhancing the Armed Forces' fighting ability by linking platforms and people and thus reducing the number of platforms required to achieve a desired military outcome. In his vision for the Royal Air Force, the Chief of the Air Staff described an agile and adaptable force structure, capable of delivering success across the spectrum of operations, from high-end warfighting to the support of humanitarian operations. The RAF is responding to these challenges, even while supporting operations in Iraq and Afghanistan.

There has been a step change in capability over the last ten years, delivered through changes to organisation, processes, culture and equipment. A key driver has been the changing operating environment, which increasingly now involves irregular warfare where the opponent only presents himself fleetingly, in different guises, and employs widely varying operational tactics. But the risk of regular warfare still exists. Against this background, the enduring tasks of Air Power to 'find, identify, fix and strike' the enemy, has become ever more challenging. And with operational timescales often now measured in minutes rather than hours the importance of 'find and identify' has increased. This is an area where the Air Power characteristics of height, speed, reach and ubiquity can provide unique warfighting advantages.

This context clearly increases the operational importance of Intelligence, Surveillance, Target Acquisition and Reconnaissance capabilities. The Royal Air Force has therefore updated the Nimrod MR2 with an enhanced electro-optical suite and introduced Predator Unmanned Air Vehicles into service in support of the joint campaign. The provision of the LITENING III pod on the Tornado GR4 has greatly enhanced its ability to support ground forces directly by providing live video feed to ground-based troops via a remote viewing terminal, enabling rapid identification and targeting of enemy forces. In the near future, this capability will be further enhanced by introduction of the new ASTOR System to provide all-weather air-to-surface radar surveillance of the battlefield. These enhancements, coupled with improvements in Air-Land integration and programmes to blend and share sensor information across platforms, will provide unprecedented levels of situational awareness for future fighting forces. This will then ensure that decisions are translated into decisive action at the right time in the right place.

The changing nature of likely targets and better understanding of the effect of an action have in turn generated a need to change the way in which an enemy is targeted. Since its inception Air Power has played a key role in giving the Armed Forces freedom of movement and action on the ground and at sea. A show of force can often achieve the desired effect. When force is necessary precision guided munitions, which are between two to 15 times more effective than 'dumb' weapons, allow a smaller number of aircraft to engage a larger number of targets. A single Harrier GR7/9 equipped with Paveway IV 500lb bombs can engage six separate targets in all weather conditions at any time, minimising damage to civilian infrastructure and the risks to innocent bystanders. Striking the same number of targets with the earlier Harrier GR3 required four aircraft, target designation by ground forces, and was confined to daylight and clear weather. The introduction into service of Typhoon with an air-to-ground capability will provide the Royal Air Force with its first multi-role platform for thirty years, able to undertake a wide range of roles including counter-air operations, strategic air operations, integrated air operations and Intelligence, Surveillance, Target Acquisition and Reconnaissance. This flexibility will allow the RAF to produce the required effect by deploying fewer aircraft. In combination with the modernised air transport fleet (see below) this will significantly increase its ability to position aircraft, and support equipment and personnel across the globe, facilitating timely intervention in response to a crisis.

In order to use the speed and reach of air to provide this rapid global mobility, the MoD continues to invest heavily in the multi-engined aircraft fleets. The RAF's air transport capability has been significantly improved by the recently procured C-130J Hercules and increased investment in the larger C-17. Both aircraft have greater range, payload and flexibility and the capability to operate from large airfields or austere locations as the situation dictates. The C-17 can also lift very large loads across large distances, increasing the ability to deploy rapidly the Army's fighting vehicles. The RAF's older air transport aircraft, the VC10 and TriStar, continue to provide vital air transport and refuelling capability, and this will be significantly enhanced over the next decade as the A400M and Future Strategic Tanker Aircraft enter service.

This 'effects' based approach and associated technological advances meant that a smaller Royal Air Force of about 41,000 personnel will be able in future to deliver the required military capability. In turn this has given the RAF the opportunity to rationalise its command and support arrangements. The formation of a single Headquarters, Air Command, at RAF High Wycombe requires 1,000 fewer posts (military and civilian) and saves over £23M a year. The RAF Transformation Programme continues to improve working practices, processes and organisational structures. Logistics transformation, including streamlining of processes (known as leaning), the establishment of a forward and depth aircraft maintenance system and an improved relationship with industry has enabled rationalisation of support facilities. Introducing multi-skilling has produced a smaller more adaptable military workforce. The Defence Airfield Review should reduce the number of RAF bases by 40% by the end of the next decade, providing greater subsequent stability for RAF personnel and more focused expenditure on the remaining infrastructure. The resources freed up can be reinvested elsewhere in defence.

But new technology and better structures and systems are not enough to continue to deliver Air Power. People continue to be the heart of the Royal Air Force's capability, with the emphasis on a 'warfighter first' ethos. In a competitive climate for talent, the Service continues to work to ensure it remains perceived as a modern, forward thinking organisation that values and empowers its personnel. The Royal Air Force of the 21st Century is not the same as its Cold War predecessor. But it remains World Class, adapting and transforming itself to meet the challenges of today and tomorrow.

Efficiency and Change

Objective: More flexible and efficient organisations and processes to support the Armed Forces.

SR2004 Efficiency Target
Realise total annual efficiency gains of at least £2.8Bn by 2007/08, of which three quarters will be cash-releasing;
- Reduce civilian staff numbers by at least 10,000;
- Reduce the number of military posts in administrative and support roles by at least 5,000;
- Be on course to have relocated 3,900 posts out of London and the South East by 2010.

Assessment and Performance Measures

Assessment: The Department remained on course to deliver the efficiency gains and the personnel reductions and relocations agreed in the 2004 Spending Review. By 31 March 2007 over £2Bn efficiencies had been delivered, civilian staff numbers had fallen by over 11,000, military posts by some 10,000 and 1,885 posts had been relocated out of London and the South East.

Force Structure Changes:

- Cumulative efficiencies of £298M from:
  - Reductions to Type 42 Destroyer, Type 23 Frigate, mine-hunter and submarine fleets;
  - Re-roling and reduction of armoured squadrons and artillery batteries;
  - Reductions to Tornado F3 units, withdrawal of Jaguar and a reduced Nimrod fleet;
  - Restructuring of helicopter fleets and ground based air defence capability.

Corporate Services:

- Roll out of Joint Personnel Administration system to the RAF from March 2006, to the RN from October 2006, and to the Army from March 2007;
- Progressive roll out of people programme, enabling personnel staff reductions;
- Progressive implementation of Defence Resource Management Programme, enabling finance staff reductions and reduced spends on external assistance;
- Progressive roll-out of Defence Information Infrastructure.

Procurement and Logistics:

- Cumulative equipment procurement expenditure reductions of £206M;
- Cumulative Logistics efficiencies of £765M-£830M, including £250M-300M during 2006-07;
- Cumulative Whole Fleet Management efficiencies of £55M;
- Cumulative Estates Modernisation efficiencies of £62M;
- Cumulative efficiencies of £66M from other areas of procurement, including £23M from Defence Travel Modernisation.

Productive Time:

- Cumulative non cashable efficiency gains of £139M from reducing time taken to restore personnel to full fitness.

Organisational Change:

- Continuing rationalisation of TLB Headquarters and organisation.

Relocation:

- 1,885 posts relocated.

Personnel Reductions:

- Cumulative efficiencies of £239M from reduction of 10,000 military personnel;
- Cumulative efficiencies of £105M from reduction of 11,000 civilian personnel.

Efficiency and Change Programmes

141. The Department has comprehensive efficiency and change programmes that extend right across the organisation and affect every employee. They affirm the importance we attach to delivering the greatest possible military capability from the resources available for defence. Improvements in areas such as logistics and medical services are already contributing directly to an increase in our military capability. Efficiencies in process and back-office functions are being reinvested in the core programme. This chapter explains the relationships between the Change and Efficiency programmes and details our performance and progress against our efficiency targets.

Defence Change Programme

142. The purpose of the Defence Change Programme is to modernise departmental business processes to improve efficiency and effectiveness, thus maximising our investment in front-line operational capability. Launched in 2002, it now joins up the major change programmes across defence under strong central direction, to produce a single, coherent programme. In prioritising between the various change initiatives underway across the Department, the Change Programme ensures that scarce resources of people, money and skills are devoted to the most important and productive areas. On 31 March 2007 there were 20 pan-defence change programmes in all, covering almost every business process. As well as improving the way we do business, twelve of these are delivering around £1.4Bn (c. 50%) of our efficiency target (see paragraph 144). The programme is supported by investment from the Defence Modernisation Fund (DMF), a ring-fenced sum secured from HM Treasury worth some £1Bn over the three years of the Spending Review 2004 period. £604M from the DMF has been invested within the SR04 period to date (£289M in 2006-07).

143. The Defence Change Programme represents a long term commitment to improved delivery. It includes both longer standing programmes which are now beginning to deliver benefits and a number of new initiatives. It is therefore managed as a live portfolio whereby the overall DCP composition changes over time as old programmes are closed and new ones identified. The Command and Battlespace Management, Business Management System, and Royal Navy Single TLB programmes have been identified by the Change Delivery Group as sufficiently mature to be taken forward as mainstream business. In January 2007, a further four programmes were brought in:

- FLEET Transformation is a coordinated programme to reduce overheads and increase efficiency throughout the FLEET Top Level Budget Organisation through a wide range of tools, including a review of the Navy's Estate Footprint, manpower reduction and the application of LEAN techniques. The programme is due to complete in March 2011 when annual efficiencies will amount to £44M;

- Joint Helicopter Command Rationalisation (Project BELVEDERE) will rationalise the Joint Helicopter Command's Airfield Estate, reducing its footprint and running costs and delivering the optimum balance between operational effectiveness, affordability and value for money, and the impact on personnel. The programme team is currently reviewing all the options prior to seeking initial approval to proceed from the Investment Approvals Board (IAB) in early 2008;

- Germany Basing (BORONA) is a programme to implement plans to relocate soldiers and their families to the UK, taking advantage of estate opportunities arising from estate rationalisation programmes and thus implementing the endorsed Super Garrison Policy. A business case seeking approval is expected in Summer 2007 (see paragraph 320 in *Estates*);

- Defence Recruitment and Individual Training Management, which will harmonise the recruitment and individual training processes across the three Services and will be supported by the replacement of legacy Management Information by a new tri-Service recruiting and training system (DRITMIS) from November 2009. The programme team is currently evaluating the options and plan to seek initial approval from the IAB in Quarter 3 2007-08 for their recommended solution.

Efficiency Programme

144. As part of the 2004 Spending Review, we agreed to realise total annual efficiency gains of at least £2.8Bn by 31 March 2008, of which three quarters will be cash releasing. Within that target, we aim to:

- Reduce the number of our civilian staff by at least 10,000;

- Reduce the number of military posts in administrative and support roles by at least 5,000; and

- Be on course to have relocated 3,900 posts out of London and the South East by 2010.

145. Around half the target will be achieved by programmes already within the Defence Change Programme, and a further 40% from implementation of the force capability changes set out in *Delivering Security in a Changing World: Future Capabilities*, published in July 2004 (see paragraph 129 under *Future Effects*). The remaining 10% comes from other programmes including TLB commodity procurement, relocations, and work to simplify and improve the finance function. The relationship between the Efficiency Programme and the Defence Change Programme is shown below at Figure 7, together with the location of further details on specific projects.

Figure 7 Relationship of change and efficiency programmes

Efficiency Programme

Defence Change Programme		Force Capability Changes	Other
Defence Training Review Transformation (Para 223)	Defence Logistics Transformation (Paras 253-259)	Forces structure changes (Para 149)	Lyons (Para 155)
UK Military Flying Training System (Paras 167, 223)	Whole Fleet Management (Para 152)	Other manpower reductions (Para 156))	Finance (Para 296)
Business Management System (Paras 277-278)	Defence Information Infrastructure (Para 138)	Equipment procurement (Para 152)	Commodity procurement (Para 152)
Defence Intelligence Modernisation Programme (Para 139)	Estates Modernisation (Paras 324-325)		
Joint Helicopter Command Rationalisation (BELVEDERE) (Para 143)	People Programme (Paras 151, 187,194)		
Germany Basing (BORONA) (Para 143)	Joint Personnel Administration (Paras 178-183)		
FLEET Transformation (Para 143)	Defence Health Change Programme (Paras 240-242)		
Defence Recruitment and Individual Training Management (Para 143)	Defence e-Commerce (Para 152)		
	Defence Travel Modernisation (Para 152)		
	Command HQ Collocations (Para 154)		

Governance

146. The Second Permanent Under Secretary leads and oversees the Efficiency and Change programmes on behalf of the Defence Management Board. Rigorous governance structures are in place, with a particular emphasis on risks and benefits. He has overall responsibility for delivery of the Efficiency Programme, chairs the Efficiency Delivery Board, and is the Senior Responsible Owner for the Defence Change Programme. Efficiency and Change performance are reported quarterly to the Defence Management Board within the Defence Balanced Scorecard. Progress towards the Department's Efficiency target is reported to Parliament in the Department's Autumn and Spring Performance Reports, as well as in the Annual Report and Accounts. Each programme within the Defence Change Programme has a Senior Responsible Owner who is personally accountable to the Defence Management Board for maximising the delivery of benefits and reporting regularly to the programme's

Table 3: Efficiency Achievements and Plans

Programme	Achievement by 31 March 2006 (£M) [1]	Achievement by 31 March 2007 (£M) [1]	Planned Efficiency Gains by 31 March 2008 (£M) [1] [2]
Force Structure changes	106	298	388
Corporate Services	343	296	253
Military Personnel Management	16	38	85
Civilian Personnel Management*	24	30	48
Finance Function	2	16	11
Information Services*	301	212	109
Procurement and Logistics	836	1169-1219	1681
Equipment Procurement *	54	206	374
Defence Logistics Transformation	662	780-830	1002
Whole Fleet Management*	54	55	116
Estates Modernisation*	31	62	95
Other Procurement	35	66	92
Productive Time*	105	139	88
Organisational changes	0	2	8
Relocation	18	18	18
Manpower	86	344	557
RN	15	32	32
Army	18	64	88
RAF	51	143	203
Civilian	2	105	234
Adjustment [3]	-9	-68	-106
Total	1,485 [4]	2198-2248	2887

Notes:
1. Planned and Achieved Efficiencies include efficiencies during 2004-05, 2005-06, 2006-07 and 2007-08. Because of the size of the Defence Logistics Transformation Programme, the validation process takes some time and this is the reason why a range is given in the table above.
2. The targets reflect a number of revisions since the publication of the Efficiency Technical Note in December 2005 and the 2006/07 Spring Performance Report.
3. Adjustment to avoid double counting of manpower savings.
4. This has increased from £1107M reported last year following a final validation of Defence Logistics Transformation Programme. The figure has been confirmed as higher after audit.
* Efficiency gains marked with an asterisk include an element of non-cashable gains.

sponsoring Minister. They are individually supported and challenged in this by the Change Delivery Group, which formally assesses the entire portfolio of Defence Change Programmes twice yearly, and manages cross-cutting issues such as common risks and interdependencies, and loading and capacity issues.

Performance against SR04 Efficiency Target

147. The MoD's Efficiency Technical Note (published on www.mod.uk) describes the Efficiency Programme in detail and explains how we are delivering and measuring the efficiency gains. Progress continues to be made in meeting the Department's efficiency targets. By 31 March 2007 £2.225Bn of efficiencies had been delivered. Overall the Department remained on course to achieve the efficiency gains and the personnel reductions and relocations agreed in the 2004 Spending Review.

Cashable gains

148. Of the total efficiency gains achieved by 31 March 2007, 84% are cash-releasing against a requirement of at least 75% for all 2004 Spending Review efficiency targets.

Force Structure Changes

149. In *Delivering Security in a Changing World: Future Capabilities*, published in July 2004, the Department set out the transformation required to deliver better policy outcomes with smaller, more flexible and adaptable Armed Forces able to meet future defence and security challenges. The force structure changes underpinning this goal delivered efficiencies of £239M in 2006-07, for a cumulative total of £298M in addition to the £106M (£58M of which is sustainable) achieved by 31 March 2006. The force structure changes made in 2005-06 set out in last year's *Annual Report and Accounts* and further changes during 2006-07 included:

- The reduction of Type 42 Destroyer, Type 23 Frigate and mine-hunter fleets and a rationalisation of submarine capability delivered £119M of additional efficiencies;

- The re-roling and reduction of Challenger II armoured squadrons and AS90 artillery batteries, reflecting the transition from heavy to light and medium weight forces delivered £12M of additional efficiencies;

- Reductions to Tornado F3 units and withdrawal of Jaguar from 30 April 2007 in line with the introduction into service of Typhoon, and reducing costs associated with the smaller Nimrod fleet delivered £65M of additional efficiencies; and

- The restructuring of current helicopter fleets and ground based air defence capability delivered £43M of additional efficiencies.

150. Further information on force structure changes is set out at paragraphs 129-134 under *Future Effects*.

Corporate Services

151. The Department has been taking forward a range of programmes to modernise and improve the effectiveness and efficiency of its corporate services:

- Joint Personnel Administration is modernising the personnel management and administration of the Armed Forces by harmonising and simplifying a range of personnel policies and processes and by introducing a new commercial off-the-shelf information system (see paragraphs 178-183 under *Future Personnel Plans*, the essay on page 108, and the Statement on Internal Control in the Departmental Resource Accounts on page 212). Following introduction to the Royal Air Force, the system rolled-out to the Royal Navy during October and November 2006, to Army personnel professionals in March 2007, and to the rest of the Army by July 2007. It had delivered £38M of efficiencies by 31 March 2007 (£16M by 31 March 2006), mainly through reductions in RAF and Navy personnel staff. The drop in achievement (£38M) against planned efficiencies (£43M) is due to a one-off loss caused by the delay in Army rollout of the administration system which is as a result of a delay in headcount reductions;

- The People Programme will enable MoD civilians to make the best contribution to the UK's defence capability through a civilian workforce which is appropriately skilled, managed and motivated (see paragraph 187 under *Future Personnel*). Efficiency gains are being achieved through a reduction of civilian HR staff, lower maintenance costs of the human resources information system, implementation of modern and simple pay and policy processes and a reduction in administration tasks. The programme had delivered £30M of efficiencies by 31 March 2007 (£24M by 31 March 2006), mainly through HR personnel reductions. This saving is a drop against the £49M of planned efficiencies expected for 2006-07 (see paragraph 194 under *Future Personnel*);

- The Defence Resource Management Programme aims to simplify and improve current financial processes, structures and systems to reduce costs and improve decision-making (see paragraph 296 under *Finance*). The programme had delivered £16M of efficiencies by 31 March 2007 (£2M by 31 March 2006), mainly through a reduction in the number of staff in the finance function and less expenditure on external assistance;

- The Defence Information Infrastructure is delivering a modern management information infrastructure across defence (see paragraph 138 under *Future Effects*). The programme had delivered a total of £212M of efficiencies by 31 March 2007 (£301M by 31 March 2006) of which £120M is a non-sustainable in year benefit. This reflects the decreasing need to sustain legacy systems, as DII is rolled out and its functionality increased.

Procurement and Logistics

152. The Department is undertaking a range of programmes to build on Smart Acquisition, improve value for money from expenditure on the future equipment programme, increase the effectiveness, efficiency and flexibility of defence logistics activity, and modernise management of the defence estate. We are also working to improve the efficiency of commodity procurement across defence. These programmes comprise the Procurement and Logistics element of our overall efficiency programme. They do not include the substantial changes the Department is making to its acquisition processes and organisation under the Defence Acquisition Change Programme (see paragraphs 170-172 under *Future Capabilities and Infrastructure*, and the essay on *Defence Industrial Strategy* on page 101). In particular:

- *Future Capabilities* identified opportunities to improve value for money from equipment procurement expenditure. The programme had delivered £206M of efficiencies by 31 March 2007 (£54M by 31 March 2006), mainly through revised procurement strategies for the future helicopter fleet and the Future Rapid Effects System, a more efficient way to provide the offensive air capability, and reprofiled acquisition increments for indirect fire precision;

- The Defence Logistics Transformation Programme is transforming the means by which logistics support is delivered to the three Services (see paragraphs 253-259 under *Logistics*). The programme delivered £250M-300M during 2006-07 in addition to £662M (£530M of which is sustainable) achieved by 31 March 2006 through Reliability Centred Maintenance, Procurement Reform and LEANing of the support and supply chain. Work is in hand to validate the efficiencies achieved in 2006-07;

- Whole Fleet Management is providing better management of the defence land vehicle fleet and facilitating the training of force elements to the required standard on future reduced fleets. Benefits of £55M had been delivered by 31 March 2007 (total 05/06 achievement of £54M by 31 March 2006), mainly through reduced spares consumption and battery use, improved management of the vehicle fleet and productive time efficiencies. The total efficiencies possible from the Equipment Maintenance labour days work strand have reduced, reflecting that it was predominantly low-maintenance equipment going into store;

- The Estates Modernisation programme is rationalising and improving the condition of the defence estate and obtaining better value for money from estate expenditure through the introduction of Prime Contracting, the modernisation of single living accommodation and the provision of water and sewage services (see paragraphs 324-325 under *Estates*). Efficiency gains of £62M had been delivered by 31 March 2007 (£31M by 31 March 2006), mainly through personnel reductions, lower management overheads for Service families' accommodation and reduced operating costs;

- The 'Other Procurement' Initiative is extending the Defence Logistics Organisation's Procurement Reform programme across other areas of defence. It seeks to maximise the Department's buying power through aggregation of requirements; the use of reverse auctions; reduced prices; purchase avoidance; and rationalisation of contracts enabled by electronic purchasing. It had delivered £66M of efficiencies by 31 March 2007 (£35M by 31 March 2006), including £23M from the Defence Travel Modernisation programme (£12M by 31 March 2006) to deliver a modern and coherent e-booking capability.

Productive Time

153. The objective of the Defence Health Change Programme is to increase the proportion of military personnel who are fit-for-task by improving the quality of healthcare using regional rehabilitation units and other methods (see paragraphs 240-242 under *Health and Safety)*. £139M of non cashable annual efficiency gains from reducing the time taken to restore personnel to full fitness had been delivered by 31 March 2007 (£105M by 31 March 2006).

Organisational Changes

154. A number of programmes to slim down the Department's management overhead continued to be taken forward, including the continuing rationalisation of Service Headquarters and other organisations. Benefits of £2M had been delivered by 31 March 2007. The Royal Navy's Fleet Headquarters stood up in April 2006 and is on track to deliver its headcount reductions and efficiencies. The Royal Air Force Collocated Headquarters opened in October 2006, had achieved 35% headcount reductions by the end of the year, and is on track to meet its overall target by 31 March 2008. Work is also in hand to reorganise Land Command and the Adjutant General's Department and establish a new collocated Headquarters (Project Hyperion), to take forward further rationalisation of the new Defence Equipment and Support Organisation, and to make further reductions to the Head Office. These are all expected to deliver further efficiencies, but not by 31 March 2008.

Hurricane Gate Guardian at RAF Air Command

Relocations

155. The Department remained on track to deliver a net reduction of 3,900 posts in London and the South East by 2010. 1,885 posts had been relocated by 31 March 2007 (1,229 by 31 March 2006).

Personnel Reductions

156. The changes in force structures and equipment capability and the Change and Efficiency programmes are producing further substantial personnel reductions:

- The number of military personnel will reduce by over 10,000 between April 2005 and April 2008, enabling the withdrawal of over 5,000 military administrative and support posts (see paragraph 178 under *Future Personnel Plans)*. By 31 March 2007 personnel numbers had been reduced by 10,000, generating efficiency savings of £239M (£84M by 31 March 2006);

- The Department plans to reduce civilian personnel numbers by 15,000[1] by 31 March 2008 (see paragraph 310 under *Manpower)*. By 31 March 2007 a reduction of 11,020 had been achieved (over 6,000 by 31 March 2006), generating efficiency savings of £105M (£2M by 31 March 2006).

Maintaining service quality

157. All programmes contributing efficiency savings are required to demonstrate that where inputs have been reduced, the quality of outputs is being maintained. Examples of this include:

- Performance under the Defence Logistics Transformation Programme is monitored against Customer-Supplier Agreements with Front Line Commands, including measures such as improved delivery timelines and increased availability of vehicles and aircraft;

- Monitoring of service support availability and response times delivered by the Defence Information Infrastructure programme, the accessibility and quality of services in line with business requirements, and customer satisfaction surveys;

- Joint Personnel Administration performance against Service Level Agreements between the Armed Forces Pay and Administration Agency which delivers the programme and the single Service customers; and

- The number of vehicles available for use under Whole Fleet Management.

1 This is based on agreement with Treasury and includes Trading Fund reductions, but excludes Locally Engaged Civilians in operational areas.

Further sources of information

158. Additional information on Efficiency and Change is available from the following sources:

- *Delivering Security in a Changing World: Future Capabilities* available at www.mod.uk;
- Quarterly PSA reports at www.mod.uk;
- *SR2004 Efficiency Technical Note* available at www.mod.uk;
- *2004 Spending Review: Stability, Security and Opportunity for all: investing for Britain's long-term future* (CM 6237 on 12 July 2004) available at www.hm-treasury.gov.uk;
- *The independent review of Public Service Relocations – Well Placed to Deliver? – Shaping the Pattern of Government Service by Sir Michael Lyons* available at www.hm-treasury.gov.uk;
- *The Gershon review: Releasing Resources for the Frontline: Independent Review of Public Sector Efficiency* (July 2004) available at www.hm-treasury.gov.uk.
- National Audit Office report *The Efficiency Programme: A Second Review of Progress* (HC 156) available at www.nao.org.uk;
- NAO report on *Transforming Logistics Support for Fat Jets* (HC 825) available at www.nao-org.uk.

Essay – Change in Defence

Since the early 1990s, the MoD has pursued a continuing programme of restructuring and modernisation to adapt to the strategic challenges emerging since the end of the Cold War, and to the public sector reform agenda to improve effectiveness and value for money. Over this period the size of the Armed Forces and the defence Civil Service have reduced by over a third, while supporting a level of sustained operational activity higher than at any time since the end of the Second World War.

There are four main strands to defence modernisation:

● the Defence Change Programme, pulling together the other major change programmes within Defence (see paragraphs 142-143 under *Efficiency and Change*);

● implementation of the Future Capabilities work stemming from the 2003 Defence White Paper *Delivering Security in a Changing World* (see the chapter on *Future Effects* on pages 129-134);

● the Defence Acquisition Change Programme, implementing the reforms necessary to deliver the Defence Industrial Strategy (see in particular paragraphs 170-172 under *Future Capabilities and Infrastructure*, and the essays on the Defence Industrial Strategy on page 101 and the Defence Technology Strategy on page 114.

● implementation of the Action Plan responding to the Departmental Capability Review (see paragraph 276 under *Business Management* and the essay on the Capability Review on pages xx-xx).

Together these represent a coherent approach to modernisation and improvement that both respond to wider Government initiatives to improve the delivery of public services and enable the Department to deliver maximum military capability as effectively as possible within the defence budget.

Defence Change Programme

The Defence Change Programme was established in 2002. It is a portfolio of programmes and projects to improve and modernise the Department. It provides central direction and a coherent framework for the wide range of change initiatives across defence, and for any new initiatives, prioritising them to ensure that resources are devoted to the most important and productive areas, and providing "challenge and support" to ensure they deliver. In total, it has so far delivered just over £1.3Bn worth of savings.

Future Capabilities

In July 2004 the Department announced an extensive re-structuring of the Armed Forces to adapt them to meet new potential threats through smaller, lighter and more capable forces. This included reductions in the surface fleet and rationalisation of our submarine capability; modification of the role and a reduction in the number of tank squadrons and heavy artillery batteries, an increased Armoured Reconnaissance capability and development of an Interim Medium Armoured capability; and reductions to Tornado F3 units and the Nimrod fleet, the withdrawal of Jaguar, and the introduction into service of Typhoon. The helicopter fleet has also been restructured.

Defence Acquisition Change Programme

The Defence Acquisition Change Programme builds on earlier acquisition reform to meet the continuing challenge set out in the December 2005 Defence Industrial Strategy to improve performance in a changing industrial, technological and operational environment. It involves major changes in process, organisation and behaviours on four main themes:

● removing the barriers between consideration of new equipment procurement and equipment support to plan delivery of equipment capability through the life of the system. A key element was the formation of the Defence Equipment and Support organisation from the Defence Procurement Agency and Defence Logistics Organisation;

- undertaking more comprehensive capability planning in the MoD Head Office, looking for solutions that consider both new and existing equipments' potential, examine affordability and support through-life from the outset, and assess the impact on the non-equipment aspects of capability, such as manpower and training;

- developing a closer relationship with Defence Industry, to share the Department's future intent more clearly and understand industrial constraints more effectively while becoming more commercially astute and aware in business dealings; and

- improving the skills, qualifications and experience of defence staff to deliver a leaner, high-performing acquisition system. A programme of new training, Human Resources reform and behaviours work has been set up to do this.

Way Forward

The Department continues to look for ways to improve effectiveness and value for money further, including in the Comprehensive Spending Review. The Capability Review was generally positive, but highlighted areas for further development including strengthening corporate leadership, clarifying and simplifying the strategic operating model and improving engagement across Whitehall and with industrial partners.

The comprehensiveness of the Department's change, restructuring and modernisation programmes has affected every employee. Virtually every part of the Department is involved. The Department continues to pursue improvement, including substantial further reductions in administrative costs and efficiencies in logistics, corporate services and estates, to improve the delivery of military capability and release resources for reinvestment in the Front Line. But the pace and volume of change will continue to be managed carefully to ensure that key outputs, and particularly support to operations in Iraq and Afghanistan, continue to be delivered.

Future Capabilities and Infrastructure

Objective: Progress future equipment and capital infrastructure projects to time, quality and cost estimates

Public Service Agreement Target (SR2004 Mod Target 6 and SR2002 MoD Target 7)
Deliver the Equipment Programme to cost and time by achieving in 2005-06:
- At least 97% of Key User Requirements, for all Category A to C Projects that have passed Main Gate Approval, to be achieved throughout the PSA period.
- An average in-year variation of forecast In Service Dates for all Category A to C Projects that have passed Main Gate Approval, to be no more than 0.5 months.
- An average in-year variation of forecast costs for Design and Manufacture phase for all Category A to C projects that have passed Main Gate approval, of less than 0.3%.

Assessment and Performance Measures

Assessment: The Department invested about £5.3Bn in equipment for the Armed Forces over the year, and over £2Bn in supporting infrastructure. Equipment acquisition performance continued to improve. For the second year running the Department met or exceeded its Public Service Agreement targets for equipment procurement, despite them being more demanding than those for 2005-06. The Department continued to invest heavily in strategic infrastructure. Significant changes to improve acquisition were made under the Acquisition Reform programme, including the establishment of the new Defence Equipment and Support organisation in April 2007.

At least 97% of Key User Requirements, for all Category A to C Projects that have passed Main Gate Approval, to be achieved:

- 99% of Key User Requirements achieved (97% 2005-06)

On average, less than 0.3% in-year variation of forecast costs for Design and Manufacture phase of projects over £20M:

- 0.0% average increase in costs measured against estimated cost at beginning of year (0.2% average increase 2005-06)

No more than 0.5 months in-year slippage of forecast In-Service Dates for projects over £20M:

- 0.5 months average slippage (0.7 months 2005-06)

DPA delivery of at least 93% of planned in-year asset deliveries, by value:

- 102% of planned in-year assets delivered (107% 2005-06)

Equipment Procurement

159. The Equipment Programme, of some £5.5-6.0Bn a year, delivers battle-winning equipment to the Armed Forces. It is rigorously reviewed every two years, as part of the MoD's overall planning and programming process, to ensure that the Department makes the best possible use of available resources and provides the UK Armed Forces with the capabilities they need for operations today and in the future. Table 4 sets out the Department's performance against the 2004 Spending Review Public Service Agreement targets, and the Defence Procurement Agency's performance against its complementary Key Targets. This performance has been certified by the National Audit Office. In 2006-07 the Department and the Defence Procurement Agency met all the acquisition targets for the second consecutive year, despite several targets being more challenging than those for 2005-06.

Public Service Agreement Targets

160. The 2004 Spending Review target for equipment acquisition covers a broad range of projects in order to provide a comprehensive picture of the Department's overall performance in delivering the Equipment Programme. It comprises all projects with a capital value greater than £20M that have passed their main investment decision point but not yet reached their In-Service Dates at the start of the financial year (a total of 44 projects in 2006-07). In 2006-07 the equipment required was managed to cost and with minimal slippage in expected in service date (see table 4 below), more than meeting the PSA Equipment Acquisition targets for the year.

RFA Mounts Bay Leaving Portsmouth Dockyard

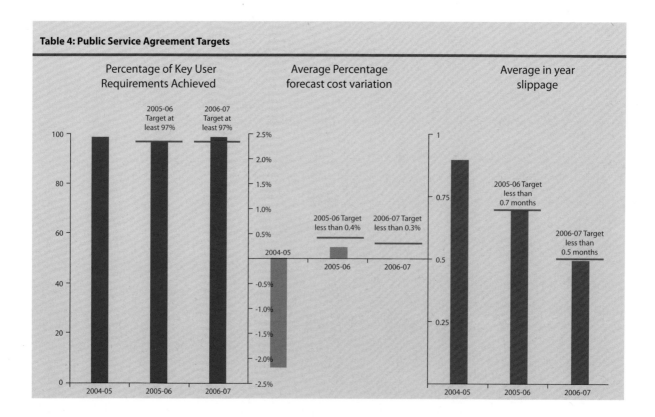

Table 4: Public Service Agreement Targets

Defence Procurement Agency Key Targets

161. The Defence Procurement Agency met all of its Key Targets in 2006-07 for the second consecutive year (see table 5 below). These included the target set used to measure the Department's performance against its PSA targets. Further details on the Agency's performance can be found in the *DPA Annual Report & Accounts*. Summary information on the performance of major equipment projects by capability area is contained in Annex G and detailed information on these projects is continued in the annual *Major Projects Report* published by the National Audit Office. The Defence Procurement Agency ceased to exist on 31 March 2007 with the formation of the Defence Equipment and Support organisation as part of the Enabling Acquisition Change Report 2006.

Table 5: PSA and Defence Procurement Agency Key Targets and Achievements

	2006-07	2005-06	2004-05
Predicted achievement of Key User Requirements[1]	**97%**	**97%**	**N/A**
Met	**99%**	**97%**	
Equivalent DPA Key Target	97%	97%	97%
Met	99%	97%	99%
Average In-Year variation of costs not to exceed[1]	**0.3%**	**0.4%**	**N/A**
Met	**0.0%**	**0.2%**	
Equivalent DPA Key Target	0.5%	0.6%	0%
Met	0.0%	0.2%	-2.2%
Average In-Year slippage of In-Service Dates not to exceed[1]	**0.5 months**	**0.7 months**	**N/A**
Met	**0.5 months**	**0.7 months**	
Equivalent DPA Key Target	0.9 months	1.0 months	0.9 months
Met	0.5 months	0.7 months	0.9 months
Asset delivery achievement (percentage by value of planned asset deliveries)	>93%	>90%	85%
Met	102%	107%	100%
i) Asset Turnover Ratio (months)[2]	<52 months	<83 months	<70 months
Met	47 months	70 months	59 months
ii) Assets delivered per £ of Operating Costs[3]	>£15.44	>£13.20	>£10.72
Met	18.58	15.29	£14.36
iii) Assets produced per £ of Operating Costs[4]	>£18.01	>£23.16	>£16.23
Met	20.63	23.87	£19.13

Notes:
(1) All projects over £20M that have passed their main investment decision point, but not yet achieved ISD at the start of the financial year.
(2) This is an approximation of how many months assets/equipment sit on the DPA balance sheet before they are finished and delivered. A decreasing number indicates improving efficiency.
(3) This measures the assets/equipment delivered to the DPA's customers against the DPA's operating costs. An increasing number indicates improving efficiency.
(4) This measures the assets added to the Balance Sheet over the DPA's operating cost. An increasing number indicates improving efficiency.

Deliveries and key contracts placed

162. The Defence Procurement Agency delivered new equipment valued at £4.98Bn during the year (£3.30Bn in 2005-06), with eleven new projects formally accepted into service. This represented 102% of the asset value planned for delivery in-year and exceeded a target of 93% asset delivery achievement. Key milestones achieved during the year included:

- Delivery of three 16,000 tonne auxiliary landing ships, RFA Mounts Bay, Largs Bay and Cardigan Bay;

- Delivery of the Guided Multiple Launch Rocket System on schedule, with its associated Future Fire Control System;

- Delivery of Titan and Trojan armoured vehicles under the Engineer Tank Systems under a £250M project;

- Delivery of 192 large fuel and water tanker lorries;

- Delivery of 10,700 Bowman tactical communications systems and other infantry weapons and equipment;

- Delivery of 16 Typhoon combat aircraft;

- Delivery of Automatic Lightweight Grenade Launchers to soldiers on operations under an Urgent Operational Requirement;

- Ordered twelve sophisticated Nimrod MRA4 patrol aircraft under a £1.1Bn contract;

- Entered a Strategic Partnering Arrangement and Business Transformation Incentivisation Agreement with AgustaWestland, placing a £1Bn contract for 70 Future Lynx helicopters;

- Placed a £450M contract for 28 Hawk 128 Advanced Jet Trainers;

- Contributed £325M to an £830M programme with Typhoon partner nations to transform the aircraft by providing it with advanced multi-role capabilities, and placed a £73M contract to equip Typhoon for autonomous all weather precision ground attack strike;

- Placed a £300M contract for the provision of a 20 year service covering aerial targets for the armed forces;

- Increased the supply of battlefield helicopters under contracts valued at up to £235M for six new Merlin aircraft and the conversion of eight Chinook Mk3s to the battlefield support role;

- Placed a £140M contract to refine and develop the design of the Future Aircraft Carrier;

- Placed a £127M contract for a technology demonstration programme named Taranis, to investigate key technologies for next generation unmanned air vehicles;

- Ordered a fifth C-17 transport aircraft and agreed that MoD will buy out leases on the RAF's four existing C-17s in 2008;

- Placed a £250M contract for more than 2,000 new design versatile trucks to support the Armed Services;

- Signed a Memorandum of Understanding for the Production, Sustainment and Follow-on Development for the next phase of the Joint Combat Aircraft project;

- Placed a £65M contract for new design of more effective robot bomb disposal vehicles;

- Placed a £56M contract for advanced new targeting pods for Typhoon aircraft;

- Launched the second Type 45 destroyer, Dauntless;

- Launched the first new generation Skynet 5 strategic communications satellite;

- Delivered the first Airborne Stand Off Radar aircraft and ground stations for training.

163. Since April 2007, the following deliveries and key contracts have been placed:

- A £200M contract for HMS Audacious, the fourth of the Astute class submarines;

- Approval of a PFI solution to replace the RAF's fleet of VC10 and TriStar aircraft;

- Launch of HMS Astute – the Royal Navy's newest super-submarine; and

- The selection of the Army's Future Rapid Effect System vehicles to participate in trials to find designs which offer the greatest protection.

Bowman – the UK's future tactical communications system

Urgent Operational Requirements

Capital Infrastructure

164. The Department invests heavily in strategic infrastructure to support defence outputs. In order to improve the decision making process regarding priorities for investment in infrastructure, the Department has brigaded funding for major infrastructure in the Non Equipment Investment Plan. This is used to make informed judgements on the relative priority of competing infrastructure proposals. It comprises about 70 projects costing around £2.5Bn a year, mainly consisting of a wide range of estate programmes costing some £2Bn a year, including estate maintenance projects such as the Regional Prime Contracts and project Aquatrine (see paragraphs 326-327 under *Estates*); and estate modernisation programmes such as Project SLAM to improve the standard of single living accommodation (see paragraph 318 under *Defence Estates*), Allenby/Connaught (see paragraph 323 under *Defence Estates*), the Defence Training Review (see paragraph 223 under *Personnel Management*), and a number of projects underpinning Top Level Budget organisations' rationalisation and collocation programmes (see paragraph 154 under *Efficiency and Change*). It also includes major Information System projects costing about £500M a year, such as the Defence Information Infrastructure to provide a coherent IS network across defence (see paragraph 138 under *Future Effects*), the Human Resource Management System (see paragraph 192 under *Future Personnel Plans*), and Joint Personnel Administration (see paragraph 178 under *Future Personnel Plans*, the essay on page 108, and the Statement on Internal Control in the *Departmental Resource Accounts* on page 212).

Private Finance Initiative

165. The Private Finance Initiative (PFI) remains a significant delivery tool in the provision of innovative and efficient services for defence. The Department remains committed to involving the private sector where appropriate, and using PFI where the requirement is for long-term services based around the provision or refurbishment of a capital asset or equivalent that can be funded by third party finance. The new MoD Project Agreement was published during the year, based upon Standardisation of PFI Contracts version three which is the standard contract and guidance that project teams have to use when drafting their PFI contracts, allowing for a more efficient and effective procurement of PFI updated from Version two, produced in 2003). Standardisation and improvements to the procurement process are producing better value for money and at the same time helping to drive down the length of the bidding process and bid costs – when a significant proportion (around 60-70%) of contract is common to all projects, standardisation of these elements of the contract will help reduce both procurement time and cost and these elements of the contract do not have to be renegotiated each time a new project commences. The Department signed one PFI deal in 2006-07 with the Northwood Development project with a capital value of £162M, bringing total private sector capital investment through PFI to over £5.8Bn. Further details on signed PFI transactions are in note 1.27 to the Departmental Resource Accounts on page 233. The Private Finance Unit also supported two public private partnerships, MoDEL (MoD Estates in London) and the Combined Aerial Targets Service projects, to reach contract close during the reporting year. At the 2007 Public Private Finance Awards, the MoD Private Finance Unit won Best Government Team, MoDEL won Best Public Sector Project Team and the Judges' Award for Innovation; Combined Aerial Target Service won best UK Deal to Sign; and C Vehicles won the best Operational Defence Scheme. The Defence Sixth Form College PFI was also highly commended in the category of Operational Project with the Best Design.

Launch of Skynet 5

166. The Department received a total gain of £2.2M from the refinancing of the PFI projects for the Very Low Frequency Naval Communications Service (VLF) in December 2006 and the Tornado GR4 Synthetic Training Service (TSTS) in March 2007. These were undertaken in compliance with the Voluntary Code on Refinancing. The Department's forward PFI programme (see Table 6) has an estimated capital value of approximately £4Bn to £6Bn.

Table 6: Major PFI Projects in Procurement as at 31 March 2006

Project Name

Corsham Development Project
Defence Training Rationalisation Project
Future Provision of Marine Services
Future Strategic Tanker Aircraft
Search and Rescue (Helicopter) Project
(new for 2006-07)
UK Military Flying Training System

Integrating Future Capabilities

167. The introduction of new and enhanced military capability does not simply mean the purchase of new equipment. It also involves the integration of equipment with all the other components that contribute to defence capabilities: Training, Concepts and Doctrine, Organisation, Personnel, Infrastructure, Information and Logistics. These components are known as the Defence Lines of Development, and Interoperability is also considered when any of them is being addressed. Directors of Equipment Capability are accountable for the coherent delivery of all components of new or enhanced military capability in the programmes for which they are responsible. Five major, equipment-led capability change programmes (UK Military Flying Training System, Medium Weight Capability, Rotorcraft Capability, Combat ID and Carrier Strike), which have individual projects of significant complexity at their core and/or requiring integration have Senior Responsible Owners responsible to the Defence Management Board for the coherent through-life development and management progress on these projects has been as follows:

- Following analysis of the industry bids for the **UK Military Flying Training System** received in August 2005, the Department announced in November 2006 that the Ascent Consortium (Lockheed Martin and VT Group) was the Preferred Bidder (see paragraph 223 under *Personnel Management*);

- On **Medium Weight Capability**, to ensure the coherent and effective implementation of Armoured Fighting Vehicle programmes, the MoD has established the Sustaining Armoured Vehicles Coherence Pathfinder programme. Additionally, the new DE&S has established an Armoured Fighting Vehicle team to provide an improved focus on armoured vehicles, particularly the Future Rapid Effect System (FRES) and force protection more generally. The FRES programme is in its Initial Assessment Phase (IAP) and continues to make good progress with all key decision milestones achieved on time and all of the Technology Demonstrator Programmes performing well against their contract schedules. The Acquisition Strategy was approved and announced by Min(DES) in November 2006, and the initial wave of three competitions has formally been launched. Candidate Utility vehicles will undertake proving trials this summer, with the outcome to be announced in November 2007. The MoD intends to build on the successes achieved during the IAP, driving the programme forward at pace.

- Significant steps have been made to improve the availability of **Rotorcraft Capability** including a decision in principle to buy six recently delivered EH101 Merlin Helicopters from Denmark, which subject to concluding negotiations should be available for operations within twelve months. This will increase the UK's Merlin helicopter fleet by 25%. Additionally a decision has been made to convert the Chinook Mk3 aircraft for use in an operational battlefield support role, thus increasing our operationally available Chinook fleet by 20% within two years.

- The Department's **Combat Identification** programme is addressing current operations as well as establishing enduring capability for the long term. The Bowman secure tactical radio communications system has been deployed on operations in Afghanistan as well as Iraq and is supporting situational awareness. Other equipment deployed to meet specific operational requirements includes blue force tracking systems, improved targeting pods for ground attack aircraft and ground-to-air radios which enable UK forces to talk directly to Coalition aircraft. For the long term, the Department has continued to work closely with the United States and other NATO partners on achieving interoperable Combat Identification solutions. For example, the principal allies have reached consensus on a technical solution for a target identification system. In addition, the Department is actively involved in preparing for Exercise BOLD QUEST, a multinational technology demonstration due to be held in the United States in September 2007 that will help to inform UK decisions on investment in interoperable capability and will explore a more networked approach to Combat Identification.

- The **Carrier Strike programme** (comprising Joint Combat Aircraft (JCA), Future Carrier (CVF), a Maritime Airborne Surveillance and Control component, and associated enablers) made good progress. The Joint Strike Fighter (JSF) is our current choice for JCA, and in December 2006, the Minister for Defence Procurement signed a multilateral Memorandum of Understanding on the next phase of the JSF programme, for production, sustainment and follow-on development. This included a detailed bilateral agreement on operational sovereignty, following the successful conclusion of negotiations with the US Government on UK operational sovereignty of JSF to ensure that the MoD will be able to operate, maintain, repair and upgrade the UK's aircraft independently. JSF's flight test programme also began in December with the successful first flight of a Conventional Take-Off and Landing variant. In the CVF programme, work to mature the risks, costs and contractual framework for building the carriers enabled steady progress in continuing negotiations with industry.

Boeing's prototype of the new Joint Strike Fighter

Acquisition Reform

Defence Industrial Strategy

168. The Defence Industrial Strategy (DIS) provides the blueprint for the future of defence acquisition. Under the DIS the Department is driving the transformation of the acquisition processes as well as working with industry to ensure the industrial base is lean, efficient and sustainable. The Department has completed a comprehensive review of the internal acquisition processes – the Enabling Acquisition Change study and are now taking forward a Defence Acquisition Change Programme aimed at embedding a through life approach in all aspects of acquisition and planning. The Defence Technology Strategy has been completed and published. Amyas Morse has been appointed as the first Defence Commercial Director, with a remit to transform our relationship with industry. This process began with the signature of a Strategic Partnering Agreement with Agusta Westland in the helicopter sector on 22nd June 2006, and has been followed by the signature of a foundation contract with BAE Systems for the fixed wing sector on 1st March 2007. Further partnering agreements will follow. The Department also welcomed industry's commitment to reform through formation of Team Complex Weapons in the complex weapons sector on 19th July 2006 and Team CBRN on 5 September 2006.

169. It was reported last year that the Defence Industrial Strategy White Paper, published in December 2005, set out a significant acquisition reform agenda, and that implementation was underway. The strategy provided greater clarity for industry on forward planning and how the MoD would take into account broader industrial issues in acquisition decisions and set out how the Department and industry need to change. A considerable amount of progress has been made over the last year. There has been significant developments in Sector areas including the formation of 'Team Complex Weapons' to manage capacity in this important area. Good progress continues to be made in other sectors and it is intended to pursue progress in the Maritime, Armoured Fighting Vehicles and General Munitions sectors over the course of 2007-08.

Defence Acquisition Change Programme

170. In response to the Defence Industrial Strategy's call for internal change, the Enabling Acquisition Change report was published in July 2006. This made a wide ranging set of recommendations aimed at improving the delivery of capability to the front line and value for money to the tax-payer. Following a period of consultation, the recommendations of the report were endorsed by Ministers and implementation of the recommendations is being taken forward under the Defence Acquisition Change Programme.

171. The report sought to introduce changes that would help improve the way in which the MoD plans, buys and supports military capability throughout its life (Through Life Capability Management). The report also recommended changes to process, organisation, culture and behaviours to bring a greater unity of purpose across the planning and acquisition communities. This means that in future the Department will consider how a defence capability – for example, a deep strike capability – should be delivered and supported through its entire life. The benefits of this new approach include a better understanding of the capabilities required to deliver defence objectives and their affordability, and increased coherence and agility in the planning and delivery of capability across all of the Defence Lines of Development. The change programme has been working to challenging deadlines with the majority of changes in place by April 2007. The most visible sign of progress to date has been the creation of Defence Equipment & Support, through merging the Defence Procurement Agency and the Defence Logistics Organisation. Launched on 2 April 2007 DE&S is responsible for equipment throughout its life, from design, through delivery to disposal, and is led by the Chief of Defence Materiel. Other changes have been introduced by the Defence Acquisition Change Programme including changes to the financial planning process, capability planning and the approvals and scrutiny process.

172. But the Defence Acquisition Change Programme is not just focussing on process or organisation. It recognises the importance of having the right skills in acquisition and a major programme of upskilling in key areas such as commercial will commence in the course 2007-08 (see paragraph 190 under *Future Personnel*). The Defence Management Board are committed to the success of the change programme recognising that successful change will require strong leadership and the demonstration of the right culture and behaviours of all of those involved in acquisition. We are working closely with Industry and other stakeholders to ensure that the reforms lead to enduring change.

Key Supplier Management

173. Sustained progress has been made with the Key Supplier Management initiative, which provides a vehicle for cementing coherent strategic relations with our major suppliers and a process for measuring and driving performance improvement and better decision-making. A start has been made in developing high-level negotiating strategies with the most strategically important defence suppliers to ensure that we adopt a sensibly 'joined-up' approach that recognises the full breadth of our current and potential business with each company. We have also paid attention to the lower-tier suppliers that contribute to and underpin defence capability. We have been working to develop our 'intelligent customer' status by capturing a better understanding of our supply networks and dependencies in each sector of the

Defence Industry, and we have provided support to prime-level suppliers in initiatives (such as the Society of British Aerospace Companies' *21st Century Supply Chains* programme) to help make industrial supply networks more robust, responsive and effective.

Defence Exports

174. The Defence Export Services Organisation helped the UK Defence Industry to win defence export orders worth £5.5Bn in 2006. This was the UK's best performance since 1998. Significant new export business was also secured through MoD's Industrial Participation Programmes, under which overseas companies place work in the UK as a result of winning orders from MoD. This provides UK companies with competitive bidding opportunities in markets where there might otherwise be some barriers to entry. BAE Systems and Rolls-Royce continue to have success in the United States with further orders associated with JSF development and the supply of aero engines. BAE Systems also won an order to supply Saudi Arabia with Tactica armoured vehicles and a C4I system. Moreover, with the signing in 2005 of an understanding, we are looking forward to a stronger partnership, modernising Saudi Arabia's Armed Forces, including by supplying Typhoon aircraft. Three Sandown Class Minehunters, withdrawn from Royal Navy service, were sold to Estonia and early in 2007, the VT Group signed a contract with Oman to supply three Ocean Patrol Vessels, with the first ship scheduled for handover around 2010. The second of three ex-Royal Navy Type 23 frigates sold to Chile was handed over in a ceremony attended by their Minister of National Defence in March 2007.

Further sources of information

175. Additional information on Future Capabilities and Infrastructure is available from the following sources:

- *Defence Industrial Strategy* available at www.mod.uk
- *Enabling Acquisition Change Report at* www.mod.uk
- quarterly PSA reports to HM Treasury at www.mod.uk;
- UK Defence Statistics 2007 available at www.dasa.mod.uk (from September 2007);
- Defence Procurement Agency Corporate Business Plan 2005 available at www.mod.uk;
- DPA Annual Report and Accounts 2006-07 available at www.mod.uk (from July 2007);
- the Public Accounts Committee 26th Report Ministry of Defence: The rapid procurement of capability to support operations (HC 70 on 30 June 2005) available at www.publications.parliament.uk;
- Annual Report on United Kingdom Strategic Export Controls published in July 2005 available at www.fco.gov.uk;
- NAO Report: Driving the Successful Delivery of Major Defence Projects: Effective Project Control is a Key Factor in Successful Projects(HC 30 on 19 May 2005) available at www.nao.org.uk;
- NAO Major Projects Report 2006(HC 595-I on 25 November 2005) available at www.nao.org.uk;
- NAO Report Progress in Combat ID(HC 936 on 3 March 2006) available at www.nao.org.uk;
- NAO Report Using the contract to maximise the likelihood of successful project outcomes (HC 1047 on 7 June 2006) available at www.nao.org.uk;
- Defence Industrial Strategy White Paper (Cm 6697 on 15 December 2005) available at www.mod.uk;
- Defence Departmental Investment Strategy available at www.mod.uk;
- Enabling Acquisition Change: An examination of the Ministry of Defence's ability to undertake Through Life Capability Management available at www.mod.uk;
- The Acquisition Handbook (Edition 6, October 2006) available at www.mod.uk;
- Delivering Security in a Change World: Future Capabilities available at www.mod.uk.

Essay – Implementing the Defence Industrial Strategy

The Defence Industrial Strategy, launched in December 2005, aims to promote a sustainable industrial base that retains in the United Kingdom those industrial capabilities needed to ensure national security. The Strategy recognised that achieving this required the MoD also to change, to be more open in its dealings with industry, particularly about its future plans. These underlying principles of clarity and transparency over future requirements and the need for an effective MoD/Industry relationship now inform all defence acquisition business. The Department is now more focussed on through-life issues, and more joined up in its acquisition activity and in its dealings with industry. But The Strategy is not just about the MoD. The Treasury, Department of Trade and Industry (now the Department for Business, Enterprise and Regulatory Reform) and the Foreign Office, were involved in its creation and played a role in its implementation. This both produced more effective policy making and strengthened the business relationships with these Departments. It has also been welcomed and supported by Parliament.

The MoD's Defence Acquisition Vision is to achieve a step change in the delivery of military capability and value for money within three years. This is no small task, but there has been a good start. The necessary unified, strategic leadership of acquisition has been established, with a clear sense of corporate ownership and collegiate decision-making at the highest level. And acquisition development has made progress, underpinned by core processes consistently applied, streamlined approval processes, and a through life approach in our planning and delivery.

2006 saw radical change in the way the MoD approached its acquisition business and its relationship with its suppliers. The first Defence Commercial Director was appointed with a remit to lead transformation of the relationship with industry, to work with industry and Allies to retain and protect critical capabilities and operational sovereignty, and to consolidate the Department's position in the marketplace and maximise its leverage by brokering tough commercial deals which deliver best long-term value for money, informed by the wider commercial context.

During the year the Defence Acquisition Change Programme put in place the majority of the recommendations of the June 2006 Enabling Acquisition Change Report. The new DE&S (Defence Equipment and Support) was created on time, merging the Defence Procurement Agency and the Defence Logistics Organisation. A new financial planning process and a single, integrated planning process have been established to address the delivery of capability long term. The focus now is to bringing these changes to life through the practical demonstration of benefits and tackling the critical enablers - people and information. There is an agreed skills plan and upskilling of MoD acquisition staff has now started. Progress on this will be closely monitored and evaluated. The Department is also working with the Defence Industries Council to build closer working relationships with industry. The Defence Industrial Strategy was also the platform for the Defence Technology Strategy (see the essay on page 114), which sets out how the Department will focus on emerging technologies and promote innovation, based on greater transparency, to encourage industry to plan, invest in ideas and take risks.

Industry has also been changing, if not always quite as fast as it or the Department would like. Achievements include partnering arrangements for Armoured Vehicles and helicopters, progress in the Fixed Wing and Maritime sectors (see below), and the formation of `Team Complex Weapons':

- The Strategy challenged the maritime industry to reduce overheads and invest in the facilities and skills needed to meet the demands of the Royal Navy's future warship programme. Industry acknowledges the need to collaborate and be realistic about future defence orders, because beyond the relatively healthy programme prospects of the next five to ten years, the market will get smaller. The Department is determined to press home the need for managed reform to improve efficiency and productivity and avert an otherwise very difficult situation arising in the next decade. But further integration is needed. Financial engineering and mergers will not, on their own, deliver the required benefits. The Department will encourage and support consolidation proposals which add value, transform the business and deliver the substantial performance improvement the sector needs;

- In the Fixed Wing sector military capability will increasingly be achieved through enhancements to in-service aircraft. The Defence Industrial Strategy highlighted that the Department does not envisage a need for UK design and build of a further generation of manned fast jet aircraft beyond Typhoon and the Joint Strike Fighter. This will have a long term impact on industry, which is why the Department is committed to negotiating the terms of a Long Term Partnering Agreement with BAE Systems by the end of 2007. A key illustration of this intent was the signing in December 2006 of the contract to build an experimental Unmanned Air Vehicle called TARANIS through a Technology Demonstrator Programme jointly funded by the MoD and an industry team led by BAE Systems. Steady progress is being made and a Foundation Contract was signed in March 2007. More generally, the Strategy has helped the Department and BAE Systems develop of a more constructive business relationship.

The Defence Industrial Strategy recognised the important role of Small and Medium Sized Enterprises in the defence supply chain, and the need for a combined effort to identify innovative companies and their capabilities and improve engagement with them. The Society of British Aerospace Companies "Supply Chain 21" initiative, aimed at making it easier for them to enter the defence market, is precisely the sort of arrangements the Strategy intended to stimulate. Work is also underway, in close consultation with defence industry representatives, including small and medium sized companies, to review MoD policy on their engagement and analyse market drivers and behaviours in the supply chain.

The Defence Industrial Strategy is here to stay. Experience shows that its fundamentals are right. It must, however, be kept up to date, and the Department and industry must both change further. A review is therefore being undertaken, which is planned to produce an update to coincide with the second anniversary of the Strategy in December 2007.

Future Personnel Plans

Objective: Develop the skills and professional expertise we need for tomorrow

Assessment and Performance Measures

Assessment: There was considerable progress in delivering the Service Personnel Plan. The Joint Personnel Administration system was rolled out successfully across all three Services, although there were significant temporary accounting problems during the year. Service personnel terms and conditions continued to improve, including a good pay settlement and introduction of the Operational Allowance. The Armed Forces Act simplifying and harmonising military law received the Royal Assent. The civilian People Programme also continued to make progress, with a particular focus on support to operations and improving acquisition skills, and the new People Pay and Pensions Agency was successfully launched.

Deliver the Service Personnel Plan – More holistic and flexible military personnel administration systems:

- JPA was rolled out on time to the RAF from April 2006, to the Royal Navy during October and November 2006, to Army personnel professionals in March 2007, and to the rest of the Army by July 2007;
- Significant accounting problems arising during the year were successfully resolved, but represented a temporary failure in financial control.

Deliver the Service Personnel Plan – Develop the military personnel package:

- A fundamental review of the Terms and Conditions of Service to improve working arrangements was started;
- Further development of the Operational Welfare Package continued;
- The Armed Forces Pay Review Body recommendations of: an increase in basic salary of 3.3%, and 9.4% for the lowest paid; an introduction of new Financial Retention Initiatives for Royal Marines and Infantry; and an increase of 3.3% in specialist pay rates; were all implemented;
- Introduction of new Operational Allowance;
- Royal Assent was given to Armed Forces Act in November 2006, creating a single system of Service law.

Deliver the Service Personnel Plan – Better Understanding of People

- Research programme continues.

Deliver the People Programme:

- People Pay and Pensions Agency was established 1 April 2006, and achieved its target of 90% of its business on time and to quality;
- Civilian Workforce Strategy was published in November 2006;
- Civilian Support to Operations programme was launched in November 2006;
- Production of Acquisition Skills Growth Plans;
- A more flexible employment framework was developed to support the Defence Equipment and Support organisation on its establishment in April 2007.

103

Service Personnel Plan

176. In September 2006 a revised Service Personnel Plan was published. This was developed from the previous Plan published in 2004, and provides a structure for the delivery of Service personnel policy over the next 15 years. It reflects the challenges and opportunities that cultural and demographic changes are likely to pose to delivering sufficient, capable and motivated personnel across the Armed Forces in order to provide the required operational capability.

177. Work in 2006-07 focused on developing opportunities for flexibility and choice for Service personnel, both in terms of career patterns and in terms of remuneration and benefit packages available to them. This was done through a continuing fundamental review of the Terms and Conditions of Service. There were also further improvements to the Operational Welfare Package (see paragraph 24 under *Personnel Management*). However ensuring that the Armed Forces have the right number of personnel with the right skills and the willingness to use them requires working across a broader range of issues. The Department therefore also continued to take forward the other key workstrands initiated in 2004;

- developing more comprehensive and flexible manpower accounting and administration processes, in particular through the implementation and exploitation of the facilities provided by the Joint Personnel Administration system (see paragraphs 178-183 below and the essay on page 108);

- making better use of Reserve and Regular personnel, integrating them more effectively (see paragraphs 222-223 under *Personnel Management*) and working to encourage young people to serve in the Armed Forces (see paragraphs 109-111 under *Wider Government*), and the essay on maximising Service Diversity on page 173;

- taking forward the strategy for training and education (see paragraphs 220-221 under *Personnel Management*);

- delivering the strategy for Health through the Defence Health Change Programme (see paragraph 246 under *Health and Safety*);

- improving single and family living accommodation and developing a more coherent Defence estate (see paragraphs 318-321 under *Estate*); and

- gaining a better understanding of the aspirations and expectations of Service personnel, both now and in the future, to inform policy and resource decisions (see paragraph 186).

Joint Personnel Administration

178. Joint Personnel Administration (JPA) is a major programme to modernise the personnel management and administration of the Armed Forces (see the essay on page 108). The system covers both 'front office' pay and personal administration processes for every member of the Armed Forces, and the 'back office' financial and manpower accounting processes. Overall it will allow over 1,400 jobs to be removed from the administrative organisations of the Armed Forces. Together with the associated business improvements this will generate savings of approximately £100M per year once steady state is reached. By 31 March 2007 it had delivered £38M of efficiencies, mainly through reductions in Royal Air Force and Royal Navy personnel staff (see paragraph 151 under *Efficiency and Change*).

179. The programme was rolled out incrementally over the year to manage risk effectively, particularly the relationship with the roll out of the underpinning Defence Information Infrastructure programme. As reported last year, the Department deliberately decided to delay roll out of the system to the Royal Navy until October 2006 and to the Army until March 2007 in order to reduce the risks involved. JPA was therefore rolled out progressively to the RAF from April 2006, to the Royal Navy during October and November 2006, to Army personnel professionals in March 2007, and to the rest of the Army by July 2007

180. As with any project of this complexity, there were inevitably some technical issues to overcome when the 'front office' systems went live. The system performed well initially on roll out to the RAF, however once large numbers of self-service users accessed the system, it slowed unacceptably. This was resolved through a series of software fixes that produced full functionality and acceptable system performance levels from the middle of May 2006 onwards.

181. Despite these problems the first RAF pay run using JPA was achieved in April 2006 as planned. This again generated a number of problems, particularly regarding flying pay and expenses, mainly as a result of errors in the original data entered on the system. These problems were resolved as quickly as possible and measures were put in place to ensure that those individuals affected were not financially disadvantaged.

182. All of these initial difficulties were overcome well before the end of the year, by when JPA was delivering a much simplified and improved personnel administration capability for the RAF. A number of lessons were learned from this, and JPA roll out to the Royal Navy and Royal Marines in the autumn of 2006 and to the Army from the spring of 2007 went much more smoothly. The first Royal Navy payroll in November 2006 and the first Army payroll in April

2007 were both successful, and the system has since continued to perform well.

183. Unfortunately, roll out of the back office financial manpower and accounting processes did not go as smoothly and a number of more fundamental problems were identified. In particular, the financial reporting information required was not initially available. These had a temporary impact on the Department's ability to exercise full financial control and created a significant risk to the timeliness and quality of the Departmental Resource Accounts. Once these issues had been identified, mitigation plans to resolve the core problems were produced and implemented successfully. By the end of the financial year full financial control had been re-established, but the problems had been of sufficient importance and duration that they represented a significant failure in financial control that required specific reference in both the Department's and Armed Forces Personnel Administration Agency (AFPAA's) Statements on Internal Control. Work to resolve a number of less fundamental accounting issues by the autumn of 2007 continues and remains on track.

Military Personnel Package

184. The independent Armed Forces' Pay Review Body (AFPRB) 2007 report was published on 1 March 2007. It recommended an increase in the basic military salary of 3.3% for all ranks, restructuring the pay range to give those on the lowest pay level an increase of 9.4%, new financial retention incentives for the Royal Marines and Infantry Other Ranks, and an extension of the existing incentive scheme for Aircrew. It also recommended an increase of 3.3% to Specialist Pay rates (such as Flying Pay, Submarine Pay and Diving Pay) and increases to food and accommodation charges. Its recommendations were implemented in full, effective from 1 April 2007, as were those of the 2007 Senior Salaries Review Body, including an increase in Senior Officers' basic pay of 2%. The AFPRB also endorsed the Operational Allowance introduced in October 2006 (See paragraph 6 under *Current Operations*).

185. In November 2006 the new Armed Forces Act received Royal Assent. This harmonised, streamlined and modernised the military justice and discipline system across all three Services under a single system of service law. It also introduced a Complaints Commissioner to hear complaints involving bullying and unacceptable behaviour. This will improve the transparency of the military complaints process and increase confidence in Service procedures. The target date for full implementation is December 2008. Work is in hand to develop and roll out the regulations, manuals and training required to ensure that the legislation works effectively in practice. The Act also pardoned over 300 soldiers who were executed in World War One.

Better Understanding People

186. The Department continued to take forward its programme of research to gain a better understanding of behaviour, and examine how changes to the Armed Forces and the wider environment within which they live and work are likely to affect issues such as recruitment, morale and retention. This included research to identify how the aspirations and expectations of personnel change as they progress through their careers. Research also continued into the nature and extent of sexual harassment in the Armed Forces in partnership with the Equal Opportunities Commission, (see paragraphs 306-307 under *Manpower*). The information produced is used to inform policy development and decisions on the allocation of resources.

Civilian Personnel Developments

People Programme

187. Work continued to take forward the People Programme, which is the major change programme to implement the Civilian Personnel Strategy launched in 2002. Its aims to:

- develop the skill and behaviours that individuals will need in the future;

- develop managers' ability to deliver through their teams;

- modernise the delivery of personnel services; and

- modernise Human Resources to move from policing and processing to strategic planning and support.

The programme remains challenging, but on track.

Skills and Behaviours

188. Skills Champions are personnel appointed within the Department to provide a functional, strategic overview of skills shortages within particular functional areas (such as project management, engineering and science) to inform top level discussions with Corporate HR, Civilian Workforce Advisors in the Top Level Budget organisations and the Personnel Director as Civilian Workforce Process Owner.

189. While the numbers of civilians who deploy on operations is small compared to that of Service men and women, demand for civilians with the right skills has continued to grow. They routinely carry out a number of roles in operational theatres in direct support of military operations, including as political advisers and civil secretaries, finance and claims officers, fire fighters, police officers, commercial experts, intelligence and scientific analysts, estates staff, and media and communication specialists. On average about 170-200 civilians are deployed at any one time. Reflecting this requirement, in November 2006 the Department successfully launched the Support to Operations programme. This has strengthened the capacity to recruit the right people for these roles and provide them with the best possible support. Together with the very extensive communications campaign that preceded its official launch, this programme is effectively closing the gap between the supply of, and demand for, suitably qualified and motivated volunteers. The challenge now is to maintain the flow of volunteers in the medium term.

Civil Servants working in Baghdad

Acquisition Skills

190. Considerable work was taken forward on developing Acquisition skills in support of the Defence Acquisition Change Programme;

● The six Skills Champions involved in this area completed an initial broad assessment of the current and future skills requirement in their areas and the key skills gaps. They then developed Skills Growth Plans to address these gaps. These plans provide a strategic perspective of the skills requirement, set out measures to address the identified skills gaps, and provide a basis for estimating the level of new investment required. As such they are entirely consistent with the recommendations of the Department's Capability Review. In parallel the Department developed a

more flexible employment framework to support the Defence Equipment and Support organisation on its launch on 1 April 2007 and is investing some £7M for acquisition up-skilling in 2007-08;

● A formal programme to take forward the upskilling element of the Defence Acquisition Change Programme was launched by the Defence Academy in June 2007 working in partnership with LogicaCMG and Cranfield University. This is focused primarily on training civilian and military staff in key roles at the awareness/practitioner level, across the acquisition community. In line with the aims of the Defence Industrial Strategy, it also aims to increase the level of joint training with industry and will significantly enhance the recent Guide to Acquisition Training and Education (see paragraph 320 under *Personnel Management*).

● The Acquisition Operating Framework is a website that was developed during the year and rolled out in June 2007. It will act as a key enabler for the wider benefits of the Defence Acquisition Change Programme by improving consistency in application of policy and best practice. It will achieve this by establishing a strong professional doctrine for the acquisition community and by defining the obligations of organisations and individuals within that community. It will be embedded throughout the organisation, bringing with it real accountability for delivering against its requirements. Leaders and teams within the acquisition community will be expected to comply with its requirements. This will be measured from April 2008, linked to the impact on business performance.

Developing Managers

191. People management is a fundamental line management responsibility, and a key theme during 2006-07 was to improve the professionalism of managers in this role. The Department continued to develop the civilian appraisal and development review processes, while also introducing a new set of improved products that define the line management role and better equip line managers to effectively carry out their responsibilities.

Modernising Personnel Services

192. In April 2006 the People Pay and Pensions Agency was established to provide transactional services and casework support across the Department. Over the year it continued to grow in size, coverage and customer acceptance as an organisation with high standards for service, quality, responsiveness

and availability, maturing from providing routine administrative services to developing and launching a significantly more complex and sensitive discipline, harassment and grievance service. By the end of the year it was meeting its target of completing 90% of its business on time and to quality. It is also delivering a major programme to modernise its IT infrastructure on time and to quality, working towards Full Operating Capability on time and developing a subsequent continuous improvement programme. Together with the associated business improvements this is on course to generate savings of approximately £305M.

RAF and Civilian Personnel working together

Strategic Planning

193. During the year the Department launched a review of how civilian talent was managed at a corporate level, working closely with the Cabinet Office on succession planning and leadership development; and developed measures to increase the rate of internal promotions to the Senior Civil Service and feeder grades (see paragraph 227 under *Personnel Management*).

The 2006 Civilian Workforce Strategy, agreed in November 2006, identified a series of strategic priorities for improving the civilian contribution to defence over the next five years. Its key themes were the continuing need to improve civilian defence leaders' ability to see through complex and transformational change, the importance of further developing the professional skills required to realise the vision of the Defence Industrial Strategy, and the need to ensure that the Department continued to bring in and develop new talent at certain management levels, in appropriate skill areas within the context of the continuing wider civilian staff reduction process. These themes were broadly affirmed by the Department's Capability Review in March 2007 and reflected in the associated action plan (see essay on page 147).

Efficiency

194. By 31 March 2007 the People Programme had delivered £30M of efficiencies, mainly through reductions in civilian personnel staff (see paragraph 151 under *Efficiency and Change*). During the 2006/07, scrutiny of the People Programme, including a Defence Internal Audit, concluded that the Department was on track to deliver the hard input efficiencies in line with the original approval of the programme. However the audit found there was room for better definition of the soft benefits and for improved data collection and analysis of these benefits. The Department has reduced to £30M the efficiencies claimed for 2006-07, and to £48M those forecast for 2007/08. This demonstrates the rigour applied to ensure efficiency claims are supported by adequate evidence. Work is in hand to implement the recommended improvements.

Further sources of information

195. Additional information on Future Personnel Plans is available from the following sources:

– Quarterly PSA reports to HM Treasury at www.mod.uk
– UK Defence Statistics – www.dasa.mod.uk
– Statement of Internal Control at www.mod.uk
– AFPAA Annual Report and Accounts – www.mod.uk
– Armed Forces Pay Review Body Report – www.mod.uk
– Senior Staff Review Body Report – www.mod.uk
– An overview of the Military Criminal Justice System and the Armed Forces Act 2006 on www.mod.uk
– Civilian Workforce Strategy 2006 at www.mod.uk
– Capability Review at www.civilservice.gov.uk
– Capability Review – The Department's Response at www.mod.uk
– Acquisition Operating Framework at www.mod.uk

Essay – Joint Personnel Administration

2006-07 saw the successful rollout of Joint Personnel Administration (JPA) to the Armed Forces – one of the key projects in the MoD's Defence Change Programme and a major contributor to the Efficiency Programme. JPA has involved significant policy, process and organisational change. These included establishment of a shared service centre to support military personnel, the Joint Personnel Administration Centre (JPAC), and the replacement of over 250 bespoke legacy systems with a single Commercial Off The Shelf software package.

JPA was initiated because the cost, risk and hindrance to business change from continuing with antiquated IT platforms had become unsustainable. The different rules that applied in each Service were an increasing source of irritation on joint operations, and the different processes prevented administrators from one Service supporting personnel from another. The fragmented nature of the personnel systems and inconsistencies in the data they contained made it impossible to fully exploit the information that was held. Consequently in June 2001 the Defence Management Board set a vision and strategy for JPA that it harmonise and simplify policy in all aspects of pay and personnel administration across all three Services, underpinned by a world standard commercial software package providing a single authoritative and integrated source of reliable, accurate and up to date personnel information. At the individual level, this meant one complete whole-life record for every Serviceman or woman which they are able to access online, and self-service facilities to undertake many administrative functions themselves without having to submit paper forms. This entailed deliberate risk, since the linkages needed to produce a more efficient and effective system also meant that incorrectly entering personal data could lead directly to incorrect payment of allowances. At the Departmental level, JPA would produce a comprehensive up-to-date picture of the size and shape of the Armed Forces for the first time, with data captured only once at source and transmitted electronically with minimal intervention. Over time the data within JPA will build up to provide the Department with a rich supply of management information to support operational decisions and the development of evidence based policy.

The strategy for delivery was to redesign radically many existing processes, ensuring that by harmonising them wherever possible, by keeping policy as simple as possible and by aligning with commercial practice wherever possible the cost of ownership would be reduced to the benefit of the front line, and that the Department and Services would create an environment more agile in responding to change initiatives. The service delivery was based on self-service, automation and centralisation of routine activity leading to considerable benefits in terms of quality of information and ease of operation. These were then expected to produce eventual financial benefits of around £100M a year.

There have been few, if any, business change projects of such complexity anywhere else in the private or public sectors. Many personnel policies and regulations have been revised, a new set of business processes designed and new organisations established. The supporting software application is one of the largest Oracle HR implementations worldwide, makes the fullest use of the functionality of the software, and is the largest single payroll. The system contains around 350,000 records (and over one million if pensioners are included) and supports 250,000 users worldwide from the regular and reserve forces. Nowhere has a more complex dataset – around 24 million pieces of data – been so successfully migrated.

JPA has now been successfully implemented for all three Services over the year, to the Royal Air Force in April 2006, the Royal Navy in October 2006 and the Army from March 2007. It has also been successfully deployed to units in Bosnia, Iraq and Afghanistan as well as on board Royal Navy ships, and all reports indicate that it is working well. Peak usage has so far seen over 3,650 users logged-on to the system at any one time and over 11,000 users in a day. The JPAC is typically handling 16,000 calls a week, with significantly more at peak periods.

JPA is extremely powerful and the new underpinning business processes are not yet fully understood. Attention is therefore now turning to fully exploiting the opportunities and wider information potential it offers. In particular work is continuing to ensure that the new culture and working practices are embedded, and that the right training and communications are in place to help all personnel learn how to use JPA effectively according to their requirements and responsibilities, and get the best from it.

Science Innovation and technology

Objective: Exploit new technologies

Assessment and Performance Measures

Assessment: The defence science and technology community provided essential support to help counter the increasing threat from improvised explosive devices on operations, and to counter terrorism activities. In addition to a continuing peer reviewed, high quality and well managed research programme of almost £500M a year, a considerable programme of work was taken forward to implement the Science and Technology aspects of the Defence Industrial Strategy, including the launch of programmes to stimulate innovation in defence research.

Support to Operations:

- Scientific support provided to commanders in the field and operational Headquarters;
- Counter Terrorism Science and Technology Centre achieved full operational capability.

Support to Current and Future Equipment Programmes:

- High degree of customer and stakeholder satisfaction with research programme;
- Research collaboration with allies work enhanced capability for our armed forces, de-risked novel and new technologies, and increased awareness of developing opportunities and threats from new technologies across the world;
- Continuing support to MoD investment decisions through scrutiny and analysis, and implementation of Defence Acquisition Change Programme Approvals and Scrutiny Workstream.

Research:

- Launch of Defence Technology Strategy, including the Competition of Ideas and the Grand Challenge;
- Publication of study into Maximising Benefit from Defence Research and extension of Peer Review approach to wider Research and Development programme;
- £498M of research contracts awarded (£480M in 2005-06);
- 85% of research projects were aligned to the Department's strategic guidance and defence technology strategy;
- Continued development of Defence Technology Centres and Towers of Excellence in partnership with industry and academia;
- 90% of Research Projects of sufficient quality or better, and 22% classed as world-leading;
- Majority of research is well managed using best practice project management techniques;
- Good medium term exploitation of research in defence and industry;
- Continued broadening of research supplier base.

196. Science, innovation and technology throughout defence is primarily provided through the Science Innovation Technology Top Level Budget organisation. This is the focus for creating battle-winning technology for the front line and bringing rigour to decision making, both at Head Office and in the field. Its work underpins the United Kingdom's defence capability by providing scientific support to decision making, developing and implementing technical solutions, supporting operations with analysis, and reducing risk. Military and commercial technological developments across the world are monitored to identify upcoming threats and opportunities to enhance the United Kingdom's defence capabilities. International research collaboration with allies facilitates cost and risk minimisation and expands our research capabilities. Defence Research enhances existing technologies, identifies and develops emerging technologies, and supports their cost effective implementation.

Support to Operations

197. The Armed Forces faced an increasing threat from improvised weapons and explosive devices during the year. Such devices currently account for the greatest loss of coalition forces in Iraq from enemy action. The Department therefore drew on its science and technology resources to provide commanders in-theatre advice and improved protective measures, and a major countermeasures research programme improved the Armed Forces' ability to detect and thus deal with such devices. Scientific Advisers and Operational Analysis teams were deployed with UK forces in Iraq and Afghanistan throughout the year. Their work focussed on campaign assessment, analysis of significant events and scientific advice on force protection and trials. The Operations Support Coordination Cell at Dstl Porton Down provided a 24 hour service to the teams in both Iraq and Afghanistan, gathering and relaying responses from the experts within the Dstl and wider communities. An example of this was when, following modelling, advice was provided to British commanders on the ground on how to operate against an urban facility while minimising damage to surrounding buildings.

198. Following its launch in April 2006, good progress has been made in establishing MoD's new Counter Terrorism Science and Technology Centre as the United Kingdom's focal point for counter terrorism science and technology research. It established an innovative research programme and let some 25 contracts with Government laboratories, industry and universities on a diverse range of topics including countering improvised explosive devices, Chemical Biological Radiological and Nuclear forensics, and social network analysis. It led the work to develop responses to

the increasing operational threat from improvised explosive devices. It also provided valuable support to technology acquisition and counter terrorism operations at home and abroad. It made a number of valuable contributions to other Government Departments, in particular to the Home Office in their development of the United Kingdom's Counter-Terrorism Science and Innovation Strategy. Defence scientific staff provided important specialist support to the Metropolitan Police, Home Office, and the Health Protection Agency following a case of poisoning with radioactive Polonium 210 in London in November 2006. As well as deploying experts in the field, much of the forensic analysis carried out on the radioactive samples was undertaken at the Atomic Weapons Establishment Aldermaston.

'Wheelbarrow' searching for Improvised Explosive Devices

Effective Support to Current and Future Equipment Programmes

199. Defence research investment provides technology options to meet defence capability needs and expertise to assist defence business and acquisition. Defence science and technology personnel continued to support decision making by providing technical scrutiny of the defence equipment programme. This included developing techniques to analyse future helicopter options and to improve the planning and deployment of medical assets on operations. An integrated programme of research, analysis and experimentation was also put in place to support the identification of friendly and hostile forces in the operational theatre. This includes work from Dstl and industry, and collaborative research with our Coalition partners through the Technical Cooperation Programme.

Quality of Advice

200. The study into *Maximising Benefit from Defence Research* demonstrated that there is a high degree of customer and stakeholder satisfaction with the programme. This is corroborated by the peer review conclusions of the quality of defence research (see paragraph 208 below).

International Collaboration

201. The Defence Technology Strategy restated the Department's intention to obtain enhanced value for money through collaboration with international partners, and clarified the Department's approach. The MoD's key collaborative partner is the United States. During 2006-07 there were 62 collaborative projects (of which 13 were established in-year), 155 formal information exchange arrangements and 30 international personnel exchanges. These programmes provided enhanced capability for our armed forces, helped de-risk novel technologies, and increased awareness of developing opportunities and threats from new technologies across the world. The International Technology Alliance between the MoD and US Army aims to build close collaborative relationships between governments, industry and academia in both nations, to research state-of-the-art technology and encourage its application in military and dual-use systems. The preferred bidder for this work is a consortium of 24 industrial and academic organisations from the United States and United Kingdom led by IBM.

Better Business Cases

202. The Defence Acquisition Change Programme is taking forward the conclusions of the Enabling Acquisition Change review (see paragraphs 170-171 under *Future Capabilities and Infrastructure*). It includes workstreams on Approvals and Scrutiny and on Research and Development which will significantly affect how the Department manages science and technology. The Approvals and Scrutiny project is addressing the requirement for a slicker, more effective process, delivering better Business Cases and more robust scrutiny. The Research and Development project is working to provide transparency from strategy to delivery, increased access to Science for acquisition, a coherent research and development approach to Through Life Capability Management, an increased rate of pull-through from research into capability and a more responsive research and development environment.

Research

203. The Defence Industrial Strategy emphasised the need to ensure that research is aligned to capability needs. Following that the Department undertook a study into *Maximising Benefit from Defence Research*, covering the £500M annual research programme. Over 240 individual research projects were subjected to external peer review and the results were published in September 2006 (see paragraph 208). This established a proven methodology which the Department can use in future reviews of the research programme, and a benchmark against which future performance can be assessed. In the light of this the Department is conducting a wider review of the product of MoD's approximately £2.5Bn annual research and development investment, drawing on the same methodology.

204. The Defence Industrial Strategy also promised a major review of the Department's approach to future research and technology. This was delivered in November 2006 with the publication of the *Defence Technology Strategy*. This set out clearly the MoD's research and development priorities, and provided a strategic view of the UK's defence research and development requirements for up to the next ten years. The strategy will enable the MoD and industry to plan their investment in research and development cooperatively, rapidly bringing the benefits of advanced technology to the front line. It also launched two initiatives to stimulate innovation in defence research. The Competition of Ideas aims to expose and seek solutions to defence problems that need innovation and the injection of new ideas from a wide range of potential UK suppliers. The Grand Challenge aims to create a system with a high degree of autonomy that can detect, identify, locate and report a comprehensive range of military threats in an urban environment. Details are set out in the essay on the Defence Technology Strategy on page 114.

205. During the year £498M of research contracts (£480M in 2005-06) covered work including:

- The ability of airborne pilots to command several Unmanned Aerial Vehicles (UAV) each capable of launching attacks, was successfully demonstrated in a trial where an RAF Tornado pilot remotely commanded an autonomous UAV (a specially adapted passenger aircraft) and three virtual aircraft in a simulated mission;

- Medical counter measures currently require individuals to take pre-treatment in anticipation of a nerve agent attack. Research undertaken demonstrates the possibility of countering nerve agent attack without the use of pre-treatment;

111

- World-leading armour research supports both existing platforms and future programmes. The research team played a key role in providing successful upgrades for vehicles deployed in operational theatres.

- The British Experimental Rotor Programme (BERP) IV rotor blades on a RAF Merlin Mk3 helicopter demonstrated improved aircraft performance;

- The Joint Convoy Operations Virtual Environment (JCOVE) concept capability demonstrator was exploited to provide a deployable mission preparation training solution for units deploying to both Iraq and Afghanistan this year. The system was delivered to the users from concept in nine months and is providing specific convoy and combat training as an integral part of pre-deployment training;

- Research work on integrated helicopter survivability, drawing on the research programme and associated studies continues to deliver significant benefits in terms of increased survivability and availability of helicopters to British forces deployed in Iraq and Afghanistan. Dstl staff have deployed into Iraq to undertake further trials and to optimise the application of this equipment and tactics.

The Unmanned Ariel System

Alignment with Defence Needs

206. Recent analysis has shown that there is a correlation between the quality of military equipment and prior investment by governments in defence Research and Development. The research programme is reviewed to ensure that work is aligned to defence needs and meets critical success factors. The *Maximising Benefit from Defence Research* report concluded that 85% of research projects were aligned to the Department's strategic guidance and its technology strategy. About half of the remainder were aimed at helping identify capability gaps and to formulate research requirements. The remainder have now been realigned or discontinued as appropriate.

207. The Defence Technology Strategy stated that the changing threat itself can often be driven by advances in science and technology. It is therefore vital to monitor science and technology developments, to target research at areas of relevance and develop innovative new ways of meeting our defence capability requirements. The Department has a number of initiatives, such as rapid assistance to operations, the Defence Technology Centres and Towers of Excellence, all aimed at developing a better understanding of the critical capabilities we require and the ways in which they can be most effectively delivered:

- Towers of Excellence are selective partnerships with industry and academia, directing resources into priority areas of technology research- guided weapons, electro-optic sensors, synthetic environments, radar, under water sensors and electronic warfare. The development of technology through to a final product and more general technology transfer to industry are a major benefit of operating Towers of Excellence.

- Defence Technology Centres are examples of an alternative partnering approach which are jointly funded by MoD and industry (usually as consortia). The Centres are based around topics (Electromagnetic Remote Sensing, Data and information Fusion, Human Factors Integration and Systems Engineering for Autonomous Systems) which are critical to defence and where investment is likely to produce significant returns. A range of suppliers, including small and medium sized enterprises and academia provide input to the Centres, which are managed to allow a flexible response to merging needs and priorities.

The Cornershot weapon which can fire around corners

Quality of Research

208. For the *Maximising Benefit from Defence Research* report external peer reviewers assessed a third of the projects in the research programme. They concluded that over 90% were of sufficient quality or better. 70% high or world class with 22% being classed as world-leading, providing the United Kingdom with a competitive edge internationally. Nearly half were deemed good quality research that would have merited publication in a top tier research journal, . Fewer than 8% of projects were found to be of poorer quality, for a number of reasons. The Department is working to ensure that projects assessed to be low quality or unlikely to meet their objectives are reviewed with a view to cancellation where appropriate in order to allow the resources to be reallocated to emerging higher priority projects. There remains scope for further improvement in research quality, and the introduction of greater competition (see paragraph 209 below) should help in this regard.

Exploitation of Technology

209. The *Maximising Benefit from Defence Research* study found that in the medium term, exploitation of research has been good and that there is increasingly widespread use of exploitation planning for current research. Just over half the current projects assessed showed evidence that they had had an impact or were likely to in future. A small sample of mid-90s research projects was also reviewed. In the case of projects intended to provide innovative solutions, nearly half were assessed as having led to a new or improved capability, and over two-thirds of such work subsequently had unexpected exploitation within defence or led to spin off into the civil sector. 50% of innovative projects produced Intellectual Property Rights taken up by industry.

Programme Management

210. The study also conducted an assessment of research suppliers' project management. This showed that the majority of research is well managed using best practice project management techniques. This reflects a number of initiatives designed to improve research project management, such as the introduction of ISO 9001 standards.

Supplier Management

211. In July 2006 the Department staged an Academic Engagement event, with 250 attendees, specifically aimed at increasing participant knowledge and understanding of defence and explaining how academia can work with the MoD. Of the delegates who gave feedback, 88% felt that the event successfully fulfilled its objectives. The Department also strengthened its campaign to reach out to and broaden the supply base. In 2002-03 around 90% of the MoD research was done in Dstl or QinetiQ. The Department remains on target to compete 60% of the research programme across industry and academia by 2009-10. The annual Research Acquisition Organisation 'Suppliers day' has become a major event in the Defence Research calendar as the Department has increased the use of open competition. The aim is to ensure that the Department's supplier base is better informed of opportunities in the research programme. Compared to 250 attendees in 2004, in November 2006 it attracted over 500 representatives of major defence companies, Small and Medium sized Enterprises, and academia, with 84% of delegate feedback agreeing that the event was informative and worthwhile. More are expected next year.

Further sources of information

212. Additional information on Science Innovation and Technology is available from the following sources:

- UK Defence Statistics at www.dasa.mod.uk;
- *Defence Industrial Strategy* at www.mod.uk;
- *Defence Technology Strategy* at www.mod.uk;
- *Maximising Benefit from Defence Research* at www.mod.uk;
- Information on Competition of Ideas at www.ideas.mod.uk;
- Information on Grand Challenge at www.Challenge.mod.uk;
- Information on The MoD Counter Terrorism Science & Technology Centre at www.ctcentre.mod.uk;
- Information on Science Technology Innovation at www.science.mod.uk;
- Defence Science and Technology Laboratory Annual Report and Accounts 2005/06 available at www.mod.uk.
- The Effects of Defence R&D on Military Equipment Quality Middleton, Burns et al., Published in the journal of Defence and Peace Economics April 2006

Essay – Defence Technology Strategy

In December 2005 the Defence Industrial Strategy set in hand a review of the Department's approach to Research and Technology. The conclusions of that review were published as the Defence Technology Strategy in October 2006. This represents the first clear statement of the MoD's overall research and development intent, setting out those technologies that are a priority for defence, and identifying where the United Kingdom should maintain an appropriate sovereign capability. It brings clarity to the Department's research and development priorities, and provides a strategic view of defence research and development requirements for the next ten years. This gives industry and academia a better understanding of where the Department will invest its limited research budget, thereby encouraging increased industry investment in areas important to defence.

The Defence Technology Strategy aims to provide ways of improving the capabilities of our Armed Forces into the future, particularly highlighting those technologies we need to develop to underpin Through-Life Capability Management. The Department is likely to continue to resource technology development with significant defence potential, but turning this into deployable equipment requires significant industrial funding as well. The Defence Technology Strategy enables the Department and industry cooperatively to plan investment in research and development, bringing the benefits of advanced technology to the frontline more rapidly. The Department is working with the National Defence Industry Council on principles for further development.

Structure of the Defence Technology Strategy follows the format of the Defence Industrial Strategy:

- Part A provides a strategic context. The UK faces adversaries who rapidly change their tactics and employ ever more varied, advanced and innovative technologies. This demands rapid evolution in our response, both tactically and in the technologies we deploy to combat the threats.

- Part B addresses the examination of our research and development effort and needs. It is the culmination of detailed analysis often through workshops of experts from industry, academia and MoD, examining each particular sector

- Part C lays out how the Strategy will be taken forward.

The Defence Technology Strategy is based on the industrial sectors of the Defence Industrial Strategy, and identifies the technologies for each. Analysis of technology requirements show that there are common technology themes to many of the sectors, identified as Cross-Cutting Technologies – those areas that underpin all capability requirements. There is also a section on emerging technologies which includes areas that are not necessarily critical for any specific sector or capability as yet, but as they develop further will undoubtedly be widely exploitable.

In particular the Strategy announced two major initiatives to stimulate innovation in defence research:

- The Competition of Ideas is designed to expose and seek solutions to defence problems that need innovation and the injection of new ideas from a wide range of potential United Kingdom suppliers. With an initial budget of £10M per annum, it aims to inspire the best innovators from across the UK to bid for a contract to develop further their ideas to meet key defence challenges. It attracted over 450 applications including from universities and small and medium sized enterprises. More information is available at www.ideas.mod.uk;

- The Grand Challenge is a major science and technology competition directly relevant to the military challenges faced by the UK Armed Forces. It aims to provide an opening into the UK defence market for new suppliers and investors. The current challenge is "*to create a system with a high degree of autonomy that can detect, identify, locate and report a comprehensive range of military threats in an urban environment*". This has received significant interest from across the UK science and technology base, large and small companies, research laboratories and academic science faculties. The Grand Challenge will culminate in a competitive physical demonstration of the various systems in the summer of 2008. The winner will receive the R J Mitchell trophy, named after the innovative designer of the Spitfire – decisive technology in the Battle of Britain. Further details can be found at www.challenge.mod.uk.

The Defence Technology Strategy emphasises the importance of developing and maintaining high quality science and engineering skills relevant to defence technologies. A Skills Growth Plan to identify any professional skills gaps in science and engineering skills across the MoD has now been produced, and the Department has worked with the Royal Society to identify candidates for postdoctoral research fellowships under a one-year pilot scheme.

Overall, the Defence Technology Strategy works on three levels:

- Making the UK defence science and technology a great sector to work and invest in, enriching the science and technology skill base of the UK;

- Ensuring that for each innovation we derive, it is exploited at the earliest opportunity for the front line. In current operations, the technology employed in improved body armour, medical treatments and in countering improvised explosive devices continues to transform how we deliver our capability in an evolutionary manner;

- Clearly identifying those technologies which we need, for national security reasons, to retain in the UK, and, where these are threatened, developing sustainment strategies to foster and maintain them.

Enabling Processes

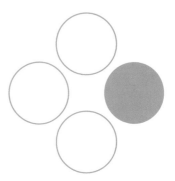

Personnel Management

Objective: Manage and Invest in our people to give their best.

Public Service Agreement Target (SR2004 MoD Target 5)
Recruit, train, motivate and retain sufficient military personnel to provide the military capability necessary to meet the Government's strategic objectives and achieve manning balance in each of the three Services by 1 April 2008.

Assessment and Performance Measures

Assessment: The continuing high operational tempo has meant that the Army and the Royal Air Force did not meet individual or unit harmony guidelines. There were further improvements in providing for the welfare of young recruits, a continuing effort to improve Basic Skills, and significant progress with major military training rationalisation. Service personnel career satisfaction remained broadly constant. Work continued to improve Civil Servants' management and leadership skills. Civilian staff satisfaction levels fell over the year, but remained high overall.

Harmony – No more than 660 days of Separated Service for RN personnel over a rolling 3 year period; Fleet units to spend a maximum of 60% time deployed in a 3 year cycle:

- Fewer than 1% of Royal Navy personnel exceeding the separated service guideline;
- The Royal Navy continued broadly to meet tour interval guidelines.

Harmony – No more that 415 days separated service for Army personnel over a rolling 30 month period; 24 month average interval between unit tours:

- 13.4% of Army personnel exceeding the separated service guideline;
- Infantry average tour interval of 21.0 months (20.6 in 2005-06); Royal Artillery 20.7 months (19.0 in 2005-06); Royal Engineers 21.2 months (31 in 2005-06); Royal Signals 18.4 months (27.6 in 2005-06); Royal Logistic Corps 23.3 months (23.7 in 2005-06).

Harmony – No more than 2.5% of RAF personnel to exceed 140 days separated service over a rolling 24 month period; unit tour intervals to be no less than 16 months:

- 6.2% of RAF personnel exceeding the separated service guideline;
- RAF Regiment Field Squadrons average tour intervals around 10.5 months (12 months 2005-06); Air Combat and Service Support units also breaching guidelines; Nimrod, Air Transport and Air-to-Air Refuelling squadrons heavily tasked.

Individual Personnel Development – Basic Skills: New entrants below national Level 2 for adult literacy and/or numeracy to be screened and assessed; All new entrants below Entry Level 3 in literacy and numeracy to achieve this before starting phase 2 training; All new entrants to achieve national Level 1 standard:

- All new entrants without Level 2 literacy or numeracy qualifications assessed;
- All Royal Navy and Royal Marine recruits below Level 1 standard receive remedial training. Virtually all recruits undertake apprenticeship schemes delivering at least level 1 qualifications;
- Entry Level 3 and Levels 1 and 2 in the Army not yet measured. Operational commitments constraining ability to release soldiers for remedial training. Army is establishing Basic Skills tutors and improving links with Further Education providers to supply local support and training;
- All RAF recruits required to have at least Level 1 qualifications. 90% of those joining go on to undertake Apprenticeship or advanced Apprenticeship.

Career Satisfaction – 5% improvement in overall satisfaction levels for Service Personnel:

- 65% of Royal Navy personnel, (63% 2005-06), 70% of Army Officers and 57% of Soldiers (73%/56% 2005-06), and 63% of RAF Officers and 56% Other Ranks (65%/55% 2005-06) were satisfied or very satisfied with Service life.

Career Satisfaction – Maintain 70% career satisfaction rate for civilians:

- Average civilian satisfaction of 68% in 2006-07 (71% 2005-06);
- 65% on average satisfied with MoD as an employer (77% 2005-06);

213. We ask a great deal of our people. Managing them well embraces a range of activities including recruitment, initial and career training, and career planning, particularly for Service personnel in relation to the time between operational tours. If they are to deliver what is required, we need to give them the necessary skills to do the job, provide a career path and listen to their views and act accordingly.

Service Pay and Conditions

Operational Welfare Package

214. The welfare of Service personnel is of the highest priority, reflecting the direct link between morale and operational capability. Through the Operational Welfare Package the Department provides support to personnel to safeguard their emotional and physical well-being as far as the operational environment, technical constraints and the availability of resources permit. Wherever possible they receive 30 minutes of free telephone calls per week to anywhere in the world; free e-mail and internet access; a free Forces Aerogramme letter and electronic letter service, a subsidised postal packet service (free in the run up to Christmas); access to televisions, radios, DVD players and video gaming machines; British Forces Broadcasting Service television and radio transmissions; books, newspapers, magazines and board games; Combined Services Entertainment live shows and celebrity visits; rest and recuperation; showers and a laundry; the provision of basic shop facilities; a Christmas box; financial assistance to home units to assist with families' welfare; concessionary families' travel; and Post Deployment Leave. The nature of some operations in Iraq and Afghanistan means that personnel are often deployed to a forward operating base where facilities are necessarily more basic, but even there the Department provides a minimum of IRIDIUM satellite telephones and TEXTLINK e-mail/ SMS messaging terminals. Key improvements to the package during 2006-07 included a 50% increase in the welfare telephone allowance from 20 to 30 minutes per week and a 700% increase in welfare internet connection speeds. Work continues to replace and upgrade all internet machines and infrastructure at main bases occupied by UK forces in Iraq; increase the number of welfare telephones available by 20% and the number of welfare internet terminals by 50%; and trial Wi-fi by the NAAFI and SSVC.

Harmony Guidelines

215. Each Service also sets guidelines for the maximum time Service personnel should spend away from their families (known as individual separated service), and the minimum time that units should have between operational deployments (known as tour intervals). These differ to reflect the nature of specific single Service skills sets and the way they deploy on operations. They are based on the routine level of concurrency that the Armed Forces are resourced and structured to sustain (see paragraphs 42-43 under *Current Operations*). Since they have been operating at or above this level since 2002 this has inevitably constrained their ability to meet harmony guidelines, particularly for personnel in certain pinch point specialist trades required for almost every operation. This is monitored carefully.

Unit Harmony

216. All three Services breached their unit harmony guidelines during the year, with the Army most and the Royal Navy least affected;

- The Royal Navy continued broadly to meet its unit tour interval harmony guidelines;

- Tour intervals for certain Army units continue to exceed the guideline of a 24-month average interval between tours. Over the year the average position improved slightly for most units, falling in the summer of 2006 before improving over the autumn and winter. The average tour interval for Infantry units in 2006-07 was 21 months (20.6 months in 2005-06) within a range from twelve to 37 months, with the Armoured Infantry most likely to be below the target interval. Where possible and appropriate the Army continued to use other Arms in their secondary role as Infantry to relieve the pressure. Average tour intervals in 2006-07 for Royal Armoured Corps, Royal Artillery, Royal Engineer, Royal Signals and Royal Logistic Corp units were respectively 28.6 months (24 months in 2005-06); 20.7 months (19 months in 2005-06); 21.2 months (31 months in 2005-06); 18.4 months (27.6 in 2005-06); and 23.3 months (23.7 in 2005-06). Some specialist units, particularly in Combat Service Support pinch point trades had shorter tour intervals;

- Against a guideline of 16 months, RAF Regiment Field Squadrons had tour intervals of around 10.5 months (around twelve months in 2005-06). While not generally breaking harmony guidelines, some fast jet squadrons were close to the boundary. The Nimrod, Air Transport and Air-Air Refuelling Squadrons remained heavily tasked, but this cannot be quantified in terms of the unit tour interval because the units remained UK-based while their aircraft and personnel deployed in and out of theatre as required. Air Combat and Service Support units also breached the guidelines, as did many other personnel deployed in support of formed units.

Air-Air refuelling squadrons are heavily tasked

Individual Separated Service

217. The Joint Personnel Administration system was introduced across all three Services in 2006-07. This collates separated service records for every individual on a consistent basis for the first time. However, while the data is immature and the system beds in, all figures are provisional. Subject to that caveat, all three Services breached their guidelines for the length of time individuals were away from home to some degree, with the Army the most and the Royal Navy least affected. There were greater shortfalls in identified pinch point trades in all three Services (see paragraphs 299-300 under *Manpower*):

- Although some individuals were approaching the threshold by the end of the year, fewer than 1% of Royal Navy personnel overall breached the guideline of no more than 660 days over a three-year rolling period;

- 13.4% of Army personnel were exceeding the guidelines of no more than 415 days separated service in any 30 month rolling period (a fall from 14.5% in 2005-06);

- 6.2% of Royal Air Force personnel breached the guideline of no more than 140 days detached duty in 12 months (4.6% in 2005-06).

Service Personnel Development

218. The Department introduced a new policy on the management of training to make training and education more coherent and effective. This is intended to ensure that there are clearly identified responsibilities and accountabilities; provide for better use of resources; improve assurance that training meets the operational and business needs; and ensure that the Department meets its duty of care responsibilities for inexperienced trainees. The training provided to Service personnel, whether basic or more advanced, also contributes towards the Government's wider skills objectives (see paragraph 105 under *Wider Government*).

Duty of Care and Welfare

219. The Department and the Armed Forces are responsible for ensuring the wellbeing and safety of all Service personnel. Following the Blake Report in March 2006 a substantial number of measures to improve the way young Service personnel are looked after have been taken forward, and building on existing work, some £73M more has been invested. A "Train the Trainer" package has been developed to be delivered to all new instructors before they take up their duties in the training environment, including modules on instructional technique, coaching and motivation, and the care of trainees. Instructional staff will be trained at the new Army Staff Leadership School at Alexander Barracks near Woking, which opened in June 2007. This will provide professional mentoring, counselling and teacher training skills to trainers, particularly those who work with new recruits. As part of improvements to care for trainees in initial training establishments, revised policies were endorsed to bring consistency to remedial training, improve weapon security, and minimise and clarify the use of trainees as armed guards. Additional Military Provost Guard Service

posts were also established to reduce the requirement for routine armed guarding by recruits. The training environment and programme were improved to reduce risks to trainees and improve support to all Service personnel. With particular reference to young trainees over 100 extra supervisory posts (nine Navy and 93 Army) have been established to support the implementation of the revised supervisory care policy, and the High Energy Training Supplement for all recruits in Phase 1 training has also been upgraded. (Further information can be found in the essay on *Duty of Care and Welfare* on page 135). Most of the actions arising from the Blake Report and previous reports have now been completed or are nearing completion. Measures to ensure that junior soldiers will be trained in an environment tailored to their needs are also being implemented, addressing a key recommendation within the Report. The Department is committed to maintaining the improvements achieved and addressing areas where performance can be further improved. Mechanisms have been put in place to ensure this happens, including internal monitoring by the Defence Individual Training Capability Team and external inspection by an enlarged OFSTED inspectorate incorporating the Adult Learning Institution.

Army Staff Leadership School

Basic Skills – Literacy & Numeracy

220. During 2006-07 the Department strengthened links with the Learning and Skills Council to improve support to young Service personnel, in particular to help those with poor literacy and numeracy. A new Basic Skills Policy for the Armed Services was endorsed which provides for early identification and systematic support to such personnel. This was reinforced by a new policy on Defence Specific Learning Difficulties, with which poor Basic Skills are often associated. All new entrants to the Armed Services without formal Level 2 literacy or numeracy qualifications[1] were assessed during 2006-07. Screening ensures that those individuals whose ability levels put them at most risk

are not taken into training until they have adequately improved their basic skills. All new entrants assessed as below Entry Level 3 literacy and numeracy (the level expected of an eleven year old) should achieve this before starting phase 2 training. All new entrants below Level 1 literacy and numeracy qualifications[2] are expected to achieve this within three years of joining, and Level 2 qualifications within a further five years or as required for career progression:

- All Royal Navy and Royal Marine recruits below Level 1 standard receive remedial training, and virtually all recruits undertake apprenticeship schemes that deliver at least Level 1 qualifications;

- Poor Basic Skills are a particular issue for the Army, which estimates that out of about 13,000 recruits a year, about 1,100 have only reached Entry Level 2 literacy and numeracy skills (those expected of a 7 year old) and a further 3,200 Entry Level 3. The Army is therefore establishing Basic Skills tutors and improving links with Further Education providers to supply local support and training for those with weak literacy and numeracy skills. Achievement of Entry Level 3 and Levels 1 and 2 in the Army has not yet been measured. Heavy operational commitments are constraining the ability of units to release soldiers for remedial Basic Skills training, but provision for this in operational theatres has improved;

- All Royal Air Force recruits are required to have Level 1 qualifications on joining, and 90% go on to undertake an apprenticeship or an advanced apprenticeship.

All three Services also provide assessment and training for those already serving with identified needs.

Basic Skills – Information and Communication Technology

221. Both operational and business success increasingly require: the availability and management of information; rapid communication over networks; and computer users with the necessary competencies. These comprise the three dimensions of a Network Enabled Capability (see paragraph 136 under *Future Effects*). The Department has invested heavily in the technology required to deliver this capability. Military personnel must therefore have a minimum level of proficiency suited to their role to operate a computer, and to input or access information and information services. The Department is therefore developing a policy on computer users' training, testing and accreditation. Personnel are categorised

1 A Level 2 qualification is the normal educational standard expected to enter into skilled employment and is equivalent to GCSE (Grade A-C).

2 Level 1 qualifications are equivalent to GCSE (Grades D-G).

as either basic, standard or advanced. The basic skill level is the minimum all personnel need to be able to use mandatory systems such as the Defence Information Infrastructure and the Joint Personnel Administration system from time to time. The standard skill level is the minimum competency required for regular computer users, with the British Computer Society's European Computer Driving Licence and its associated Level 2 Certificate for IT Users as proof of competency. The advanced skill level is for specialist Information System roles. The policy for occasional and regular users should be fully implemented for new entrants by September 2008, with all military and civilian personnel compliant by 2012. Significant progress towards full implementation has already been achieved. During 2006-07 over 99% of recruits to the Royal Navy, Royal Marines and Royal Air Force achieved the Standard Skill Level qualification, and all Army recruits were trained to the requisite level as occasional users.

Individual Military Training

222. In order to spread best practice and to ensure high quality and consistency across the Armed Forces, there are specific training policies for the eight Common Military Skills subjects[3]. These are common to at least two of the Services and require initial and continued training for the majority of personnel regardless of their career specialisation. The skills, knowledge and attitudes developed during this training are fundamental, and are particularly pertinent on deployed operations. Harmonising these requirements has facilitated their being more efficiently delivered. During 2006-07 the Defence Language Training Policy was also updated to include Cultural Awareness. This is now covered in detail in all pre-deployment training, tailored to the specific theatre of operation.

Recruits at a Weapons/Skill at Arms lesson

3 Chemical, Biological, Radiological and Nuclear Defence; Equality and Diversity; First Aid; Personal Weapons Handling and Shooting; Physical Development (including physical education, adventurous training and sport); Security; Avoiding Substance Misuse; and the Law of Armed Conflict.

Training Efficiency and Rationalisation

223. The Department is taking forward two major training modernisation, efficiency and rationalisation programmes designed to provide better, more cost effective long term specialist military training:

- The Defence Training Review will provide more cost-effective training and improved accommodation and facilities using best practice learning techniques in newly created national centres of excellence for each specialism. By harmonising training currently delivered by the Services individually it will also rationalise and improve the quality and efficiency of the training estate (see paragraph 328 under *Estate*) without reducing supervisory care at training establishments. Rationalisation is planned to be completed in 2012, and the whole programme is expected to produce benefits of approximately £2Bn over a 25 year period. It comprises two packages. Package One covers; Aeronautical Engineering; Communications and Information Systems; and Electro-Mechanical Engineering. Package Two covers Logistics; Joint Police and Personnel Administration; and Security, Languages, Intelligence and Photography. Following a robust and detailed evaluation of the Bidders' proposals in response to the Invitation To Negotiate, it was announced in January 2007 that Metrix was selected as the Preferred Bidder for Package One and Provisional Preferred Bidder for Package Two. Since then work has focused on examining whether Package Two can be made affordable through developing synergies and efficiencies in a Whole Programme Solution while still protecting the original terms of the procurement. Good progress has been made in negotiations with Metrix but it is not yet clear whether such a solution is affordable and deliverable. The results are likely to be announced later in 2007.

- The UK Military Flying Training System programme is working to replace the present flying training arrangements for the Royal Air Force, Fleet Air Arm and Army Air Corps with a single tri-Service military flying training system to train fast jet, helicopter and multi-engine aircraft pilots, weapons system operators and rear crew up to the point of their entry into Operational Conversion Units for frontline aircraft. In October 2006 the Department placed a contract with BAES for Hawk 128 Advanced Jet Trainers (see paragraph 162 under *Future Capabilities and Infrastructure*), which will form a key part of the flying training system. In November 2006 the Ascent Consortium (Lockheed Martin and VT Group) was appointed Preferred Bidder for the Training Service Partner, with a view to awarding a contract during 2007. The training system will be built incrementally to achieve full service provision in 2014, with significant investment over the next six years generating substantial improvements in efficiency and effectiveness from the next decade onwards.

Winch Training Exercise

Skills and Development Initiatives

224. The main focus during 2006-07 was to improve further the management and leadership skills of civilian managers, as this is central to improving delivery of defence capability by the Department. A standardised and clear definition of what is expected of managers was developed and appropriate tools, techniques, training and processes are being promulgated during 2007, including 'A Guide to Managing People', designed to help individuals develop themselves to become more effective managers. The majority of this work builds on existing good practice and will be further developed in the future to reflect the findings of the Cabinet Office Capability Review (see the essay on page 147). The Department also developed an enhanced Development Review process for staff, to be launched in 2007. This will give development a higher profile, bring together the currently separate reviews of skills and personal development, improve

performance management arrangements, and help gather more complete data on the skills held by our civilian workforce. Current managers at all levels have a significant role to play in all this, including coaching and mentoring future generations of managers and leaders.

225. In December 2006 the Department launched a Skills Management Information service, building on the Single Skills Framework and the post and personal skills profiles introduced in 2005-06. This service gives skills stakeholders, such as Skills Champions and Personnel Business Partners, the capability to inform future skills planning through structured analysis of the data contained in skills profiles. Analysis of the skills information in the electronic Personal Training and Development Plan introduced for all civilian personnel during 2006 have helped to identify skills gaps which are being addressed.

226. From April 2007 the Department extended to all civilian staff a Career Consultancy Service successfully trialled during 2006-07. This provides impartial career and development support and advice to staff, and helps them search for learning and job opportunities. A voluntary scheme to make mentoring available to all civilians in the Department was also introduced during the year. It is now open to any civilian manager who would like to be a mentor, and to any civil servant in the Department who would like to be mentored as part of their development. The Department also continued to develop its capacity to help civilian support staff improve their literacy and numeracy skills where necessary.

Development Schemes

227. The Department continued to operate a number of internal management development schemes such as MIDIT (Means of Identifying and Developing Internal Talent) for Band C and D staff, the Band B Development Scheme for those assessed as having strong potential to reach the Senior Civil Service, and the Acquisition Leadership and Development Scheme (see paragraph 230). The Department also participated in the Civil Service Fast Stream programme for individuals with the potential for rapid promotion to Band B and subsequent promotion to the Senior Civil Service in due course. At the end of the year a broader look at the operation of all of civilian development schemes across defence was announced as part of a wider review of how talent is managed within the Department. The Department also continued to support personal development programmes such as the Druidstone Prince's Trust community venture and Project Raleigh. It also operated the New Horizons programme to give junior ethnic minority staff the skills and confidence that they need to progress. It is intended to expand this scheme to include other under-represented groups in the future. The Department was heavily

involved during the year with the development and subsequent introduction of the new Cabinet Office Leaders Unlimited scheme aimed at helping under-represented groups reach the Senior Civil Service. Seven individuals were accepted onto the programme following assessment.

228. The Defence Industrial Strategy recognised the need to maintain a strong supply of scientists, engineers and technologists. The Department supports the wider government initiatives set out in the *Science Innovation Investment Framework 2004-2014: next steps*, working with the Department for Trade and Industry,[4] the Treasury and the Department for Education and Skills.[5] The 2006 Defence Engineering and Science Group Graduate Scheme recruited 64 graduate engineers and scientists and will be responsible for their personnel management over their two years of Initial Professional Development. Other sponsorship schemes include bursaries and undergraduate sponsorships for students taking engineering and science courses.

Joint Training

Defence Academy

241. The Defence Academy continued to take forward education across the Services and Civil Service, supporting departmental objectives in a number of areas. The launch of the Academy's *Shrivenham Papers* and the continued demand for research and educational products are helping to cement the Academy's reputation within the academic and defence worlds. At the component college level, there were a number of developments during 2006-07. The Royal College of Defence Studies introduced a flexible approach to linking in with the Higher Command and Staff Course to allow attendance on both courses in a single year. The Defence College of Management and Technology is the lead provider of education and training for acquisition and wider defence business and as such support the Defence Acquisition Change Programme. In April 2007 it produced a new publication, The Guide to Acquisition Training and Education, to help acquisition staff find the right training course from the over 200 that are available. This was an important step in developing a coherent acquisition training and education curriculum. It also supported a number of other key change programmes, such as the People Programme and the Resource Management Skills Framework. At the Joint Services Command and Staff College the Advanced Command and Staff Course was reorganised on a fully joint, postgraduate basis for members of all the Services, focusing more on Security Sector Reform, International Terrorism, Homeland

4 DTI become the Department for Business, Enterprise and Regulatory Reform on 28 June 2007
5 DFES become the Department for Children, Schools and Families; and the Department for Innovation, Universities and Skills, on 28 June 2007

Security & Resilience, and Effects Based Operations. The Armed Forces Chaplaincy Centre introduced a number of new initiatives in response to the increased operational tempo. The Advanced Research and Assessment Group continued to introduce new initiatives to keep it at the cutting edge of its subject, enhance its reputation for innovative thinking, and increase its capacity to contribute to policy and syllabus development in the Department and the Academy.

Acquisition Leadership Development Scheme

230. This year membership of the Defence Acquisition Leadership Scheme has risen to 753, including civilian, military and industry members, of whom 508 were alumni members who had completed one or more sections of the course and were eligible to return to continue should they wish to do so. From September 2007 the Acquisition Leadership Development Scheme will merge with the DE&S Management Development Programme to become a new and flexible, leadership development framework. This will take the best developmental elements from both schemes to produce a regular supply of candidates with the leadership capability and skills to compete for and perform strongly in team leader roles across the acquisition community. It will also include an expanded psychometric portfolio, and explore the benefits of executive coaching, short-term interchange and the delivery of developmental projects.

Investors in People

231. Work went forward to prepare for a corporate assessment of the whole Department against the Investors In People standard to begin in June 2007. This will evaluate the effectiveness of the programmes in place to improve organisational performance through the development and leadership of people. Lower level assessments continued throughout the year, with a number of areas gaining or keeping recognition. Evidence from these will support the corporate assessment.

Career Statisfaction

Service Personnel

232. All three Services run continuous attitude surveys to assess and monitor the attitudes of serving personnel. The most recent surveys were undertaken in the Royal Navy in July and August 2006, in the Army between September 2006 and January 2007, and in the Royal Air Force between February and November 2006 (see table 7). Satisfaction with Service life in the Royal Navy increased by 2% overall to 65%. In the Army it decreased for Officers by 3% to 70% and increased

for Soldiers by 1% to 57%. In the RAF satisfaction with Service life decreased by 3% to 62% among Officers but remained stable among Other Ranks at 55%.

Table 7: Percentage of those reported to be satisfied or very satisfied with Service life.

	2006-07	2005-06
RN	65% (RM 76%)	63%
Army	70% Officers, 57% Other Ranks	73% Officers, 56% Other Ranks
RAF	62% Officers, 55% Other Ranks	65% Officers, 55% Other Ranks

233. The main sources of satisfaction and dissatisfaction are shown in Tables 8 and 9. These have changed little. Job security, challenge and excitement, responsibility and pensions entitlements dominated the Royal Navy and Army positive retention factors, and enjoyment of life the Royal Air Force's. Negative retention factors continued to reflect the high levels of operational commitment and, for the Royal Air Force, the very substantial drawdown and restructuring programme under way. Reflecting the increasingly joint nature of the military environment, the three Service strands of feedback are being harmonised to enable joint and single Service personnel policy development to be informed by objective and timely analysis of joint attitudinal data, and each Service to understand the specific concerns and needs of its own people. A Tri-Service Attitude Survey was developed during the year and will be conducted later in 2007.

Table 8: Sources of Satisfaction

	Top indicators in 2006-07 surveys	Top indicators in 2005-06 surveys
RN + RM	Security of employment (RN 87%, RM 91%) Amount of responsibility (RN 80%, (RM 84%) Accuracy of assessment of appraisal report (76%) Variety of tasks in current role (RM 77%)	Security of employment (86%) Amount of responsibility (78%) Accuracy of assessment of appraisal report (73%)
Army	Job security (Officers 79%, Other Ranks 72%) Excitement (Officers 69%) Pension entitlements (Other Ranks 62%)	Job security (Officers 73%, Other Ranks 71%) Challenging job (Officers 71%) Pension entitlements (Other Ranks 61%)
RAF	Enjoyment of life in the RAF (86%) Tour length of Operational deployments (81%) Number of days annual leave (71%) Adequacy of training for your Service job (71%)	Enjoyment of life in the RAF (85%) Adequacy of training (over 72%) Leave Allowance (68%)

Table 9: Sources of Dissatisfaction

	Top indicators in 2006-07 surveys	Top indicators in 2005-06 surveys
RN + RM	Current X factor rate of 13% (RN 54%, RM 66%) The quality of equipment (RN 46%) Amount of fun in the Service (RN 41%) The X-factor method of payment meets its objectives (RM 53%) Ability to plan their own long term life (RM 50%)	Current X factor rate of 13% (RN 48%, RM 58%). Amount of fun in the Service (RN 46%) Ability to plan their own long term life (RN 44%) Medical treatment in units (RM 63%)
Army	Impact of Army lifestyle on personal and domestic life (Officers 62%, Other Ranks 49%) Effect of operational commitment and overstretch (Officers 59%, Other Ranks 42%)	Impact of Army lifestyle on personal and domestic life (Officers 62%, Other Ranks 47%) Effect of operational commitment and overstretch (Officers 55%, Other Ranks 38%)
RAF	Effects of overstretch (85%) and gapping of posts (71%) on the RAF as a whole Effects of civilianisation and contractorisation (73%) Effects of overstretch (63%) and gapping of posts on own working group (53%)	Effects of Overstretch (85%) and gaping of posts (72%) Effects of civilianisation and contractorisation (75%) Impact of change on the RAF (56%)

234. There were a significant number of Industrial Tribunal applications by part-time members of the Royal Irish Regiment (Home Service) in relation to their non-pensionable status. Redresses of Grievance were lodged with the Army Board by about 1,100 part-time and former part-time members of the Regiment, claiming unequal treatment when compared to full-time colleagues, particularly in relation to the Normalisation Settlement package.

Civilian Personnel

235. The Civilian Attitude Survey provides evidence on the commitment of the civilian workforce to the work of the Department (both intellectually and emotionally), how well civilian staff are managed and whether the changes being implemented through the People Programme are having the intended results:

- Overall, civilian **Engagement** remained positive during the year. The vast majority of civilian staff remained aware of the Department's aims and of how they contributed to them. Marginally under two thirds were satisfied with the MoD as an employer. But although the overall positive response rate remained consistent with previous years, there was a statistically significant reduction in overall satisfaction with the MoD as an employer. It is not yet clear whether this was a one-off result or

the beginning of a trend, and it is being investigated as part of the assessment of the impact of work to strengthen the corporate leadership of the Department and pursue the diversity agenda. Key driver analysis continued to show that satisfaction with MoD as an employer was closely correlated with pride in working for defence, a belief that the MoD as a whole is well managed, a sense of being treated with fairness and respect and a feeling that one's contribution is valued;

- Quality of **Management** is central to employees' engagement with their work. The results of the 2006-07 surveys confirmed those of previous years. Line managers almost universally believed that managing their team was central to their role, that they were encouraged to manage and develop their team and that their performance should, in part, be judged on this. Three quarters of staff reported a trusting relationship with their line manager and a similar proportion believed their line manager was responsive to individuals' needs. Despite that, only around 60% believed their team was well managed, and fewer than half believed their line manager fulfilled their development responsibility and that they received regular and constructive feedback on their performance. Work is in hand to build on line managers' basic commitment in order to achieve a step change in the degree of professionalism they bring to their role, with a series of new materials being rolled out in July 2007. But long term success will require a real cultural change;

Table 10: Civilian Career Satisfaction

	2007-06	2005-06[1]	2004-05
Considering everything, how satisfied are you with MoD as an employer?	65%	77%	73%
Are you aware of the MoD's aims and objectives?	87%	73%	80%
How do you rate your understanding of how your job contributes to the MoD's aims and objectives?	82%	94%	90%
I have access to the type of training I need to carry out my job properly.	66%	83%	65%
My job makes good use of my skills and abilities.	76%	70%	71%
I can express my views and ideas and have them taken seriously by Managers.	71%	72%	70%
Do you regard MoD as an equal opportunities employer?	76%	90%	89%
Individuals who make greater relative contributions towards achieving business outputs should receive a greater financial reward.	70%	73%	74%
The MoD's current performance pay arrangements reward better performance	16%	22%	16%
The move to introduce a more flexible percentage split for the reward of performance is the right thing to do.	N/A	54%	56%
Average positive rates for each year[2]	**68%**	**71%**	**70%**

Notes
1. 2005-06 results originate from a survey undertaken in Autumn 2006
2. The average positive response rate is based upon questions shown in the table.

- The most far reaching policy and process changes introduced under the **People Programme** relate to matching people to posts. During the year the Department moved to a largely self-service competitive internal recruitment market supplemented by intervention only in limited cases, in order to provide a cost effective means of matching people and their skills to posts. Over 80% of staff believed that competing for jobs in the internal job market should give them the freedom to apply for jobs they are attracted to. Nearly two thirds of managers believed they should have a greater choice from which to select the best candidate (with fewer then 15% disagreeing). Annual performance bonus arrangements remained a challenging issue, as in most large organisations. But even though only 16% of staff supported the current arrangements, 70% endorsed the principle of assessment of relative contributions providing a basis for financial reward. It is not realistic to expect results in this area to be as positive as in others. The Department nevertheless remains committed to delivering a system which staff regard as fair and transparent, and performance bonus arrangements have been overhauled to provide more flexibility and restore bonus decisions to line management wherever possible.

236. The Department is committed to good employee relations. At the April 2007 meeting of the Defence Whitley Council the Combined Council of Civil Service Unions stated that they believed employee relations had reached crisis point and that they were in formal disagreement with the Department. In a message to all civilian staff the Permanent Secretary disagreed that relations were at crisis point, stressed the value the Department attached to the work of all civilian staff in support of defence, and emphasised the Department's commitment to the full Trade Union consultation process.

Further Sources of Information

237 Additional information on Personnel management is available from the following sources:

- Quarterly PSA reports to HM Treasury at www.mod.uk;
- Armed Forces Pay Review Body Report at www.mod.uk;
- Review Body on Senior Salaries at www.mod.uk;
- UK Defence Statistics at www.dasa.mod.uk;
- The Blake Review at www.official-documents.gov.uk;
- The Government's response to the Blake Report at www.mod.uk;
- Defence Academy Shrivenham Papers at www.defac.ac.uk;
- DGCP Civilian and Continuous Attitude Survey Annual Report available at www.mod.uk;
- Continuous Attitude Surveys (CAS): Results for Service Personnel available at www.mod.uk;
- Science Innovation Investment Framework 2004-2014: next steps available at www.hm-treasury.gov.uk.

Essay – Defence and National Skills

With about 300,000 military and civilian staff, the Ministry of Defence is one of the United Kingdom's largest employers and plays a crucial role in contributing to the national skills base, having always invested in the training and education of its personnel. The Armed Forces recruit approximately 18,000 young people every year from a broad educational background. For those joining with few or no qualifications, they are given the chance to succeed; indeed, defence is one of the few areas of employment where an individual can join with no qualifications at all and, with the correct motivation, leave with marketable skills and experience – a fact recently acknowledged in the Government's March 2007 Green Paper on raising the participation age[1]. This responded to the December 2006 conclusions of the Leitch Review of Skills[2] sponsored by the Chancellor of the Exchequer, which reported that national skills remain fundamentally weak by international standards with competitors in the global economy advancing much more rapidly. The Department is engaged in the debate on implementation of Lord Leitch's recommendations. The fundamental change his report advocates, that learning be viewed as a continual work related activity, is already embedded in Service culture and the Ministry of Defence. The increasing complexity of defence business requires a wide spectrum of skills and competencies to deliver operational effect. This demands that defence personnel acquire the necessary skills through adequate investment in training and education.

Basic Skills

The emphasis placed on Skills for Life (also known as Basic Skills) has become more important across the increasingly sophisticated, technological and networked defence environment. Sailors, soldiers and airmen are expected to manage and coordinate complex tasks and equipment, often in the most hostile of environments where friends' and colleagues' lives can be in danger. Those with poor Basic Skills can struggle to understand verbal or written instructions, make simple calculations, or record information. They often find the training and education necessary to do their job difficult, taking longer to assimilate the required skills or in some cases failing to reach the required standards and leaving the Armed Forces. Those with higher levels of literacy and numeracy can work with less supervision, use their initiative more, and are more confident in demanding and complex environments. Service personnel joining technical trades, which comprise the vast majority of Royal Navy and Royal Air Force posts, and those who join as officers, have a good level of education upon entry. The Army faces a greater challenge, as it recruits several thousand personnel a year with no more than basic levels of literacy and numeracy. The Armed Forces and the MoD Civil Service work to raise the Basic Skills levels of personnel identified with weaknesses (see paragraphs 220-221 under *Personnel Management*) and resources have been allocated to support more extensive Basic Skills delivery in the Army. All this supports the overall Skills Agenda. The link between Basic Skills and operational effectiveness will be further explored in a five-year study staring later in 2007 sponsored by the Department for Education and Skills.[3]

Vocational Skills and Qualifications

All defence training and education is driven by operational and business need. Training within defence has a heavy emphasis on work-based learning. There are over 2,500 different courses, ranging from half a day to up to four years long. The Armed Forces favour apprenticeship schemes that provide a National Vocational Qualification, a technical certificate, and certain key skills. These latter not only cover literacy, numeracy and IT skills, but also develop problem solving and the ability to work with others, and provide improvements to self-learning and performance. In 2006-07 over 5,700 personnel completed apprenticeships and nearly 2,500 completed advanced apprenticeships, with significant numbers in key areas such as engineering, communications, transport, health care, customer care and public services. This is more than comparable with the training performance of the best private sector employers.

1 *Raising Expectations: Staying in Education and Training Post-16*, *available at* www.dfes.gov.uk
2 *Prosperity for all in the global economy – world class skills*, available at www.hm-treasury.gov.uk.
3 DFES became the Deparment for Children, Schools and Families; and the Department for Innovation, Universities and Skills, on 28 June 2007

Since much of what Service personnel do on a daily basis requires vocational skills, the Armed Forces put great store in accrediting the training and education carried out by military personnel to nationally recognised vocational qualifications. This not only provides external assurance that military training is high quality. It also helps recruiting and retention. Parents of young recruits are assured that the training and education provided by the Armed Forces leads to nationally recognised qualifications. Service personnel, having gained nationally recognised transferable skills, are content to stay longer in the Armed Forces and acquire greater experience before leaving to work in the civil economy. Opportunities to gain nationally recognisable academic and vocational qualifications continue throughout a military career. Service personnel can also make use of the Learning Credits Scheme (see paragraph 108 under *Wider Government*) to gain vocational and academic qualifications for their personal development. The training of MoD civil servants is similarly accredited, wherever possible, to nationally-recognised qualifications.

The Future

The Department is committed to playing a leading part helping to shape and influence the development of national qualifications and the wider skills vision, working closely with the Department for Education and Skills,[3] the Qualifications and Curriculum Authority, the Cabinet Office, relevant Sector Skills Councils and the Learning and Skills Council. Current defence policies and practice provide a strong foundation for the future.

Health and Safety

Objective: A safe environment for our staff, contractors and visitors.

Public Service Agreement Target (SR2004 MoD Target 5)
Recruit, train, motivate and retain sufficient military personnel to provide the military capability necessary to meet the Government's strategic objectives and achieve manning balance in each of the three Services by 1 April 2008.

Assessment and Performance Measures

Assessment: Further improvements were made to military medical support during the year, the number of patients assessed by Regional Rehabilitation Units and the proportion of Service personnel medically downgraded nevertheless continued to increase, and the Department did not meet its target of 90% 'fit for task' by April 2007. The Civilian sickness absence rate continued to fall, remaining comparable with private sector performance. Defence safety management systems were judged to be generally robust, the number of deaths attributable to health and safety failures fell during the year, and the Department remained on course to meet Government targets for improved Health and Safety performance by 2010. But the Department did not achieve its own target of no deaths attributable to Health and Safety failures.

Reduce number of Service personnel medically downgraded:

- Service personnel reported 'fit for task' fell from 87.8% to 85.9% during 2006-07 (target 90% on 1 April 2007);
- Complex Rehabilitation and Amputee Unit at Headley Court fully operational in June 2006;
- Reserves Mental Health Programme operational in November 2006;
- Military Managed Ward Unit opened at Selly Oak Hospital in December 2006;
- 7,168 patients assessed at Regional Rehabilitation Units during 2006-07, and 705 (9.8%) referred for fast-track surgery.

Reduce level of civilian sickness absence:

- Civilian non-industrial sickness absence rate fell from 7.3 days to 6.7 days (target 7.3 days);
- Civilian industrial sickness absence rate fell from 11.9 days to 10.8 days.

No fatalities attributable to Health and Safety failures:

- 6 deaths reported as attributable to Health and Safety failures (8 in 2005-06);
- 2 Crown Censures against MoD during 2006-07 (1 in 2005-06).

Reduce the number of serious injuries by 10% against previous year:

- 706 serious injuries during the year, producing target for 2007-08 of no more than 635.

Other Developments

- Updated Safety, Health and Environmental Protection Policy in December 2006;
- Health and Safety Gap Analysis concluded in January 2007;
- *The Defence Health Strategy* issued in March 2007;
- Introduction of Corporate Manslaughter legislation in summer 2006 with exemptions for military operations and training in support of operations;
- Expanded work to minimise Road Traffic Accidents and analyse their causes;
- Smoking banned across Defence Estate from 1 January 2007.

Health of Service Personnel

238. The Armed Forces must have personnel fit and able to carry out the tasks required of them. When people are not fit, it is important to identify this and provide the necessary care for their recovery. On 2 March 2007, the Service Personnel Board issued *The Defence Health Strategy*, which sets out the responsibilities of everyone in defence, including the chain of command, the medical services and the individual, for the promotion and enhancement of health.

239. The Department continued to improve the care provided to injured personnel. Defence medical personnel deployed to Afghanistan during the year won awards for Hospital Doctor of the Year and Paramedic of the Year. The British Field Hospital in Camp Bastion, Helmand Province, is equipped to deal with severe trauma casualties, including the first British Computerised Tomography scanner in Afghanistan, a range of advanced mobile digital X-ray machines and innovations such as new self-applied combat tourniquets, new clotting agents, and new rapid drug delivery systems that reduce the time it takes to put in a drip. There were continuing improvements to medical capability on deployed operations, backed up by an Aeromedical Evacuation team widely regarded as providing an exceptional service, and which is also used to recover Canadian and Dutch casualties in Afghanistan. Military personnel who sustain a serious physical injury on operations overseas are usually aeromedically evacuated back to the United Kingdom for treatment by the University Hospital Birmingham NHS Foundation Trust. This includes Selly Oak Hospital, which is at the leading edge in the medical care of the most common types of injuries (such as polytrauma) our casualties sustain. Recognising the value to military patients of recovering alongside their comrades, in December 2006 the Department established a Military Managed Ward within one of the larger trauma/orthopaedic wards at Selly Oak, with a combined military and civilian team to care for those military patients whose clinical condition allows for it.

240. On 1 June 2006, the new Complex Rehabilitation and Amputee Unit at the Defence Medical Rehabilitation Centre, Headley Court, became fully operational. Since then, over 40 amputees have been treated in the Unit, receiving individually tailored prosthetic limbs and adaptations, as well as associated rehabilitation care. For the more common range of injuries the Defence Medical Services continued to build on the scheme introduced in April 2003 to provide fast track access to routine surgery, cutting down on often lengthy waits for assessment, diagnosis and surgical treatment, and contributing to the numbers available for deployment. 7,168 patients were assessed at Regional Rehabilitation Units during 2006-07 of whom only 705 (9.8%) required onward referral to fast-track orthopaedic surgery. The rest were successfully managed with rehabilitation alone. The development of this programme has allowed Headley Court to focus on the most complex rehabilitation cases, including amputees and neurological rehabilitation for brain-injured patients.

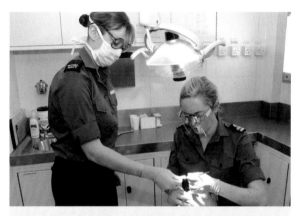

HMS ALBION's Dental Department

241. The Defence Medical Services continued to provide mental health support through 15 military Departments of Community Mental Health in the UK (plus satellite centres overseas), ensuring better access to specialised mental heath support within or close to an individual's unit or home. This also enables defence mental health staff to work within their local Service community, which is more closely aligned with their operational role. In-patient care is provided regionally by the private Priory group of hospitals. (For further information on the provision of medical support to veterans see paragraphs 120-124 under *Wider Government*).

242. Over the year the proportion of Armed Forces personnel reported as 'fit for task' (that is, fully able to carry out the task that they were posted to their unit, ship or establishment to perform) fell by a further 1.9%, from 87.8% on 31 March 2006 to 85.9% at 31 March 2007, against a target of 90% on 1 April 2007. The reduction reflected the continuing high operational tempo, as the level of fitness required for personnel to be able to deploy on combat operations is both more demanding and more strictly enforced than that required in less a challenging environment. Reporting systems have also been improved further. The position in the Army was more marked, with the number reported as fully fit falling from 84.2% on 31 March 2006 to 82.7% on 31 March 2007. Of those not fully fit only 0.5% were unfit for any task, with the remaining 16.8% not fully fit for their primary task able to carry out other duties in their units.

Reserves

243. The new Reserves Mental Health Programme became operational in November 2006. Any member of the Reserve Forces demobilised since January 2003 following deployment overseas is eligible for a dedicated mental health assessment programme offered by the Defence Medical Services. In the event that individuals are assessed as having a combat-related mental health condition, they are offered outpatient treatment by the Defence Medical Services, who have particular expertise in this area. If a case is particularly complex or acute and requires in-patient care, the Defence Medical Services will assist in arranging access to NHS treatment. The Programme is based at the Reserves Training and Mobilisation Centre at Chilwell in Nottinghamshire. As at 31 March 2007, a total of 96 enquiries had been received by the Centre. Most were resolved without an individual needing to attend for formal assessment, but 16 individuals had been assessed by this date, of whom eight were referred for treatment at one of MoD's own Departments of Community Mental Health (see previous paragraph).

Civilian Sickness

244. The Department introduced a new reporting process during the year that improved the quality of sick absence data. In 2006-07 the MoD's civilian sickness absence rate was 6.7 working days per non-industrial employee, (costing £47.5M) against a target of (no more than) 7.3 days. This compares favourably with other large Civil Service and commercial organisations. The most recent Cabinet Office figures reported an average of 9.8 days lost per staff year in 2005 across the Civil Service, with other very large departments ranging from 10.3 to 12.6 days. The most recent Confederation of British Industry (CBI) survey reported an average of seven working days per employee lost across the UK workforce (and eight days in organisations with over 5,000 employees). The most recent Chartered Institute of Personnel and Development Absence Management Report indicated an average of eight days lost per employee. The MoD also lost an average 10.8 Industrial average working days to sickness absence, (costing some £13.1M) down from 11.9 days in 2005. The CBI survey reported an average of eight working days lost per employees among manual workers. The Department has not previously had a target for Industrials because since the MoD employs over 80% of all Civil Service Industrial staff they have not been taken into account in comparisons with other Government Departments. However, from 2007-08 reported figures will be based on new Cabinet Office definitions for the whole of the MoD workforce bar those employed in trading funds.

245. Under the People Programme (see paragraph 187 under *Future Personnel Plans*) the Department continued to develop policy for and delivery of Occupational Health and Absence Management services. Occupational Health support and advice is already available to all MoD civilian staff. The Department's approach to occupational health is being reviewed in advance of the award of a contract in 2008 Every major business area was set a tailored target to reduce its absence levels further.

Health and Safety

246. The Secretary of State issued an updated Policy on Safety, Health and Environmental Protection in December 2006. This emphasises the importance of delivering high standards of safety, health and environmental performance, which are critical to the generation of battle winning people and equipment. The Department remained on track to meet the improvement targets for 2010 set in the joint Government/Health and Safety Commission initiative *Revitalising Health and Safety*, launched in June 2000. At its best, health and safety management in defence compare well with best practice elsewhere, as demonstrated by the award of the Sir George Earle prize to HM Naval Base Devenport in 2006 by the Royal Society for the Prevention of Accidents, and of the International Safety Award to HM Naval Base Clyde in May 2007 by the British Safety Council. The Department nevertheless commissioned a Strategic Gap Analysis in 2006 from Professor Richard Taylor, an independent safety expert with many years' experience in senior roles in high hazard industries such as nuclear power. This reported to the Defence Environment and Safety Board in January 2007 and provided a strategic view of safety and environmental management performance benchmarked against outside industry. It concluded that MoD's safety management system was generally clear and robust, and that the areas of highest hazards (nuclear, explosives, and aviation safety) appeared to be well managed, but that there was room for improvement in some areas, including performance measurement. The new Incident Recording and Information System to be launched in January 2008 will provide more effective analysis of accident statistics and better assessment of performance. In November 2006 the Royal Air Force was awarded the British Horse Society Safety award for the organisation that has done most to promote equestrian safety. This reflects the Department's response to death of Heather Bell in 2003, who was thrown from her horse when an RAF helicopter passed by at low level. The Department has set up a freephone telephone number for horse riders to call to find out if low level helicopter operations are planned to take place in an area they wanted to ride, and donated

£14,000 for high-visibility equipment for horses and riders.

HM Naval Base Clyde with the International Safety Award

Corporate Manslaughter

247. The Department has worked closely with the Home Office on the development of the draft Corporate Manslaughter legislation currently before Parliament, which aims to strengthen corporate responsibility for safety management. The Department strongly supports this goal, and the imperative of ensuring that the risks and benefits of particular activities to the delivery of operational capability continue to be properly balanced. In this context it is essential that the legislation does not inadvertently compromise the military judgment of commanders on operations, or the duty of care to military personnel to ensure that they are properly trained and prepared for what they are expected to do and may have to face on operations. There are accordingly certain limited but vital exemptions in the draft legislation covering military operations and training in support of operations.

Avoiding Fatalities

248. The Revitalising Health and Safety initiative set a target of a 10% reduction in deaths by 2010 against the 1999-2000 baseline. In that year 16 on-duty, workplace injury-related deaths were reported. Six were reported in 2006-07 (see below), but the low number means that single multi-fatality events can seriously skew the figures. In 2005, the Department set itself the further target of no deaths attributed to health and safety failures. A full investigation is carried out after every death, and during 2006-07 six fatalities were reported as attributed to such failures: a motorcycle display team rider hit by a bike while supporting a display; two soldiers crushed beneath armoured fighting vehicles in Afghanistan; a Royal Logistic Corps driver crushed

beneath a vehicle on Salisbury Plain; a contractor working on the defence estate in Northern Ireland; and a Private soldier on a physical training test. There were two Crown Censures[6] against the MoD during 2006-07, relating to the deaths of two Army soldiers crushed between armoured fighting vehicles in 2003 and 2004. These recognised and welcomed the action taken subsequently to improve the work procedures, communications and training deficiencies that were identified as root causes of the incidents.

Road Traffic Accidents

249. The largest single non-operational cause of deaths and serious injuries in the Armed Forces is Road Traffic Accidents, on and off duty. In 2006 there were nine deaths in on-duty and 50 deaths in off-duty Road Traffic Accidents, compared to eleven such deaths on-duty and 41 such deaths off-duty in 2005. Although these are not the result of health and safety failures they remain a significant concern, particularly for the Army, which has taken steps to reduce them including the use of targeted radio and television advertisements and road safety campaigns. The Defence Analytical Services Agency is also conducting a more detailed analysis to identify underlying causes, which will enable them to be addressed. There is a possibility that increased risk-taking by Service personnel returning from operational tours could be responsible for some of these accidents. The work is therefore focusing particularly on the pattern of road traffic accidents among personnel returning from operational tours and looking at the circumstances behind them, including the degree to which 'operational service' might have affected perceptions of risk of personal injury.

Minimise Serious Injuries

250. The Revitalising Health and Safety initiative also set a target of a 10% reduction in serious injuries by 2010 against the 1999-2000 baseline. 60 serious injuries per 100,000 employees were reported in that year. In 2005-06 76 serious injuries per 100,000 employees were reported. This increase is partly explained by the increased reporting rates for all injuries, following the introduction of call centres in most of the major TLBs. In 2005 the Department set itself a target to reduce the number of serious injuries by 10% each year against the previous years' performance, with 2006-07 the baseline. There were 706 serious injuries[7] during the year, producing a target

6 Crown Censure is the Health and Safety Executive's procedure to censure a breach of health and safety obligations for which, but for Crown Immunity, it would have prosecuted the employer with a realistic prospect of conviction.
7 Defined as "a reportable major injury" under the Health and Safety Executive's Reporting of Injuries, Diseases and Dangerous Occurrences Regulations.

for 2007-08 of no more than 635. With the introduction of call centres across the Department and the Armed Forces reporting of injuries has improved. This has produced a clearer understanding of what causes such accidents of which the largest cause is 'slips, trips and falls', followed by 'physical movement' (including sports and training injuries).

Smoking

251. Reducing smoking and tobacco-related harm is a key Government objective. The Scottish Executive introduced a smoking ban in all enclosed public places and workplaces in Scotland in March 2006, at which time the Department banned smoking in enclosed premises on defence sites in Scotland and the RN surface fleet worldwide. Both Wales and Northern Ireland followed suit in April 2007, and England's legislation comes into affect in July 2007, in advance of which the Department banned smoking in enclosed premises on the entire defence estate (including overseas) from 31 December 2006, except in designated bedrooms and family quarters, and RN submarines and the RFA will become smokefree by 1 July.

Further sources of information

252. Additional Information on Health and Safety is available from the following sources:

- Health and Safety Policy at www.mod.uk
- CBI/AXA Absence and Labour Turnover Survey 2007, available at www.nhsplus.nhs.uk
- CIPD Annual Survey Report 2006: Absence Management, available at www.cipd.co.uk/surveys
- Annual *Analysis of Sickness Absence in the Civil Service* available at www.civilservice.gov.uk
- *Safety Health and Environmental Protection in the Ministry of Defence – A Policy Statement by the Secretary of State for Defence* available at www.mod.uk
- Revitalising Health and Safety, available at www.hse.gov.uk
- Draft Corporate Manslaughter legislation at www.parliament.uk
- UK Defence Statistics, available at www.dasa.mod.uk
- DASA annual summary of incident statistics at www.dasa.mod.uk
- Sustainable Development Annual Report available at www.mod.uk.
- House of Commons Public Accounts Committee report on Reserve Forces, HC729, available at www.publications.parliament.uk

Essay – Duty of Care and Welfare in Initial Training

The Department has a continuing duty of care towards Service personnel, particularly those under the age of 18. Just over one year on from the publication of the Deepcut Review significant improvements have been made to the environment in which recruits and trainees are trained and to the way they are managed, including to the support provided at a time when they may be particularly vulnerable. In its *Better Training* report published in March 2007, the Adult Learning Inspectorate commented that "substantial improvements have been made everywhere with some very marked achievements".

Initiatives to improve the training environment focused on changing the way instructors are selected, trained and developed prior to undertaking their role. The Armed Forces have tightened up their procedures for checking the personal records of Service personnel before employing them as instructors to ensure that only suitable personnel of the right quality are posted to training establishments. Current legislation does not allow for Criminal Records Bureau checks to be carried out on personnel working with recruits and trainees under the age of 18 because they are in full time employment. The Department is therefore working as a matter of urgency with the Department for Education and Skills[1] and the Home Office on changes to legislation to provide greater flexibility in carrying out such checks in future. In April 2006, a new Defence Train the Trainer course was introduced and mandated for all new instructors. A new policy on Remedial Training has been introduced which defines what behaviour to help trainees achieve required standards is legitimate, and to ensure that both instructors and trainees distinguish this from bullying or harassment, which is always unacceptable. All instructional staff will now be trained at the new purpose built Army Recruiting and Training Division Staff Leadership School at Pirbright.

There have been a number of changes to reduce the risk to the safety and wellbeing of recruits and trainees. The Department has implemented the Supervisory Care Directive across training organisations, underpinned by Unit Commander's Risk Assessment. Policy on the care of Service personnel under the age of 18 has been revised. This aims to ensure that our under 18s are properly identified, monitored and supported throughout their training and, when necessary, during their free time. It also sets out procedures to prevent them being deployed on operations outside the United Kingdom where they may become engaged in or exposed to hostilities. Real progress has been made in managing the risk of self-harm and suicide, including the introduction of pragmatic policies and the development of better awareness, knowledge and understanding. Armed guarding policy at training establishments has been updated, and a programme of transferring routine armed guarding at all Phase 2 establishments to the Military Provost Guard Service is well underway. Controls over access to firearms are now tighter and better enforced, and the risks associated with their use in training establishments managed more carefully.

As recognised by the Adult Learning Institute, the Department is committed to meeting the specific needs of those under the age of 18 and to providing them with a well organised and highly effective support service. A number of recommendations from the welfare review were implemented over the year, including the production of a new Joint Service Publication on welfare provision. There are comprehensive mechanisms in place to support Service personnel, but work on enhancing this support system continued. For example, the Army completed a trial of the 'Bullytext' system, and other more localised schemes using text messaging are now being explored to complement the well-used Confidential Support Line. A simple leaflet has been produced for Service personnel on what to do on encountering any form of bullying, who to turn to for help, sources of advice, definitions of the terms bullying and harassment and an overview of how complaints are made, responded to, investigated and dealt with. The procedures for making and dealing with complaints of bullying and harassment have also been revised. Further improvements will be made to the complaints process under Armed Forces Act 2006. These include the introduction of Service Complaint Panels with an external, independent member for the consideration of complaints making allegations of harassment and bullying, and the establishment of a Service Complaints Commissioner who will provide Service personnel and others an alternative means of raising a grievance if they do not feel comfortable, for whatever reason, in reporting it to the relevant commanding officer. Work is underway to implement this new system ahead of full implementation of Armed Forces Act 2006.

The Department has also made great efforts to keep families and partners informed as recruits pass through training, as recommended in the Deepcut Review. The Adult Learning Institute acknowledged that this has improved significantly. Families are engaged with if a young recruit has a problem, but contact with them goes far beyond keeping them informed of problems. They receive letters and phone calls about progress and forthcoming events and further information via training establishments' websites.

Achieving real and lasting change in the Armed Forces requires sustained effort. The Department remains committed to further improvements, and to maintaining the momentum so far achieved.

1 DFES became the Department for Children, Schools and Families; and the Department for Innovation, Universities and Skills, on 28 June 2007.

Logistics

Objective: Support and sustain our Armed Forces.

Assessment and Performance Measures

Assessment: The logistic support required to sustain the high tempo of operations was successfully provided against a growing requirement over the year as the forces deployed to Afghanistan increased. The logistic transformation programme continued to deliver improved support arrangements and financial efficiencies. But the continuing impact of reduced levels of support for the Royal Navy and the impact of operations on RAF aircraft meant that the level of routine logistic support provided to the Services continued to fall slightly below the target level.

Provide the logistic support required to current operations:

- Successful logistic support to operations in Iraq, Afghanistan and the Balkans, and to civilian evacuation operation from Lebanon;
- Improvements to operation of strategic airbridge to Iraq and Afghanistan;
- Improvements in consignment tracking.

Deliver 98% of logistic support for funded levels of readiness and funded support to enable force generation within planned readiness times, as set out in Customer Service Agreements with Top Level Budget Holders:

- 94.9% of logistic support outputs delivered (94.5% in 2005-06).

Provide funded logistic sustainability for future contingent operations:

- Work to introduce new Force Elements at Sustainability process to manage sustainability requirements for contingent operations;
- Work continued to ensure that the full logistic recuperation requirements and cost are understood.

Deliver Logistics efficiency savings agreed in 2004 Spending Review:

- Validated total of £662M efficiencies achieved by the end of March 2006 (target £539M);
- £225M to £300M estimated further efficiencies achieved in 2006-07 (target £175M).

Achieve a disposal sales receipt of £63 million from sales of surplus equipment and stores:

- £81.5M gross sales achieved.

Delivery of Logistics Support

253. In 2006-07, the Defence Logistics Organisation (DLO) was responsible for providing support to the front line British Armed Forces. Support to operations was the highest priority throughout the year. To achieve this, it worked closely with the Army, Navy, RAF, the Defence Procurement Agency (DPA) and other parts of the MoD and industry. At the beginning of April 2007, the DLO merged with the DPA to form Defence Equipment and Support. This means that in future there will be a single organisation centred in the Bath/Bristol area dedicated to the procurement, maintenance and sustainment of military capability.

Supporting Current Operations

254. The DLO remained focussed on support to operations and demonstrated its ability to respond to additional short notice surge requirements, including the evacuation of UK citizens and their dependants from Lebanon in July 2006 (see paragraph 28 under *Current Operations*). For most of the year the main logistic effort continued to be in support of operations in Iraq (see paragraph 28 under *Current Operations*). Incremental improvements were introduced during the year to the management of Urgent Operational Requirements, logistic command and control, asset tracking, air transport and the airbridge. As force levels built up in Afghanistan the logistic effort to support the high operational tempo (see paragraph 20 under *Current Operations*) grew substantially, including the movement of 2,800 tonnes of ammunition in late 2006. Key medical supplies were delivered including a CT scanner and 'golden hour' boxes to ensure that the best medical facilities were available (see paragraph 20 under *Health and Safety*). A total of 245 protected mobility vehicles such as MASTIFF and BULLDOG were delivered rapidly by air to Iraq and Afghanistan as they became available from September 2006. Planning is underway to support further logistic expansion in Afghanistan as a series of new capabilities are introduced into theatre during 2007, including the new Guided Multiple Launch Rocket System.

Upgraded FV430 Mk3 Bulldog vehicles arrive in Iraq

255. Over the year a significant body of work was taken forward to improve the air bridge, the operation and reliability of which has been subject to considerable military, Parliamentary and media scrutiny. To maintain the required levels of support, the operational air bridges were supplemented by air charter. This cost some £82M in 2006-07, of which some £56M was directly in support of operations in Iraq and Afghanistan. Although stretched, rotation of forces 'in-place' was successfully accomplished for both theatres, including a period of 'decompression' (time to adjust after intense combat conditions) in Cyprus for personnel returning from Afghanistan. There was also a steady improvement in consignment tracking as changes to regulations, training, and equipment began to deliver improved visibility of materiel in transit, addressing the concerns raise by the Public Accounts Committee in it report into *Assessing and reporting military readiness* in February 2006. A range of Logistic Information Systems are being introduced over the next five years that will provide the data to support full asset tracking in future.

256. Equipment that is no longer required also has to be removed from theatre. There was a series of such shipments from Iraq and Afghanistan during the year, and work was taken forward to make the reverse supply chain from both theatres function more effectively by applying the same tracking and consignment visibility processes used for outbound loads. It was also necessary to support the drawdown in the Balkans once the last major unit withdrew from Bosnia at the end of March 2007 (see paragraph 26 under *Current Operations*).

Performance against Customer Supplier Agreements

257. In 2006-07, the DLO achieved the agreed service levels for delivery against funded levels of readiness of 94.9% of its logistic support outputs, against a target of 98%, a slight increase from 94.5% in 2005-06. The shortfall against the target was principally driven by the following:

- defects and spares availability difficulties for surface ships, reflecting in part the impact of the reduced support period for the Royal Navy;

- difficulties supporting ageing Royal Fleet Auxiliary ships;

- unexpected defects with new classes of ships entering service;

- the high operational tempo affecting aircraft and spares availability for Hercules and Tornado, with significant damage sustained on operations requiring extensive repair on return home;

- difficulties in supporting the ageing Nimrod MR2 fleet, exacerbated by the loss of an aircraft in Afghanistan; and

- a shortfall in the availability of spares for the Typhoon and Hercules fleets, largely mitigated by working closely with industrial partners.

Sustainability for contingent operations

258. The last Logistic Sustainability and Deployability Audit was carried out in 2005. Resources are currently focused on providing the assets judged most likely to be needed to sustain operations and which could not be bought within assumed readiness times. Work is now underway to introduce a new logistic requirement setting and associated risk management process, known as Force Elements at Sustainability, to set sustainability targets on Defence Equipment and Support and then assess its ability to sustain the Force Elements at the required level. The intention is to assess any sustainability shortfall in capability terms and set funded sustainability targets in Service Delivery Agreements. This will then allow the Department to judge what might be made available within the relevant warning times in order to support operations up to the most demanding level envisaged in Defence Planning Assumptions, thus providing an updated assessment of our sustainability capability.

259. The Department continued to develop its ability to evaluate and articulate logistic performance and risk to ensure that decisions take full account of the logistics implications. Work also continued to ensure that the full logistic recuperation requirements and cost are understood as part of the process of restoring contingent forces' readiness to conduct a wide range of operations when the high tempo of current operations reduces.

Improving Logistics Effectiveness and Efficiency

Management of Logistics

260. Logistics is one of the enabling processes within the Department's Business Management System (see paragraphs 277-278 under *Business Management*). As process owner, the Chief of Defence Logistics was responsible during 2006-07 for the delivery of the logistics process across defence including the Equipment Capability Customer, industry, Defence Procurement Agency, Front Line Commands and the Chief of Joint Operations, as well as in the Defence Logistics Organisation. The revised Defence Logistics Programme provided the strategy and supporting delivery programme to take logistics forward. It drew together the most significant work currently underway in improving delivery of logistics across defence, including the current Defence Logistics Transformation Programme, and provides the strategic direction for logistics to meet the current and future needs of the operational commander.

The Defence Logistics Transformation Programme

261. The Defence Logistics Transformation Programme (DLTP) incorporates all logistic activity from one end of the acquisition cycle to the other. This extends from the early stages of equipment acquisition, through support in the Front Line Commands and in industry, until the final planning for and process of equipment disposal at the end of its operating life. The DLTP has operated as a single, coherent programme for more than two years, and delivered simplified, lean processes driven by the operational users; improved availability of equipment; reduced repair times and equipment holdings; and improvements in the performance of the supply chain. Its success has produced a sound understanding across the logistic community of the benefits achieved by an end-to-end support concept. Accordingly during 2006-07 there was a staged transfer and delegation of responsibility for delivering and managing further logistics transformation from the core DLTP team into

the wider Defence Logistics Organisation, the Defence Procurement Agency and the Front Line Commands. The DLTP also prepared the ground for the recognition of the importance of through-life management in the Defence Industrial Strategy and the work to implement that in the Defence Acquisition Change Programme (see paragraphs 170-172 under *Future Capabilities and Infrastructure*, and the essay on page 101). The merger of the Defence Logistic Organisation and the Defence Procurement Agency into Defence Equipment and Support in April 2007 recognised and embodied this approach and will help build on it further.

262. The programme has consistently met its efficiency targets. In the 2005-06 *Annual Report and Accounts* the estimated savings were reported as between £500M and £575M against a target of £539M by the end of March 2006. Following an internal audit to validate the efficiencies achieved, the final total rose to £662M (see table 3 under *Efficiency and Change*). This reflected identification of £55M of savings from the upkeep of warships and £30M of additional benefits in Strike Command that had not been included in the original claim, and better evidence for other benefits than had originally been assumed. A further £225M to £300M estimated further efficiencies were achieved in 2006-07, against a target of £175M. Work is in hand to validate these. In parallel with the transfer of responsibility for delivering logistics transformation (see paragraph 261), responsibility for delivery of efficiency targets is also now being delegated across the broader logistics community.

263. Examples of improved logistics effectiveness and efficiency achieved during the2006-07 are set out below. Figures are for in-year benefits delivery unless otherwise stated, and are subject to validation:

- At RAF Cottesmore, introduction of a pulse-line, partnering with industry and improved repair processes has enabled:

  – a 43% reduction in the time required to upgrade Harriers from GR7 to GR9 standard;

  – a 40% reduction in the time required to repair Harrier Pegasus engines

- The December 2005 contract with Rolls-Royce for full support and a guaranteed agreed level of availability for the Tornado RB199 whole engine delivered savings of £43M and 100% availability during 2006-07;

- Improvement in Tornado F3 deep repair and maintenance at RAF Leuchars saved £24M over ten years;

- The application of Lean thinking to the operational planning process in Afghanistan reduced the number of convoys required in-theatre by over 50%, both improving logistics efficiency and minimising risks to personnel;

- The Merlin Integrated Operational Support contract delivered £6M through payments for achieved flying hours and arrangements to incentivise agreed levels of aircraft serviceability, operational fleet aircraft numbers and training system availability;

- Adoption of lean techniques brought about a 20% increase in output for Puma helicopter deep repair and maintenance;

- The creation of a single repair facility and adoption of lean techniques led to an increase in repair capacity for Gem helicopter engines from 90 to 120 a year;

- A reduction in turnaround time for deep repair and maintenance of Apache helicopters from over 50 days to 42 days by introduction of a Lean pulse-line for depth maintenance;

- Introduction of lean techniques at RAF Odiham provided an additional 1,000 Chinook flying hours against a background of an operational tempo requiring up to 60% of the available operational Chinook fleet to be deployed on operations in different theatres for considerable periods;

- Improvements to the supply chain have reduced delivery times for routine demands in the United Kingdom and north west Europe from 28 days to an average of twelve days.

Puma Helictopter

Restructuring

264. The Defence Logistics Organisation continued to drive forward its major restructuring programme aimed at improving its efficiency and effectiveness. In July 2006, approval was granted for Phase One of the organisation's project to collocate the majority of its staff with DPA staff in the Bath/Bristol area (see paragraph 321 under *Estate*). Collocation was given further impetus by the decision, also taken in July 2006, to merge the DLO with the Defence Procurement Agency as Defence Equipment and Support in April 2007.

Defence Aviation Repair Agency

265. In May 2007 it was announced that DARA will merge with ABRO, forming a new defence support organisation from April 2008. This will include the retained Electronics Business Unit at RAF Sealand and, following market testing, the Large Aircraft Business Unit (VC10) at RAF St Athan. The DARA Transformation Team continued working to establish whether sale of DARA's Rotary and Components business might deliver better value for money for defence and longevity for the businesses. If it does not, these business units will also join the new defence support organisation.

Red Dragon

266. The Red Dragon project structure continued to play an important role in managing MoD's interest at St Athan in South Wales. In particular it worked with the Welsh Assembly Government over the future of its Aerospace Business Park following the decision in February 2006 to transfer Fast Jet maintenance and repair work from RAF St Athan to RAF Marham. In January 2007 it was announced that St Athan will be home to a new tri-service Defence Training campus under Package 1 of the Defence Training Review. The Red Dragon project will continue until October 2007 to achieve a number of intermediate objectives, following which responsibility for St Athan will transfer to Defence Estates and the Defence Training Review project.

Equipment Disposals

267. The Disposal Services Agency had a successful year, achieving £81.5M in gross sales, including £9M of repayment sales and £3M sales on behalf of other Government Departments. It met all its key targets, including the achievement of customer satisfaction scores of over 94%. Two of the three surplus Type 23 frigates sold to Chile in 2006-07 completed their refurbishment and were handed over to the Chilean Navy in November 2006 and March 2007, with the third ship due to be handed over during 2007-08. Although its function remained the same, the DSA ceased to be an agency at the end of March 2007 and became the Disposal Services Authority within Defence Equipment and Support.

Further sources of information

280. Additional Information on Logistics is available from the following sources:

– Quarterly PSA reports to HM Treasury at www.mod.uk;
– Annual *UK Defence Statistics* available at www.dasa.mod.uk;
– *SR2004 Efficiency Technical Note* available at www.mod.uk;
– The Defence Logistics Organisation Plan 2006 available at www.mod.uk;
– *Defence Logistics Programme 2006* available at www.mod.uk;
– *ABRO Annual Report and Accounts* available at www.official-documents.gov.uk;
– *DARA Annual Report and Accounts* available at www.official-documents.gov.uk;
– *Disposal Services Agency Annual Report and Accounts* available at www.official-documents.gov.uk.
– *Transforming logistics support for fast jets.* (HC825) at www.official-documents.gov.uk.

Essay – Supplying Operations

Keeping soldiers, sailors and airmen on operations housed, equipped, fed, supplied and looked after, and supplying the fuel, spares and support to keep their equipment running, is an enormous task. At the back of this is the Joint Supply Chain, providing the essential backbone that makes support to operations work. As such, it is fundamental to operational performance. In recent years there has been considerable work to reshape the Supply Chain by adopting a more integrated and joint approach to minimise waste and drive up performance.

Strategic transport is acquired by Defence Supply Chain Operation and Movements, which coordinates the movement of personnel and their supplies to operations based on the movement requirements set by the Permanent Joint Headquarters. These have then to be translated into the air, sea and land transport assets provided by a mixture of national and international operators including military units and civilian businesses and prioritised for movement. The cost of this strategic lift in 2006 was some £750M, or 2% of the defence budget. Providing air transport requires taking a multitude of factors into account. These can include aircraft serviceability, the weather, refuelling limitations, diplomatic clearance, crew availability, Defensive Aid Suite availability and airfield capacity. Air freight is moved on a combination of military and civilian aircraft to both Iraq and Afghanistan. The core of this service is provided by RAF C17 aircraft, which usually undertake six sorties per week. Commercial A300M freighters provide a further six sorties a week. Large ad hoc consignments and outsize loads are covered by hiring Antonov aircraft. 463 civilian air freighters and 454 passenger aircraft were chartered in 2006-07. All this equates to about 20 flights a week for Iraq and Afghanistan combined. RAF Brize Norton handled over 8,000 tonnes outbound to Iraq and 13,500 tonnes to Afghanistan, and about 3,400 tonnes inbound. These totals are comparable with those handled by major regional airports. This was supplemented by surface delivery options including three Defence Strategic Sealift ships. A weekly service from Southampton despatched 810 containers to Iraq in 2006-07, and Felixstowe handled 1,364 containers for Afghanistan.

The quantities involved are immense. Since the start of operations in Iraq 23 million items worth £493M have been delivered to theatre. This includes 240,000 days worth of Operational Ration Packs, fresh food costing about £21M a year, clothing costing about £13M a year, and about 27 tonnes of mail a month. Some three million items worth some £31M have so far been delivered to Afghanistan, including about 88,000 days worth of ration packs, 56 tonnes of fresh rations a month worth about £2.5M over a year, clothing costing about £7M a year, and about 18 tonnes of mail a month. This is an enormous volume of freight transported over long distances in inhospitable terrain. It also, of course, includes the provision of gift boxes for every sailor, soldier and airman deployed on operations on Christmas Day. Substantial amounts have eventually to be returned to the UK, so the reverse Supply Chain is also busy. Efforts continue to make this all work as well as possible. Since September 2006 there has been a dedicated cell to measure performance, quickly identify areas of concern, investigate them and instigate appropriate remedial action. Work to improve the line of communication reduced surface transit times to Afghanistan further from 100 days in December 2006 to an average of 71 days by the end of April 2007.

Fuel is equally essential and has its own supply chain, which delivers over 715 million litres of fuel a year to support operations and training in the UK and worldwide. The demands of military operations and the virtual non existence of a fuel supply chain in Afghanistan have required bespoke solutions. These have not constrained operations on the ground, but have required careful planning of strategic air support.

Passengers also need moving. In 2006-07 there were over 160,000 passenger movements to support operations in Iraq and Afghanistan. All personnel entering the operational theatres by air must do so in aircraft protected by Defence Aid Suites, which precludes using civilian operators. Some RAF Tristar passenger aircraft are appropriately equipped and make a number of sorties per week to Afghanistan. Personnel travelling to Iraq are flown by commercial air charter to a benign hub, from where they make the last stage of journey into Basra on protected military C130 aircraft.

There is a continuing programme of coordinated investment in Information Systems to improve supply management and control further. Front line users are seeing the benefit of more user friendly and automated systems, together with more streamlined and joint processes, improving delivery. A new Supply Priority System was introduced in 2006, which simplified the arrangements for making a 'demand'. The Joint Demand Tracking System was also rolled out to all three Services in September 2006. This allows any unit with access to the MoD's Intranet to identify the status of their demands on the supply system and the latest recorded location of the items being provided to satisfy those demands. It is proving an effective, popular and low-cost information tool and is contributing significantly to increased confidence in the Supply Chain. Further improvements are in hand, including the Management of the Joint Deployed Inventory and Consignment Visibility projects, other engineering and asset management systems such as Joint Asset Management and Engineering Solution, and work to create a service oriented architecture which will allow information systems to share data, giving both operational commanders and Integrated Project Team Leaders clear visibility of whether the equipment they are using and supporting is in the supply chain, fitted to a platform, in the home base or deployed.

Business Management

Objective: Deliver improved ways of working.

Assessment and Performance Measures

Assessment: The Department was assessed as one of the stronger departments in the Capability Review. There were significant developments in the Department's systems, process and structures. These included a new system for managing strategic risk, major changes to improve acquisition performance leading up to the establishment of Defence Equipment and Support, and the launch of a further study into streamlining the Head Office in the light of the Capability Review.

Organisation and Governance:

- Substantial programme of Defence Management Board development, including engagement with major investment decisions and Introduction of new strategic risk process;
- Launch of Defence Acquisition Change Programme in July 2006, and establishment of Defence Equipment and Support organisation in April 2007;
- Positive result from MoD Capability Review;
- Launch of programme to streamline the Head Office and how it works.

Implementation of the Business Management System:

- Business Management System incorporated into normal business;
- Establishment of new Commercial Process under Defence Commercial Director.

Top Level Organisation and Governance

269. Work continued to improve the efficiency and effectiveness of the Department's management and governance arrangements, which drive the way we work to deliver military capability. The Ministry of Defence's *Departmental Framework Document* sets out the framework within which the Department operates to deliver defence outputs, the roles, responsibilities and governance framework that underpin the business of defence, and explains how these integrate to support the delivery of the Defence Vision and defence outputs. This is summarised in Annex B on the Organisation and Management of Defence. The Department follows as closely as possible the code of good practice on *Corporate Governance in Central Government Departments.* Annual reports against the code are published on www.mod.uk in parallel with the Annual Report and Accounts.

Defence Management Board

270. Reflecting the pressures generated by the imperative of sustaining the high operational tempo while simultaneously taking forward a series of major change and efficiency programmes at home (see paragraph 144 under *Efficiency and Change*), the tempo of the Defence Management Board significantly increased during the year and it developed several initiatives to take a more strategic grip of the Department's business. In particular, as recommended by the *Enabling Acquisition Change* report, as well as continuing to oversee the development of major programmes across the Department, the Board took on

an active role in making the most significant acquisition decisions, previously considered solely by the Department's Investment Approvals Board. It also took forward a new approach to the management of strategic risk (see paragraph 271 below). In pursuit of openness where possible in the spirit of the Freedom of Information Act, the Agendas and summaries of conclusions of Defence Management Board meetings are now published on the MoD website one month in arrears, and a consolidated list of the papers considered by the Board is published at the end of the year.

Risk Management

271. Active management of risk is fundamental to the effective achievement of defence objectives, and is central to the way business is conducted within the Department. It informs operational decision making, contingency planning, investment decisions and the financial planning process. During the year the Defence Management Board established a new strategic risk approach reflecting the context within which defence operates. Strategic risks are categorised into six realms. One Board member leads work in each Realm, assessing and managing the risks and raising issues to the Board as the need arises and another (the 'Inquisitor') provides challenge to them and encourages debate in the Board (see Table 11 below). The Board reviews each of the Realms through the course of the year in order to decide whether it needs to take specific action to improve the position and to regularly consider the relationship with the risks reported by other parts of the Department which form an integral element of the Board's quarterly performance reviews.

Table 11: Defence Management Board Strategic Risks

Strategic Risk Realm	Leader	Inquisitor
Operational or other failure	Chief of Defence Staff	Non-Executive Director
Making the Defence Case	Vice Chief of Defence Staff	Finance Director
Departmental decision making	2nd Permanent Under Secretary	Chief of the General Staff
Attracting and keeping talent	Chief of the Naval Staff	Non-Executive Director
Maximising technological opportunities whilst minimising vulnerabilities	Chief Scientific Advisor	Chief of Defence Materiel
Perception of the Armed Forces – at home and abroad	Chief of the Air Staff	Non-Executive Director

272. The Department has a wide range of control and assurance processes, including the Business Management System (see paragraphs 277-278 below). The effective operation of these is overseen on behalf of the Defence Management Board by the Defence Audit Committee, underpinning the Permanent Secretary's annual Statement on Internal Control (see pages xx-xx in the *Departmental Resource Accounts*). The Audit Committee produces a separate summary of its work, in line with the Corporate Governance code of good practice, which is published on www.mod.uk in parallel with the Annual Report and Accounts.

Business Continuity Exercise

Acquisition Change

273. In response to the Defence Industrial Strategy's call for internal change, the Enabling Acquisition Change report was published in July 2006. This recommended wide ranging changes to process, organisation, culture and behaviours to bring a greater unity of purpose across the planning and acquisition communities. In particular it recommended the creation of the Defence Equipment and Support organisation, through merging the Defence Procurement Agency and the Defence Logistics Organisation (see paragraph 161 under *Future Capability and Infrastructure*, and the essay on *Defence Industrial Strategy* on page 101).

Capability Review

274. A Capability Review of the MoD as a Department of State (but not of its role as the United Kingdom's strategic military headquarters) was carried out as part of the wider Civil Service Capability Review Programme. Work began in October 2006, leading to publication of the Report on 27 March 2007. The Review produced an assessment of the Department's capability to deliver now and into the future. The Capability Review Team included business and public

sector leaders from outside Government with national recognition for their achievements and successes. In gathering evidence the team:

● interviewed over 120 members of MoD's Senior Civil Service, their military equivalents, key MoD customers from across Government and stakeholders, including in academia and industry;

● held eleven large workshops across the country, meeting with over 200 members of staff and the military;

● hosted a number of smaller ad-hoc groups of staff to discuss specific lines of enquiry in more detail;

● carried out eight visits, ranging from Basra to the Defence Procurement Agency in Abbey Wood, Fleet Headquarters in Portsmouth and Headquarters RAF Strike Command in High Wycombe;

● observed at least eight committees, including the Defence Management Board and Chiefs of Staff committee; and

● reviewed numerous publications and documentation.

275. The MoD came out of the Review as one of the stronger departments. Of the ten elements in the model of capability (see essay on page 147) the Department's capability for future delivery was assessed as 'strong' or 'well placed' in those for 'focus on outcomes', 'ignite passion, pace and drive', 'take responsibility for leading delivery and change' and 'base choices on evidence'. The elements for 'build capability', 'build common purpose', 'plan, resource and prioritise' and 'manage performance' were assessed as a 'development areas'. The elements for 'set direction' and 'develop clear roles, responsibilities and business model(s)' were assessed as 'urgent development areas'. There were no areas of 'serious concerns'.

276. The review team was impressed by the work the MoD is doing at all levels to deliver operational effect in theatre. It commented positively on the extent to which the Department is on course to meet its Public Service Agreement Targets, on the Department's existing change programmes, and on the far-reaching changes to improve acquisition skills and performance. However, the report acknowledged some significant challenges, which the Permanent Secretary and Chief of the Defence Staff have committed the Department to dealing with through the MoD Action Plan. This aims to strengthen corporate leadership, clarify and simplify the Department's operating model, and redouble efforts to build the capability of all defence personnel, military and civilian. It includes the programme of work

to streamline the Head Office and the way it works set up in early 2007.

MoD at Abbey Wood, Bristol

Implementation of the Business Management System

277. The Department has continued to implement the Business Management System (BMS) introduced in April 2005 to embed continuous improvement across the system. The process owners for the six pan-

Departmental enabling processes (logistics, civilian workforce, Service personnel, communications, financial management and commodity procurement) continued to use their authority to ensure common standards and processes where applicable across the Department. The BMS approach has now been incorporated into normal business and relevant activities are reported in the chapters on *Logistics*, *Personnel Management*, *Future Personnel*, *Reputation*, *Resources*, and *Future Capabilities and Infrastructure*. They are held to account by the Defence Audit Committee for the management of their processes as part of the assurance work underpinning the Statement on Internal Control.

278. Based on the work carried out as part of the Defence Acquisition Change Programme a new Commercial Process was established during the year. Under this the Defence Commercial Director is responsible for ensuring that a robust and effective process is in place in respect of all commercial activity across defence, together with those elements of procurement that fall within the definition of an enabling process (such as responsibility for ensuring that all commercial aspects of the procurement strategy adopted are addressed). Work is now underway to define the scope and parameters of this process and to ensure these principles are embedded within the Department.

Further sources of information

279. In addition to the Statement on Internal Control in the *Departmental Resource Accounts*, further Information on Business Management is available from the following sources:

- MoD Capability Review available at http://www.civilservice.gov.uk/reform/capability_reviews/reports.asp
- *Ministry of Defence Framework Document* available at www.mod.uk;
- *Corporate governance code for central Government departments: Code of Good Practice* available at www.hm-treasury.gov.uk;
- Defence Annual Corporate Governance Reports available at www.mod.uk;
- Defence Audit Committee Annual Reports available at www.mod.uk;
- *Enabling Acquisition Change Report at* www.mod.uk.

Essay – The Capability Review

In October 2005, the Cabinet Secretary announced that he would develop a programme of Capability Reviews to assess how well equipped departments were to meet their delivery challenges, and to provide targeted support to make any improvements required. The three main aims were:

- To improve the capability of the Civil Service to meet today's delivery objectives and be ready for the challenges of tomorrow;

- To assure the Public and Ministers that the Civil Service leadership is equipped to develop and deliver departmental strategies; and

- To help departments act on long term key development areas and therefore provide assurance on future delivery.

The reviews were to assess the capability of departments' senior leadership against ten elements across leadership, strategy and delivery using the model of capability below.

Further details are available at www.civilservice.gov.uk.

The MoD Capability Review

The MoD's was reviewed as a Department of State, but not as the United Kingdom's military strategic headquarters, which was outside the boundaries of the Capability Review process. Pre-fieldwork activities ran from October 2006 to January 2007, followed by fieldwork during February and March 2007. The Review Team was drawn from the private sector, the wider public sector and board-level members of other Government Departments, comprising:

- Alexis Cleveland, Chief Executive Pension Service, Department of Work and Pensions;

- Bill McCarthy, Director General Policy and Strategy, Department of Health;

- Sir David Henshaw, Former Chief Executive of Liverpool City Council;

- Christopher Lendrum, Chairman Barclay's Pension Funds Trustees Ltd; and

- Peter Mather, Vice President Europe, BP.

In the pre-fieldwork phase a team from the Prime Minister's Delivery Unit gathered evidence to develop a picture of the challenges the Department faced and generate Key Lines of Enquiry for the external Review Team members to use during the fieldwork phase. This process comprised:

- reviewing high level departmental documents, including the Annual Report, Service Delivery Agreements, Defence Management Board records, performance reports, staff survey results, leadership and staff development programmes, communication plans, media strategy, Strategic Guidance, efficiency targets, and business planning framework and processes;

- holding eleven workshops to gather the views and opinions of over 200 staff mainly at 1* level and above, although one workshop was arranged for about 60 Band B/C staff and another for a selection of MoD's key external stakeholders including representatives from industry;

- interviewing Ministers and members of the Defence Management Board;

- visiting locations LAND Command, Sandhurst, HQ Fleet, the Permanent Joint Headquarters, HQ Strike Command, and a three day visit to Basrah Air Station; and

- observing a range of senior meetings and committees.

This prepared the Review Team members for the fieldwork phase, which comprised an intensive two week period of interviews and assessment. They interviewed over 100 people, including the Secretary of State for Defence, other Defence Ministers, members of the Defence Management Board, senior civilian and Service personnel in MoD and other Government Departments (including the Foreign Office, Cabinet Office, the Treasury, the Department of Transport and the Department of Trade and Industry[1]), academics, senior industry representatives, and senior officials at the United Nations, NATO and the French Ministry of Defence. They presented their findings to the Defence Management Board on 21 February and then worked with the Board to develop an action plan that addressed the key findings. This was published internally, along with the Report, on 27 March 2007. The report is also at www.civilservice.gov.uk

Key findings

The Review Team acknowledged the hugely complex and challenging objectives with which the Department is grappling and the sustained high level of operational commitment. They were very impressed with the clarity of purpose they found. But they made a series of detailed observations, both of strengths and future capability challenges:

- Under **Leadership**, they observed both that the Department is held in high regard domestically and internationally, and the passion and commitment of its staff. The MoD has made significant progress towards the creation of an integrated Department, with joined-up working across all three Armed Services and the Civil Service. This continued in the great openness to change that they found throughout the Department. However, there was a clear need for the Defence Management Board to take a stronger corporate role, particularly in articulating how the overarching vision links into strategy and delivery;

- **Strategy** was a particular strength. The vision and purpose of the Department were well articulated. Defence Strategic Guidance provided a strong platform for aligning effort and prioritising departmental activity and resources. But challenges remained in developing a sense of common purpose across Whitehall and wider;

- On **Delivery**, the Department was praised for its ambitious and extensive change portfolio, and the success with which it is being delivered. But performance management systems lacked agility and there was a culture of a lack of clarity around roles, accountability and authority.

The MoD Response

The Permanent Secretary and Chief of the Defence Staff jointly welcomed the findings, and committed the Department to meeting the challenges identified. They set out four key areas in which they would drive improvements:

- To strengthen the corporate leadership of the department;

- To clarify and simplify the MoD's operating model, streamlining the head office and significantly reducing costs at the centre;

- To work more closely with other Departments across Whitehall; and

- To redouble the department's efforts to build its human capability.

Implementation of these action areas has now begun.

1 DTI became the Department for Business, Enterprise and Regulatory Reform, on 28 June 2007.

Resources

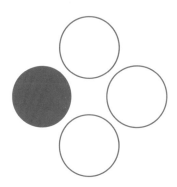

Finance

Objective: Control our expenditure within allocated financial resources, while maximising our outputs

Assessment and Performance Measures

Assessment: Total Defence expenditure during the year was some £34Bn, including a net cash requirement of some £31.4Bn. The additional cost of operations was just under £1.8Bn. The Department remained firmly in command of its finances. Overall defence expenditure in 2006-07 remained well within the total resources voted by Parliament, and the Department met all its Treasury Control Totals, but the cost of operations exceeded the resources voted to cover them by some £21M (1.4%).

In Year Departmental Financial Management

- Net resource consumption of £31,519M for provision of Defence capability against resources voted by Parliament of £32,349M;
- Net additional Resource and Capital expenditure of £1,796M on operations against resources voted by Parliament of £1,876M;
- Expenditure against war pensions and allowances of £1,038M, against resources voted by Parliament of £1,048M;
- DEL outturn of £32,009M against Resource Departmental Expenditure limit of £32,678M;
- Outturn of £6,849M against Capital Departmental Expenditure Limit of £6,999M.

Defence Budget and Spending

Departmental Outturn

280. Planned expenditure for the year was set out in the *Ministry of Defence: The Government's Expenditure Plans 2006-07 to 2007-08*, and in the Main, Winter, and Spring Supplementary Estimates voted by Parliament. Provisional outturn for the year was set out in the Public Expenditure Outturn White Paper 2006-07 which was published in July 2007. Table 12 compares final performance against the final estimates approved by Parliament, as reported in the Statement of Parliamentary Supply on page 223 of the Accounts. It includes Resource Departmental Expenditure Limit (Resource DEL), Annually Managed Expenditure (AME) and Non Budget, but does not include income payable to the Consolidated Fund, shown in Note 5 to the accounts. Total Defence expenditure in 2006-07 was contained within overall voted provision, with an overall Net Resource underspend, which includes both cash and non cash items and unallocated provisions, of £819M.

281. As set out in the explanation of variation between Estimate and Outturn in the Departmental Resource Accounts on page 199, the principal explanation for the underspend in RfR1 of £830,700,000 is due to an underspend in AME of £666,526,000 arising from a review of nuclear provisions, in preparation for the Quinquennial review of liabilities by the Nuclear Installations Inspectorate during 2007-08. There is an underspend within Resouce DEL of £148,322,000; and a small underspend of £15,852,000 in Non Budget.

Stores Accountants in the Naval Stores'

Cost of Operations

282. No formal budget is set for the cost of operations. The Department is voted additional resources (Requests for Resources 2) to cover the net additional costs of Operations and Conflict Prevention Programmed Expenditure, and the request for resources is normally made in the Supplementary Estimates which is the first occasion when the Department can reach a reasonably firm forecast of costs. Total expenditure is set out in Table 13 below. Overall expenditure in 2006-07 was £1,796M, including £956M for operations in Iraq, £56M for operations in the Balkans (Bosnia and Kosovo), and £742M for operations in Afghanistan. Additional detail is shown in Note 2 to the Departmental Resource Accounts (page 236).

Table 12: 2006-07 Parliamentary Controls (£M – rounded)

	Final Voted Provision	Net Resource Outturn	Variation
Request for Resources 1 (Provision of Defence Capability)	32,349	31,519	-830
Request for Resources 2 (net additional cost of operations)	1,427	1,448	21
Request for Resources 3 (war pensions and allowances)	1,048	1,038	-10
Net Resources	34,824	34,005	-819
Net Cash Requirement	33,746	31,454	-2,292

283. Although overall defence expenditure in 2006-07 remained well within the total resources voted by Parliament, the Department exceeded by some £21M the resources voted to cover the costs of operations (Request for Resources 2). The Comptroller and Auditor General therefore qualified the accounts in this respect. The excess is entirely against the provision for non-cash costs, for which the Department seeks a transfer from Request for Resources 1 to Request for Resources 2 at Supplementary Estimates. It mainly reflects the use of more Hellfire missiles in Afghanistan than had been forecast at the time the Department submitted Supplementary Estimates and increased depreciation charges for some military equipment damaged or destroyed on operations. Decisions by military commanders on the ground on the resources they need to use in combat cannot be constrained by the accounting consequences, and the scale of operations during the year was such that the transfer between the two categories of voted expenditure requested

of Parliament turned out to be slightly too low. The Department will identify any appropriate lessons in time to inform the production of the Winter and Spring Supplementary Estimates for 2007-08.

Resources by Departmental Aims and Objectives

284. Details of the MoD's expenditure for 2006-07 broken down against our three primary Public Service Agreement objectives are summarised in Table 14 below and set out in detail in the Statement of Operating Costs by Departmental Aims and Objectives (page 228) and Note 24 (page 256) to the Departmental Resource Accounts. It is shown net of the £56M for excess Appropriation-in-Aid and Consolidated Fund Extra Receipts included in total outturn of £33,949M in Table 14 (see Note 5 to the Defence Resource Accounts 2006-07 on page 241).

Table 13: Net Additional Costs of Operations 2006-07 (£M – rounded)

	Final Voted Estimate	Outturn	Variation
Resource			
Iraq (Op Telic)	807	787	-20
Afghanistan (Op Herrick)	516	564	48
Balkans (Op Oculus)	53	56	3
Programme Expenditure (African and Global pool)	51	41	-10
Total Resource	**1,427**	**1,448**	21
Capital			
Iraq (Op Telic)	195	169	-26
Afghanistan (Op Herrick)	254	178	-76
Balkans (Op Oculus)	0	1	1
Total Capital	**449**	**348**	-101
Total Net additional cost of Operations	**1,876**	**1,796**	-80

Table 14 Resources by Departmental Objectives 2006-07

	Net Operating Cost (£M – rounded)
Objective 1: Achieving success in the tasks we undertake	3,711
Objective 2: Being ready to respond to the tasks that might arise	26,293
Objective 3: Building for the future	2,907
(Total RfRs 1&2)	32,911
Paying war pension benefits (RfR3)	1,038
Total Net Operating Costs	**33,949**

Outturn against Departmental Expenditure Limit (Budgetary Basis):

285. In addition to the Net Resource controls set out above, against which Departmental expenditure is presented in the Departmental Resource Accounts and audited by the National Audit Office, the Department works within two Departmental Expenditure Limits (DELs) covering both the majority of the Department's operating costs (excluding some non-cash costs specifically relating to nuclear provisions) and capital expenditure. Detailed outturns by Top Level Budget Holder against their RfR1 DEL control totals are set out in Table 15 below. The Estimates figures shown in Note 2 of the Departmental Resource Accounts were based on data at the half year point, and there are inevitable movements between TLBs between then and the year end reflecting, for example, changes in budgetary responsibilities between TLBs. The total outturn for 2006-07 was contained within the RDEL with an underspend of £669M of which £180M was Near Cash. The underspend of £150M in CDEL was due to receipts from estates disposal in a PFI projects, for which there will be corresponding capital spend in later years. The RDEL underspend mainly resulted from lower than expected depreciation and write offs. The main pressures on the budget during the year were for pay costs, utilities and fuel.

Resource and Capital DEL Variances (Budgetary Basis):

286. Table 15 shows an underspend of £669M against Resource DEL and £150M against Capital DEL.

- Commander in Chief Fleet (£2M underspend Resource DEL and £5M Capital DEL): The underspend was the consequence of lower than anticipated write-offs on balance transfers which reduced spend against Resource DEL. The underspend in Capital DEL is a result of slippage in estates projects.

- General Officer Commanding (N Ireland) (£7M underspend Resource DEL): The underspend largely reflects accelerated savings from normalisation.

- Commander-in-Chief Land Command (£10M overspend Resource DEL): The reasons for the overspend included higher stock consumption and increased costs of multi activity contracts. The reason for the latter was principally an actuarially certified increase in the provision for industrial injuries pensions due to Locally Engaged Civilians in Germany.

- Air Officer Commanding-in-Chief RAF Strike Command (£13M Resource DEL overspend and £4M underspend Capital DEL): The overspend in Resource DEL was principally due to an increase in the civilian early departure provision. The underspend in Capital DEL is principally due to Defence Modernisation Fund projects.

- Chief of Joint Operations (£9M overspend Resource DEL and £2M underspend Capital DEL): The Resource DEL overspend was related to a court case settlement endorsed by HM Treasury (Gibraltar Service Police pay) and exceptional utilities inflation, mainly in BF Cyprus. The Capital DEL underspend is almost entirely due to slippage in capital works projects.

- Chief of Defence Logistics (£249M underspend Resource DEL and £8M overspend in Capital DEL): The DLO recorded a Resource DEL underspend because there was a significantly lower number of fixed asset write-offs and reduced depreciation of assets. There were also underspends on Defence Modernisation Fund projects and in infrastructure projects. The Capital DEL overspend is principally attributable to an overspend on capital spares.

- Adjutant General (£21M underspend): The underspend relates to the release of provision for future redundancy payments.

- Air Officer Commanding-in-Chief RAF Personnel & Training Command (£39M underspend Resource DEL and £7M underspend in Capital DEL): This underspend was due to a reduced number of UK civilians on loan to the US which has resulted in lower receipts and release of provision for redundancies which is no longer required. The underspend in CDEL is attributable to a reduction of funding for long service advances of pay.

- Central (£34M underspend on Resource DEL and £7M underspend on Capital DEL): The Resource DEL underspend was primarily due to the underspend on Defence Modernisation Fund projects; additional receipts have been recovered. The Capital DEL underspend is principally due to slippage of Chief of Defence Intelligence projects.

- Defence Procurement Agency (£87M overspend on Resource DEL and £10M overspend on Capital DEL): The DPA recorded a Resource DEL overspend because there was a significant number of stock write-off and depreciation of assets. The Capital DEL overspend is principally attributable to an overspend on expenditure on fighting equipment.

● Defence Estates (£116M overspend in Resource DEL and £14M in Capital DEL): There was an overspend in Indirect R DEL mainly on depreciation costs due to Quinquennial asset revaluations and offsetting impairment revisions. The overspend in Capital DEL was due to increased expenditure on estates projects.

● Corporate Science and Technology (£4M underspend Resource DEL): The underspend is due to a correction of a prior year error.

Table 15: Defence Budget Outturn against Departmental Expenditure Limits (DEL) 2006-07 (RFR1) (£M)

	DEL	Outturn	Var against DEL
Resource DEL (net of A in As)			
Allocated to TLBs:			
Commander-in-Chief Fleet	2,150	2,148	-2
General Officer Commanding (Northern Ireland)	396	389	-7
Commander-in-Chief Land Command	4,312	4,322	10
Commander-in-Chief Strike Command	1,911	1,924	13
Chief of Joint Operations	382	391	9
Chief of Defence Logistics	13,037	12,788	-249
Adjutant General	1,597	1,576	-21
Commander-in-Chief Personnel and Training Command	801	762	-39
Central (Incl CBFM)	2,206	2,172	-34
Defence Procurement Agency	2,264	2,351	87
Defence Estates	2,576	2,692	116
Corporate Science and Technology	528	524	-4
Sub total	32,160	32,039	-121
Not Allocated	518	-30	-548
Total	**32,678**	**32,009**	**-669**
of which Near Cash in RDEL	**21,832**	**21,652**	**-180**
Capital DEL (net of A in As)			
Allocated to TLBs:			
Commander-in-Chief Fleet	19	14	-5
General Officer Commanding (Northern Ireland)	2	2	0
Commander-in-Chief Land Command	76	75	-1
Commander-in-Chief Strike Command	11	7	-4
Chief of Joint Operations	6	4	-2
Chief of Defence Logistics	1,235	1,243	8
Adjutant General	15	15	0
Commander-in-Chief Personnel and Training Command	18	11	-7
Central	51	44	-7
Defence Procurement Agency	5,269	5,279	10
Defence Estates	126	140	14
Corporate Science and Technology	0	0	0
Sub total	6,828	6,834	6
Not Allocated	171	15	-156
Total	**6,999**	**6,849**	**-150**

Table 16: Reconciliation between Estimate and DEL £M

	Provision	Outturn
Resource Estimate (RfR 1)	**32,349**	**31,519**
Annually Managed Expenditure	-210	456
Non Budget	-13	3
Non Voted	552	87
Less: Consolidated Fund Extra Receipts		-56
Resource DEL (Table 15)	**32,678**	**32,009**
Capital Estimate	**7,441**	**7,198**
RfR 2	-449	-348
AME	7	0
Capital Spending by by Non Departmental Bodies	0	-1
Capital DEL (Table 15)	**6,999**	**6,849**

Reconciliation between Estimate and DEL

287. Table 16 provides a reconciliation between the outturn shown in the DEL Table 15 with the Estimate, to assist in understanding the differences between the tables presented here in the Annual Report, and those shown in the Departmental Resource Accounts. The totals shown for R DEL and C DEL are for RfR1 only. Non voted items in this table relate to the cash release of nuclear provisions which is not a Parliamentary control, but which makes up part of the Department's net cash requirement. There is a small element of non voted funding within Capital DEL.

Reconciliation between Estimates, Accounts and Budgets.

288. The Department is required to use different frameworks to plan, control and account for income and expenditure. The planning framework uses resource and capital budgets broken down into DEL and AME and these budgets are referred to throughout the Spending Review, Budget Red Book, Pre-budget Report and individual Departmental Annual Reports. Control is exercised through the Parliamentary approval of Supply in the Main and Supplementary Estimates. Some elements of DEL and AME are outside the Supply process. Equally, some expenditure is voted but outside the scope of the budgets. Audited outturn figures are reported within the Departmental Resource Accounts, prepared under the conventions of UK Generally Accepted Accounting Practice (UK GAAP), adapted for the public sector, with adjustments necessary to reconcile to either the planning or control totals. Table 17 provides the reconciliation between these three bases.

Table 17: Reconciliation of Resource Expenditure between Estimates, Accounts and Budgets (£M – rounded)

	Provision	Outturn
Net Resources Outturn (Estimates)	**34,824**	**34,005**
Adjustments to include:		
Consolidated Fund Extra Receipts in the OCS		-56
Other adjustments		
Net Operating Cost (Accounts)	**34,824**	**33,949**
Adjustments to remove:		
Voted expenditure outside the budget	-4	12
Adjustments to include:		
Other Consolidated Fund Extra Receipts		56
Resource consumption on non departmental public bodies	16	16
Unallocated Resource Provision	220	
Resource Budget Outturn (Budget	**35,056**	**34,033**
of which		
Departmental Expenditure Limits (DEL)	34,104	33,451
Annually Managed Expenditure (AME)	952	582

Major Contractual Commitments

289. As of 31 March 2007 the Department's outstanding contractual commitments (excluding those already reported within the Balance Sheet) were some £17.8Bn (see Note 25 to the Departmental Resource Accounts on page 263). This represents capital expenditure which the Department is contractually obliged to pay in future years (assuming delivery of a satisfactory product). While this is built up from more than 300 individual projects, the ten largest (see table 18 below) comprise some £11.3Bn, or 63% of the total. The Department is also committed to payments of £1.2Bn for PFI projects (see Note 27 to the Departmental Resource Accounts on page 264).

Table 18: Major Contractual Commitments as at 31 March 2007

Project	£M
Typhoon Tranche 2 Production	3,886
A400M – The RAF's Future Transport Aircraft	1,530
Future Lynx Helicopter	1,244
Support Vehicles: (6, 9, 15 Tonne Cargo, Recovery & Tanker Vehicles and Trailers)	1,146
Nimrod MRA4	838
Merlin Mk 1 Helicopter (Capability Sustainment Plus)	692
The Royal Navy's new T45 Destroyers	684
Astute Class Submarine	665
WATCHKEEPER (Unmanned Aerial Vehicles)	579
Single Living Accommodation Modernisation	538

Defence Assets

290. Under the 'Simplify and Improve' programme (see paragraph 296) on 1 April 2006 the Department centralised fixed asset management. Defence Estates now owns all land and buildings and related plant and machinery assets. Defence Equipment and Support own all single use military equipment, guided weapons, missiles and bombs, capital spares, associated plant and machinery, transport, all assets under construction, Government furnished equipments held in project accounts, and all information technology and communication equipment. This change means that while fixed assets will continue to be held and used by all TLBs whose personnel will remain responsible for their custodianship, they are now managed financially by the Single Balance Sheet Owners. This change produced a substantial redistribution of the associated non-cash resources (such as depreciation charges) from the other TLBs to Defence Estates and Defence Equipment and Support.

291. MoD's asset base is large, diverse, geographically dispersed and varies significantly in age. At any time there are many items approaching the end of their useful life and many others entering service with, in the case of fighting equipment and buildings, a life of perhaps 25-50 years. More information on their management can be found in the Departmental Investment Strategy. Details of the Department's assets and their valuation are set out in Notes 13 and 14 to the Departmental Resource Accounts on pages xx-xx. According to the 2007 National Asset Register the MoD owns about 25% of the Government's tangible fixed assets and over 90% of the Government's intangible assets. The Department's gross Tangible Fixed Assets cost increased from £110.7Bn at 31 March 2006 to £118.5Bn at 31 March 2007, an increase of £7.8Bn. Of this £5.8Bn reflected capital additions, broadly in line with last year's capital expenditure figure. Once depreciation is subtracted, the Department's tangible fixed assets were worth some £74.6Bn at 31 March 2007, an increase of £2.8Bn over the previous year. This is largely accounted for by growth in the net value of single use military equipment reflecting the continuing programme of investment in the equipment provided for the Armed Forces. The vast majority of tangible fixed assets comprise either specialist military equipment in service or being acquired (some £44.6Bn, 63% of the total); dwellings, land and buildings (some £18.4Bn, 25% of the total); transport (some £4.3Bn, 5.8% of the total); and plant and machinery (some £2.6Bn, 3.5% of the total). The net holding of intangible fixed assets (mainly comprising development costs of military equipment) at 31 March 2007 was some £24.2Bn, an increase of some £1.2Bn over the year.

Losses and Write-Offs

292. Details of losses, gifts and special payments are set out in Note 31 to the Departmental Resource Accounts (page 270). Reported losses are not necessarily indicative of a failure of control, although the Department has processes – overseen by the Defence Audit Committee – to identify any that are and learn appropriate lessons. They also result from sensible management decisions as force structures, requirements and organisations are adjusted to meet changing circumstances. The total value of new and potential losses and special payments arising in year (both closed cases and advance notifications) was £417M in 2006-07. Of this £68M was for ex-gratia redundancy payments to members of the Royal Irish Regiment (RIR) and £17M for civilian redundancy payments following normalisation in Northern Ireland, and £112M from the decision to withdraw M26 bomblets for the Multiple Launch Rocket System (MLRS) as not meeting the Government's stricter criteria for use of cluster munitions (see paragraph 87 under Policy). Without these, new and potential losses and special payments arising in year would have fallen to £237M. The Department continues to work to minimise the number of new cases that arise. Excluding gifts and payments made by the Veterans Agency the value of cases closed during the year amounted to £384M, 73% was from final closure of cases previously notified, including £195M from the 1995 decision not to proceed with the long range anti-tank guided weapons system (LR TRIGAT).

293. The losses statement also identifies potential losses that have not yet been brought to completion and have therefore been identified for formal incorporation in a future year's accounts (known as advance notifications). The costs identified are estimates, so the final loss declared may therefore be either larger or smaller. The estimated value of our advance notifications of losses and special payments continued to fall, reducing from about £607M in

2005-06 to about £486M in 2006-07. Of this, £205M (42%) is for writing-down of the value of Chinook Mark 3 helicopters, where the Department has deliberately taken a very prudent accounting approach that maximises the size of the potential write-off pending revaluation on delivery of modified aircraft, and £167M (34%) from the Northern Ireland normalisation and MLRS decisions.

2004 Spending Review Efficiency Programme

294. The Government is committed to funding the Armed Forces as they modernise and adapt to meet evolving threats and promote international stability in the changing global security environment. The 2004 Spending Review announced in July 2004 increased planned spending on Defence by an average of 1.4% per year in real terms over the three years to 2007-08, with total planned Defence spending £3.7Bn higher in 2007-08 than in 2004-05. In cash terms, the equivalent increase is £3.5Bn, an average real growth of 1.5% per year. Further modernisation of Defence is being supported through the continued provision of the Defence Modernisation Fund, amounting to £1Bn over the three years to 2007-08. Building on the existing change programme, the Department also undertook to realise total annual efficiency gains of at least £2.8Bn by 2007-08, of which three-quarters will be cash releasing, to be re-invested in Defence capability and further modernisation initiatives. As of 31 March 2007 the Department had achieved efficiency savings of £2.2Bn (subject to validation), of which 84% was cash releasing.

Wider Markets Initiative

295. The aim of the Treasury's Wider Markets Initiative is the commercial exploitation of Departments' assets which need to be retained but are not fully used. Defence activities under the initiative have grown since 1998 to the extent that the MoD is regarded by the Treasury and the National Audit Office as among the leaders in the field. Indeed, in visiting the UK in March 2007, a senior auditor charged by the French Finance Minister with assessing the scope for commercialisation in his country's public sector singled out the MoD's 2nd PUS (as the MoD's Wider Markets champion) and Wider Markets team as his one departmental port of call besides the Treasury. The importance of thinking innovatively about commercialisation opportunities in periods of particular financial pressure is emphasised from time to time at the highest levels. In 2006-07 we have continued to refine and strengthen our management processes in this expanding field, bringing to over 300 the number of practitioners put through our training course and expanding the number of commercial officers licensed to contract for sale. Much of our Wider

Markets income comes from numerous small local arrangements for the loan of manpower, equipment, land and facilities; the exploitation of our intellectual property; and the use of the military "brand" in marketing goods such as clothing. Larger projects include the Defence Communication Services Agency's exploiting of the Boxer Communication Towers; the Royal Navy's contract, in partnership with Flagship, with Network Rail for engineering apprentice training at HMS SULTAN; and the provision of surplus bulk oil storage capacity at Campbeltown and Loch Ewe to a Dutch trading company.

'Bride and Prejuduce' filmed at RAF Halton – Wider Markets

Finance Process Improvement

296. Continued improvements to the finance processes are being taken forward through the 'Simplify and Improve' programme, being delivered through the Defence Resource Management Programme (see paragraph 151 under Change and Efficiency). The creation of a Financial Management Shared Service Centre is one of the key strands of this work and it went 'live' on 1 April 2007. The Shared Service Centre is expanding further over the next year with greater integration of processes and systems for bill paying. Improvements to the Planning, Budgeting and Forecasting system have also been introduced to meet requirements from the Defence Acquisition Change Programme.

Further sources of information

297. Detailed information on the Department's financial performance is contained in the Departmental Resource Accounts in Section Two of this report. Further information is also available from the following sources:

- 2007 National Asset Register, available at www.hm-treasury.gov.uk
- 2004 Spending Review: Stability, security and opportunity for all: investing for Britain's long-term future: New Public Spending Plans 2005-2008 (Cm 6237) at www.hm-treasury.gov.uk;
- SR2004 Public Service Agreement and technical note at www.mod.uk;
- SR2004 Efficiency technical note at www.mod.uk;
- Ministry of Defence: The Government's Expenditure Plans 2006/07 to 2007/08 (Cm 6822) at www.mod.uk;
- Central Government Supply Estimates 2006-07: Main Estimates (HC 1035) available at www.hm-treasury.gov.uk;
- Central Government Supply Estimates 2006-07: Main Estimates 2006-07 Supplementary Budgetary Information (Cm 6771) available at www.hm-treasury.gov.uk;
- House of Commons Defence Committee report on Ministry of Defence Main Estimates 2006-07, HC1366, available at www.publications.parliament.uk;
- Ministry of Defence Main Estimates 2006-07: Government Response to the House of Commons Defence Committee's report, HC1601, available at www.publications.parliament.uk;
- Central Government Supply Estimates 2006-07: Winter Supplementary Estimates (HC 2) available at www.hm-treasury.gov.uk;
- House of Commons Defence Committee report on Cost of Operations in Iraq and Afghanistan: Winter Supplementary Estimate 2006-07, HC129, available at www.publications.parliament.uk;
- Cost of Operations in Iraq and Afghanistan: Winter Supplementary Estimate 2006-07: Government Response to the House of Commons Defence Committee's report, HC1317, available at www.publications.parliament.uk;
- Central Government Supply Estimates 2006-07: Spring Supplementary Estimates (HC 293) available at www.hm-treasury.gov.uk;
- House of Commons Defence Committee report on *Cost of Operations in Iraq and Afghanistan: Winter Supplementary Estimate 2006-07*, HC129, available at www.publications.parliament.uk;
- Public Expenditure Outturn White Paper 2006-07 available at www.hm-treasury.gov.uk;
- Defence Departmental Investment Strategy available at http://www.mod.uk;
- NAO Report Ministry of Defence Wider Markets Initiative available at www.nao.org.uk.

Essay – Wider Markets

It is a key principle that publicly-owned resources should be disposed of when they become surplus to requirements. But where there are assets which cannot be disposed of but are not fully used, Selling into Wider Markets, also known as "income generation" or "commercialisation", provides for their commercial exploitation. The Treasury's Wider Markets Initiative of 1998 encouraged this and undertook that any income so generated could be used by the Department earning it to support its public objectives in addition to the funds voted by Parliament. This "sweating" of our irreducible spare capacity was subsequently endorsed by the 2004 Lyons review of public sector asset management.

The MoD uses this to serve two distinct aims: helping meet the Department's core objectives, and funding local projects of benefit to the working lives of those staff who have worked to secure the income. These two priorities inevitably sometimes conflict. Striking the right balance remains a challenge for resource managers across the Department, using their considerable delegated local authority within the Top Level Budget system.

Identifying assets that can be exploited in this way has been addressed with considerable energy and imagination. Wider Markets practitioners have been deployed in local business areas in addition to a small dedicated team established in Head Office to co-ordinate the Department's overall effort. These have developed processes ranging from the marketing of products carrying the brand of an Armed Service to the provision of airfield facilities to private flyers. Whereas film companies used to chance upon a MoD-owned property for use as a shooting location, there is now a film locations website designed to inform enquirers of the wide range of land and buildings which are in use as defence assets but which have capacity available to filmmakers.

It is not yet possible to determine how much revenue has been generated. Defining precisely what activities belong under the Initiative is challenging, calculating the precise cost of each transaction to the MoD provider is complicated, and it is important not to divert disproportionate resources away from the day job. There has however been a continuous increase in the volume of Wider Markets activity across defence, which in turnover terms now probably exceeds £100M a year. The Department has also worked with its partners in the Private Finance Initiative and Public-Private Partnership arrangements to ensure that there is scope for third-party income streams as a part of each deal. One such example is the Royal Navy's contract, in partnership with Flagship, to train engineer apprentices for Network Rail. All this places the MoD among the leaders in taking up the Wider Markets Initiative, which was confirmed by the National Audit Office's January 2006 report into its implementation across the Civil Service.

The expansion of MoD's Wider Markets business has required development of effective governance processes. Venturing into the market place takes on a set of legal and other responsibilities which are new to most defence personnel. To guarantee the soundness of a deal requires a combination of good budget management, commercial competence, legal knowledge and health and safety expertise. This is provided for by the formal sign off by experts in all these fields. The Department also provides dedicated guidance and training for staff involved in this business. For instance, producing a contract for sale demands different skills to those possessed by most MoD commercial staff, who are used to buying rather than selling. The Department has therefore established internal training in contracting for sale, which is attended by outsiders as well as defence staff. A national network of practitioners across defence business areas has also been established to advise, establish best practice and communicate it to the Centre. There is also a clear Head Office military and civilian lead that this is worth doing to maximise the resources available for defence.

There are nevertheless constraints. While there is no conflict between providing defence capability and at the same time engaging to a modest extent in commercial business with a view to greater efficiency in our use of defence assets, income generation activity must not interfere with defence tasks. Income generation by Service personnel must also have a military purpose. None of these activities must risk bringing the Armed Forces or the Department into disrepute.

But the benefits are substantial, and go well beyond what, relative to the total defence budget, is a modest though useful supplementary income. Staff engaging in income generation learn skills unavailable in any other area of Departmental business. The public sees the Department making full use of the assets which it has provided. Successful transactions generate good publicity. It contributes to the Department's role in the wider community, and has created links improving cooperation with other departments. The MoD will therefore continue to look for further Wider Markets opportunities to maximise the return for defence from the assets it owns.

Manpower

Objective: to succeed in Operations and Military Tasks Today

Public Service Agreement Target (SR2004 MoD Target 5)
Recruit, train, motivate and retain sufficient military personnel to provide the military capability necessary to meet the Government's strategic objective to achieve manning balance in each of the three Services by 1 April 2008.

Assessment and Performance Measures

Assessment: The programmes to transform and restructure the Armed Forces meant that during 2006-07 military trained strength fell by 3% from just over 183,000 to just under 178,000. At the end of the year all three Services were outside Manning Balance, and there is some risk that they may not return to balance by 1 April 2008. Pinch points remained in all three Services. Recruiting increased in a challenging environment, and Voluntary Outflow rates remained broadly stable. Service Diversity continued to improve, although not yet to target levels. The Reserve Forces continued to provide the support to operations required. Civilian staff numbers continued to fall, reducing by 5.6% from 104,000 to 98,000 during the year, and the Department remained on course to achieve the Spending Review efficiency target for civilian reductions by 1 April 2008. As a result of the continuing reduction programme civilian recruitment, turnover and progression remained low, significantly constraining the Department's ability to meet civilian diversity targets.

Trained strength of Forces 98%-101% of overall requirement on 1 April 2008. As at 1 April 2007:

- RN/RM trained strength of 34,940, or 94.9 % of overall requirement (96.7% on 1 April 2006);
- Army trained strength of 99,280, or 97.5 % of overall requirement (98.8% on 1 April 2006);
- RAF trained strength of 43,550, or 96.7% of overall requirement (99.2% on 1 April 2006);
- Royal Navy Reserve trained strength of 1,640 or 77% of overall requirement (71% on 1 April 2006);
- Royal Marines Reserve trained strength of 470 or 77% of overall requirement (82% on 1 April 2006);
- Territorial Army Volunteer Reserve trained strength of 21,070 or 70% of overall requirement (69% on 1 April 2006);
- RAF Auxiliary Air Force trained strength of 1,390, or 66% of overall requirement (49% on 1 April 2006);
- Critical shortage groups remained in all three Services.

Achieve stable Voluntary Outflow rates for each Service:

- Voluntary Outflow rates stable; the RN continued to exceed the stable long term goal rate.

Civilian Workforce:

- 98,050 Full Time Equivalent civilian staff employed on 1 April 2007 (103,930 on 1 April 2006);
- 9,600 reductions achieved as at 1 April 2007, against target of 11,000 by 1 April 2008;
- Continuing limited scope for progression.

Diversity:

- Overall Service ethnic minority strength (including Commonwealth recruits) increased to 5.8% at 1 April 2007 (5.5% at 1 April 2006) against target of 8% by 2013. UK ethnic minority intake:
    - RN 2.1% (target 3.5%, 2005-06 intake 2.0%)
    - Army 3.8% (target 4.1%, 2005-06 intake 3.6%)
    - RAF 1.6% (target 3.6%, 2005-06 intake 1.5%)
- Sexual Harassment Action Plan for Armed Forces agreed with Equal Opportunities Commission;
- As of 1 April 2007 women comprised 9.3% of UK Regular Forces, and 11.2% of 2006-07 intake;
- Proportion of women grew at SCS and Band B level, but fell at Band D level. Proportion of ethnic minorities fell at SCS level, grew at Band B level and stable at Band D level. Proportion of disabled fell at SCS and Band B level and grew at Band D level. Department only meeting diversity targets for disabled at SCS level and women at Band B level.

Service Personnel Numbers

Trained Strength

298. The Department's 2004 Spending Review Public Service Agreement Target requires all three Services to achieve manning balance by 1 April 2008. Manning balance is defined as trained strength between 98% and 101% of the requirement, which itself changes over time to reflect changes in the equipment and structure of the individual Services. From 1 April 2006 to 1 April 2007, reflecting the programmes to transform and restructure the Services, the total trained strength of the Services fell by over 5,400 personnel (3.0%) and the total requirement by 2,300 personnel (1.2%):

- On 1 April 2007, the total trained strength of the Royal Navy and Royal Marines was 34,940, a shortfall of 1,860 personnel or 5.1% against the requirement of 36,800, and 3.1% below the manning balance target range. This reflects a reduction of 680 trained personnel over the year, representing an overall decline of 1.4% against the requirement since 1 April 2006. This decline arose because Gains to Trained Strength were lower than expected and it was not possible to reduce the overall requirement as fast as had originally been planned. Work has been set in hand to resolve this, but there is some risk that the Royal Navy and Royal Marines may not achieve manning balance against the reduced requirement in Defence Plan 2007 of 36,260 in April 2008;

- The Army's total trained strength on 1 March 2007 was 99,280, a shortfall of some 2,500 personnel or 2.5% against the requirement of 101,800, and 0.5% below the manning balance target range. This reflects a reduction of 1,340 trained personnel over the year, representing an overall decline of 1.2% against the requirement since 1 April 2006. This mainly reflects a high level of early departures within the Infantry and Royal Artillery and the fact that although recruiting performance continued to improve, the environment remained challenging (see paragraph 301). The Army is taking forward a wide-ranging manning action plan to improve recruitment and retention covering a range of issues from training, to welfare and recruitment, to estate infrastructure, and expects to be very close to or back within manning balance by April 2008;

- The Royal Air Force's total trained strength on 1 April 2007 was 43,550, a shortfall of 1,470 personnel or 3.3% against the requirement of 45,020, and 1.2% below the manning balance target range. This reflects a reduction of 3,390 trained personnel over the year, representing an overall decline of 2.5% against the requirement since 1 April 2006. This fall reflects the continuing RAF redundancy programme as the Service moves towards the requirement in Defence Plan 2007 of 40,790 on 1 April 2008. The RAF continues to monitor the complex picture of restructuring and outflow and expects to achieve manning balance against that reduced requirement.

Table 19 Strength and Requirement of Full Time UK Regular Forces, Full Time Reserve Service & Gurkhas

	Royal Navy/ Royal Marines			Army			Royal Air Force		
	2007	2006	2005	2007	2006	2005	2007	2006	2005
Trained Requirement	36,800	36,830	38,190	101,800	101,800	104,170	45,020	47,290	48,730
Trained Strength	34,940[p]	35,620[r]	36,400[r]	99,280[3]	100,620	102,440	43,550[p]	46,940[r]	49,210
Variation	-1,860[p]	-1,220[r]	-1,790[r]	-2,520[3]	-1,180	-1,730	-1,470[p]	-350[r]	480
Untrained Strength	4,500[p]	4,500[r]	4,440[r]	11,300[3]	11,260	10,970	2,160[p]	2,110[r]	3,020
Total UK Regular Forces	39,440[p]	40,110[r]	40,840[r]	110,580[3]	111,880	113,420	45,710[p]	49,060[r]	52,230

Notes:
1. Data from DASA.
2. p denotes provisional. Following the introduction of a new Personnel Administration System, all Naval Service and RAF data from 1 November 2006 are provisional and subject to review.
3. Due to the introduction of a new Personnel Administration System, Army data is as at 1 March 2007.
4. r denotes revised.
5. Figures are rounded to ten and may not sum precisely to the totals shown.

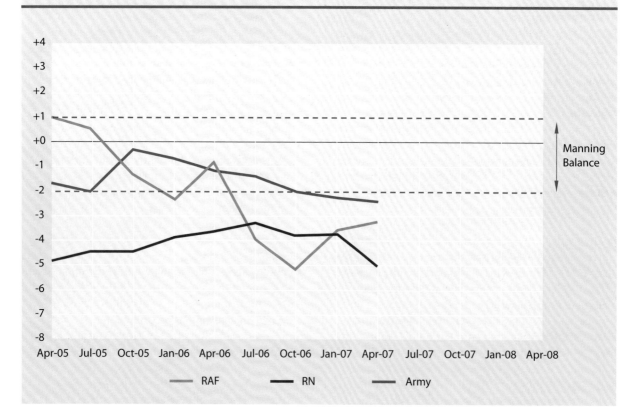

Figure 8 E1 Service manning surplus/deficit: history and forecast against MTWS as at Q4 2006/07

Manning Pinch Points

299. Within these overall manning totals there are a number of identified skills areas with insufficient trained strength to meet the specified requirement for that skill. These are known as Manning Pinch Points. This can reflect a shortage of people against the peacetime requirement, a temporary operational requirement greater than the peacetime requirement, or a combination of the two. Manning Pinch Points are managed by the individual Services, with a central working group maintaining an overview to identify trends and ensure best practice. Mitigating the operational impact of Pinch Points can in some cases require personnel to exceed harmony guidelines (see paragraph 216 under *Personnel Management*). Each Service maintains a dynamic list reflecting operational commitments and manning levels within branches and trades as they vary over time. There was a continuing shortage of Intelligence Analysts and Linguists across defence, and in addition:

- In the Royal Navy the shortages previously identified in Royal Marines Other Ranks, Mine Warfare Petty Officers, Warfare Leading Hands, and Air Engineering Technicians continued to be of concern during 2006-07, as did shortages of Divers, MERLIN personnel including Aircrew, and Fast Jet Pilots which have arisen during the

year. Their impact on Operational Capability was mitigated through proactive micro-management and prioritisation. The shortage of Nuclear Marine Engineering Watchkeepers identified in 2005-06 improved during 2006-07;

- The Army had 18 Manning Pinch Point trades in 2006-07 (24 in 2005-06). This included the Infantry, which is of particular concern, as well as Intelligence Operators and Unmanned Air Vehicle operators. Mitigation plans to manage the impact of these shortfalls are in place and the Army continued to work to reduce the total number of Pinch Points to nine by the end of 2008-09. Although some of these reflect underlying structural issues, the Army made use of levers such as Financial Retention Incentives to combat serious shortfalls, including those in the Royal Artillery and Infantry;

- The Royal Air Force continued to manage a period of deficit manning as the drawdown programme proceeded. 100% manning of senior pilots to the front line throughout 2006-07 was maintained by backfilling other posts as necessary. There were 22 critically manned Airmen trades, including Staff Nurses, Medical Administrative Assistants, Fire-Fighters, Gunners, and Weapon System Operators.

300. Across all three Services a revised Defence Medical Services requirement of 8,251 medical personnel (including those in training) was agreed in December 2006 following a review of the baseline medical personnel requirement for operations. Further work is in hand to examine reserve and retained tasks. On 1 April 2007 there were some 7,200 medical personnel. This represented a decrease of some 500 personnel over the year, and an overall shortfall of just under 1,100 or 13% against the requirement, but the revised baseline produced a reduced shortfall of some 6% in Medical Officers in 2006-07, and a small excess in Dental Officers. Despite these improvements there were continuing critical shortages in some specialist disciplines including Anaesthetics, Psychiatry, and Emergency Medicine for Medical Officers, and Emergency Medicine and Intensive Therapy Care for Nurses. Use of civilian agency contractors and close liaison with allies ensured that despite these shortfalls full medical support to operations was maintained. The Defence Medical Services continued to use a mix of Financial Retention Incentives, selective re-skilling, adapting existing training and increased recruitment to address these shortage areas.

Passing Out Parade

Recruitment and Trained Inflow

301. During the year the Royal Navy and the Army each combined their Regular and Reserves recruiting operations under single professional organisations to ensure high quality and consistent branding. In November 2006 the National Audit Office published its report on *Recruitment and Retention in the Armed Forces*, which concluded that since 2000-2001 the Services had recruited 98% of their target for intake from civilian life. Although the recruiting environment remained difficult during the year, with high employment, a prosperous and strong economy and attractive alternatives in further education, the Armed Forces continued to recruit well:

● Naval Service recruitment was about 5% lower in 2006-07 than in the previous year, in part reflecting the reducing overall requirement. A multi-media recruiting campaign accompanied by an online advertising campaign was launched in January 2007, which placed particular emphasis on shortage areas by highlighting the opportunities available for those choosing careers as engineers, aircrew and submariners;

● The Army significantly increased recruitment of Other Ranks during 2006-07, with over 1,000 more recruited, representing an increase of almost 9% over the previous year. Within this, Infantry and Royal Artillery specific initiatives produced a 25% and 29% increase in potential recruits respectively, although not all proved to have the quality or motivation needed for selection. In December 2006 the maximum age for soldier intake was increased to 33 years to align with the other Services;

Table 20: Intake to UK Regular Forces from civilian life:

	Royal Navy/Royal Marines			Army			Royal Air Force		
	2006-07	2005-06	2004-05	2006-07	2005-06	2004-05	2006-07	2005-06	2004-05
Officer Intake	320p	370	370	840	770	760	380p	320	290
Other Ranks Intake	3,430p	3,570	3,320	12,950	11,910	10,940	1,440p	1,110	1,880
Total Intake	3,750p	3,940	3,690	13,780	12,690	11,690	1,820p	1,430	2,180

Notes:
1. Data from DASA.
2. UK Regular Forces includes Nursing Services and excludes Full Time Reserve Service Personnel, Gurkhas, the Home Service battalions of the Royal Irish Regiment and mobilised reservists. It includes trained and untrained personnel.
3. All intake to UK Regular Forces includes re-enlistments and rejoined reservists.
4. 'P' denotes provisional. Due to the introduction of a new Personnel Administration System for all three services, Army data at 1 April 2007 are not available. Consequently Army data shown are for the latest 12 months available, comprising data from 1 March 2006 to 28th February 2007. All Naval Service and RAF data from 1 November 2006 are also provisional and subject to review.
5. Figures are rounded to the nearest 10 and may not sum precisely to the totals shown.

- The Royal Air Force also significantly increased recruitment by over 25% from the previous year, reflecting the approaching end of the drawdown programme. However, there were shortfalls in some trades (including Gunners and Air Traffic Control Assistants) where there were not enough applicants able to meet the requirements.

302. Once personnel have been enlisted they require training before joining the trained strength of their Service. On enlistment all recruits undergo Phase 1 training, lasting on average about twelve weeks, to provide the initial training in basic military skills and the inculcation of the Service ethos. This is followed by Phase 2 training to provide initial specialist training such that on completion they have the necessary skills for first employment in their chosen trade or specialisation. This varies from a few weeks to over a year for highly specialised training. On completion of Phase 2 training, personnel join the trained strength of their Service. This is known as Gain to Trained Strength. Inevitably the number successfully completing initial training is less than the number originally recruited, although the Department aims to keep the wastage rate to a minimum. The proportion of initial recruits who successfully progress on to units is some 78% for the Royal Navy, 49% for the Royal Marines, 67% for the Army, 94% for RAF officers and 93% for airmen. Given the variable length of Phase 2 training, there is no direct correlation between the number recruited and the Gain to Trained Strength in a given year. In 2006-07 the Naval Service and Army successfully trained more officers and about the same number of other ranks as in 2005-06, the Royal Air Force about the same number of officers and fewer other ranks. The number of Officers completing training includes those personnel promoted from other ranks as well as those recruited directly from civilian life.

Retention and Voluntary Outflow

303. The Armed Forces require sufficient turnover of personnel to maintain promotion opportunities. A certain level of early exits each year is therefore important. However, it costs significantly more to recruit and train new personnel than it does to retain existing ones. The Department does not set retention targets per se, but monitors the level of Voluntary Outflow closely against stable guideline figures derived from long term historic trends that reflect the ability to provide sustainable personnel structures and the capacity to train replacements for those who leave. Where appropriate, and particularly with regard to key Pinch Point trades, it seeks to improve retention rates through targeted Financial Retention Incentives. Overall Voluntary Outflow rates have varied little over the last few years, with only a small increase from 2005-06 to 2006-07, and a reasonable level of retention is being maintained across the Armed Forces. There are nevertheless some specific areas where the outflow rate would be too high if sustained over time. These are monitored closely to assess whether further action is necessary.

Table 21 Gains to Trained Strength

	2006-07			2005-06		
	Target	Achieved		Target	Achieved	
Naval Service Officers	410	450[p]	110%	410	370	90%
Naval Service Other Ranks	2,960	2,320[p]	79%	2,700	2,330	86%
Army Officers	1,020	960	95%	810	750	93%
Army Other Ranks	9,050	7,640	84%	9,230	7,770	84%
Royal Air Force Officers	500	400[p]	81%	370	380[r]	103%[r]
Royal Air Force Other Ranks	1,200	1,010[p]	84%	1,800	1,860[r]	103%[r]

Notes:
1. Naval Service and RAF Data from DASA. Army Figures come from the Adjutant General TLB.
2. Army numbers and target show officers completing the Royal Military Academy Sandhurst and soldiers completing Phase 2 training. This metric is used for internal management and does not match the figures produced by DASA and published in Tri Service Publication 4.
3. 'P' denotes provisional. Following the introduction of a new Personnel Administration System, all Naval Service and RAF data from 1 November 2006 are provisional and subject to review
4. r denotes revised.

Table 22 Voluntary Outflow Rates

	Stable long term Voluntary Outflow	Year ending 31 March 2007	Year ending 31 March 2006	October 1999 to October 2006
Naval Service Officers	2.0%	3.0% P	3.0%	2.5%
Naval Service Other Ranks	5.0%	6.0% P	6.0%	6.4%
Army Officers	4.1%	4.3% [3]	4.3%	3.9%
Army Other Ranks	6.2%	5.8% [3]	5.5%	5.7%
RAF Officers	2.5%	3.0% P	2.5%	2.4%
RAF Other Ranks	4.0%	4.9% P	4.8%	3.8%
Tri-Service Officers	N/A	3.6% P	3.4%	3.2%
Tri-Service Other Ranks	N/A	5.6% P	5.4%	5.4%

Notes:
1. Data from DASA
2. 'P' denotes provisional. Following the introduction of a new Personnel Administration System, all Naval Service and RAF data from 1 November 2006 are provisional and subject to review
3. Army data at 1 April 2007 are not available. Consequently Army data shown are for the latest 12 months available, comprising data from 1 March 2006 to 28 February 2007.
4. Voluntary Outflow Goals as set out in the Departmental Plan 2005-2009

Table 23 Outflow of UK Regular Forces

	Royal Navy/Royal Marines			Army			Royal Air Force		
	2006-07	2005-06	2004-05	2006-07 [3]	2005-06	2004-05	2006-07	2005-06	2004-05
Officer Outflow (Voluntary Outflow)	500 P (200 P)	520 (200)	510	1,270 (590)	1,070 (590)	1,100	850 P (270 P)	700 r (240)	700
Other Ranks Outflow (Voluntary Outflow)	3,770 P (1,670 P)	3,960 (1,670)	4,130	14,000 (4,780)	13,120 (4,620)	13,970	4,190 P (1,720 P)	3,890 r (1,840)	3,020
Total Outflow (Voluntary Outflow)	4,270 P (1,870 P)	4,490 (1,870)	4,630	15,280 (5,370)	14,190 (5,110)	15,070	5,040 P (1,990 P)	4,590 r (2,080)	3,730

Notes:
1. Data from DASA
2. 'P' denotes provisional. Following the introduction of a new Personnel Administration System, all Naval Service and RAF data from 1 November 2006 are provisional and subject to review
3. Army data at 1 April 2007 are not available. Consequently Army data shown are for the latest 12 months available, comprising data from 1 March 2006 to 28 February 2007.
4. Figures are rounded to the nearest 10 and may not sum precisely to the totals shown.

Diversity of the Armed Forces

304. The Armed Forces are committed to becoming more representative of the society they serve. But despite continuing efforts, recruitment from UK ethnic minority groups remains challenging (see the essay on Improving Service Diversity on pages 173). All three Services fell short of their ethnic minority recruiting goals (see Table 24) but overall ethnic minority representation within the Armed Forces continued to increase slowly (see Table 24). Most roles, with the exception of selective combat units, submarine and mine clearance diving, are now open to women. As of 1 April 2007, women comprised 9.3% of UK Regular Forces, and 11.2% of the total 2006-07 intake. Sexual orientation is a private matter not relevant to an individual's suitability for a career in the Armed Forces. Personnel are free to choose whether or not to disclose their sexual orientation. In line with the terms of the Civil Partnerships Act, the Services accord those who have formally registered their partnerships parity of treatment with married couples.

We Were There exhibition

305. The Armed Forces regularly review their recruiting policies with the Commission for Racial Equality and other experts in the field to ensure that they reflect best practice. During 2006, the Armed Forces again participated successfully in the Opportunity Now benchmarking scheme, which is designed to help organisations working towards gender equality and diversity to take stock of their progress and measure their development. Both the Army and the Royal Air Force received Gold Awards. The Royal Navy did not participate in 2006, but received a Silver award in 2005. The Armed Forces also again participated successfully in the Business in the Community's Race for Opportunity benchmarking scheme – a growing network of public and private sector organisations working across the UK to promote racial diversity. The Army came top among public sector organisations for the sixth consecutive year, with both the Royal Navy and RAF achieving places in the top ten. Out of the 104 public and private sector employees who participated, the Army achieved fifth place overall and the RAF tenth.

Table 24 Armed Forces UK Ethnic recruitment

	2007-06		2005-06		2004-05	
	Target	Actual	Target	Actual	Target	Actual
Navy	3.5%	2.1%	3.5%	2.0%	3.0%	2.3%
Army	4.1%	3.8%	3.9%	3.6%	3.4%	3.7%
RAF	3.6%	1.6%	3.6%	1.5%	3.1%	1.7%

Notes:
1. These figures are unaudited single Service estimates of UK ethnic minority intake.
2. The Army officer intake is measured by intake into Sandhurst

Table 25 Armed Forces ethnic minority representation

	1 April 2007	1 April 2006	1 April 2005	1 April 2004	1 April 2003
Royal Navy	2.7%[P]	2.6%	2.5%	2.4%	2.3%
Army	8.4%[3]	8.0%	7.6%	6.9%	5.9%
RAF	2.3%[P]	2.4%	2.5%	2.5%	2.6%
Armed Forces	5.8%[P]	5.5%	5.3%	4.9%	4.3%

Notes:
1. Data from DASA
2. 'P' denotes provisional. Following the introduction of a new Personnel Administration System, all Naval Service and RAF data from 1 November 2006 are provisional and subject to review
3. Due to the introduction of a new Personnel Administration System, Army data at 1 April 2007 are not available, data points shown as 1 April are the latest available, comprising data from 1 March 2007.

Table 26 Women in the Armed Forces as of 1 April 2007

Royal Navy/Royal Marines/Army/Royal Air Force	Total	Naval Service	Army	Royal Air Force
Commodore/Brigadier/Brigadier/ Air Commodore	2 (0.4%)	1 (0.9%)	1 (0.4%)	–
Captain(RN)/Colonel/Colonel/ Group Captain	39 (3.3%)	1 (0.3%)	19 (3.2%)	19 (6.1%)
Commander/Lt Colonel/Lt Colonel/ Wing Commander	200 (4.9%)	33 (3.0%)	77 (4.5%)	88 (7.1%)
Lt Commander/Major/Major/ Squadron Leader	890 (9.2%)	160 (6.6%)	460 (9.7%)	280 (10.4%)
Lieutenant/Captain/Captain/Flight Lieutenant	1,800 (14.8%)	400 (13.3%)	650 (13.8%)	750 (17.0%)
Sub Lieutenant/ Lieutenant & 2nd Lieutenant/ Lieutenant & 2nd Lieutenant/ Flying & Pilot Officer	790 (17.6%)	90 (12.7%)	430 (16.1%)	270 (24.5%)
Total Officers	**3,720 (11.6%)**	**680 (9.0%)**	**1,640 (11.2%)**	**1,410 (14.2%)**
Warrant Officer Class 1/ Warrant Officer Class 1/ Warrant Officer Class 1/Warrant Officer	130 (3.4%)	25 (3%)	67 (3.9%)	34 (2.9%)
Warrant Officer Class 2/Warrant Officer Class 2/ Warrant Officer Class 2	220 (4.0%)	1 (0.1%)	220 (4.7%)	N/A
Chief Petty Officer/Colour Sergeant/ Staff Sergeant/Flight Sergeant/ Chief Technician	580 (4.1%)	160 (3.6%)	300 (5.1%)	110 (3.3%)
Petty Officer/Sergeant/Sergeant/Sergeant	1,690 (7.7%)	330 (7.7%)	740 (7.1%)	630 (9.1%)
Leading Rate/Corporal/Corporal/Corporal	3,400 (11.1%)	650 (10.4%)	1,490 (9.7%)	1,270 (13.9%)
Lance Corporal	1,520 (9.2%)	2[4] (0.4%)	1,520 (9.4%)	N/A
Able Rating/Marine/Private/ Junior Technician/Leading & Senior Aircraftman	5,360 (10.0%)	1,810 (13.0%)	1,340 (5.2%)	2,210 (15.9%)
Junior Private/Aircraftman	1,060 (8.8%)	N/A	910 (8.2%)	150 (16.1%)
Total Other Ranks	**13,960 (8.8%)**	**2,970 (9.5%)**	**6,590 (7.2%)**	**4,400 (12.4%)**
Grand Total	**17,680 (9.3%)**	**3,650 (9.4%)**	**8,230 (7.7%)**	**5,810 (12.8%)**

Notes:
1. Data from DASA
2. Following the introduction of a new Personnel Administration System, all data are provisional and subject to review
3. Figures are rounded, (except for those less than 100 so as not to obscure the data). Due to the rounding methods used, figures may not always equal the sum of the parts. When rounding to the nearest 10, numbers ending in 5 have been rounded to the nearest multiple of 20 to prevent systematic bias. Percentages have been calculated from unrounded figures.

Sexual Harassment

306. Harassment of any kind is unacceptable in the Armed Forces and incompatible with the Services' core values and standards. It damages individual and team cohesion, and undermines operational effectiveness. In June 2005, the Secretary of State and the Chief of the Defence Staff signed an Agreement with the Equal Opportunities Commission on *Preventing and Dealing Effectively with Sexual Harassment in the Armed Forces*. This aims to create a working environment in which sexual harassment is not tolerated; to ensure that Service Personnel who experience sexual harassment feel able to complain and have confidence in the complaints process; and to monitor the nature and extent of harassment in the Armed Forces in order to correct deficiencies and build upon the strengths of our policies and processes. The Agreement runs until June 2008, at which time the Commission will decide whether it needs to take further action.

307. In the first phase of the Agreement, the Department conducted extensive research, including a survey of all Servicewomen. The results made clear that we had a serious problem that required urgent attention and, in light of these findings, an Action Plan was agreed with the Commission in May 2006 and it reviewed progress with the Chiefs of Staff in May 2007. Over the year complaints procedures were revised to make them more accessible and robust, further surveys were conducted, guidance was issued on appropriate sanctions in harassment cases, attitudes to equality and diversity were incorporated into appraisal reporting criteria, a system of career monitoring for parties to harassment cases was introduced, and a comprehensive review of equality and diversity training was begun. All senior officers are now required to undertake mandatory equality and diversity training provided by the Defence Academy. The Department continues to monitor progress to identify areas requiring further development.

First female Beefeater

Reserves Personnel

308. The Government aims to have capable, usable, integrated and relevant Reserve Forces supporting their Regular counterparts on operations overseas. The Reserves are not a contingency force but an integral part of defence capability to be drawn upon for use on enduring operations where necessary. As a matter of policy the Services seek only to mobilise willing personnel, and not to call out individuals more than one year in five. This has generally been achieved, although there have been instances where it has not been possible. The operational utility of the Reserves is borne out by their continuing contribution in 2006-07 to operations in Iraq, Afghanistan, the Balkans, and in support of the Government's counter-terrorist objectives. During the year an average of 1,250 reservists drawn from all three Services were in mobilised service at any one time. Of these, about two thirds were serving in operational theatres, integrated into regular forces either as reservist sub-units or as individuals. A small number served in the United Kingdom in direct support of operations or backfilling posts to allow regular personnel to be posted to operations. The remainder were mainly on Pre Deployment Training or Post Operational Leave. In addition, there were some 1,600 personnel on Full Time Regular Service commitments embedded within regular units and formations, including in operational theatres when their unit was deployed.

Table 27: Reserves

	April 2007[1]	April 2006
Regular Reserves		
Naval Service	9,600	10,400
Army	33,800	32,100
Royal Air Force	7,300	7,800
Volunteer Reserves		
Royal Navy Reserve		
Trained Strength Requirement	2,340	2,440
Trained Strength	1,640	1,740
Manning Balance	77%	71%
Royal Marines Reserve		
Trained Strength Requirement	600	600
Trained Strength	470	490
Manning Balance	77%	82%
Territorial Army		
Trained Strength Requirement	30,270	30,270
Trained Strength	21,070	20,830
Manning Balance	70%	69%
Royal Auxiliary Air Force		
Trained Strength Requirement	2,100	2,210
Trained Strength	1,390	1,080
Manning Balance	66%	49%

Notes:
1. Following the introduction of a new Personnel Administration System, all data for April 2007 are provisional and subject to review.
2. Figures are rounded to the nearest ten. Totals may therefore not always equal the sum of the parts.

309. The continuing use of Reserves to augment the Regular Forces requires a sufficient supply of Reservists to be available to undertake these tasks. The current strengths of the Reserve Forces is shown in table 27. None of the Volunteer Reserve Forces met their manning balance target of at least 95% of the trained strength requirement. Numbers are stable overall. The Department and the Services are therefore working hard to increase levels of recruitment and retention in the Reserve Forces, including improving the medical support available to them (see paragraph 243 under *Health and Safety*).

Civilian Personnel

Staff Numbers

310. The Department remained on course to exceed the 2004 Spending Review efficiency target to reduce the number of civilian posts in administrative and support roles by 11,000 (including 1,000 Locally Engaged Civilians) by the end of March 2008 (see paragraph 156 under *Efficiency and Change*). Current plans provide for reduction of about 12,800 civilian posts, of which 9,600 had been achieved by 31 March 2007. The total number of civilians employed by the Department (including its Trading Funds and Locally Engaged Civilians) fell by 5.6% from 103,930 Full Time Equivalents on 1 April 2006 to 98,050 on 1 April 2007. This represented a reduction of nearly 5,000 staff based in the United Kingdom and some 900 Locally Engaged Civilians elsewhere. The Department continued to make every effort to minimise and, where possible, avoid compulsory redundancies. The majority of the planned reductions are being delivered through

resignations, normal retirements and transfers out of the Department (including staff transfers to private contractors on Transfer of Undertaking and Protection of Employment terms), supplemented by recruitment limitations (see paragraph 311 below) and voluntary early release schemes. When staff find themselves without a post they are managed through a Department-wide Redeployment Pool, which gives them priority consideration when filling new or vacant posts. Staff leaving the Department under early release schemes have access to a MoD-funded Outplacement Service. Staff who are retiring attend a workshop on "Planning for Retirement".

Civilian Recruitment and Turnover

311. Reflecting the planned reduction programme, recruitment in 2006-07 continued to fall, but at a slower rate than previously (see Table 28). (Additional recruitment information, in accordance with the Civil Service Commissioners' Recruitment Code, is at Annex F on page 316.) The Department continued in particular to maintain targeted recruitment in certain specialist functions, and to ensure an adequate supply of potential future senior managers. The combination of the continuing reduction programme, the demographic profile of the Department's civilian personnel, and the low level of recruitment meant that the Department's staff turnover rate in 2006-07 was only 6.7%[1], compared to a labour turnover rate in the private sector of 14.7% in 2006.

Table 28: Civilian Recruitment

	2006-07		2005-06		2004-05	
	Non Industrial	**Industrial**	**Non Industrial**	**Industrial**	**Non Industrial**	**Industrial**
Total Number of staff recruited	2,860	1,070	3,510	1,130	5,480	1,700
Number and percentage of women recruited	1,250	250	1,510	290	2,440	470
	43.7%	23.7%	43.1%	25.6%	44.6%	27.4%
Number and percentage of ethnic minorities recruited[2]	120	30	170	20	130	20
	6.5%	4.2%	7.2%	3.0%	4.2%	2.3%
Number and percentage of people with disabilities recruited[3]	10	~	10	~	40	20
	0.4%	~	0.3%	~	0.7%	1.2%

Notes:
1. Data from DASA
2. The recruitment statistics shown are for all permanent and casual civilian personnel including Trading Fund staff. No recruitment information is available for Royal Fleet Auxiliary or Locally Engaged Civilian personnel.
3 Percentage of staff recruitment is based on known declarations of ethnicity and excludes staff with unknown or undeclared ethnicity.
4. Percentage of staff recruitment is based on known declarations of disability status and excludes staff with unknown or undeclared disability status.
5. ~ = Strength of less than ten or percentage based on strength of less than ten.
6. All figures are on a Full Time Equivalent basis.
7. All figures have been rounded to meet Freedom of Information requirements and protect confidentiality.

1 This is based on civilian inflow from all sources, including inward transfers from other Departments not reflected in the totals in table 28 above.

Civilian Progression

312. Progression rates remained hampered by the low rate of turnover, unfavourable demographic profile and continued reduction in staff numbers. The problem was particularly acute at the Senior Civil Service level (where the proportion of MoD staff is significantly lower than in the Civil Service as a whole), with 19 promotions to the SCS in 2006-07 (16 in 2005-06). Similar constraints also apply at lower levels. To ensure that the Department promotes the right people it was decided during the year to introduce an assessment centre from 2008 to assess and select for the Senior Civil Service, in line with the approach taken for promotion to Bands D (junior management) and B (middle management).

MoD Women's Network meeting

Table 29: Percentage of Women, Ethnic Minority and Disabled Non-Industrial Civilian MoD Staff

	1 April 2007		1 April 2006		1 April 2005		1 April 2004	
	Target	Achieved	Target	Achieved	Target	Achieved	Target	Achieved
Total Senior Civil Servants in the MoD[4]								
Women	15.0	12.2	15.0	10.1	15.0	9.2	13.0	8.8
Ethnic Minorities	3.2	2.1	3.2	2.6	3.2	2.2	3.0	2.2
Disabled	2.0	2.1	2.0	2.9	2.0	3.3	1.9	3.0
Band B								
Women	18.0	20.6	18.0	19.1	16.0	18.5	15.0	16.6
Ethnic Minorities	3.5	2.5	3.5	2.3	3.0	2.4	2.7	2.5
Disabled	4.0	2.4	4.0	2.7	4.0	2.4	3.6	2.0
Band D								
Women	40.0	37.2	40.0	38.5	40.0	37.6	38.0	36.1
Ethnic Minorities	4.0	3.2	4.0	3.2	4.0	2.9	3.5	2.9
Disabled	6.0	4.7	6.0	4.3	6.0	4.2	5.8	4.2

Notes:

1. Data from DASA

2. Percentages of Ethnic Minority Staff have been calculated as percentages of staff with known ethnicity status

3. Percentages of Disabled staff have been calculated as percentages of total staff, to be comparable with set targets. This differs from the methodology used in all external publications and in the recruitment table where percentages of Disabled staff are calculated from staff with known disability status.

4. Senior Civil Service data covers SCS and equivalent analogue grades e.g. medical consultants.

Civilian Diversity

313. In the light of these significant constraints, the Department's diversity performance did not change significantly during the year and it continued to miss the majority of its diversity targets (see Table 29). Work continued to improve this, focused around the Cabinet Office's 10 Point Plan to improve diversity in the Civil Service and the requirement to be compliant with Equality and Diversity related legislation. This included ensuring that the governance arrangements and measurement and evaluation frameworks support action to increase diversity at senior levels. In addition a single Equality and Diversity Scheme and associated Action Plans were also published in 2006. The Department's commitment and approach is favourably recognised. The Government's Action Plan for implementing the Women and Work Commission recommendations quotes the MoD's Manifesto for Civilian Women as an exemplary initiative for encouraging culture change. Opportunity Now has included MoD in the 100 Exemplar Employers and awarded the Department a Gold Standard, Race for Opportunity awarded us the Gold Standard (up from silver in 2005), and Stonewall placed the Department 72nd out of top 100 employers in their Workplace Equality Index. The Department also won two Civil Service Diversity Awards. Notwithstanding all of this, the 10 Point Plan targets remain very challenging, and it seems likely that while the Department will achieve the SCS targets for women (15%) and disabled (4%), it is unlikely to achieve the target for Ethnic minorities (3.2%) in the short term, despite slowly increasing representation in the feeder grades.

Further sources of information

314. Additional information on Manpower is available from the following sources:

- Quarterly PSA reports at www.mod.uk
- Q2 Autumn Performance Report at www.mod.uk
- GEP (Government Expenditure Plan) at www.mod.uk
- NAO report on Reserve Force (HC 964) available at www.nao.org.uk
- NAO report on recruitment and retention in the Armed Forces (HC 1633) available at www.nao.org.uk
- House of Commons Public Accounts Committee Report *Recruitment and Retention in the Armed Forces (HC43)* available at www.publications.parliament.uk
- House of Commons Public Accounts Committee Report on Reserve Forces (HC 729) available at www.publications.parliament.uk
- UK Defence Statistics and TSP series available at www.mod.uk & www.dasa.mod.uk
- Race Equality Scheme available at www.mod.uk
- Sexual Harassment available at www.mod.uk
- Agreement between MoD and EOC available at www.mod.uk
- Civil Service 10 point diversity plan available at www.mod.uk
- Civilian Workforce Strategy available at www.mod.uk
- Unified Diversity Strategy available at www.mod.uk

Essay – Improving Service Diversity

The Armed Forces aim to be manned by personnel from all sectors of the United Kingdom's diverse communities. This reflects both the moral obligation to reflect the society which they serve and the practical need to be able to recruit effectively from all parts of that society to provide trained personnel in the future. Against that background, through a succession of Partnership Agreements with the Commission for Racial Equality, the goal is to achieve 8% ethnic minority representation by 2013. By 1 April 2007 the Services had reached 5.8% representation, a 0.3% increase on the previous year. Within the overall representation target there is an annual UK ethnic minority recruiting goal to recruit at 0.5% above the previous year's achievement level for each Service, or roll forward the previous year's target, whichever is greater.

All three Services have a dedicated and specialist team promoting military careers amongst the UK's ethnic minority and faith communities. Each team undertakes a range of initiatives and participates in diverse cultural events both nationally and (in particular) at local level. For example:

- The Royal Navy's Diversity Action Team work ranges from giving presentations in schools and colleges and to Community and Faith leaders to organising and operating five-day Personal Development Courses, attending careers, and cultural and religious festivals and events, and engaging potential recruits and their gatekeepers;

- The Army's Diversity Action Recruiting Team provides role models to young members of the ethnic minority and faith communities at recruiting events throughout the country. They add credibility to the recruiters' outreach work within minority communities. Within the Team there are Community Liaison Officers who engage with and develop relationships with 'influencers' in minority communities in their respective regions. The Team participates in some 650-700 events each year;

- The Royal Air Force's Motivational Outreach Team is responsible for promoting the Service in major ethnic minority communities. Their work is augmented by Careers Liaison Officers, Community Careers Liaison Officers and a network of Youth Activity Liaison Officers across the UK. They participate in schools' careers conventions, festivals and sporting events, and visits to youth organisations and Air Training Corps and Combined Cadet Force squadrons. They also arrange visits for ethnic minority personnel to RAF stations.

Although they are making determined and sustained efforts, the Services are not recruiting as many ethnic minority recruits as they would wish. Results of recent public opinion surveys have shown that increasing parental and gatekeeper disapproval of the Armed Forces as a career, particularly within the minority communities. The Services are addressing this directly through harmonised tri-Service working to improve communications and to build up their reputation with ethnic minority and religious communities, and by conducting research on how best to inform minority communities. They are engaged in top level communications with religious leaders. For example, in January 2007 the Chief of Defence Staff met with Dr Muhammad Abdul Bari, the Secretary General of the Muslim Council of Britain, and with in February 2007 with Dr Khalid Ahmed, the High Sheriff of London. They sponsored an award at the annual Muslim News Awards for Excellence, and all three Services were well represented at the Awards dinner in April 2007. And the Department's 'We Were There' exhibition, which aimed to inform young people of the part played by soldiers of ethnic minority origin in the United Kingdom's military history, has been a resounding success as it has been rolled out across the UK.

The Armed Forces are committed to giving all individuals the opportunity to practice their faith wherever possible. Every effort is made to allow personnel to celebrate religious festivals and holidays, to comply with specific religious dress codes or dietary requirements, and to fast when required. Members of the Armed Forces are normally allowed to fast and pray in circumstances where this would not jeopardise operational effectiveness or health and safety. Where practical, areas of worship are made available in all Service establishments, including ships and submarines. In most circumstances, arrangements can be made for daily prayer. The Armed Forces aim to cater for the religious dietary requirements of all Service personnel. Halal, Kosher and vegetarian meals can be provided by Service messes and are available in Operational Ration Packs for operations and exercises. The first MoD civilian chaplains to the Armed Forces from the Buddhist, Hindu, Muslim and Sikh faith communities began work in October 2005 (the Services have had an honorary officiating chaplain from the Jewish faith under long-standing arrangements).

The Armed Forces are working hard to develop an organisational culture that welcomes racial diversity and the highest priority is being placed on rooting out unacceptable behaviour. There is a continuing constructive dialogue with the Commission for Racial Equality, and meetings take place regularly. They remain committed to increasing ethnic minority representation. This is demonstrated by the fact that all three Services were in the top ten in Race for Opportunity's annual benchmarking report for 2006. But there is still some way to go.

Estate

Objective: Maintain an estate of the right size and quality, managed in a sustainable manner, to achieve Defence objectives.

Assessment and Performance Measures

Assessment: The quality of the estate – including single living and family accommodation – continued to improve, but there is a long way yet to go to achieve target standards for single living accommodation across the estate. New estate management arrangements began to bed down, albeit with some teething problems. A substantial rationalisation and relocation programme continued with several major announcements during the year. Good progress with environmental stewardship and conservation.

Improving the Estate – Improve Single Living Accommodation to Grade 1 standard by delivering 2,000 Grade 1 bed spaces through Project SLAM and 5,400 Grade 1 bed spaced through other projects:

- 2,207 new-build bed spaces delivered in 2006-07 through Project SLAM;
- 3,615 new-build bed spaces delivered in 2006-07 through parallel projects.

Improving the Estate – Improve Service Families Accommodation in the Great Britain by upgrading 1,200 family houses to Standard 1 for condition:

- 1,215 Service families houses upgraded in 2006-07;
- 59% of the long term core stock at Standard 1 for condition, and over 95% at Standards 1 or 2 for condition.

Managing the Estate – Improved standard of routine maintenance:

- Effective implementation of new Housing Prime Contract (England and Wales only) after a poor start;
- Regional Prime Contracts beginning to improve reactive maintenance and efficiency;
- Introduction of improved arrangements for Training, Overseas and Volunteer estates.

Managing the Estate – Relocation of 3,900 posts outside of London and the South East by 2010:

- Major estate rationalisation programme in progress;
- 1,885 posts relocated outside of London and South East.

Sustainable Development – Natural Resource Protection and Environmental Enhancement:

- Development of Sustainability Environmental Appraisal Tools Handbook and Defence Related Environmental Assessment Methodology;
- Continuing roll-out of environmental management systems;
- 81% of Sites of Special Scientific Interest in England at target condition (target 95% by 2010). Condition elsewhere in UK also improving;
- 70% of listed buildings and 73% of Scheduled Monuments (62% 2005-06) in good or fair condition;
- Increased access to Defence land.

The Defence Estate

315. The Ministry of Defence is the one of the largest landowners in the United Kingdom, with an estate of some 240,000 hectares (about 1% of the UK mainland). Some 80,000 hectares of this comprise a varied built estate including naval bases, airfields, living accommodation for nearly 200,000 military personnel, scientific facilities, storage and distribution centres, communications facilities, and offices, making the Department the UK's largest property manager. Reflecting the long history of the Armed Forces, the estate contains a substantial number of listed buildings (see paragraph 335). The rural estate (some 160,000 hectares) comprises mainly training areas, and ranges on undeveloped land, often of particular environmental or archaeological significance (see paragraph 335). The Department has rights to use about a further 196,000 hectares in the UK, mainly for training. The Department also manages an overseas estate mainly comprising the garrisons and training facilities in Germany, Cyprus, the Falkland Islands and Gibraltar, as well as facilities in Ascension Island, Belize, Brunei, Nepal, Singapore and the United States. The Armed Forces regularly use major training facilities in Canada, Cyprus, Germany, Norway, Poland and Kenya. The Department invests over £2Bn a year (about 1% of UK construction industry annual turn over) in the estate, in April 2006 the Department's estate-related assets were worth some £18.9Bn.

Improving the Estate

316. The defence estate exists solely to support the Armed Forces in delivering military capability. The Defence Estate Strategy 2006 – In Trust and On Trust, published in March 2006, set out the principles by which it is managed and developed. The estate is kept under review to ensure that it remains the right size and quality to support the delivery of defence capability, is managed and developed effectively and efficiently in line with acknowledged best practice, and is sensitive to social and environmental considerations. The Department therefore continued to take forward an extensive estate improvement programme during 2006-07, including:

- the award of the PFI contract in April 2006 for Project Allenby/Connaught, to provide modern living and working accommodation for some 18,000 military and civilian personnel in Aldershot and the Salisbury Plain Training Area. Service delivery began in July 2006. The Project includes a particular focus on Single Living Accommodation and will provide over 11,000 soldiers with new and refurbished ensuite bedspaces during the period 2006-16;

- in May 2006 the Woodbridge Airfield redevelopment in Suffolk was handed over for occupation to 23 Engineer Regiment (Air Assault). The project was recognised as a demonstration project both for construction excellence and environmental management;

- the award in July 2006 of a £1.15Bn PFI contract for the redevelopment, management and operation of the Permanent Joint Headquarters site at Northwood in north London;

- the award of the contract for Project MoDEL (Ministry of Defence Estate in London) in September 2006. The Project will contribute to consolidation of the defence estate in Greater London through development of an integrated Anchor Site at RAF Northolt, relocation of London based units and disposal of sites rendered surplus. It will initially invest over £180 million in the redevelopment of RAF Northolt;

- in September and October 2006 personnel from 16 Air Assault Brigade moved into new accommodation at Colchester Garrison on return from Afghanistan, with completion of the first phase of the Colchester PFI Garrison Project ten weeks ahead of schedule. This included 2,232 new junior ranks en-suite single living accommodation;

- the selection in October 2006 of the preferred bidder for the £800M PFI project to rebuild, refurbish and manage state-of-the-art communication and technical support facilities at Corsham in Wiltshire, and provide new offices for 2,000 staff and en-suite single living accommodation for 180 Service personnel. The underground tunnels at Corsham are an important link to Cold War history and the Department continued to work with English Heritage and the contractor to ensure their preservation.

Moving into new accommodation at HMS Neptune, Clyde

Service Accommodation

317. Service personnel and their families deserve good quality accommodation. It forms an important part of their overall package of terms and conditions and plays a significant role in retention. The MoD owns or manages an overall stock of 72,000 houses worldwide and 168,000 single living units, spread across more than 200 sites in 16 countries. There are problems with some Service accommodation; too much is old, not well adapted for modern lifestyles, or in a poor physical condition. Recognising this, around the end of the last decade the Government substantially increased the base standards required for living accommodation. This created a huge block of work that the Department is addressing by investing money in new or upgraded facilities (see paragraphs 318-319 below). £700M was spent on housing and other accommodation in 2006-07 and over £5Bn more is planned over the next decade. But tackling all the shortcomings will take considerable time, particularly given the continuing need to balance investment in accommodation against other defence priorities. The Department is also exploring whether there are further ways to help Service personnel buy their own property where they want to and can afford it, such as through the long service advance of pay scheme. The Department has also been setting up better long term maintenance arrangements (see paragraph 326 below), and taking forward a substantial rationalisation programme (see paragraphs 320-321).

Single Living Accommodation

318. The Department is providing a greatly improved living environment including mostly single rooms with en-suite facilities through a combination of the Project SLAM (Single Living Accommodation Modernisation) and a large number of parallel projects. The first phase of Project SLAM, which will upgrade some 10,000 single bed spaces in the UK by April 2008, was awarded in December 2002. The second follow-on phase, to upgrade a minimum of a further 5,000 bed spaces by April 2013, was awarded in January 2007. 2,207 bedspaces were delivered in 2006-07 against a target of 2,000, bringing the total delivered by Project SLAM by 31 March 2007 to nearly 7,800. Other projects to modernise Single Living Accommodation at specific locations in the UK and overseas delivered 3,615 bedspaces during 2006-07, including over 500 overseas, against a target of 5,400 bed spaces. In all, just under 20,000 single living bed spaces have been built or upgraded since April 2002 and over 22,000 more will be delivered over the next three years.

Service Families Accommodation

319. Work also continued to improve the overall standard of Service Families Accommodation in the United Kingdom. Over 12,000 properties have been upgraded over the last six years, and the percentage of housing stock at Standard 1[2] has risen from 41% in April 2001 to 59% in April 2007. 36% are at Standard 2, and only 140 houses (0.3% of the total stock) are at the lowest standard. The Department is planning to upgrade up to a further 900 properties by April 2008, and to conduct a full condition based survey of all its Service Family Accommodation to inform future investment priorities. During 2006-07 1,215 properties were upgraded to Standard 1 for Condition against an increased target of 1,200, bringing the total upgraded to Standard 1 since April 2003 to over 6,700. On 1 April 2007, the long-term core stock comprised about 26,900 properties at Standard 1 (26,000 in April 2006), 16,000 at Standard 2 (16,000 in April 2006), 1,800 at Standard 3 (2,000 in April 2006) and about 140 at Standard 4 (130 in April 2006). The slight increase in the number of properties overall mainly comprises accommodation for families returning to Great Britain from Germany and Northern Ireland as the number of military personnel stationed there has fallen.

Cooked-to-order omelettes in Rock's Barracks, Suffolk

2 Standard for Condition is calculated from 102 different attributes in 8 categories: Health & Safety, Sanitary, Kitchen, Energy Efficiency, Building Fabric, Electrical, Security and Bedroom:

- Standard 1 properties achieve standard 1 in all eight categories;
- Standard 2 properties are at least standard 2 in each category, and usually reach standard 1 in at least five. Required improvements might include a thermostatic shower, new kitchen, or better loft insulation;
- Standard 3 properties are standard 3 in at least one category, but are usually standard 1 or 2 in at least half. Required improvements might include a new kitchen, bathroom, upgraded loft and plumbing insulation;
- Standard 4 properties typically achieve a standard of 4 in five or fewer categories. Required improvements might include a new bathroom, electrical system, kitchen, insulation upgrade, and health & safety review.

Managing the Estate

Rationalisation, Relocation and Disposals

320. As set out in The Defence Estate Strategy 2006, the MoD is working towards an estate of fewer but larger sites. Since 1999, the Department has achieved accrued disposal receipts of nearly £2.1Bn, including accrued gross Estates disposal receipts of £394M (£258M in 2005-06) during 2006-07. Work has also begun on producing an Estate Development Plan looking forward over the next 20 years, to be completed by the end of 2007. This will enable the Department and the Armed Forces to plan estate requirements across defence in a more geographically coherent manner, with defence establishments mainly located away from London and the South East of England. The goal is to develop defence communities in environments where civilian and military personnel and their families want to live and work both now and in the future, whilst recognising the sustainable development needs of others. In this context:

- the Royal Navy has already largely concentrated its facilities around Portsmouth, Plymouth and on the Clyde, and the Naval Base Review is continuing;

- the Army's long term goal is to achieve coherence across the formations in which it deploys. In the longer term it aims to develop 'super garrisons' along the lines of Aldershot, Catterick, Colchester, and around Salisbury Plain to concentrate formations and units in a coherent, efficient and effective manner to improve military output. It continues where possible to consolidate dispersed units onto existing major garrisons and bring back further units from bases in Germany to the UK (project BORONA – see paragraph 143 under Efficiency and Change). It is considering the potential to establish further 'super garrisons' in major recruiting areas where there is not at present a large military presence, such as in the West Midlands. With Security Normalisation the Army's presence in Northern Ireland is reducing from an Operational Theatre Headquarters to Regional Brigade proportions, with an appropriate estate to support regional and deployable Army structures. The Joint Helicopter Command is considering the scope to establish a Support Helicopter Main Operating Base (Project Belvedere), which would have implications for Lyneham, Dishforth, Wattisham, Gutersloh, Benson and Odiham;

- the Royal Air Force is already largely focused on its Main Operating Bases, but the increased capabilities of future aircraft may enable longer term rationalisation onto fewer, larger "hub" airfields. In particular RAF Brize Norton is being developed as the prime Defence Air Port of Departure and will become the Air Transport and Air to Air refuelling hub.

321. Major rationalisation programmes underway during the year included:

- the establishment of an Acquisition Hub in the Bristol/Bath area was approved in September 2006 in line with the decision to establish Defence Equipment and Support (see paragraph 161 under Future Capabilities and Infrastructure, and the essay on Defence Industrial Strategy on page 101). Over the next five years this will involve relocating about 2,000 logistics posts from their current locations;

- work to establish a new collocated single Army Headquarters (Project Hyperion) (see paragraph 131 under Future Effects). Subject to further work and final decisions later this year this will probably be set up on 1 April 2009 at the Andover site being vacated by logistics personnel;

- the opening of the new Royal Air Force Collocated Headquarters at RAF High Wycombe in October 2006, which became the headquarters of the single RAF Air Command in April 2007 (see paragraph 134 under Future Effects). The remaining RAF Personnel Management personnel from RAF Innsworth will move to High Wycombe in early 2008;

- the announcement in January 2007 that St Athan in South Wales will be home to a new tri-service Defence Training campus under Package 1 of the Defence Training Review (see paragraph 223 under Personnel Management), with substantial reductions at the sites where this training is currently delivered. Depending on the results of negotiations on Package 2 the training estate may eventually reduce from about 30 to ten sites;

- as part of the wider Defence Intelligence Modernisation Programme (see paragraph 139 under Future Effects), the Programme to Rationalise and Integrate Defence Intelligence Service Estate, which aims to collocate a number of Defence Intelligence units on a single site, passed its initial gate in July 2006;

- the selection in August 2006 of Lichfield as the preferred location for the Midlands Medical Accommodation project. This will consolidate the headquarters of the Defence Medical Education and Training Agency and 33 Field Hospital from Gosport, the headquarters of the Royal Centre for Defence Medicine from Birmingham, and the Defence Medical Services Training Centre from Aldershot.

322. There have already been very substantial reductions in the number of posts in London and the South East of England. The number of defence civilians in and around London fell from nearly 50,000 in 1993 to about 24,000 in 2006, and the number of headquarters buildings in London from more than 20 in 1990 to three, four office buildings in central London having been disposed of in the last four years. In line with the Government's goals under the Lyons review to make further reductions in London and the South East, the Department continued to take forward a number of projects to reduce its footprint within Greater London. In September 2006 a contract was awarded for Project MoDEL to rationalise a number of defence sites in Greater London at RAF Northolt and Woolwich (see paragraph 316 above). In Spring 2007 a streamlining study was set up to identify how to reduce the MoD Head Office in London following the Capability Review and taking account of the new TLB headquarters arrangements (see paragraph 274 under Business Management). An understanding was reached with a prime bidder through a competitive process for the disposal of Chelsea Barracks, although the details are commercially confidential until completion in 2008. Under the Lyons review, the Department plans to relocate about 5,000 defence posts out of London and the South East of England between April 2005 and March 2010 (against a target of 3,900). 1,229 had been relocated by April 2006, and a further 656 were relocated during 2006-07, for a total of 1,885 as at 31 March 2007. These reductions will be offset to some degree by the establishment of the new Army and RAF headquarters at Andover and High Wycombe, both of which involve moving posts into the South East.

Other Ranks living accommodation at Tidworth Garrison

323. The Department continued to develop its close relationship with English Partnerships to support the Government's wider regeneration goals. In particular, during the year Defence Estates and English Partnerships worked on developing the Connaught Barracks site in Dover as an exemplar of sustainable carbon neutral housing development. They also worked together with Local Authorities, the Greater London Authority, other Government Departments and Strategic Government Bodies to maximise the regeneration potential of the surplus sites in London released by project MoDEL, which will free up around 100 hectares of predominantly brownfield land within the M25 on which thousands of new homes could be built.

Housing Management

324. The MoD is managing some 72,000 Service Family Accommodation (SFA) properties, of which some 49,000 are in the United Kingdom. Nearly 45,000 of these are long-term core stock. There are around 20,000 moves in and out of SFA each year in the UK. Accommodation charges are recommended by the Armed Forces Pay Review Body. About 9,000 properties in Great Britain were vacant in April 2007 (including some 2,500 held pending decisions on rationalisation opportunities or possible unit redeployments). The proportion of vacant properties is known as the management margin and, discounted by those properties identified for disposal over the next year, it is used to measure housing management efficiency. Against a target of 10% it increased from 13.9% to 15.5% over the year.

325. The service provided to military families in England and Wales changed significantly during January 2006 with the roll-out of the new Housing Prime Contract for repair and maintenance of SFA. The initial service was not up to the required standard, reflecting a greater backlog of work than calculated, teething problems with the contractor's IT systems, and difficulties in reorganising the supply chain around the new arrangements. The Department agreed a number of measures with the contractor to rectify the problems. These proved effective and performance levels improved markedly over the year. 97% of emergency calls are now responded to within three hours where there is an immediate health and safety risk and in every case any make-safe process are completed within 24 hours; 82% of urgent calls are responded to within five working days; all helpdesk calls are answered in less than two minutes; and reported missed appointments have fallen below 1%. The Department also rolled out the redesigned and estate-focused Housing Customer Attitude Survey in late 2006, including to overseas occupants. This showed that customer satisfaction levels have

improved, with a 94% level of satisfaction reported (29% excellent, 49% good and 16% satisfactory).

Estate Maintenance

326. Between 2003 and 2005 the Department let five Regional Prime Contracts (RPC) for the delivery of maintenance and construction of the built estate in Great Britain, covering Scotland, the South West, the South East, the East, and Central England and Wales. These replaced over 600 individual contracts. They provide single points of responsibility for the management and delivery of projects and integrated estate services on most defence establishments. All are making progress. The National Audit Office found in its recent report on Managing the Defence Estate: Quality and Sustainability, that civilian and Service personnel are very satisfied with their core elements and that reactive maintenance has improved. However, the Defence Management Board decided that in order to meet financial pressures arising from significantly increased fuel costs it was necessary to reduce by £13.5M the amount available in 2006-07 for the non-accommodation elements of the Regional Prime Contracts. During the year Top Level Budget organisations injected £45M for a range of minor new works to address their local priorities. Prime Contracting aims to deliver 30% through life value for money improvements in estate management by 2012 through improved planning, supply chain management, incentivisation, continuous improvement, economies of scale and partnering. This is measured by the new Estate Performance Measurement System (which the National Audit Office concluded will make a vital contribution to the Department's ability to manage the estate once further work has been done to allow it to be rolled out effectively). Initial data still being validated from RPC Scotland (the most mature contract) indicates that it has so far achieved between 3% and 5% against the 2003-04 baseline. RPC Scotland has also successfully trialled a Single Business Delivery Model to provide a consistent approach to planning and delivery.

327. Water and wastewater management is now provided across the defence estate in Great Britain through three contracts (one for Scotland; one for the Midlands, Wales and South West England: and one for the North East and South East of England) under the 25-year PFI Project Aquatrine. This has transferred environmental risk to those in the private sector best placed to manage it and enabled the Department to focus better on its core activities. It is enabling new capital investment such as new or upgraded fire mains and water and sewage treatment works at a number of locations, and will provide the Department for the first time with accurate water consumption data. This data

will enable the Department to put in place steps to reduce consumption by 25% by 2020 (relative to 2004-05 levels) in line with the Government's sustainable development targets. Last year the Department consumed about 24.2 million cubic meters of water, which included domestic, commercial and industrial use and some distribution losses. The Department is developing a plan to achieve the 25% reduction target. Some of the reduction will come from Aquatrine service providers' work to reduce leakage and the rest from reductions in Departmental consumption.

Defence Training Estate

328. The Defence Training Estate (DTE) was formed on 1 April 2006 from the merger of elements of training facilities previously owned and managed by all three Services, the Defence Logistics Organisation and Defence Estates. DTE and its strategic partner, Landmarc Support Services Ltd, now provide the Armed Forces with the majority of their UK based training and associated support services, including equipment support, catering, air traffic control, range control, simulation, and booking and allocation services. The Department is considering whether and how to incorporate remaining training facilities in the United Kingdom, Europe and in the rest of the world.

Overseas Estate

329. Management of the built estate on the Permanent Joint Operating Bases overseas will be provided through a series of Integrated Service Provider contracts. Contracts for the South Atlantic Islands and Cyprus were rolled out during 2006. Implementation of the Gibraltar contract was delayed until January 2007 while the Department considered an In-House option. During the year the Department also reviewed the procurement of Facilities Management services in Germany, and how best to fulfil our host nation obligations to US Visiting Forces in the UK while providing demonstrable value for money.

Volunteer Estate

330. Following a review, Defence Estates became responsible in April 2007 for the strategic management of the Volunteer Estate (the 4,500 widely dispersed buildings that accommodate the UK's Reserve Forces and Cadets) to meet the operational requirement. Delivery of estate service will continue to be provided by the 13 Reserve Force and Cadet Associations. These arrangements will ensure more stable funding, enable management on a national basis so that resources go to areas of greatest need, facilitate better planning by

the Associations, and produce greater consistency in the service customers receive.

Relationship with Industry

331. In the spirit of the Defence Industrial Strategy (see essay on page 101) the MoD has recognised that effective and constructive engagement with industry is essential to improve performance, generate best value for money, and cement collaborative relationships. Defence Estates have developed a Supplier Management Strategy to facilitate effective engagement with the construction and facilities management industry. This focuses on supplier associations, individual supplier relationships and developing relationships with wider industry:

- **Supplier Associations.** These aim to create an environment and culture change through which shared business improvement, resourced by all, provides tangible benefits both to defence and industry. 13 collaborative projects have been launched so far;

- **Individual Supplier Relationships.** There are a number of strategically important suppliers operating on the defence estate. The Department continued to work with them to improve coherence and interaction at both the strategic and project level;

- **Relationships with Wider Industry.** The Department is working to be more transparent about its future estate and infrastructure requirements in order to allow industry to provide better informed bid, resource and investment planning. This will then give the Department a clearer understanding of industry's capacity to deliver. Defence Estates worked closely with the Office of Government Commerce to capture public sector demand and assess industry's capacity to deliver national construction programmes, including the Olympics infrastructure, up to 2015. This concluded that industry should not face any significant capacity constraints given that many large projects such as Heathrow Terminal five and the Channel Tunnel Rail Link were scheduled to wind-down or complete before work associated with the Olympics began.

Sustainable Development: Natural Resource Protection and Environmental Enhancement

332. As a major landowner, the Department faces considerable environmental responsibilities and challenges. It works to manage these and implement the targets set out in *Sustainable Operations on the*

Government Estate in 2006 and its own wider sustainable development goals through the use of Integrated Estate Management Plans. Sustainability appraisals and environmental assessments must be completed for all policies, programmes and projects and the Department has developed a comprehensive Sustainability Environmental Appraisal Tools Handbook and a Defence Related Environmental Assessment Methodology to give Project Managers the necessary advice, guidance and procedures to follow. These initiatives have been widely recognised across Government as representing best practice. The Department is progressively developing and introducing Environmental Management Systems that comply with ISO 14001 at all major defence sites. These require site managers to identify impacts of site occupation, to set targets to reduce significant impacts and to monitor and report progress through an annual management review and periodic audit. Over 500 were in place covering over 80% of defence personnel by the end of the year. The Department conducted 147 sustainability and environmental appraisals and assessments in 2006. A range of internal and external general and specialist environmental management training is provided for defence personnel where necessary, some of which contributes towards membership of the Institute of Environmental Management and Assessment (reported under management of water and wastewater in paragraph 327).

Biodiversity

333. During the year the MoD published its Biodiversity Strategic Statement for the Defence Estate. The estate includes 174 Sites of Special Scientific Interest. The quality of these continued to improve, with 81% in England, 68% in Scotland, 75% in Wales and 57% in Northern Ireland meeting the target condition against the Government target of 95% by 2010. The Department has also set a goal that 80% of the Ministry of Defence sites with significant biodiversity interest should have an integrated land or rural management plan by 2008.

Biodiversity at Salisbury Plain

Land condition

334. A small proportion of defence land is contaminated. The Department is working to complete desktop assessments. Over 3,000 Land Quality Assessment Reports have been produced, which include all priority sites (such as those to be disposed, and those known or suspected to pose the most significant risk) but it is unlikely that desktop assessment work will be completed by the end of 2007 for all parts of the defence estate as originally planned.

Conservation and Access

335. The Department owns over half the Government's historic assets, including over 800 historic buildings in the UK of which 782 are listed. In the 2005 English Heritage Biennial Conservation Report there were 28 defence entries in the Buildings at Risk register. Four have since been removed: two by repair or reuse, and two by disposal. The Department also owns over 9,000 archaeological monuments (of which more than 900 are scheduled), and nine registered parks and gardens. In total the Department is responsible for 1,056 scheduled monuments. At 31 March 2007, 70% of the Department's listed buildings and 73% of Scheduled Monuments were in good or fair condition. The condition of a further 16% of listed buildings and 5.5% of scheduled monuments was unknown and the Department is committed to establishing this by April 2008. A number of defence sites have been designated as or are located within Conservation Areas and parts of the MoD estate lie within nine World Heritage Sites including the City of Bath, Hadrian's Wall and St Kilda. The Overseas estate also contains important historic features, such as classical remains in Cyprus and historic buildings in Gibraltar (a candidate World Heritage Site). Responsible management of these nationally and internationally important historic assets is an important strand of the Department's sustainable development strategy. A delivery plan has been put in place to strengthen the condition-monitoring of our historic estate and ensure heritage is appropriately considered within programmes and projects. Progress is reported within the MoD Heritage Biennial Report.

336. The Department seeks to provide as much public access for recreation to defence land as is consistent with safety and security obligations and the delivery of the military capability for which the land is held. A new permissive bridleway in the North Yorkshire Moors through the RAF Fylingdales estate was opened in April 2007. The MoD also launched its new access website in 2006, which provides members of the general public with timely and up to date information about opportunities for accessing and in particular walking on, the defence estate. In November 2006 Defence Estates won the British Horse Society Access award for the public agency that has done most for equestrian access. A network of some 180 voluntary Conservation Groups support the Department by monitoring habitats and species, providing input to management plans and carrying out practical work in support of nature conservation and archaeology on the rural estate. More detailed information can be found in both the Annual *Stewardship Report on the Defence Estate* and the defence conservation magazine *Sanctuary*.

Further sources of information

339. Additional Information of Estate is available from the following sources:

- Quarterly PSA reports at www.mod.uk;
- UK Defence Statistics, available at www.dasa.mod.uk;
- NAO Report Managing the Defence Estate (HC 25 of 25 May 2005)
- NAO Report on Managing the Defence Estate: Quality and Sustainability (HC154 of 23 March 2007) available at www.nao.org.uk;
- Evidence to Public Accounts Committee on Managing the Defence Estate: Quality and Sustainability on 14 May 2007, to be published as HC537-I, available at www.parliament.uk;
- Evidence to House of Commons Defence Committee on The Work of Defence Estates on 15 May 2007, to be published as HC 535-I, available at www.parliament.uk;
- 2007 Stewardship Report on the Defence Estate available at www.defence-estates.mod.uk (to be published in September 2007);
- The Defence Estate Strategy 2006 – In Trust and On Trust available at www.defence-estates.mod.uk;
- DE Corporate Plan 2006-2011 available at www.defence-estates.mod.uk;
- DE Information Booklet at www.defence-estates.mod.uk;
- MoD Access and Recreation website at www.mod.uk/access;
- Defence Estates Annual Report and Accounts at www.defence-estates.mod.uk;
- Defence Estates Framework Document at www.defence-estates.mod.uk;
- Securing the Future – UK Government sustainable development strategy, CM 6467 available at www.sustainable-development.gov.uk;
- Sustainable Development Annual Report 2006 available at www.mod.uk
- MoD Sustainable Development Delivery Strategy for Non-Operational Energy available at www.mod.uk;
- MoD Sustainable Development Action Plan – February 2006 and revised version July 2007 available at www.mod.uk;
- Biodiversity Strategic Statement for the Defence Estate at www.defence-estates.mod.uk;
- Safety, Health and Environmental Protection in the Ministry of Defence – Policy Statement by the Secretary of State for Defence – January 2007 available at www.mod.uk
- OGC report on Construction Demand / Capacity Supply 2005 – 2015 available at www.ogc.gov.uk;
- Sanctuary at www.defence-estates.mod.uk;
- Information on accessing the defence estate available at www.access.mod.uk;
- Sustainable operations on the Government Estate available at www.sustainable-development.gov.uk

Essay –Environmental Management on the Defence Estate

A haven for Britain's wildlife is perhaps not the first image that springs to mind when thinking of the Ministry of Defence. But the Department's 160,000 hectares of rural estate, of training areas, small arms ranges, test and evaluation ranges and aerial bombing ranges, is just that. It includes 174 Sites of Special Scientific Interest, 41 Special Protection Areas; 65 Special Areas of Conservation; and 26 RAMSAR listed wetlands of international importance. It also includes over half of the Government Historic estate.

Managing this biodiversity rich and internationally important asset is a daunting responsibility. The MoD aims to be an exemplar in its stewardship, balancing the delivery of military training to support operational commitments with protecting the natural environment. And there can be some seemingly perverse benefits. For example, tanks cut tracks; but flooded tank tracks provide a perfect habitat for the rare British Fairy Shrimp, a tiny crustacean dependent on temporary pools of standing water. While the Department is focused on supporting military capability, it is also able to create and retain the natural environment. Areas are left to rest and Sites of Special Scientific Interest placed out of bounds where necessary, and the Department works with its tenants to ensure their farming practices work with rather than against nature.

The annual MoD Sanctuary Awards illustrate the range of achievements well. They encourage efforts that benefit wildlife, archaeology, or community awareness of conservation on the MoD estate. The winners in 2006 were Holcombe Moor Heritage Group, for their work on historic landscape assessment at Holcombe Moor Training Area, Bury near Manchester. This project turned back the clock on a mosaic of stone walls and hedges to reveal a variety of historic farmsteads and enabled the development of the landscape to be traced from medieval times to the present. The joint runners up were for improvement work to the Site of Special Scientific Interest at Predannack, and the recreation of an Iron Age cornfield by the Leconfield Conservation Group. Working with the National Trust, Cornwall Wildlife Trust and Natural England significant environmental improvements were made at the Royal Naval Air Station Predannack in Cornwall by clearing large areas of scrub and drilling a solar-powered bore hole to provide water to allow the grazing of cattle, benefiting the flora and general wellbeing of the land. The Leconfield Carrs Conservation group promoted greater community awareness of the Iron Age and Romano-British history of their area. The group held an open day with demonstration of excavations and historic foods, including pigeon and snails.

The Department has Environmental Management Systems in place for over 80% of the Training Estate to ensure that environmental management commitments are properly balanced. Some 120 sites with significant biodiversity interest, including all the most complex and largest training areas, have Integrated Land Management Plans. These take a holistic approach, comprising a number of component plans addressing different aspects including biodiversity, forestry, and heritage integrated through a single costed action plan with timescales. They are developed through consultation to create a sense of ownership and a balanced approach to what are often conflicting pressures.

This integrated approach has delivered a positive approach to environmental management which is delivering excellent results, for example:
● At Sennybridge Army Training Area in mid Wales, a 90km permissive bridle path was built encircling the Training Area. Working with a range of stakeholders including the Wales Tourist Board, Welsh Development Agency, and Powys County Council, the project significantly improved access to the MoD estate in this area;
● At Otterburn in Northumberland the Department is delivering a flagship visitor information project for the Otterburn Training Area, in association with Northumberland National Park Authority. The new www. otterburnranges.co.uk website provides further information;
● On Salisbury Plain the Department has worked to increase the breeding population of the endangered Stone Curlew. This helped raise the overall UK population to 377 pairs, the most recorded in recent years, and was welcomed by the Royal Society for the Protection of Birds. Also on Salisbury Plain the Raptor and Owl Nest box project has led to 73 breeding pairs recorded, with the 1000th owlet ringed. In 1987 only one barn owl with three owlets was recorded.

The Department has also made significant progress improving the quality of the Sites of Special Scientific Interest for which it is responsible. Since 2003 the proportion of sites in favourable or favourable recovering condition has improved from 53% to 82%. Innovation is often the key to success. For example, at Warcop in Cumbria the Department is using radio-controlled collars to make sure sheep are grazing in the right places in order to manage and keep Helbeck Wood and Appleby Fells in the right condition. Similar approaches are used to manage Highland cows and calves at Barry Buddon in Scotland, with White Park Cattle on Salisbury Plain and in Dorset, with Shetland Ponies at Penhale in Cornwall; and with Scottish Blackface sheep in Suffolk.

183

Reputation

Objective: Enhance our reputation with our own people and externally.

Assessment and Performance Measures

Assessment: Considerable work went into external and internal communications and accountability during the year. The overall reputation of the Armed Forces and MoD rose among the public and remained very high among military and civilian personnel. But the favourability ratings on how well the Forces are equipped and personnel are looked after are a cause for concern.

Continuing Improvement in overall ratings of our reputation of MoD and UK Armed Forces among the UK public:

- Favourable ratings for Armed Forces of 76% (64% in March 2006); unfavourable ratings of 3% (5% in March 2006);
- Favourable ratings for MoD of 44% (38% in March 2006); unfavourable ratings of 13% (14% in March 2006).

Continuing improvement in overall scores of our reputation among Service and civilian personnel:

- 85% of Service and civilian personnel thought that the Armed Forces were a Force for Good;
- 73% of Service and civilian personnel thought that the MoD was a Force for Good.

Defence in the Public Eye

337. The activities of the MoD and our Forces have been constantly in the public eye during a busy year for defence. The Department continued to work to ensure that Parliament, the public, the media and other stakeholders were presented with the information they need to understand what the MoD and the Forces are doing and why. The main focus of parliamentary and public attention has been on operations in Iraq and, increasingly, in Afghanistan and the Department arranged visits by MPs and journalists to these theatres. Polling of public opinion shows that it remains strongly favourable towards the Armed Forces (see paragraph xx below).

Defence Communication Strategy

338. A Defence Communications Strategy was approved by the Defence Management Board during the year. This aims to enhance the reputation of the MoD and Armed Forces both internally and externally using all the communications channels at our disposal. It includes increased focus on internal communications, more emphasis on use of new media and regional and local media, more effective use of imagery, greater attention to the management of key stakeholders, a more coherent approach to branding, increased skills and professionalism for those involved in communications, and greater priority on measuring the effectiveness of our efforts. The strategy should enable a more joined up communications effort across defence against a common set of priorities, specifically: demonstrating success on operations; showing that Service personnel are valued and are equipped for the tasks they are asked to do; demonstrating that the MoD provides value for money to the taxpayer and the contribution that defence makes to the country, and showing that it is an open Department of State. The Department is now putting in place the necessary structures and work to implement the strategy.

Communicating the Work of the Department and Armed Forces

339. Significant policy changes and adjustments to force levels are announced to Parliament. Defence Ministers made a number of such announcements during the course of the year including on revised force levels in Iraq, Afghanistan and Bosnia. Defence is debated several times a year in both Houses of Parliament, Ministers answer oral questions on defence issues once a month and have provided written answers to over 4,800 parliamentary questions, as well as providing Written Ministerial Statements on important defence issues. The Department also gave written and oral evidence to the Select Committees of the House of Commons and House of Lords. (see Annex A on pages xx-xx). The Armed Forces Parliamentary Scheme provided a mechanism for MPs to spend time with the Armed Forces, including in operational theatres. Ministers and MoD officials also answered over 14,000 letters from MPs, peers and members of the public. Last year the Department received 3,185 requests for information under the Freedom of Information Act, representing 18% of the total received by Whitehall. 83% were answered within statutory timescales. 70% resulted in full release of the requested information and it was necessary to decline in full, only 11% of requests made under the Act, compared with 60% and 19% respectively for Whitehall.

340. Defence Ministers, together with military personnel and officials, participated regularly in academic fora on defence and security issues. They also delivered speeches to a range of national and international audiences, placed a number of articles on defence issues in the national and regional media and gave several media briefings on topical issues. Day to day engagement with the regional and national media is conducted by Defence Press Officers who are responsible for notifying the media of newsworthy events, arranging facilities, responding to questions from journalists and supplying facts. The MoD wants the media to have access to UK personnel on operations and arranged regular visits to Iraq, Afghanistan and the Balkans. The Defence Media Operations Centre provides training for military and civilian personnel before they take up operational media posts and has a surge capacity to provide additional support in times of peak demand. During the year it deployed teams of personnel to Iraq and Afghanistan, and supported the 90th Anniversary commemorations of the Battle of the Somme and the 25th Anniversary of the Falklands.

2006 RAF Waddington Air Show

341. The single Services delivered over 250 formal presentations in town halls, conference centres and schools across the county. 780 public events were conducted, ranging from the Mountbatten Festival of Music to air shows. The Services have continued to develop new and innovative ways of engaging with the public, for example through developing merchandising strategies, specialist documentaries and feature articles, greater use of new and alternative media, book deals and parliamentary and stakeholder engagement. The Defence Schools Team visited over 460 schools. It will be replaced at the end of this year by an innovative e-learning package called Defence Dynamics which will communicate defence messages into schools through lesson plans for the National Curriculum. The Defence Web has been refreshed and now receives 1.5 million page views every month, whilst the Service sites attract over two million individual visitors.

342. The Department's prime communications focus over the last year was explaining the UK's role as part of the UN endorsed coalition effort in Iraq (see paragraphs 7-15 under *Current Operations*) and in support of the democratically elected government in Afghanistan (see paragraphs 16-24 under *Current Operations*). There was also a considerable communications effort to support the Government's announcement to renew the nuclear deterrent (see paragraph 77 under *Policy*, and the essay on page 50); and to explain the support provided to Service personnel, for example on accommodation (see paragraphs 318-319 under *Estate*); medical services (see paragraphs 239-242 under *Health and Safety*); recruitment and retention (see paragraphs 301-303 under *Manpower*); and the quality of the equipment used by the Armed Forces, how it has improved and how it is contributing to operational success (see paragraph 162 under *Future Capabilities and Infrastructure*). Commemorative events have continued to be good vehicles to link past achievements with current capabilities as well as recognise the sacrifice of those who died. The key events were the Somme and Falklands Anniversaries. There have been a record number of documentaries as the broadcast media has expanded. These have ranged from current affairs programmes on current operations to series about the Royal Marines, Grenadier Guards and the GR4 Tornado Force.

Table 30 External Opinion Survey headlines

Armed Forces	March 2007	March 2006	Ministry of Defence	March 2007	March 2006
Overall favourable impression of Armed Forces	76%	64%	Overall favourable impression of MoD	44%	38%
Overall unfavourable impression of Armed Forces	3%	5%	Overall unfavourable impression of MoD	13%	14%
UK Armed Forces are among the best in the world (average for RN/Army/RAF)	82%	N/A	UK Armed Forces are well equipped	26%	37%
UK needs strong Armed Forces	88%	80%	MoD gives the taxpayer value for money	39%	34%
UK Armed Forces help make the world a safer place	76%	73%	MoD is as open as it can be about its activities	47%	31%
UK Armed Forces have the highest professional standards	74%	69%			
UK Armed Forces look after their people	57%	61%			
UK Armed Forces make a positive contribution to the UK through their activities at home	84%	44%			

Reputation among UK Public

343. Public support is important to the Armed Forces and to the achievement of Defence Objectives. The MoD carries out regular public opinion surveys, using an independent polling company, to track the reputation of the Armed Forces. The latest survey, conducted by Ipsos MORI in March 2007 showed public support for the Armed Forces, at 76% favourability, at its highest level since January 2003. There is overwhelming support (88%) for the UK needing strong Armed Forces, and 82% agree that our Forces are amongst the best in the world. But public perceptions on how well the Forces are equipped and personnel are looked after are far less positive and a cause for concern.

Internal Communication

344. Good internal communication is vital to defence business, to the MoD's reputation as a top class employer which values its people, and to delivering defence change programmes. During the year there were a number of major internal campaigns aimed at explaining the most important changes to the people most affected, including on the merger of the Defence Procurement Agency and Defence Logistics Organisation into the new Defence Equipment and Support organisation (see paragraph 161 under *Future Capabilities and Infrastructure*) , the mergers of the Service Headquarters Commands, changes to medical services (see paragraphs 239-240 under *Health and Safety*), the MoD Capability Review (see paragraphs 274-276 under *Business Management*, the introduction of the tri-service Joint Personnel Administration (see paragraphs 178-183 under *Future Personnel*), and developments in civilian personnel management (see paragraph 187 under *Future Personnel*). These campaigns have been conducted while continuing to provide defence personnel with honest, straightforward and timely information on military operations in Iraq, Afghanistan and elsewhere.

345. Defence in-house corporate publications are among the best in their field. In the twelve months to October 2006, the Armed Services and MoD collected some 21 separate awards for their corporate in-house communications, including the Building Public Trust Award for Telling it Like it is in the Public Sector for the MoD Annual Report and Accounts for 2005-06.

Reputation among Service and Civilian Personnel

346. The Department carries out periodical surveys of the views of defence personnel– Service and civilian – on aspects of defence and the Armed Forces. The most recent poll in spring 2007 showed that confidence that the Services and MoD act as a Force for Good remained high (85% and 73% respectively), but, as with the public, there is a less positive perception as to how well people feel they are looked after and equipped.

347. Our external and internal surveys pre-dated the illegal seizure of 15 naval personnel by Iran on 23 March and the events that followed their release on 4 April. The media handling of these events - particularly the decision to allow two Naval ratings to be paid by the media for their stories - led the Secretary of State to instigate a review of media access to defence personnel. This was led by Mr Tony Hall, the Chief Executive of the Royal Opera House and formerly the BBC's Director of News and Current Affairs.

348. The outcome of Mr Hall's review was announced on 19 July, and his report published (see separate essay). On the media handling of this particular episode, he concluded that there was a collective failure of judgement or an abstention from judgement within the MoD that led to media payments to detainees being permitted. Mr Hall recommended that in future such payments should not be allowed and this should be made clear in Departmental and Service instructions. He was also clear that responsibility for dealing with major newsworthy events should rest with MoD centrally and that the department should work to improve its relations with the media. All of the review's recommendations were accepted and they are now being implemented as a matter of urgency.

Table 31 Internal Opinion Survey headlines

Armed Forces	%	Ministry of Defence	%
UK Armed Forces are a Force for Good	85	MoD is a Force for Good	73
UK Armed Forces are among the best in the world (average for RN/Army/RAF)	79	UK Armed Forces equipment is satisfactory	46
UK needs strong Armed Forces	98	MoD gives the taxpayer value for money	57
UK Armed Forces help make the world a safer place	82	MoD is as open as it can be about its activities	62
UK Armed Forces have the highest professional standards	80	MoD looks after its civilian employees	54
UK Armed Forces look after their people	38		
UK Armed Forces make a positive contribution to the UK through their activities at home	90		
UK Armed Forces training is world class	70		

Further sources of information

349. Additional Information on Reputation is available from the following sources:

- Detailed Opinion Surveys published on www.mod.uk;
- Defence image database at www.defenceimagedatabase.mod.uk;
- *Navy News* at www.navynews.co.uk;
- *Soldier Magazine* at www.soldiermagazine.co.uk;
- *RAF News* at www.rafnews.co.uk.

Essay – Media Access to Personnel – The Hall Report

In April 2007 the Secretary of State announced an independent review of the media handling of the detention of Royal Navy personnel by Iranian authorities in March 2007 and its aftermath, including the decision to allow those involved to sell their stories. This was led by Mr Tony Hall, Chief Executive of the Royal Opera House and formerly the BBC's Director of News and Current Affairs. His report was published in June 2007, and is available at www.mod.uk. The Department will implement its recommendations in full.

The intention of the review was to provide a calm and dispassionate assessment of what happened in order to learn the lessons and improve the ability of the MoD and the Services to handle similar events in future. It was not looking to apportion blame for the decision to allow media payments to the returning detainees. The report made it plain that there was a 'collective failure of judgment or an abstention from judgment' within the Department in allowing this to happen.

The report identified the following key lessons:

- In the future media payments to serving military or civilian personnel for talking about their work should not be allowed. Work is underway to make detailed amendments to Service and MoD regulations and guidance to reflect this conclusion, pending which the interim ban on such payments announced by the Secretary of State in April 2007 will continue to apply;

- Clear responsibility should lie with the MoD centrally, rather than the single Services, to lead on the media handling of such episodes and the Department must be fully equipped to deal with them. The manning and structure of the press office and related procedures are now being reviewed to make sure that media handling is adequately dealt with in future

- MoD should work to establish improved relations with the media. This really matters. Defence is always in the news, and the public need to get an accurate understanding of the important work the Armed Forces do, and the challenges they face.

The report identified some broader themes. Perhaps most crucial is the huge change over the last 25 years in the context in which media coverage of operations takes place. Media access has increased significantly, and the agenda has changed. The focus on the individual, for example, inevitably clashes with the service ethos of group first, and the desire to present instantaneous news from the heart of the action can conflict with the need for operational security. This means that while it is clearly in the interests of both the MoD and the media to cooperate, tensions exist. The Department must manage these tensions better and work to increase mutual confidence with the media. But the report is also clear that the Department needs to help the media develop a better understanding of defence issues so that they can be set in context.

The Armed Forces are in a difficult position. A balance has to be found between openness and risks to security and the over-riding ethos in the services which puts the interests of the whole above those of the individual. The MoD recognises that it must explain, as far as possible, what it is doing to the public, and often the best and most compelling account is provided by soldiers, sailors and airmen rather than senior officers, politicians or civil servants. But in circumstances like this episode individual Service personnel (and where necessary their families) must be supported and get the right protection from intrusion. The report identified that work was needed to establish a clearer policy on the naming of individuals and their families in cases of this kind. This is underway. It recommended that the Department work more closely with the Press Complaints Commission in the future.

The report also made a number of recommendations on the need for clearer decision-making processes. Unequivocal understanding of who should sanction what is essential. The Capability Review published in March 2007 also highlighted this. The Department had therefore already been looking at how to clarify responsibilities and improve accountability.

The report said that acceptance of payments from the media offended the public and their view of the special place of the Armed Forces in British life. It also ran contrary to what the Armed Forces believe they stand for: the team versus the individual, and selfless service on behalf of the nation. The Department has sought to learn the lessons from the media handling of this difficult episode, and to be open and accountable in doing so. The report offered clear, detailed recommendations, all of which have been accepted. Some have already been implemented, and the great majority of the rest should be implemented by the end of the year.

189

Departmental Resource Accounts 2006-07

Section 2:

Notes to the Accounts

The Annual Report

History and Background

The present Ministry of Defence (MoD), the Department, was formed by the amalgamation in 1964 of the Ministry of Defence, the Admiralty, the War Office and the Air Ministry, and the inclusion in 1971 of the Ministry of Aviation Supply. In 1973, the operations of the Atomic Weapons Establishment were transferred from the UK Atomic Energy Authority to the MoD.

Principal Activity

The principal activity of the Department is to deliver security for the people of the United Kingdom and the Overseas Territories by defending them, including against terrorism, and act as a force for good by strengthening international peace and stability. This is achieved by working together to produce battle-winning people and equipment that are:

- fit for the challenge of today,

- ready for the tasks of tomorrow, and

- capable of building for the future.

Further definition of the Departmental Objectives in terms of outputs is given in the Statement of Operating Costs by Departmental Aim and Objectives and in its supporting Note to the Accounts – Note 24.

Departmental Boundary[1]

At 31 March 2007, the Department consisted of 12 (2005-06:13) Top Level Budget (TLB) Holders; the merger of the Commander in Chief Fleet and 2nd Sea Lord organisations on 1 April 2006 created a single Naval TLB. The TLBs are responsible for providing forces and support services required for a modern defence force and are detailed in Note 2 to the accounts – Analysis of Net Resource Outturn. Within the TLBs, there were 57 (2005-06: 55) reporting entities, known as management groupings, recording accounting balances and transactions and producing detailed management accounting information as part of in-year financial management and planning and budgeting processes. One of the aims of the Department's Simplify and Improve initiative is to reduce the workload on finance staff. Consequently, whilst accounting transactions are still attributed to the management group level for in-year management purposes, reporting for the annual financial accounts is now normally completed only at TLB level.

There are 17 on-vote Defence Agencies (listed in Note 35), a reduction of 3 from 2005-06 following the removal of agency status on 1 April 2006 from: the Naval Recruiting and Training Agency, the Army Training and Recruiting Agency and the RAF Training Group Defence Agency as these training organisations became an integral part of their respective Services' TLBs. Defence Agencies publish their own accounts. All on-vote agencies are also management groupings, except for the Defence Procurement Agency and Defence Estates, which are TLBs, and the Disposal Services Agency and the Defence Transport and Movements Agency, which form part of larger management groupings. Further information relating to the Defence Agencies can be found at Annex E to the Annual Report and Accounts.

Also included within the Departmental Boundary are Advisory Non-Departmental Public Bodies (NDPBs) sponsored by the Department; these are listed at Note 35 – Entities within the Departmental Boundary.

There are 5 (2005-06: 5) Executive Defence Agencies established as Trading Funds, and owned by the Secretary of State for Defence, at 31 March 2007. These Trading Funds produce their own accounts and fall outside the Departmental Boundary. Further details are at: Note 15 – Investments, Note 32 – Related Party Transactions and at Annex E. On 22 May 2007 the MoD announced the decision to merge two of the Trading Funds, ABRO and the Defence Aviation Repair Agency, with effect from April 2008, to form a new defence support group providing a maintenance repair, overhaul and upgrade capability in support of the Armed Forces.

The Department also sponsors 5 Executive Non Departmental Public Bodies (NDPBs), which are self accounting and produce their own accounts. They receive Grants-in-Aid from the MoD and fall outside the Departmental Boundary. Further details are at Note 32 – Related Party Transactions.

1 The Departmental Boundary in this context relates to the boundary of the Departmental Resource Accounts.

The Oil and Pipelines Agency and the Fleet Air Arm Museum are Public Corporations sponsored by the Department, which fall outside the Departmental Boundary.

On 10 February 2006, QinetiQ Group plc was successfully floated on the London Stock Exchange, via an Initial Public Offering (IPO). The IPO completed the process of transforming the MoD in-house research and development organisation into an international defence technology and security company. QinetiQ Group plc is outside the Departmental Boundary; details of the MoD's remaining shareholding in the company are set out at Note 15 – Investments and Note 32 – Related Party Transactions.

Pension Liabilities

The transactions and balances of the Armed Forces Pension Scheme (AFPS) (including the Gurkha Pension Scheme, the Non-Regular Permanent Staff Pension Scheme, and the Reserve Forces Pension Scheme) and the Armed Forces Compensation Scheme are not consolidated in these financial statements. The report and accounts of the AFPS are prepared separately; further information is available on the website:
http://www.official-documents.gov.uk/document/hc0506/hc15/1508/1508.asp.

The Department's share of the transactions and balances of other pension schemes to which employees belong (e.g. under Civil Service Pension (CSP) arrangements, the NHS Superannuation Scheme and the Teachers' Pension Scheme) is also not consolidated in these accounts; separate accounts are prepared for the schemes and details can be found on the following websites:
www.civilservice-pensions.gov.uk/
www.dfes.gov.uk/aboutus/reports/
www.nhspa.gov.uk/site/index.cfm

Further information on the various pension schemes can be found in the Remuneration Report and at Note 9 – Staff Numbers and Costs.

Future Developments

The Department has comprehensive efficiency and change programmes that extend right across the Department and affect every employee. The details of many of these programmes are set out in the section on Efficiency and Change in the Annual Performance Report, which forms the first part of the MoD Annual Report and Accounts.

In July 2006, Ministers announced plans to establish a new organisation, Defence Equipment & Support (DE&S), to carry out integrated defence equipment procurement and support. DE&S will be formed by merging the activities carried out by the Defence Procurement Agency and the Defence Logistics Organisation. As part of the re-organisation, agency status will be removed from: the Disposal Services Agency, the Defence Procurement Agency, the Defence Communications Services Agency, the British Forces Post Office and the Defence Transport and Movements Agency, with effect from 1 April 2007.

Progress on the collocation and rationalisation of the operational command headquarters and the personnel & training headquarters of the Services has continued. The collocation of the RAF's Strike and Personnel and Training Commands, in October 2006, was followed by their merger to form a single Air Command with its Headquarters at RAF High Wycombe, on 1 April 2007. Project Hyperion is taking forward the re-organisation of the Army's Land and Adjutant General Commands with progressive collocation to a new Land Forces Headquarters planned to be completed by March 2009. GOC Northern Ireland ceases to be a TLB Holder from 1 April 2007.

The process of organisation review continues to identify opportunities to reduce the number of on-vote Agencies. Agency status will be removed from: the Defence Bills Agency, Defence Estates and the Duke of York's Royal Military School with effect from 1 April 2007. The merger of the Veterans Agency and the Armed Forces Personnel Administration Agency to form the Service Personnel and Veterans Agency (SPVA), with effect from 1 April 2007, will also reduce the number of Agencies. MoD's programme of efficiency and business change including extensive organisational restructuring and rationalisation is likely to reduce the number of Agencies still further.

Joint Personnel Administration (JPA) will modernise the personnel management and administration of the Armed Forces by harmonising and simplifying a range of personnel policies and processes and by introducing new information systems. Roll-out of JPA to the RAF in April 2006 was followed by the RN in November 2006 and the Army at the end of March 2007.

The Defence Resource Management Programme (DRMP) aims to simplify and improve current financial processes, structures and systems to reduce costs and improve decision-making. As part of the Programme, the Financial Management Shared Service Centre (FMSSC), which took over the responsibilities of the Defence Bills Agency, was formally established in April 2007. The FMSSC is also responsible for fixed asset processing, cash and banking services and the preparation of the annual accounts. During 2007, the FMSCC will undertake changes to accounts payable processes and systems as part of the DRMP.

Management

The Ministers who had responsibility for the Department and the composition of the Defence Management Board (DMB) during the year ended 31 March 2007 are shown on pages 202 to 203 in the Remuneration Report.

Fixed Assets

During 2006 the intangible and tangible fixed assets and related provisions, contingent liabilities and reserves, held on individual TLB Fixed Asset registers, were transferred to Single Balance Sheet Owners based on the category of asset managed:

- Land and Buildings – Defence Estates

- Single Use Military Equipment – Defence Logistics Organisation

- Plant & Machinery – Defence Logistics Organisation

- Transport – Defence Logistics Organisation

- IT & Communications – Defence Communication Services Agency

- Equipment Related Assets Under Construction – Defence Procurement Agency

Changes in fixed asset values during the year are summarised at Notes 13, 14 and 15 (Intangible Assets, Tangible Fixed Assets and Investments) to the accounts. Note 1 – Statement of Accounting Policies provides details of the accounting policies relating to fixed assets.

Research and Development

Research and development expenditure is incurred mainly for the future benefit of the Department. Such expenditure is primarily incurred on the development of new single use military equipment and on the improvement of the effectiveness and capability of existing single use military equipment.

In accordance with SSAP13, "Accounting for Research and Development" (as adapted for the public sector by HM Treasury's Financial Reporting Manual (FReM), paragraphs 5.3.6 to 5.3.8), amounts spent on research are not capitalised, and certain development expenditure is expensed. The amounts are included at Note 10 – Other Operating Costs.

Capitalised development expenditure is included in Intangible Assets, where appropriate, and shown in Note 13.

Net Expenditure

The Operating Cost Statement shows net expenditure of £33,948,669,000 which has been charged to the General Fund. Cash voted by Parliament for the provision of Defence Capability (RfR 1), Conflict Prevention (RfR 2) and War Pensions Benefits (RfR 3) amounting to £31,683,881,000 has been credited to the General Fund (Note 21).

Dividends

Details of dividends and loan interest received on investments can be found at Notes 11, 12 and 15 (Income, Net Interest Payable and Investments) to the accounts.

195

Payments to Suppliers

The Department's bills, with the exception of some payments to suppliers by units locally, are paid through the Defence Bills Agency (DBA). In 2006-07, the DBA met its target by paying 99.95% of all correctly submitted bills within eleven calendar days, ensuring that the Department is in compliance with its statutory obligation under the Late Payment of Commercial Debts (Interest) Act 1998. Commercial debt interest paid during the year amounted to £8,603 (2005-06: £14,709) and included interest paid by units locally of £23 (2005-06: £48).

Departmental Reporting Cycle

The MoD's main Departmental Report presented to Parliament each year comprises the *Ministry of Defence Annual Performance Report* (which forms the first section of the Annual Report and Accounts and sets out the MoD's performance, against the objectives stated in the Statement of Operating Costs by Departmental Aim and Objectives, over the year and developments since the year end, where appropriate) and *The Government's Expenditure Plans: Ministry of Defence*, which sets out planned expenditure over the following year. The MoD's financial performance is also reported to Parliament in the explanatory memorandum to the Main Estimates, and in the *Public Expenditure Outturn White Paper*. Performance against Public Service Agreement and Efficiency targets is reported to Parliament during the year in the Autumn Performance Report. The latest copy of *The Government's Expenditure Plans: Ministry of Defence* can be found at the website:
http://www.mod.uk/DefenceInternet/AboutDefence/CorporatePublications/BusinessPlans

Financial Instruments

The Department does not trade or enter into any speculative transactions in foreign currencies. Forward contract commitments entered into to cover future expenditure in foreign currencies are stated at Note 28 – Financial Instruments.

Provision of Information and Consultation with Employees

The MoD has a strong Whitley committee structure through which employees' representatives, in the form of recognised industrial and non industrial trades unions (TUs), are consulted on and informed of all matters likely to affect our civilian personnel. This structure is supported by formal policy and procedures for consulting and informing TUs. We also advocate the development of informal relationships with the TUs to discuss ideas together. Our policy makes clear that consulting the TUs is not a substitute for dealing with personnel direct, and vice versa. Managers and project leaders, for example, are encouraged to use all media available, including cascade briefings, newsletters and intranet websites/email. In respect of Service personnel, the process operates through the chain of command, with no formal representation through the TUs. Additional information on communication, internal and external, is provided in the Reputation section of the Annual Performance Report, which forms the first part of this Annual Report and Accounts.

Management Commentary

Performance

The Annual Performance Report forms the first part of the MoD Annual Report and Accounts and provides the detailed information set out, as best practice, in the Accounting Standards Board's (ASB's) Reporting Statement: Operating and Financial Review.

The Performance Report uses the Defence Balanced Scorecard structure to:

● describe Defence strategies, objectives and activities, and how they are managed and delivered in the legislative, regulatory and external environments in which we operate;

● provide a forward looking view of performance and development for the reporting year, with sections on Current and Future Operations as well as Future Capabilities;

● set out information on the availability and use of resources, covering: finance, manpower and estate as well as aspects such as reputation and the Wider Markets Initiative.

The Annual Performance Report also describes some of the risks and uncertainties which might affect performance.

The Statement on Internal Control describes the Department's risk and control framework and its relationship to the Performance Management System. The Departmental approach to Performance Management is detailed in Annex D to the Annual Report and Accounts.

Environmental, Social, Community, Employee and Other Matters

The preface to the Annual Report and Accounts summarises senior managers' views of how the document sets out the Department's work to realise the Defence Vision, highlighting all relevant matters. Some specific aspects mentioned in the ASB's Reporting Statement that are covered by the Performance Report are:

● **Social and Community Issues** – included in the sections: Current Operations e.g. Crisis Response Operations and Military Aid to the Civil Authorities and Wider Government, e.g. Defence in the Wider Community and Young People: Building Skills and Raising Expectations.

● **Environmental** – aspects are included in the Sustainable Development sections under Estate and Wider Government and in the essay on Defence and Climate Change. The MoD owns a large, varied and complex estate, with most of the UK's indigenous habitat types, exceptional biodiversity and some of the finest archaeology in the country. Further information on how the MoD is undertaking its responsibility for stewardship of the estate in the UK and overseas including links to, *Sanctuary*, the annual MoD Conservation magazine can be found at the MoD Conservation Office website:
http://www.defence-estates.mod.uk/conservation/index.php

● **Employees** – information is provided in the sections: Manpower, Personnel Management, Health and Safety and Future Personnel Plans and in the essay on Joint Personnel Administration. Information on policy and numbers of disabled staff can be found in the Manpower section and at Annex F – Government Standards.

● **Performance Indicators** – these are included at the start of each section of the Performance Report where the Objective, Public Service Targets, Performance Measures and the Assessment against the measures are set out. Additional information can be found in the *MoD Departmental Plan 2005-2009* available on the website: www.mod.uk/DefenceInternet/AboutDefence/CorporatePublications/BusinessPlans and in the Summary of Progress against SR2004 Public Service Agreement Objectives and Targets at the beginning of the Performance Report.

- **Contractual Arrangements** – some of the Department's major contractual commitments are detailed in Note 27 to the accounts – Private Finance Initiative (PFI) Commitments. The Defence Science and Technology Laboratory, the UK Hydrographic Office, the Met Office, the Defence Aviation Repair Agency and ABRO are Executive Defence Agencies financed by Trading Fund; they provide essential services to the Department. Further information on Trading Funds is at Annex E to the Annual Report and Accounts. Details of significant contracts relating to the management of the Defence Estate are included in the Estate section of the Performance Report.

- **Spending Review** – the financing implications of significant changes following the Department's Spending Review are set out in *The Government's Expenditure Plans 2006-07 to 2007-08: Ministry of Defence*, which, with the MoD Annual Report and Accounts, comprise the MoD's Departmental Report. *The Government's Expenditure Plans 2006-07 to 2007-08: Ministry of Defence* and the *MoD Investment Strategy* are available on the websites:
http://www.mod.uk/DefenceInternet/AboutDefence/CorporatePublications/BusinessPlans/
GovernmentExpenditurePlans
and http://www.mod.uk/DefenceInternet/AboutDefence/CorporatePublications/PolicyStrategy/
DefenceDepartmentalInvestmentStrategy.htm

- **Contingent Liabilities** – Details of Contingent Liabilities disclosed under Financial Reporting Standard (FRS) 12 and additional liabilities included for Parliamentary Reporting and Accountability are at Notes 29 and 30 to these accounts.

Reconciliation of Resource Expenditure Between Estimates, Accounts and Budgets

	2006-07 £M Estimate	2006-07 £M Outturn	2005-06 £M Estimate	2005-06 £M Outturn
Net Resources Outturn (Estimates)	34,824	34,005	36,839	34,862
Adjustments to include:				
Consolidated Fund Extra Receipts in the OCS	-	(56)	-	(468)
Other adjustments				
Net Operating Cost (Accounts)	34,824	33,949	36,839	34,394
Adjustments to remove:				
voted expenditure outside the budget	(4)	12	(2,349)	(1,060)
Adjustments to include:				
other Consolidated Fund Extra Receipts	-	56	-	468
resource consumption of non departmental public bodies	16	16	24	24
unallocated Resource Provision	220	-	-	-
Resource Budget Outturn (Budget)	35,056	34,033	34,514	33,826
of which				
Departmental Expenditure Limits (DEL)	34,104	33,451	33,727	32,937
Annually Managed Expenditure (AME)	952	582	787	889

Financial Position

The Statement of Parliamentary Supply – Summary of Resource Outturn on Page 223 compares Estimate and Outturn (net total resources). A detailed explanation of the variances against the Departmental Expenditure Limit is shown in paragraphs 285 to 286 within Finances in the Performance Report.

Request for Resources (RfR) 1, Provision of Defence Capability, provides for expenditure primarily to meet the MoD's operational support and logistics services costs and the costs of providing the equipment capability required by defence policy. Within RfR1, the Estimate and Outturn for Operating Appropriations in Aid are shown as equal amounts. Any Appropriations in Aid in excess of the Estimate are shown at Note 5, and these will be surrendered to the Consolidated Fund. This RfR is made up from three different controls:

● Resource Departmental Expenditure Limit (DEL), which consists of items such as pay, equipment support costs, fuel and administrative expenses, as well as non cash items such as depreciation, cost of capital and movements in the level of provisions;

● Annually Managed Expenditure (AME), which covers programmes that are demand-led, or exceptionally volatile in a way that could not be controlled by the Department, and where the programmes are so large that the Department could not be expected to absorb the effects of volatility in its programme, such as movements in nuclear provisions; and

● Non Budget costs, items of expenditure which are subject to Parliamentary but not Treasury control, and therefore outside DEL and AME. The majority of the costs relate to changes in the discount rates for pensions and other long term liabilities.

The net outturn for Total Resources is £34,004,995,000 against an Estimate of £34,824,389,000; an underspend of £819,394,000.

The net outturn for RfR1, Provision of Defence Capability is £31,518,502,000 against an Estimate of £32,349,202,000; an underspend of £830,700,000. The variance against the Estimate results from an underspend of £148,322,000 against Resource DEL; an underspend of £666,526,000 in Annually Managed Expenditure (AME); and an underspend of £15,852,000 in Non Budget.

RfR2, Conflict Prevention, shows a net outturn of £1,448,420,000 against an Estimate of £1,427,526,000; an overspend of £20,894,000. This excess relates to non-cash costs, such as depreciation charges for military equipment and the firing of guided weapons, missiles and bombs in Afghanistan, which were higher than forecasted at the time the Estimates were prepared.

RfR3, War Pensions Benefits shows a net outturn of £1,038,073,000 against an Estimate of £1,047,661,000; a small underspend of £9,588,000. This RfR provides for the payment of war disablement and war widows' pensions in accordance with relevant legislation, this is all AME. The costs of administering war pensions are borne by RfR1.

The non-operating Appropriations in Aid show a net outturn of £498,287,000 against an Estimate of £556,152,000, which assumed higher fixed asset disposals in 2006-07.

The Net Cash Requirement shows a net outturn of £31,454,292,000, against an Estimate of £33,746,251,000; an underspend of £2,291,959,000.

Other Areas

The Department's Accounts include a note (Note 31) on Losses and Special Payments. The nature of the losses and special payments, as defined in Government Accounting, varies from year to year depending on the circumstances arising and decisions made by the Department during the year. Cases brought forward from last year are shown separately in order properly to identify the cases arising during the year. Further details on this Statement are included in the Resources Section of the Departmental Performance Report.

The Department is required to have a professional revaluation of its land and building fixed assets every five years, and manages this process through a rolling programme. The current revaluation programme is due to complete in 2007-08 and is currently under review to ensure that it is being carried out effectively and at minimum cost.

Details of directorships and other significant interests held by Ministers are set out in The Register of Lords' Interests and The Register of Members' Interests which are available on the UK Parliament website: http://www.parliament.uk/about_commons/register_of_members__interests.cfm

Details of directorships and other significant interests held by Defence Management Board members are included at Note 32 – Related Party Transactions.

Auditor

The financial statements for the Department are audited by the Comptroller and Auditor General under the Government Resources and Accounts Act 2000. The Certificate and Report of the Comptroller and Auditor General on the financial statements are set out on pages 217 to 222. The audit fee is disclosed in Note 10 – Other Operating Costs.

Statement as to Disclosure of Information to Auditors

So far as I, the Accounting Officer, am aware, there is no relevant audit information of which the Department's auditors are unaware, and I have taken all the steps that I ought to have taken to make myself aware of any relevant audit information and to establish that the Department's auditors are aware of that information.

Bill Jeffrey
Accounting Officer   **16 July 2007**

Remuneration Report

Remuneration Policy

The Review Body on Senior Salaries provides independent advice to the Prime Minister and the Secretary of State for Defence on the remuneration of senior civil servants and senior officers of the Armed Forces.

The Review Body also advises the Prime Minister from time to time on the pay, pensions and allowances of Members of Parliament; on Peers' allowances; and on the pay, pensions and allowances of Ministers and others, whose pay is determined by the Ministerial and Other Salaries Act 1975.

In reaching its recommendations, the Review Body has regard to the following considerations:

● the need to recruit, retain and motivate suitably able and qualified people to exercise their different responsibilities;

● regional/local variations in labour markets and their effects on the recruitment and retention of staff;

● Government policies for improving the public services including the requirement on departments to meet the output targets for the delivery of departmental services;

● the funds available to departments as set out in the Government's departmental expenditure limits; and

● the Government's inflation target.

The Review Body takes account of the evidence it receives about wider economic considerations and the affordability of its recommendations.

Further information about the work of the Review Body can be found at www.ome.uk.com.

There is an established departmental procedure for the appointment of all Non-Executive Directors (NED). This requires a visibly fair and open recruitment and selection process with appointment on merit, thus mirroring the Civil Service Commissioners' Recruitment Code for permanent employees to the Civil Service. NEDs appointed to the Defence Management Board (DMB) receive a Letter of Appointment setting out, amongst other things, details of remuneration.

Performance and Reward

The basic salary and annual increases of the civilian members of the DMB, which could include a bonus payment, are performance related and are set by the Permanent Secretaries Remuneration Committee and the MoD's Main Pay Committee.

Pay and management arrangements for members of the Senior Civil Service (SCS) reward individuals for delivery and personal achievement. These arrangements include an objective-setting regime complementary to the Department's performance management system and a performance-related incremental pay system.

Up to two thirds of the SCS population will receive a bonus with the highest level of award limited to the top ten percent assessed as making the greatest contribution; the ceiling for the bonus payments is six and a half percent (2005-06 five percent) of the SCS paybill.

All senior military officers (except for Legal Branch 2-star officers, medical and dental officers and those in the Chaplaincy branches) are paid under the Performance Management and Pay System (PMPS). Depending on their performance, individuals can be awarded a double increment, a single increment or no increment and progress accordingly up the incremental pay range for their rank. The average value of one incremental rise under the PMPS is 2.4% of salary. The award of increments is recommended by the Senior Officers' Remuneration Committee, chaired by the Department's Permanent Under Secretary.

Whilst Non-Executive remuneration is not directly linked to performance, in part to avoid any suggestion that an employee/employer relationship exists, NED performance should nevertheless be reviewed annually. The aim of any review is to consider the impact of the NED on the performance of the board, recognise the contribution of the NED and identify ways this could be improved, and provide feedback.

Senior Managers' Contracts

Civil Service appointments are made in accordance with the Civil Service Commissioners' Recruitment Code, which requires appointments to be on merit on the basis of fair and open competition but also includes the circumstances when appointments may otherwise be made. Further information about the work of the Civil Service Commissioners can be found at www.civilservicecommissioners.gov.uk.

Unless otherwise stated below, the officials covered by this report hold appointments which are open-ended. Early termination, other than for misconduct, would result in the individual receiving compensation as set out in the Civil Service Compensation Scheme.

For the NEDs appointed to the DMB, the Department has employed recruitment consultants to search for suitable candidates based upon a specification drawn up by senior officials. Short listed candidates are then interviewed by a selection panel (Permanent Under Secretary and Chief of the Defence Staff) with the successful candidate chosen on merit and appointed to the Board for a period of three years.

NEDs are not employees and, therefore, do not have a contractual relationship with the Department but rather are appointees who receive a Letter of Appointment setting out: their role, period of appointment, standards and any remuneration.

The Chief of Defence Procurement and the Chief Scientific Adviser are recruited on three year fixed term appointments. The conditions covering the termination of their employment are set out in their contract documents.

The Chief of the Defence Staff, Vice Chief of the Defence Staff and Single-Service Chiefs of Staff are appointed on the recommendation of the Secretary of State for Defence to the Prime Minister. The final approval of the appointee lies with Her Majesty The Queen.

Senior Military members of the Management Board hold appointments which are competed for by the 3 Services. Once selected for the appointment, they will usually hold the post for between 3 and 4 years.

Management

Ministers who had responsibility for the Department during the year were:

Secretary of State for Defence
The Right Honourable Des Browne MP was appointed as Secretary of State for Defence on 6 May 2006; prior to this, the Secretary of State for Defence was The Right Honourable Dr John Reid MP.

Minister of State for the Armed Forces
The Right Honourable Adam Ingram MP.

Minister of State for Defence Equipment and Support
Lord Drayson.

Parliamentary Under Secretary of State for Defence and Minister for Veterans
Derek Twigg MP was appointed as Parliamentary Under Secretary of State for Defence and Minister for Veterans on 7 September 2006.

The following also served as the Parliamentary Under Secretary of State for Defence and Minister for Veterans during the financial year: Tom Watson MP, 6 May 2006 to 5 September 2006, prior to 6 May 2006 the Minister was Don Touhig MP.

Recent ministerial changes
On 29 June 2007, The Right Honourable Bob Ainsworth MP was appointed as Minister of State for the Armed Forces, replacing The Right Honourable Adam Ingram MP.

The composition of the Defence Management Board (DMB), as at 31 March 2007 was:

Permanent Under Secretary of State
Bill Jeffrey CB
(appointed 21 November 2005).

Chief of the Defence Staff
Air Chief Marshal Sir Jock Stirrup GCB AFC ADC DSc FRAeS FCMI RAF
(appointed 28 April 2006, vice, General Sir Michael Walker GCB CMG CBE ADC Gen).

First Sea Lord and Chief of the Naval Staff
Admiral Sir Jonathon Band KCB ADC
(appointed 7 February 2006).

Chief of the General Staff
General Sir Richard Dannatt KCB CBE MC ADC Gen
(appointed 29 August 2006, vice, General Sir Mike Jackson GCB CBE DSO ADC Gen).

Chief of the Air Staff
Air Chief Marshal Sir Glenn Torpy KCB CBE DSO ADC BSc(Eng) FRAeS RAF
(appointed 13 April 2006, vice, Air Chief Marshal Sir Jock Stirrup GCB AFC ADC DSc FRAeS FCMI RAF).

Vice Chief of the Defence Staff
General Sir Timothy Granville-Chapman GBE KCB ADC Gen
(appointed 22 July 2005).

Second Permanent Under Secretary of State
Sir Ian Andrews CBE TD
(appointed 4 March 2002).

Chief of Defence Procurement
Sir Peter Spencer KCB
(appointed 1 May 2003).

Chief of Defence Logistics
General Sir Kevin O'Donoghue KCB CBE
(appointed 1 January 2005).

Chief Scientific Adviser
Professor Sir Roy Anderson FRS
(appointed 1 October 2004).

Finance Director
Trevor Woolley CB
(appointed to the DMB 24 June 2004).

Non-Executive Directors
Charles Miller Smith, Chairman of Scottish Power (appointed 20 May 2002).
Philippa Foster Back OBE, Director of the Institute of Business Ethics (appointed 24 July 2002)*.
Paul Skinner, Chairman of Rio Tinto plc and Rio Tinto Limited (appointed 1 June 2006).
Ian Rushby, Group Vice President and General Auditor of BP (appointed 29 January 2007).

*Chairman of the Defence Audit Committee.

Ministerial Salaries, Allowances and Taxable Benefits

(This section has been subject to audit)

	2006 – 07 Salary* £	2006 – 07 Benefits-in- kind (to nearest £100)*	2005 – 06 Salary* £	2005 – 06 Benefits-in- kind (to nearest £100)*
Secretary of State for Defence: The Rt Hon Des Browne MP (from 6 May 2006) *Full year equivalent salary*	68,642 *75,963*	Nil		
The Rt Hon Dr John Reid MP (to 5 May 2006) *Full year equivalent salary*	7,321 *75,651*	Nil	67,653 *74,902*	Nil
Minister of State for the Armed Forces: The Rt Hon Adam Ingram MP	39,405	Nil	38,854	Nil
Minister of State for Defence Equipment and Support: Lord Drayson †	Nil	Nil	Nil	Nil
Parliamentary Under Secretary of State for Defence and Minister for Veterans: Derek Twigg MP (from 7 Sep 2006) *Full year equivalent salary*	17,002 *29,909*	Nil		
Tom Watson MP (from 6 May 2006 to 5 Sep 2006) *Full year equivalent salary*	9,942 *29,786*	Nil		
Don Touhig MP (to 5 May 2006) *Full year equivalent salary*	2,883 *29,786*	Nil	26,320 *29,491*	Nil

*Disclosures cover the period during which individuals served as Ministers in the MoD.
† Lord Drayson does not receive the Ministerial salary of £80,970 to which he is entitled.

Ministers who, on leaving office, have not attained the age of 65 and are not appointed to a relevant Ministerial or other paid office within three weeks, are eligible for a severance payment of one quarter of the annual Ministerial salary being paid. Two payments were made in 2006-07 (2005-06 – One).

Ministerial Salary

'Salary' includes: gross salary; performance pay or bonuses; overtime; London weighting or London allowances; recruitment and retention allowances; private office allowances; ex-gratia payments and any other allowance to the extent that it is subject to UK taxation.

The figures above are based on payments made by the Department and thus recorded in these accounts. In respect of Ministers in the House of Commons, the Department bears only the cost of the additional Ministerial remuneration; the salary for their services as an MP – £60,277 pa with effect from 1 November 2006 (£59,686 pa with effect from 1 April 2006; £59,095 pa with effect from 1 April 2005) and various allowances to which they are entitled are borne centrally. The arrangements for Ministers in the House of Lords are different in that they do not receive a salary but rather an additional remuneration, which cannot be quantified separately from their Ministerial salaries. This total remuneration, as well as the allowances to which they are entitled, is normally paid by the Department and would therefore, normally, be shown in full above.

Benefits-in-kind for Ministers

Ministers' private use of official cars is exempt under the rules governing the definition of taxable benefits-in-kind. Where Ministers are provided with living accommodation and a taxable benefit-in-kind arises, its value is calculated in accordance with HM Revenue & Customs regulations.

Ministerial Pensions

(This section has been subject to audit)

Figures for **2006-07 in bold**. The real increase in the value of the accrued pension compared to the 2005-06 value, is shown in italics (in bands of £2,500).

	Total Accrued Pension at Retirement as at 31 Mar 07 £000	CETV* at 31 Mar 06 or Date of Appointment if Later £000	CETV at 31 Mar 07 or on Cessation of Appointment if Earlier £000	Real Increase in CETV £000
Secretary of State for Defence: The Rt Hon Des Browne MP (from 6 May 2006)	**5-10** *0-2.5*	49	63	7
The Rt Hon Dr John Reid MP (to 5 May 2006)	**10-15** *0-2.5*	181	197	14
Minister of State for the Armed Forces: The Rt Hon Adam Ingram MP	**5-10** *0-2.5*	119	146	18
Minister of State for Defence Equipment and Support: Lord Drayson †	Nil	Nil	Nil	Nil
Parliamentary Under Secretary of State for Defence and Minister for Veterans: Derek Twigg MP (from 7 Sep 2006)	**0-5** *0-2.5*	21	24	2
Tom Watson MP (from 6 May 2006 to 5 Sep 2006)	**0-5** *0-2.5*	8	9	1
Don Touhig MP (to 5 May 2006)	**0-5** *0-2.5*	50	51	1

† Lord Drayson is not a member of the Parliamentary Contributory Pension Fund.
* CETV – Cash Equivalent Transfer Value.

Pension benefits for Ministers are provided by the Parliamentary Contributory Pension Fund (PCPF). The scheme is statutory based (made under Statutory Instrument SI 1993 No 3253, as amended). Ministers who are Members of Parliament may also accrue an MP's pension under the PCPF; this pension is not included in the table above. The accrued pension quoted is the pension the Minister is entitled to receive when they reach the age of 65, or immediately on ceasing to be an active member of the scheme if they are already 65.

The arrangements for Ministers provide benefits on an 'average salary' basis, taking account of all service as a Minister. The accrual rate has been 1/40th since 15 July 2002 (or 5 July 2001 for those that chose to backdate the change). Ministers, in common with all other members of the PCPF, can opt for a 1/50th accrual rate and a lower rate of employee contribution.

Benefits for Ministers are payable at the same time as MPs' benefits become payable under the PCPF or, for those who are not MPs, on retirement from Ministerial office from age 65. Pensions are increased annually in line with changes in the Retail Prices Index. Members pay contributions of 6% of their Ministerial salary if they have opted for the 1/50th accrual rate, and 10% if they have opted for the 1/40th accrual rate. There is also an employer contribution paid by the Exchequer representing the balance of cost. This is currently 26.8% of the Ministerial salary.

The Cash Equivalent Transfer Value (CETV)

This is the actuarially assessed capitalised value of the pension scheme benefits accrued by a member at a particular point in time. The benefits valued are the member's accrued benefits and any contingent spouse's pension payable from the scheme. It is a payment made by a pension scheme or arrangement to secure pension benefits in another pension scheme when the member leaves a scheme and chooses to transfer the pension benefits they have accrued in their former scheme. The pension figures shown relate to the benefits that the individual has accrued as a consequence of their total Ministerial service, not just their current appointment as a Minister. CETVs are calculated within the guidelines and framework prescribed by the Institute and Faculty of Actuaries.

The Real Increase in the Value of the CETV

This is the increase in accrued pension due to the Department's contributions to the PCPF and excludes increases due to inflation and contributions paid by the Minister, and is calculated using common market valuation factors for the start and end of the period.

Defence Management Board – Salaries, Allowances and Taxable Benefits in Kind

(This section has been subject to audit)

	2006 – 07 Salary* £000	2006 – 07 Benefits-in-kind (to nearest £100)**	2005 – 06 Salary* £000	2005 – 06 Benefits-in-kind (to nearest £100)**
Permanent Under Secretary of State Bill Jeffrey CB (from 21 Nov 05)	175-180	29,600	55-60	10,800
Full year equivalent salary			*155-160*	
Chief of the Defence Staff Air Chief Marshal Sir Jock Stirrup GCB AFC ADC DSc FRAeS FCMI RAF (from 28 Apr 06)	190-195	32,200		
Full year equivalent salary	*205-210*			
Chief of the Defence Staff General Sir Michael Walker GCB CMG CBE ADC Gen (now The Lord Walker of Aldringham) (to 27 Apr 06)	15-20	Nil	200-205	38,000
Full year equivalent salary	*215-220*			
First Sea Lord and Chief of the Naval Staff Admiral Sir Jonathon Band KCB ADC (from 7 Feb 06)	155-160	26,000	20-25	3,900
Full year equivalent salary			*140-145*	
Chief of the General Staff General Sir Richard Dannatt KCB CBE MC ADC Gen (from 29 Aug 06)	100-105	10,900		
Full year equivalent salary	*170-175*			
Chief of the General Staff General Sir Mike Jackson GCB CBE DSO ADC Gen (to 28 Aug 06)	70-75	14,700	170-175	28,100
Full year equivalent salary	*180-185*			
Chief of the Air Staff Air Chief Marshal Sir Glenn Torpy KCB CBE DSO ADC BSc(Eng) FRAeS RAF (from 13 Apr 06)	140-145	24,100		
Full year equivalent salary	*145-150*			
Chief of the Air Staff Air Chief Marshal Sir Jock Stirrup GCB AFC ADC DSc FRAeS FCMI RAF (to 12 Apr 06)	5-10	900	145-150	27,600
Full year equivalent salary	*155-160*			
Vice Chief of the Defence Staff General Sir Timothy Granville-Chapman GBE KCB ADC Gen (from 22 Jul 05)	150-155	25,500	95-100	18,400
Full year equivalent salary			*140-145*	
Second Permanent Under Secretary of State Sir Ian Andrews CBE TD	145-150	Nil	135-140	25,700

	2006-07 Salary* £000	2006-07 Benefits-in-kind (to nearest £100)**	2005-06 Salary* £000	2005-06 Benefits-in-kind (to nearest £100)**
Chief of Defence Procurement Sir Peter Spencer KCB***	140-145	36,800	135-140	29,400
Chief of Defence Materiel General Sir Kevin O'Donoghue KCB CBE	145-150	Nil	135-140	Nil
Chief Scientific Adviser Professor Sir Roy Anderson FRS	145-150	22,100	135-140	18,900
Finance Director Trevor Woolley CB	130-135	Nil	125-130	Nil
Non-Executive Directors	Fees		Fees	
Charles Miller Smith	25-30	Nil	25-30	Nil
Philippa Foster Back OBE	25-30	Nil	25-30	Nil
Paul Skinner (from 1 Jun 06)	20-25	Nil		
Full year equivalent	*25-30*			
Ian Rushby (from 29 Jan 07)	0-5	Nil		
Full year equivalent	*25-30*			

*Salary, in bands of £5,000, includes gross salary, performance pay (paid in-year but based on performance in an assessment period ended prior to the start of the financial year) and allowances paid.

** Benefits-in-kind figures for civilian members of the DMB represent the taxable benefit attributed to the private use of official cars. For Service members of the DMB, the benefits-in-kind are the taxable benefits relating to the occupation of Official Service Residences. The Department has an arrangement with HM Revenue and Customs where MoD pays the tax liability that would ordinarily be paid by the individual on the benefits-in-kind; this tax liability is included in the figures in the table.

*** Sir Peter Spencer received a payment as compensation for Compulsory Early Retirement.

Defence Management Board – Pension Benefits

(This section has been subject to audit)

2006-07 figures are in bold. The real increase in the pension, from 2005-06, and where applicable the real increase in the lump sum payment, are shown in italics.

	Total Accrued Pension at Retirement as at 31 Mar 07 £000	CETV at 31 Mar 06 or Date of Appointment if Later £000	CETV at 31 Mar 07 or on Cessation of Appointment if Earlier £000	Real Increase or (Decrease) in CETV £000
Permanent Under Secretary of State Bill Jeffrey CB	Pension **70-75** *2.5-5* Lump Sum **210-215** *7.5-10*	1,583*	1,725	66
Chief of the Defence Staff Air Chief Marshal Sir Jock Stirrup GCB AFC ADC DSc FRAeS FCMI RAF (from 28 Apr 06)	Pension **105-110** *27.5-30* Lump Sum **315-320** *82.5-85*	1,462	2,061	565

	Total Accrued Pension at Retirement as at 31 Mar 07 £000	CETV at 31 Mar 06 or Date of Appointment if Later £000	CETV at 31 Mar 07 or on Cessation of Appointment if Earlier £000	Real Increase or (Decrease) in CETV £000
Chief of the Defence Staff General Sir Michael Walker GCB CMG CBE ADC Gen (now The Lord Walker of Aldringham) (to 27 Apr 06)	Pension **100-105** *0-2.5* Lump Sum **305-310** *2.5-5*	1,604	1,641	32
First Sea Lord and Chief of the Naval Staff Admiral Sir Jonathon Band KCB ADC	Pension **80-85** *5-7.5* Lump Sum **240-245** *15-17.5*	1,434	1,568	127
Chief of the General Staff General Sir Richard Dannatt KCB CBE MC ADC Gen (from 29 Aug 06)	Pension **70-75** *2.5-5* Lump Sum **220-225** *12.5-15*	1,440	1,525	100
Chief of the General Staff General Sir Mike Jackson GCB CBE DSO ADC Gen (to 28 Aug 06)	Pension **75-80** *0-2.5* Lump Sum **230-235** *2.5-5*	1,161	1,191	15
Chief of the Air Staff Air Chief Marshal Sir Glenn Torpy KCB CBE DSO ADC BSc(Eng) FRAeS RAF (from 13 Apr 06)	Pension **65-70** *15-17.5* Lump Sum **205-210** *47.5-50*	530	743	173
Vice Chief of the Defence Staff General Sir Timothy Granville-Chapman GBE KCB ADC Gen	Pension **75-80** *5-7.5* Lump Sum **235-240** *17.5-20*	1,184	1,298	96
Second Permanent Under Secretary of State Sir Ian Andrews CBE TD	Pension **50-55** *2.5-5* Lump Sum **130-135** *0-2.5*	947*	1,025	44
Chief of Defence Procurement Sir Peter Spencer KCB	Pension **5-10** *0-2.5* Lump Sum **N/A**	104*	145	32
Chief of Defence Materiel General Sir Kevin O'Donoghue KCB CBE	Pension **75-80** *5-7.5* Lump Sum **230-235** *15-17.5*	1,298	1,314	106

	Total Accrued Pension at Retirement as at 31 Mar 07 £000	CETV at 31 Mar 06 or Date of Appointment if Later £000	CETV at 31 Mar 07 or on Cessation of Appointment if Earlier £000	Real Increase or (Decrease) in CETV £000
Chief Scientific Adviser Professor Sir Roy Anderson FRS	Pension **0-5** *0-2.5* Lump Sum **N/A**	53*	93	33
Finance Director Trevor Woolley CB	Pension **45-50** *0-2.5* Lump Sum **135-140** *0-2.5*	740*	771	5
Non-Executive Directors Charles Miller Smith Philippa Foster Back OBE Paul Skinner Ian Rushby	N/A N/A N/A N/A	N/A N/A N/A N/A	N/A N/A N/A N/A	N/A N/A N/A N/A

*The factors used to calculate the CETV for members of the PCSPS were revised for 2006-07, following advice from the Cabinet Office. The figures for 31 March 2006 have been recalculated using the new factors and this has led to changes to the figures published last year.

Civil Service Pensions

Pension benefits are provided through the Civil Service pension arrangements. From 1 October 2002, civil servants may be in one of three statutory based 'final salary' defined benefit schemes (classic, premium, and classic plus). The schemes are unfunded with the cost of benefits met by monies voted by Parliament each year. Pensions payable under classic, premium, and classic plus are increased annually in line with changes in the Retail Prices Index. New entrants after 1 October 2002 may choose between membership of premium or joining a good quality 'money purchase' stakeholder arrangement with a significant employer contribution (partnership pension account). The accrued pension quoted is the pension the member is entitled to receive when they reach 60, or immediately on ceasing to be an active member of the scheme if they are already 60.

Employee contributions are set at the rate of 1.5% of pensionable earnings for classic and 3.5% for premium and classic plus. Benefits in classic accrue at the rate of 1/80th of pensionable salary for each year of service. In addition, a lump sum equivalent to three years' pension is payable on retirement. For premium, benefits accrue at the rate of 1/60th of final pensionable earnings for each year of service. Unlike classic, there is no automatic lump sum although members may give up (commute) some of their pension to provide a lump sum. Classic plus is essentially a variation of premium, but with benefits in respect of service before 1 October 2002 calculated broadly as per classic.

The partnership pension account is a stakeholder pension arrangement. The employer makes a basic contribution of between 3% and 12.5% (depending on the age of the member) into a stakeholder pension product chosen by the employee. The employee does not have to contribute but, where they do make contributions, the employer will match these up to a limit of 3% of pensionable salary (in addition to the employer's basic contribution). Employers also contribute a further 0.8% of pensionable salary to cover the cost of centrally-provided risk benefit cover (death in service and ill health retirement).

Further details about the Civil Service pension arrangements can be found at the website www.civilservice-pensions.gov.uk.

Armed Forces Pension Scheme (AFPS)

From 6 April 2005, a new Armed Forces Pension Scheme (known as AFPS 05) was introduced for all new members of the Armed Forces; those in service before this date have been given the opportunity to transfer, from AFPS-75, to the new scheme. Both schemes are defined benefit, salary-related, contracted out, occupational pension schemes. The AFPS is non-contributory for members; the cost of accruing benefits are met by the employer at rates approximately equivalent to 36.3% (Officers) and 21.8% (Other Ranks) of pensionable pay. Members are entitled to a taxable pension for life and a tax-free pension lump sum if they leave the Armed Forces at or beyond either the Early Departure Point or the Immediate Pension Point. If a scheme member leaves before these points, they will be entitled to a preserved pension and related lump sum.

Further details about Armed Forces Pensions can be found at the website www.mod.uk/DefenceInternet/AboutDefence/Issues/Pensions/

Cash Equivalent Transfer Value

A Cash Equivalent Transfer Value (CETV) is the actuarially assessed capitalised value of the pension scheme benefits accrued by a member at a particular point in time. The benefits valued are the member's accrued benefits and any contingent spouse's pension payable from the scheme. A CETV is a payment made by a pension scheme or arrangement to secure pension benefits in another pension scheme or arrangement when the member leaves a scheme and chooses to transfer the benefits accrued in their former scheme. The pension figures shown relate to the benefits that the individual has accrued as a consequence of their total membership of the pension scheme, not just their service in a senior capacity to which disclosure applies. The pension details include the value of any pension benefit in another scheme or arrangement which the individual has transferred to the AFPS or Civil Service pension arrangements and for which a transfer payment commensurate with the additional pension liabilities being assumed has been received. They also include any additional pension benefit accrued to the member as a result of their purchasing additional years of pension service in the scheme at their own cost. CETVs are calculated within the guidelines and framework prescribed by the Institute and Faculty of Actuaries.

Real Increase in CETV

This reflects the increase in CETV effectively funded by the employer. It does not include the increase in accrued pension due to inflation, or contributions paid by the employee (including the value of any benefits transferred from another pension scheme or arrangement) and uses common market valuation factors for the start and end of the period.

Bill Jeffrey
Accounting Officer

16 July 2007

Statement of Accounting Officer's Responsibilities

Under the Government Resources and Accounts Act 2000, HM Treasury has directed the Ministry of Defence to prepare for each financial year resource accounts detailing the resources acquired, held or disposed of during the year and the use of resources by the Department during the year.

The accounts are prepared on an accruals basis and must give a true and fair view of the state of affairs of the Department and of its net resource outturn, resources applied to objectives, recognised gains and losses, and cash flows for the financial year.

In preparing the accounts, the Accounting Officer is required to comply with the requirements of the *Government Financial Reporting Manual* and in particular to:

- observe the Accounts Direction issued by HM Treasury, including the relevant accounting and disclosure requirements, and apply suitable accounting policies on a consistent basis;

- make judgements and estimates on a reasonable basis;

- state whether applicable accounting standards, as set out in the *Government Financial Reporting Manual*, have been followed, and disclose and explain any material departures in the accounts; and

- prepare the accounts on a going-concern basis.

HM Treasury has appointed the Permanent Head of Department as Accounting Officer of the Department. The responsibilities of an Accounting Officer, including responsibility for the propriety and regularity of the public finances for which the Accounting Officer is answerable, for keeping proper records and for safeguarding the Department's assets, are set out in the Accounting Officers' Memorandum issued by HM Treasury and published in *Government Accounting*.

Statement on Internal Control

1. Scope of responsibility

As Accounting Officer, I have responsibility for maintaining a sound system of internal control that supports the achievement of Departmental policies, aims and objectives, set by the Department's Ministers, whilst safeguarding the public funds and Departmental assets for which I am personally responsible, in accordance with the responsibilities assigned to me in Government Accounting.

During the Financial Year 2006-07, the Department's outputs were delivered through 12 Top Level Budget areas, each managed by a military or civilian Top Level Budget (TLB) Holder, together with 5 Trading Fund Agencies. The Department also has 5 executive Non-Departmental Public Bodies (NDPB) and two Public Corporations with delegated responsibilities. Included within the TLBs are 17 on-vote Defence Agencies whose Chief Executives are responsible for producing annual accounts which are laid before Parliament but which also form part of the Departmental Resource Accounts. TLB Holders operate within a framework of responsibilities delegated by me. To assist me in assessing the adequacy of control arrangements across the Department, TLB Holders submit to me an annual statement of Assurance, endorsed by their Audit Committee and Management Board, also covering the Agencies for which they are responsible[2]. Both the Veterans' Agency (VA) and Armed Forces Personnel Administration Agency (AFPAA) (which merged on 1 April 2007) are administered within the Central TLB. The VA manages the War Pensions Benefits Programme. AFPAA manages the pay and provides administrative support for Service personnel. It also manages the Armed Forces Pensions and Compensation schemes (AFPS/AFCS), for which I am also Accounting Officer, which are accounted for separately to the main Departmental Resource Accounts. The Agencies' Chief Executives are directly accountable for the delivery of all these services.

The 5 MoD Trading Funds (the Defence Aviation Repair Agency, ABRO, the Defence Science and Technology Laboratory (Dstl), the UK Hydrographic Office, and the Met Office) fall outside the Departmental Accounting Boundary and their Chief Executives are Accounting Officers in their own right. They therefore publish their own Statements on Internal Control together with their Annual Accounts. Given their close integration into the Department's business, and their extensive use of Departmental personnel and assets, their Chief Executives also provide to me the Statement on Internal Control prepared for their annual Accounts. Although sponsored by the Department, the 5 Non Departmental Public Bodies and 2 Public Corporations also fall outside the Departmental Boundary and their accounts are also published separately. The NDPBs and one Public Corporation (the Fleet Air Arm Museum) each operate within a financial memorandum agreed between their respective Boards of Trustees and the Department. The other Public Corporation (Oil and Pipelines Agency) has a Board of Directors on which the Department is represented.

Ministers are involved in the delivery of outputs, including the management of risks to delivery, through their routine oversight of the Department. They also chair a variety of internal Boards which review the performance of the Trading Funds, the primary on-vote Agencies, including during 2006-07 the Defence Procurement Agency and Defence Estates which were also TLBs. In particular, all 5 Trading Fund Agencies report to Advisory Boards chaired by MoD Ministers. Ministers are consulted on all key decisions affecting Defence, including major investment decisions and on operational matters. Command and administration of the Armed Forces is vested in the Defence Council by Letters Patent, chaired by the Secretary of State for Defence, and beneath that in the Service Boards, chaired by a Minister. Membership of the Defence Council comprises all Defence Ministers and the executive members of the Defence Management Board. The Chief of Defence Staff is the Government's and the Secretary of State's principal advisor on military operations and is responsible for the maintenance of military operational capability and for the preparation and conduct of military operations, including managing the risks to successful outcomes. The Chiefs of Staff Committee is chaired by the Chief of Defence Staff and is the main forum in which the collective military advice of the Chiefs is obtained on operational issues. The individual Service Chiefs also advise the Chief of Defence Staff, the Secretary of State and, when required, the Prime Minister on the operational employment of their Service.

---

2 For the Defence Procurement Agency and Defence Estates, which were both agencies and Top Level Budgets in the year ending 31 March 2007, this was discharged by submission of the Statement on Internal Control prepared for their own annual Accounts.

2. The purpose of the system of internal control

The system of internal control is designed to manage risk to a reasonable level rather than to eliminate all risk of failure to achieve policies, aims and objectives; it can therefore provide only reasonable and not absolute assurance of effectiveness. The system of internal control is based on an ongoing process designed to identify and prioritise the risks to the achievement of Departmental policies, aims and objectives, to evaluate the likelihood of those risks being realised and the impact should they be realised, and to manage them efficiently, effectively and economically. The system of internal control has been in place in the Department for the year ended 31 March 2007 and up to the date of approval of the annual report and accounts, and accords with Treasury guidance.

3. Capacity to handle risk

Active management of risk is fundamental to the effective achievement of Defence objectives, and is central to the way business is conducted within the Department. It informs operational decision making, contingency planning, investment decisions and the financial planning process. The major strategic risks are regularly considered by the Defence Management Board and risk forms an integral element of the quarterly performance reviews. Guidance on the Department's approach to risk is detailed in a Joint Service Publication, which is periodically reviewed and updated. This sets out the Department's corporate governance and risk management policy statement and strategy to be cascaded down through Top Level Budget Holders, and provides extensive guidance to staff on definitions, criteria and methods available for risk assessment and management. It is made available to all personnel in either hard copy or via the Department's intranet. Individual training, at both awareness and practitioner level, is available to all staff via the Department's in-house training provider.

4. The risk and control framework

The Defence Management Board manages the top level risks to the Department through a structured series of discussions of the major risks through the course of the year. The Department's Performance Management System provides the overall framework for the consideration of risks within the Defence Balanced Scorecard and lower level scorecards, providing a means for the identification, evaluation, control and reporting of risk against a balanced assessment of Departmental objectives. Key Departmental objectives, performance indicators and targets are defined by the Defence Management Board for each year and cascaded to Top Level Budget Holders through Service Delivery Agreements. Performance is monitored and discussed quarterly at Defence Management Board and lower level management board meetings, including explicit consideration of key risks.

The Department has a high tolerance of risk which is based predominantly in its purpose, preparedness and willingness to undertake military operations with potentially fatal consequences for both adversaries and UK Service personnel. Risk appetite is determined through the advice given to Ministers on operations, through the decisions taken as part of the Department's bi-annual planning round including assessing any gaps against Planning Assumptions, and demonstrated through the limits and controls placed on individual investment projects as part of the Department's Investment Approval process and the total number of projects.

5. Review of effectiveness

As Accounting Officer, I have responsibility for reviewing the effectiveness of the system of internal control. My review of the effectiveness of the system of internal control is informed by the work of the internal auditors and the executive managers within the Department who have responsibility for the development and maintenance of the internal control framework, and comments made by the external auditors in their management letter and other reports. I have been advised on the implications of the result of my review of the effectiveness of the system of internal control by the Defence Management Board and the Defence Audit Committee and a plan to address weaknesses and ensure continuous improvement of the system is in place.

The following processes are in operation in order to maintain and review the effectiveness of the system of internal control:

- A Defence Management Board, which meets approximately twice a month to manage the plans, performance and strategic direction of the Department, comprising the senior members of the Department and at least two external independent members.

- A Defence Audit Committee, chaired by an external independent member of the Defence Management Board, which reviews the Department's risk-based approach to internal control. The Committee itself has also adopted a risk based approach in its assurance work process, co-ordinating the activities of internal audit, and drawing on reports from pan-Departmental process owners and specialist assurance sources, including:

  - 2nd Permanent Under Secretary, as the Chair of the Defence Environment and Safety Board (including Scientific risks);

  - the Chief of Defence Material (formerly the Chief of Defence Logistics) for the logistics process;

  - the Finance Director for departmental financial and planning systems;

  - the Deputy Chief of the Defence Staff (Personnel) for Service personnel processes;

  - the Personnel Director for civilian personnel processes;

  - the Director General Media and Communication for communications processes;

  - the Director General Security and Safety as the Departmental Security Officer, for security and business continuity;

  - the Director General of Defence Acquisition Policy for acquisition processes;

  - the Director of Operational Capability;

  - Defence Internal Audit, including the Defence Fraud Analysis Unit;

  - the Director of Internal Management Consultancy; and

  - the National Audit Office.

- A Strategic Risk Register and a Departmental risk register, supported by operational-level risk registers, which complement the Defence Balanced Scorecard. Departmental risks are routinely reviewed by the Defence Management Board in the context of its regular reviews of Departmental programmes. The Departmental risk management process has been reviewed and approved by the Defence Audit Committee.

- Through Top Level Budget Holders, a cascaded system for ensuring compliance with legal and statutory regulations. Each TLB holder is supported by an Audit Committee, including and, in all bar one case[3], chaired by non-executive directors and at which representatives from the internal and external auditors are present. Like the Defence Audit Committee these committees focus their activities to provide advice on wider-business risk and assurance processes.

- A Business Management System, with responsibility for the effective and efficient operation of the key pan-Departmental processes, such as Finance and Human Resources (military and civilian), including the identification of risks within these processes and the maintenance of effective controls to manage them, assigned to functional heads or process owners. Process Owners are responsible directly to the Defence Management Board.

- Through Top Level Budget Holders, a cascaded system for ensuring that business continuity plans are in place, and that these plans are tested on a regular basis.

3 Reflecting the particular circumstances in Northern Ireland, ,the General Officer Commanding Northern Ireland Top Level Budget Audit Committee was chaired by the Civil Secretary, but contained two Non-Executive Directors with direct access to the Management Board and the TLB Holder. On 1 April 2007 the TLB was absorbed into the Land TLB and the separate Audit Committee disestablished.

- An annual risk-based programme of internal audit provided by Defence Internal Audit, who are the primary source of independent assurance, which is complemented by the activity of the Directorate of Operational Capability, which provides independent operational audit and assurance to the Secretary of State and the Chief of Defence Staff. On the basis of the audit work conducted during the year, Defence Internal Audit offered Substantial Assurance that the systems of internal control, risk management and governance reviewed are operating effectively across the Department.

- The Department's external audit function is provided on behalf of Parliament by the Comptroller and Auditor General, supported by staff from the National Audit Office (NAO). The Accounting Officer and NAO staff see all Defence Audit Committee papers and attend its meetings, and there was no relevant audit information that the NAO were not already aware. Additionally the Accounting Officer held periodic private discussions with Internal Audit and with non-executive members of the Defence Audit Committee. The NAO see all relevant Top Level Budget papers and attend TLB Audit Committee meetings.

- Annual Reports providing measurable performance indicators and more subjective assessments on the Health of Financial Systems from all Top Level Budget Holders and key functional specialists. Improvements have continued to be made to our financial control during the year, although longstanding difficulties with the Oracle fixed asset accounting module, exacerbated by the migration of the Defence Logistic Organisation's Managed Equipment Fixed Asset Register onto Oracle, generated some temporary difficulties in processing fixed asset data during the year. These were successfully resolved, and the Department has a programme of work to prevent their recurrence. The Department has delivered its outputs within the resources voted by Parliament notwithstanding the pressure generated by the high level of operations.

- The Department remained within the Treasury's Total Departmental Expenditure Limit. However, the high level of operations has resulted in a small excess (1.4%) on Request of Resources 2, due to the higher than expected non-cash costs (mainly depreciation charges), in part as the result of increased firing of Hellfire missiles in Afghanistan. Although there was no breach of the Net Cash Requirement, the consequence of the excess is a technical qualification of the Accounts. Whilst the National Audit Office has acknowledged that policy and guidance is sound, the Department has put in place a series of measures to prevent this reoccuring.

- Significant developments in Business Continuity Management, in particular the further development of effective policy and processes to ensure that Business Continuity is an integral part of the planning and management processes undertaken across all areas of Department. Significant improvements in this area have been made in the course of the year.

- The Department has designed and implemented a number of changes to its processes as it implements the Defence Acquisition Change Programme. This has ranged from the development of new Through Life Capability Management processes, new planning and approvals processes and, the merger of the Defence Procurement Agency and Defence Logistics Organisation Top Level Budgets in April 2007 to form the new integrated procurement and support Organisation: Defence Equipment and Support. It has been an achievement to deliver all this change within 12 months

- An effective governance structure and performance management system that addresses the risks arising from the introduction of the general right of access to information from January 2005 under the Freedom of Information Act.

Significant Internal Control Issues

Joint Personnel Administration

During the past year the Armed Forces Personnel Administration Agency achieved three extremely significant milestones by rolling out the Joint Personnel Administration (JPA) system to the Royal Air Force (RAF) from April 2006, the Royal Navy (RN) from November 2006, and the Army from the end of March 2007. Initial teething problems with RAF specialist pay and expenses were overcome and the first RN payroll in November 2006 was successful. There are now no systemic problems with the delivery of RAF and RN pay and allowances. However, following RAF go-live a number of concerns about JPA support to Departmental financial and manpower accounting processes, and some weaknesses in AFPAA internal controls were identified. These have had a temporary impact on the Department's ability to exercise full financial control and increased the risk to the timeliness and quality of the Departmental Resource Accounts. Following identification of these issues mitigation plans were put into effect and action taken to resolve them such that full financial control had been re-established before year end. AFPAA (now the Service Personnel Veterans Agency) continues to work with the MoD finance community to resolve the outstanding issues.

Bill Jeffrey
Accounting Officer   **16 July 2007**

The Certificate of the Comptroller and Auditor General to the House of Commons

I certify that I have audited the financial statements of the Ministry of Defence for the year ended 31 March 2007 under the Government Resources and Accounts Act 2000. These comprise the Statement of Parliamentary Supply, the Operating Cost Statement and Statement of Recognised Gains and Losses, the Balance Sheet, the Cashflow Statement and the Statement of Operating Costs by Departmental Aim and Objectives and the related notes. These financial statements have been prepared under the accounting policies set out within them. I have also audited the information in the Remuneration Report that is described in that report as having been audited.

Respective responsibilities of the Accounting Officer and auditor

The Accounting Officer is responsible for preparing the Annual Report, which includes the Remuneration Report, and the financial statements in accordance with the Government Resources and Accounts Act 2000 and HM Treasury directions made thereunder and for ensuring the regularity of financial transactions. These responsibilities are set out in the Statement of Accounting Officer's Responsibilities.

My responsibility is to audit the financial statements and the part of the remuneration report to be audited in accordance with relevant legal and regulatory requirements, and with International Standards on Auditing (UK and Ireland).

I report to you my opinion as to whether the financial statements give a true and fair view and whether the financial statements and the part of the Remuneration Report to be audited have been properly prepared in accordance with HM Treasury directions issued under the Government Resources and Accounts Act 2000. I report to you whether, in my opinion, certain information given in the Annual Report, which comprises a Management Commentary, is consistent with the financial statements. I also report whether in all material respects the expenditure and income have been applied to the purposes intended by Parliament and the financial transactions conform to the authorities which govern them.

In addition, I report to you if the Department has not kept proper accounting records, if I have not received all the information and explanations I require for my audit, or if information specified by HM Treasury regarding remuneration and other transactions is not disclosed.

I review whether the Statement on Internal Control reflects the Department's compliance with HM Treasury's guidance, and I report if it does not. I am not required to consider whether this statement covers all risks and controls, or to form an opinion on the effectiveness of the Department's corporate governance procedures or its risk and control procedures.

I read the other information contained in the Annual Report and consider whether it is consistent with the audited financial statements. I consider the implications for my certificate if I become aware of any apparent misstatements or material inconsistencies with the financial statements. My responsibilities do not extend to any other information.

Basis of audit opinions

I conducted my audit in accordance with International Standards on Auditing (UK and Ireland) issued by the Auditing Practices Board. My audit includes examination, on a test basis, of evidence relevant to the amounts, disclosures and regularity of financial transactions included in the financial statements and the part of the Remuneration Report to be audited. It also includes an assessment of the significant estimates and judgments made by the Accounting Officer in the preparation of the financial statements, and of whether the accounting policies are most appropriate to the Department's circumstances, consistently applied and adequately disclosed.

I planned and performed my audit so as to obtain all the information and explanations which I considered necessary in order to provide me with sufficient evidence to give reasonable assurance that the financial statements and the part of the Remuneration Report to be audited are free from material misstatement, whether caused by fraud or error, and that in all material respects the expenditure and income have been applied to the purposes intended by Parliament and the financial transactions conform to the authorities which govern them. In forming my opinion I also evaluated the overall adequacy of the presentation of information in the financial statements and the part of the Remuneration Report to be audited.

Votes A

The Ministry of Defence's Votes A is presented annually to Parliament to seek statutory authority for the maximum numbers of personnel to be maintained for service with the armed forces. Note 36 to the Accounts shows that the maximum numbers maintained during 2006-07 for the Naval, Army and Air Force Services in all active and reserve categories were within the numbers voted by Parliament. My role is to inform Parliament whether or not the approved Estimates (Vote A) have been exceeded. My staff have reviewed the information supporting actual numbers provided in the note to the financial statements and I am content that the numbers provided for in the Estimates have not been exceeded.

Opinions

Audit Opinion

In my opinion:

- the financial statements give a true and fair view, in accordance with the Government Resources and Accounts Act 2000 and directions made thereunder by HM Treasury, of the state of the Department's affairs as at 31 March 2007, and the net cash requirement, net resource outturn, net operating cost, operating costs applied to objectives, recognised gains and losses and cashflows for the year then ended;

- the financial statements and the part of the Remuneration Report to be audited have been properly prepared in accordance with HM Treasury directions issued under the Government Resources and Accounts Act 2000; and

- information given within the Annual Report, which comprises a Management Commentary, is consistent with the financial statements.

Qualified Audit Opinion on Regularity arising from expenditure in excess of amounts authorised

As explained more fully in the attached report, Parliament authorised a Request for Resources for the Ministry of Defence relating to Conflict Prevention in the Appropriation Acts 2006 and 2007. A net total provision of £1,427,526,000 was authorised, and against this authorised limit, the Ministry of Defence incurred net resource expenditure of £1,448,420,000 as shown in the Summary of Resource Outturn in the Resource Accounts for 2006-07, and have thus exceeded the authorised limit.

In my opinion, with the exception for net resource expenditure of £20,894,000 in excess of the amount authorised for the Request for Resources 2: Conflict Prevention, referred to in my Report, in all material respects, the expenditure and income have been applied to the purposes intended by Parliament and the financial transactions conform to the authorities which govern them.

Details of this matter are explained more fully in my Report below.

John Bourn
Comptroller and Auditor General   **18 July 2007**
National Audit Office
157-197 Buckingham Palace Road
Victoria
London SW1W 9SP

Report of the Comptroller and Auditor General to the House of Commons

Excess Vote

Introduction

1. The principal activity of the Ministry of Defence (the Department) is to deliver security for the people of the United Kingdom and the Overseas Territories by defending them, including against terrorism, and to act as a force for good by strengthening international peace and stability (Departmental Annual Report, 2006-2007).

2. For 2006-07, the Department had three Requests for Resources by which it was voted resources by Parliament. These were:

- Request for Resources 1: Provision of Defence Capability. This covers expenditure primarily to meet the Department's operational support and logistics services costs and the costs of providing the equipment capability required by defence policy.

- Request for Resources 2: Conflict Prevention. This accounts for conflict prevention and peacekeeping activities and includes the additional costs of current operations being undertaken not only in Iraq and Afghanistan but in other parts of the world such as the Balkans and Africa.

- Request for Resources 3: War Pensions Benefits. This Request for Resources provides for the payment of war disablement and war widows' pensions in accordance with relevant legislation.

3. This report describes the background and circumstances leading to the qualification of my audit opinion on the Ministry of Defence's 2006-07 Resource Accounts.

Purpose of Report

4. In 2006-07 the Department expended more resources than Parliament had authorised on Request for Resources 2. In so doing, the Department breached Parliament's control of expenditure and incurred what is termed an "excess" for which further parliamentary authority is required. I have qualified my opinion on the Department's 2006-07 Resource Accounts in this regard.

5. The purpose of this Report is to explain the reasons for this qualification and to provide information on the causes, extent and nature of the breach to inform Parliament's further consideration.

My responsibilities with regard to the breach of regularity

6. As part of my audit of the Department's financial statements, I am required to satisfy myself that, in all material respects, the expenditure and income shown in the Resource Accounts have been applied to the purposes intended by Parliament and conform to the authorities which govern them; that is they are "regular". In doing so I have had regard to Parliamentary authority and in particular the supply limits Parliament has set on expenditure.

7. By incurring expenditure that is unauthorised and is thus not regular, the Department have breached Parliament's controls.

Background to the excess

8. Parliament authorises and sets limits on departmental expenditure on two bases – 'resources' and 'cash'. Such amounts are set out in Supply Estimates for which Parliament's approval is given in Annual Appropriation Acts.

9. By this means Parliament has authorised three Requests for Resources for the Department. For each Request for Resources, Parliament thereby authorises amounts for current (rather than capital) expenditure which are net of forecast income, known as "operating Appropriations in Aid". Parliament also sets limits on the amount of operating Appropriations in Aid that can be applied towards meeting expenditure. The amounts authorised therefore represent a limit on the net current expenditure that may be incurred under each Request for Resources.

Limits

10. The limits described above for the Department were set out in the Main Supply Estimates for 2006-07 (HC1035, 2005-06), as amended by the Winter and Spring Supplementary Estimates (HC2 & HC293, 2006-07). The limit for Request for Resources 2 was set at net expenditure of £1,427,526,000 together with a limit on Appropriations on Aid of £15,557,000. These limits were authorised in the Appropriation Act (No 2) 2006 and 2007. The breach reported below is against this limit. The Net Cash Requirement for the Department was not breached.

Breach of limit on Request for Resources 2

11. The Statement of Parliamentary Supply for the accounts shows net expenditure on Request for Resources 2 of £1,448,420,000 which is £20,894,000 (1.44 per cent) in excess of the amount authorised. Operating income authorised to be appropriated in aid of expenditure on this Request for Resources was limited to £15,557,000. This amount was wholly earned and applied. The Department also earned during the year from these income sources an additional £5,047,000.00. This is shown as excess Appropriations in Aid on Note 5 on page 53 of the accounts. It is proposed to ask Parliament to increase the limit on Appropriations in Aid by this amount to allow it to be applied towards meeting the excess on this Request for Resources, and to authorise the balance of £15,847,000 as additional use of resources by an Excess Vote.

Details and causes

12. The rest of my report covers:

● the costs attributable to Request for Resources 2;

● forecasting of costs ;

● the resulting requests for Resources by the Department;

● causes of the excess and action proposed by the Department.

The costs attributable to Request for Resources 2

13. Broadly, Request for Resources 2 comprises the additional costs of current operations throughout the world over and above that which would have been borne under normal conditions. This Request for Resources therefore for example includes:

● stocks consumed in operational theatres for example fuel, food and munitions;

● the costs of additional equipment support eg servicing of vehicles;

● additional pay such as the operational bonus to which military personnel are entitled. The standard pay costs of military and civilian personnel serving in operational theatres are included within RfR1.

● costs such as depreciation and cost of capital charges relating to assets and equipment in use on operations which under Government Accounting rules are sometimes called "non-cash costs".

14. The costs allocated to Request for Resources 2 are reduced to recognise that some activities that would normally have taken place such as training and exercises will not have been carried out and therefore some costs will not have been incurred. These "savings" have therefore been deducted from the total costs recognised. Receipts recognised under Request for Resources 2 include repayments by, for example, other government departments or for supplies made available to allies in operational theatres.

Estimating and recording costs for Request for Resources 2

15. The Department employs a comprehensive methodology to record the income and expenditure attributable to Request for Resources 2. This process initially takes the information provided through the Department's main financial systems and allocates this to the different Requests for Resources. The apportionment of the net additional costs to Request for Resources 2 is complex and requires judgement. The Department has issued detailed guidance to staff to assist the process and the results are reviewed for completeness and consistency.

16. The nature of the operations whose resources are attributed to Request for Resources 2 makes it difficult to anticipate the final costs as the tempo of operations inevitably fluctuates. Some of the costs of operations are able to be assessed with a high degree of accuracy, for example the additional costs of equipment support and additional personnel costs as well as the costs of activities foregone. However other significant costs such as the levels of stock consumption will depend in part on information provided by personnel in operational theatres and this increases the complexity of the reporting process where there may be more urgent operational priorities.

The resulting requests for Resources by the Department

17. Because of the factors outlined above, the Department provided Parliament with a Request for Resources in the main Estimates voted on in May only in respect of operations in the Balkans; for 2006-07 this was £27 million (net). The bulk of its forecast expenditure, including that for Iraq and Afghanistan, for the year in question was provided part way through the year via the Winter Supplementary Estimates (net additional funding of £1.04 billion) made in November 2006. This was 3 months in advance of their request in the previous year. The Department provided a final request for additional resources (of £340m) in the Spring Supplementary estimates approved by Parliament in February 2007. As in previous years, this included a transfer from Request for Resources 1 to Request for Resources 2 for items such as depreciation and cost of capital which the Department can only assess later in the year.

18. As noted in its Annual Report for 2005-06, the Department included in its 2005-06 Spring Supplementary Estimate a contingency of some £69 million to ensure it had sufficient funding to cater for the potential impact of a rapidly changing operational situation. In the event only a proportion of the contingency was utilised and the Department completed the year with a net surplus on Request for Resources 2 of some £45 million. In 2006-07 no contingency was made following discussions between the Department and Treasury.

Causes of the excess and actions taken or proposed to be taken by the Department to help prevent a recurrence

19. The excess on Request for Resources 2 was primarily the result of operational activity in both Afghanistan and Iraq being substantially higher than originally forecast. The unpredictability in activity levels is a significant cause of the underlying difficulties in forecasting Request for Resources 2 and in particular gave rise to additional depreciation and cost of capital charges[4]. The main items were the firing (and consequent accelerated depreciation) of more Hellfire missiles than expected, particularly in Afghanistan, and the incomplete capture of depreciation costs associated with the operational use of capital spares.

20. The Department is undertaking a detailed review of the treatment of asset depreciation and stock consumption in operations, focusing particularly on Urgent Operational Requirements, in order to understand the origin of the issues which gave rise to the excess. It will take account of the results of this exercise when preparing the 2007-08 Supply Estimates. The policy and guidance is sound, but the Department should take steps to improve the application of the process in operational situations.

---

4 In February 2007, in the Spring Supplementary, an increase was approved by Parliament of £42 million for cost of capital and depreciation associated with equipment procured under Urgent Operational Requirement arrangements. Actual expenditure under this category was some £60 million.

21. The Department has already identified some useful improvements in both the forecasting and the accounting for Request for Resources 2:

● The relevant guidance to its major departmental groupings[5] and budget holders will be reissued, and the importance of accounting properly for even urgent requirements will be stressed;

● There will be an increased focus on accurate forecasting at the mid-year point, in time for Spring Supplementary Votes;

● At the mid year point, the Department will carry out a robust review of stock and spares consumption charged to Request for Resources 2, and the depreciation of equipment damaged or destroyed in conflict, and of weapons fired, to ensure that the accounting is accurate and provides a firm base for forecasts; the department has invited my staff to review this exercise with them.

Summary and Conclusions

22. The Department has incurred an excess vote on Request for Resources 2 due to the factors outlined above for which it now plans to seek Parliamentary approval. The Department is putting into place procedures that will address the weaknesses that have been identified to minimise the possibility of an excess occurring in the future.

John Bourn
Comptroller and Auditor General   **18 July 2007**
National Audit Office
157-197 Buckingham Palace Road
Victoria
London SW1W 9SP

5 These are called "Top Level Budgets or TLBs".

Statement of Parliamentary Supply

Summary of Resource Outturn 2006-07

Request for Resources	Note	Estimate			Outturn			2006-07 Net Total Outturn compared to Estimate Savings/ (Excess)	2005-06 Total Outturn
		Gross Expenditure	A in A *	Net Total	Gross Expenditure	A in A *	Net Tota		
		£000	£000	£000	£000	£000	£000 I	£000	£000
1	2	33,827,383	1,478,181	32,349,202	32,996,683	1,478,181	31,518,502	830,700	32,737,691
2	2	1,443,083	15,557	1,427,526	1,463,977	15,557	1,448,420	(20,894)	1,055,848
3	2	1,047,661	-	1,047,661	1,038,073	-	1,038,073	9,588	1,068,595
Total resources	3	36,318,127	1,493,738	34,824,389	35,498,733	1,493,738	34,004,995	819,394	34,862,134
Non operating cost A in A				556,152			498,287	57,865	374,320

*Appropriation in Aid (A in A)

Net Cash Requirement 2006-07

	Note	Estimate	Outturn	2006-07 Net Total Outturn compared to Estimate Savings/ (Excess)	2005-06 Total Outturn
		£000	£000	£000	£000
Net Cash Requirement	4	33,746,251	31,454,292	2,291,959	30,603,297

Summary of Income Payable to the Consolidated Fund

(In addition to appropriations in aid, the following income relates to the Department and is payable to the Consolidated Fund (cash receipts being shown in italics)).

	Note	Forecast 2006-07		Outturn 2006-07	
		Income	Receipts	Income	*Receipts*
		£000	£000	£000	*£000*
Total	5	-	-	56,326	*56,326*

The notes on pages 229 to 279 form part of these accounts.

223

Further analysis of the variances between Estimate and Outturn is at Note 2 and a summary of the overall financial position, including an explanation of the main variances identified above, is provided both in the Management Commentary and the following paragraphs. A detailed explanation of the Department's financial performance in relation to HM Treasury's Departmental Expenditure Limits is included within Resources in the Performance Report.

Request for Resources (RfR) 1, Provision of Defence Capability, provides for expenditure primarily to meet the MoD's operational support and logistics services costs and the costs of providing the equipment capability required by Defence policy. Within RfR1, the Estimate and Outturn for Operating Appropriations in Aid are shown as equal amounts. Any Appropriations in Aid in excess of the Estimate are shown at Note 5, and these will be surrendered to the Consolidated Fund.

The net outturn for Total Resources is £34,004,995,000 against an Estimate of £34,824,389,000; an underspend of £819,394,000. The variance against the Supply Estimate results from an underspend of £127,428,000 against Resource DEL; an underspend of £676,114,000 in Annually Managed Expenditure (AME); and an underspend of £15,852,000 in Non Budget.

The principal explanations for the underspend in RfR1 of £830,700,000 is due to an underspend in AME of £666,526,000 arising from a review of nuclear provisions, in preparation for the quinquenial review of liabilities by the Nuclear Installations Inspectorate during 2007-08. There is an underspend within Resource DEL of £148,322,000.

RfR2, Conflict Prevention, shows a net outturn of £1,448,420,000 against an Estimate of £1,427,526,000; an overspend of £20,894,000. The excess relates to non-cash costs, such as depreciation charges for military equipment and the firing of guided weapons, missiles and bombs in Afghanistan, which were higher than forecasted at the time of the Estimates were prepared.

RfR3, War Pensions Benefits shows a net outturn of £1,038,073,000 against an Estimate of £1,047,661,000; a small underspend of £9,588,000. This RfR provides for the payment of war disablement and war widows' pensions in accordance with relevant legislation, this is all AME. The costs of administering war pensions are borne by RfR1.

The non-operating Appropriations in Aid show a net outturn of £498,287,000 against an Estimate of £556,152,000, which assumed higher fixed asset disposals in 2006-07. This is made up principally of £105,000,000 lower than expected actual capital receipts within the Defence Procurement Agency; and £53,000,000 higher than expected capital receipts within the Defence Logistics Organisation.

The Net Cash Requirement shows a net outturn of £31,454,292,000, against an Estimate of £33,746,251,000; an underspend of £2,291,959,000. This results from planned working assumptions made in the Spring Supplementary Estimates that did not materialise.

Operating Cost Statement

for the year ended 31 March 2007

	Note	2006-07 £000	2005-06 £000
Staff costs	9	11,204,262	11,254,851
Other operating costs	10	20,764,796	20,171,162
Gross operating costs		31,969,058	31,426,013
Operating income	11	(1,429,392)	(1,390,997)
Net operating cost before interest		30,539,666	30,035,016
Net interest payable	12	167,096	1,252,150
Cost of capital charge	21	3,241,907	3,106,369
Net operating cost		33,948,669	34,393,535
Net resource outturn	3	34,004,995	34,862,134

Statement of Recognised Gains and Losses

for the year ended 31 March 2007

	Note	2006-07 £000	2005-06 £000
Net gain on revaluation of intangible fixed assets	22	(602,077)	(312,151)
Net gain on revaluation of tangible fixed assets	22	(2,629,943)	(1,888,608)
Net (gain)/loss on revaluation of stock	22	385,024	(225,073)
Net (gain)/loss on revaluation of investments	22	9,991	(242,590)
Receipts of donated assets and gain on revaluation	22	(59,233)	(111,753)
Net gain on change in the discount rate of pension scheme	21	(50,600)	-
Recognised gains for the financial year		(2,946,838)	(2,780,175)
Prior year adjustment*			(4,348,036)
Recognised gains since the last Annual Accounts			(7,128,211)

* Gain arising from the transfer of civil nuclear liabilities to the Nuclear Decommissioning Authority on 1 April 2005. Further details can be found in the *Ministry of Defence Report and Accounts 2005-06*.

The notes on pages 229 to 279 form part of these accounts.

225

Balance Sheet

as at 31 March 2007

	Note	31 March 2007		31 March 2006	
		£000	£000	£000	£000
Fixed Assets					
Intangible assets	13	24,162,622		22,982,695	
Tangible fixed assets	14	74,600,538		71,774,958	
Investments	15	500,062		514,132	
			99,263,222		95,271,785
Current Assets					
Stocks and work-in-progress	16	5,321,394		6,052,227	
Debtors	17	3,237,419		2,921,155	
Cash at bank and in hand	18	473,676		1,018,245	
		9,032,489		9,991,627	
Creditors: amounts falling due within one year	19	6,738,594		6,449,389	
Net current assets			2,293,895		3,542,238
Total assets less current liabilities			101,557,117		98,814,023
Creditors: amounts falling due after more than one year	19	975,146		1,057,601	
Provisions for liabilities and charges	20	5,771,881		6,274,944	
			6,747,027		7,332,545
Net assets			94,810,090		91,481,478
Taxpayers' equity					
General fund	21		75,434,183		72,490,177
Revaluation reserve	22		17,129,769		16,635,683
Donated assets reserve	22		2,013,539		2,113,028
Investment reserve	22		232,599		242,590
			94,810,090		91,481,478

Bill Jeffrey
Accounting Officer

16 July 2007

The notes on pages 229 to 279 form part of these accounts.

Cash Flow Statement

for the year ended 31 March 2007

	Note	2006-07	2005-06
		£000	£000
Net cash outflow from operating activities	23.1	(24,671,233)	(23,865,060)
Capital expenditure and financial investment	23.2	(6,767,865)	(6,222,278)
Payments of amounts due to the Consolidated Fund		(119,654)	(736,501)
Financing	23.4	31,014,183	31,403,673
Increase/(decrease) in cash at bank and in hand	23.5	(544,569)	579,834

The notes on pages 229 to 279 form part of these accounts.

Statement of Operating Costs by Departmental Aim and Objectives

for the year ended 31 March 2007

Aim

The principal activity of the Department is to deliver security for the people of the United Kingdom and the Overseas Territories by defending them, including against terrorism; and to act as a force for good by strengthening international peace and stability.

In pursuance of this aim, the Department has the following objectives:

	Gross £000	Income £000	2006-07 Net £000	Gross £000	Income £000	2005-06 Net £000
Objective 1: Achieving success in the tasks we undertake	4,014,273	(303,275)	3,710,998	3,984,890	(420,801)	3,564,089
Objective 2: Being ready to respond to the tasks that might arise	27,373,390	(1,081,131)	26,292,259	27,526,586	(925,270)	26,601,316
Objective 3: Building for the future	2,952,325	(44,986)	2,907,339	3,204,461	(44,926)	3,159,535
	34,339,988	(1,429,392)	32,910,596	34,715,937	(1,390,997)	33,324,940
Paying war pensions benefits	1,038,073	-	1,038,073	1,068,595	-	1,068,595
Total	35,378,061	(1,429,392)	33,948,669	35,784,532	(1,390,997)	34,393,535

See additional details in Note 24.

The notes on pages 229 to 279 form part of these accounts.

Notes to the Accounts

1. Statement of Accounting Policies

Introduction

1.1 These financial statements have been prepared in accordance with the generic Accounts Direction issued by HM Treasury under reference DAO(GEN)12/06 on 19 December 2006 and comply with the requirements of HM Treasury's Financial Reporting Manual (FReM), except where HM Treasury has approved the following departures to enable the Department to reflect its own particular circumstances:

The Operating Cost Statement is not segmented into programme and non-programme expenditure.

The FReM's requirement for Departments to prepare accounts that present the transactions and flows for the financial year and the balances at the year end between "core" department and the consolidated group in respect of the Operating Cost Statement (and supporting notes) and Balance Sheet (and supporting notes) has not been applied. Since agencies falling within the Departmental Boundary are on-vote and embedded within the Departmental chain of command, HM Treasury permits them to be treated as an integral part of the "core" Department. Throughout these accounts, the consolidated figures for the Ministry of Defence (including its on-vote agencies) are deemed to represent those of the "core" Department.

The Department has not fully complied with the FReM emissions cap and trade scheme accounting requirements on grounds of materiality. Rather than registering an asset and liability to reflect its holding of allowances and its obligation to pay for emissions discharged, the Department has reflected the purchase and sales of allowances as expenditure and income within the Operating Cost Statement. All other costs associated with the scheme, such as compliance checking, are also charged to the Operating Cost Statement.

Although FRS 15, as interpreted by the current FReM, requires that all tangible fixed assets be subject to a quinquennial revaluation by external professional valuers, the 2007-08 FReM permits entities to use the most appropriate valuation methodology available, including that of applying appropriate indices, to uplift non-property fixed assets to current values. Since it is considered that a truer and fairer representation of the values of the Department's non-property fixed assets may be achieved by using appropriately robust indices, rather than a mixture of indices and quinquennial professional revaluation, this approach has been applied to the 2006-07 accounts.

Accounting Convention

1.2 These financial statements are prepared on an accruals basis under the historical cost convention, modified to include the revaluation of certain fixed assets and stocks.

Basis of Preparation of Departmental Resource Accounts

1.3 These financial statements comprise the consolidation of the Department, its Defence Supply Financed Agencies and those Advisory Non Departmental Public Bodies (NDPBs) sponsored by the Department, which are not self-accounting. The Defence Agencies and the Advisory NDPBs sponsored by the Department are listed in Note 35.

1.4 Five of the Department's agencies are established as Trading Funds. As such, they fall outside Voted Supply and are subject to a different control framework. The Department's interests in the Trading Funds are included in the financial statements as fixed asset investments. Executive NDPBs operate on a self-accounting basis and are not included within the consolidated accounts. They receive grant-in-aid funding from the Department, which is treated as an expense in the Operating Cost Statement.

1.5 The Department's interest in QinetiQ Group plc, formerly a Self-Financing Public Corporation, is included in the financial statements as a fixed asset investment.

1.6 The Armed Forces Pension Scheme (AFPS) is not consolidated within these financial statements. Separate accounts are prepared for the AFPS.

1.7 Machinery of Government changes which involve the merger of two or more Departments into one new Department, or the transfer of functions or responsibility of one part of the public service sector to another, are accounted for using merger accounting in accordance with Financial Reporting Standard (FRS) 6.

Net Operating Costs

1.8 Costs are charged to the Operating Cost Statement in the period in which they are incurred and are matched to any related income. Costs of contracted-out services are included net of recoverable VAT. Other costs are VAT inclusive, although a proportion of this VAT is recovered via a formula agreed with HM Revenue and Customs. Surpluses and deficits on disposal of fixed assets and stock are included within Note 10 – Other Operating Costs.

1.9 Income from services provided to third parties is included within operating income, net of related VAT. In accordance with FRS 21, as interpreted by the FReM, Trading Fund dividends are recognised as operating income on an accruals basis, whilst other dividends are recognised in the year in which they are declared.

Fixed Assets

1.10 The Department's fixed assets are expressed at their current value through the application of the Modified Historical Cost Accounting Convention (MHCA). Prospective indices, which are produced by the Defence Analytical Services Agency, are applied at the start of each financial year to the fixed assets which fall within the categories listed below. These indices, which look ahead to the subsequent Balance Sheet date, are also adjusted to reflect the difference between the actual change in prices in the prior year and the earlier prediction.

– Land (by region and type);

– Buildings – Dwellings (UK and specific overseas indices);

– Buildings – Non Dwellings (UK and specific overseas indices);

– Single Use Military Equipment – Sea Systems;

– Single Use Military Equipment – Air Systems;

– Single Use Military Equipment – Land Systems;

– Plant and Machinery;

– Transport – Fighting Equipment;

– Transport – Other;

– IT and Communications Equipment – Office Machinery and Computers; and

– IT and Communications Equipment – Communications Equipment.

1.11 Property fixed assets are also subject to a quinquennial revaluation by external professional valuers in accordance with FRS 15, as interpreted by the FReM.

1.12 Assets under construction are valued at cost and are subject to indexation. On completion, they are released from the project account into the appropriate asset category.

1.13 The Department's policy on the capitalisation of subsequent expenditure under FRS15 is to account separately for material major refits and overhauls, when their value is consumed by the Department over a period which differs from that of the overall life of the corresponding core asset and where this is deemed to have a material effect on the carrying values of a fixed asset and the depreciation charge.

1.14 Subsequent expenditure is also capitalised, where it is deemed to enhance significantly the operational capability of the equipment, including extension of life, likewise when it is incurred to replace or restore a component of an asset that has been treated separately for depreciation purposes.

Intangible Fixed Assets

1.15 Pure and applied research costs are charged to the Operating Cost Statement in the period in which they are incurred.

1.16 Development costs are capitalised where they contribute towards defining the specification of an asset that will enter production, and those not capitalised are charged to the Operating Cost Statement. Capitalised development costs are amortised, on a straight line basis, over the planned operational life of that asset type, e.g. class of ship or aircraft. Amortisation commences when the asset type first enters operational service within the Department. If it is decided to withdraw the whole or a significant part of an asset type early, then a corresponding proportion of any remaining unamortised development costs is written off to the Operating Cost Statement, along with the value of the underlying tangible fixed assets. For development costs, a significant withdrawal of assets is deemed to be 20% or greater of the net book value of the underlying asset class.

Tangible Fixed Assets

1.17 The useful economic lives of tangible fixed assets are reviewed annually and adjusted where necessary. The Departmental capitalisation threshold is £10,000, and this is applied when deciding whether to register an asset on the Fixed Asset Register (FAR). The decision to record an asset on a FAR normally takes place at the point of initial acquisition.

1.18 In these financial statements, Guided Weapons, Missiles and Bombs (GWMB) and Capital Spares are categorised as fixed assets and subject to depreciation. The depreciation charge in the Operating Cost Statement also includes the cost of GWMB fired to destruction. The principal asset categories and their useful economic lives, depreciated on a straight line basis, are:

	Category	Years
Land and Buildings	Land	Indefinite, not depreciated
	Buildings, permanent	40 – 50
	Buildings, temporary	5 – 20
	Leasehold	Shorter of expected life and lease period
Single Use Military Equipment (including GWMB)	Air Systems – Fixed Wing	13 – 35
	Air Systems – Rotary Wing	25 – 30
	Sea Systems – Surface Ships	24 – 30
	Sea Systems – Submarines	28 – 32
	Land Systems – Armoured Vehicles	25 – 30
	Land Systems – Small Arms	10 – 15
Plant and Machinery	Equipment	10 – 25
	Plant and Machinery	5 – 25
Transport	Air Systems – Fixed Wing	25 – 35
	Air Systems – Rotary Wing	15 – 32
	Sea Systems – Surface Ships	20 – 30
	Land Systems – Specialised Vehicles	15 – 30
	Land Systems – Other Standard Vehicles	3 – 5
IT and Communications Equipment	Other Machinery	3 – 10
	Communications Equipment	3 – 30
Capital Spares	Items of repairable material retained for the purpose of replacing parts of an asset undergoing repair, refurbishment, maintenance, servicing, modification, enhancement or conversion	As life of prime equipment supported
Operational Heritage Assets *		As other tangible fixed assets

*Operational Heritage Assets are included within the principal asset category to which they relate.

Donated Assets

1.19 Donated assets (i.e. those assets that have been donated to the Department or assets for which the Department has continuing and exclusive use, but does not own legal title, and for which it has not given consideration in return) are capitalised at their current valuation on receipt and are revalued/depreciated on the same basis as purchased assets.

1.20 The Donated Assets Reserve represents the value of the original donation, additions and any subsequent professional revaluation and indexation (MHCA). Amounts equal to the donated asset depreciation charge, impairment costs and deficit/surplus on disposal arising during the year, are released from this reserve to the Operating Cost Statement.

Impairment

1.21 The charge to the Operating Cost Statement in respect of impairment arises on the decision to take a fixed asset out of service and sell it; on transfer of a fixed asset into stock; on reduction in service potential or where the application of MHCA indices causes a downward revaluation below the depreciated historical cost, which is deemed to be permanent in nature. Any reversal of an impairment cost is recognised in the Operating Cost Statement to the extent that the original charge, adjusted for subsequent depreciation, was recognised in the Operating Cost Statement. The remaining amount is recognised in the Revaluation Reserve.

Disposal of Tangible Fixed Assets

1.22 Disposal of assets is principally handled by two specialist agencies: Defence Estates for property assets and the Disposal Services Agency for non-property assets.

1.23 Property assets identified for disposal are included at the open market value, with any write down in value to the net recoverable amount (NRA) charged to the Operating Cost Statement against impairment whilst any increase in value to the NRA is credited to the Revaluation Reserve. On subsequent sale, the surplus or deficit is included in the Operating Cost Statement under surplus/deficit on disposal of fixed assets.

1.24 Non-property assets are subject to regular impairment reviews. An impairment review is also carried out when a decision is made to dispose of an asset and take it out of service. Any write down in value to the NRA is charged to the Operating Cost Statement against impairment whilst any increase in value to the NRA is credited to the Revaluation Reserve. The surplus or deficit at the point of disposal is included in the Operating Cost Statement under surplus/deficit on disposal of fixed assets. Non-property assets, where the receipts on sale are anticipated not to be separately identifiable, are transferred to stock at their NRA and shown under assets declared for disposal. Any write down on transfer is included in the Operating Cost Statement under impairment.

1.25 Disposals exclude fixed assets written off and written on. These items are included within other movements in Notes 13 and 14 (Intangible and Tangible Fixed Assets).

Leased Assets

1.26 Assets held under finance leases are capitalised as tangible fixed assets and depreciated over the shorter of the lease term or their estimated useful economic lives. Rentals paid are apportioned between reductions in the capital obligations included in creditors, and finance costs charged to the Operating Cost Statement. Expenditure under operating leases is charged to the Operating Cost Statement in the period in which it is incurred. In circumstances where the Department is the lessor of a finance lease, amounts due under a finance lease are treated as amounts receivable and reported in Debtors.

Private Finance Initiative (PFI) Transactions

1.27 Where the substance of the transaction is such that the risks and rewards of ownership remain with the Department, the assets and liabilities are reported on the Department's Balance Sheet. Unitary charges in respect of on-balance sheet PFI deals are apportioned between reduction in the capital obligation and charges to the Operating Cost Statement for service performance and finance cost. Where the risks and rewards are transferred to the private sector, the transaction is accounted for in the Operating Cost Statement in accordance with FRS 5 and HM Treasury Guidance.

1.28 Where assets are transferred to the Private Sector Provider, and the consideration received by the Department is in the form of reduced unitary payments, the sales value is accounted for as a prepayment. This prepayment is then reduced (charged to the Operating Cost Statement) over the course of the contract, as the benefits of the prepaid element are utilised.

Investments

1.29 Investments represent holdings that the Department intends to retain for the foreseeable future. Fixed asset investments are stated at market value where available; otherwise they are stated at cost. In the case of Trading Funds (which are not consolidated into the Department's resource accounts), the value of loans and public dividend capital held by the Department is recorded at historic cost. In February 2006, QinetiQ Group plc became a listed company. The MoD's investment in QinetiQ Group plc is now recorded at market value. Details of the QinetiQ Group plc investment are given in Note 15. Investments may either be equity investments, held in the name of the Secretary of State for Defence, or medium or long-term loans made with the intention of providing working capital or commercial support.

1.30 Joint Ventures would be accounted for using the Gross Equity method of accounting. Under this method, the Department's share of the aggregate gross assets and liabilities underlying the net equity investments would be shown on the face of the Balance Sheet. The Operating Cost Statement would include the Department's share of the investee's turnover. The Department currently has no Joint Ventures.

Stocks and Work-in-Progress

1.31 Stock is recognised on the Department's Balance Sheet from the point of acquisition to the point of issue for use, consumption, sale, write-off or disposal. The point of consumption for Land stocks is the point at which stock is issued from depots. For Air stocks, the point of consumption is when stocks are issued from final depots such as an airbase, and for Naval stocks it is when the stock item is used.

1.32 Stock is valued at current replacement cost, or historic cost if not materially different. Provision is made to reduce cost to net realisable value (NRV) where there is no expectation of consumption or sale in the ordinary course of the business. Stock provision is released to the Operating Cost Statement on consumption, disposal and write-off.

1.33 Internal work in progress represents the ongoing work on the manufacture, modification, enhancement or conversion of stock items and is valued on the same basis as stocks. External work in progress represents ongoing work on production or repair contracts for external customers and is valued at the lower of current replacement cost and NRV.

1.34 Assets declared for disposal include stock held for disposal and those non-property fixed assets identified for disposal where receipts are not anticipated to be separately identifiable.

1.35 Stocks written-off, included within Other Operating Costs, represent the book value of stock which has been scrapped, destroyed or lost during the year, and also adjustments to bring the book values into line with the figures recorded on the supply systems.

Provisions for Liabilities and Charges

1.36 Provisions for liabilities and charges have been established under the criteria of FRS 12 and are based on realistic and prudent estimates of the expenditure required to settle future legal or constructive obligations that exist at the Balance Sheet date.

1.37 Provisions are charged to the Operating Cost Statement unless the expenditure provides access to current and future economic benefits, in which case the provision is capitalised as part of the cost of the underlying facility. In such cases, the capitalised provision will be depreciated and charged to the Operating Cost Statement over the remaining estimated useful economic life of the underlying asset. All long-term provisions are discounted to current prices using the rate advised by HM Treasury. The rate for financial year 2006-07 is 2.2% (2.2% for 2005-06). The discount is unwound over the remaining life of the provision and shown as an interest charge in the Operating Cost Statement.

Reserves

1.38 The Revaluation Reserve reflects the unrealised element of the cumulative balance of revaluation and indexation adjustments on fixed assets and stocks (excluding donated assets and those financed by Government grants). The Donated Asset Reserve reflects the net book value of assets that have been donated to the Department.

1.39 The Investment Reserve represents the value of the Departmental investment in QinetiQ Group plc on flotation, and the subsequent movement in market valuation as at 31 March 2007.

1.40 The General Fund represents the balance of the Taxpayers' Equity.

Pensions

1.41 Present and past employees are mainly covered by the Civil Service pension arrangements for civilian personnel and the AFPS for Service personnel. There are separate scheme statements for the AFPS and Civil Service pensions as a whole.

1.42 Both the AFPS and the main Civil Service pension schemes are unfunded defined benefit pension schemes, although, in accordance with the HM Treasury FReM, the Department accounts for the schemes in its accounts as if they were defined contribution schemes. The employer's charge is met by payment of a Superannuation Contribution Adjusted for Past Experience (SCAPE), formerly known as an Accruing Superannuation Liability Charge (ASLC), which is calculated on the basis of the current pay of serving personnel. The SCAPE represents an estimate of the cost of providing future superannuation protection for all personnel currently in pensionable employment. In addition, civilian personnel contribute 1.5% of salary to fund a widow/widower's pension if they are members of classic, and 3.5% if they are members of premium. The Department's Balance Sheet will only include a creditor in respect of pensions to the extent that the contributions paid to the pension funds in the year fall short of the SCAPE and widow/widower's pension charges due. Money purchase pensions delivered through employer-sponsored stakeholder pensions have been available as an alternative to all new Civil Service entrants since October 2002.

1.43 The pension schemes undergo a reassessment of the SCAPE contribution rates by the Government Actuary at four-yearly intervals. Provisions are made for costs of early retirement programmes and redundancies up to the minimum retirement age and are charged to the Operating Cost Statement.

1.44 The Department operates a number of small pension schemes for civilians engaged at overseas locations. Since 1 April 2003, they have been accounted for in accordance with FRS 17 – Retirement Benefits. The pension scheme liability is included within the total provisions reported at Note 20 – Provisions for Liabilities and Charges, and following a change in policy by HM Treasury, the gain on the change in the discount rate at 31 March 2007 is shown in the General Fund and the Statement of Recognised Gains and Losses. Gains or Losses arising from discount rate changes prior to 2006-07 have been charged to the Operating Cost Statement.

1.45 The disclosures required under FRS 17 for the main pension schemes are included in: the Remuneration Report, Note 9 – Staff Numbers and Costs, and on the websites of the Civil Service Pension Scheme and the Armed Forces Pension Scheme (see Note 9 paragraphs 9.3 and 9.4).

Early Departure Costs

1.46 The Department provides in full for the cost of meeting pensions up to the minimum retirement age in respect of military and civilian personnel early retirement programmes and redundancies announced in the current and previous years. Pensions payable after the minimum retirement age are met by the Armed Forces Pension Scheme for military personnel and the Civil Service pension arrangements for civilian personnel.

Cost of Capital Charge

1.47 A charge, reflecting the cost of capital utilised by the Department, is included in the Operating Cost Statement and credited to the General Fund. The charge is calculated using the HM Treasury standard rate for financial year 2006-07 of 3.5% (2005-06: 3.5%) in real terms on all assets less liabilities except for the following, where the charge is nil:

- Donated assets and cash balances with the Office of HM Paymaster General (OPG).

- Liabilities for the amounts to be surrendered to the Consolidated Fund and for amounts due from the Consolidated Fund.

- Assets financed by grants.

- Additions to heritage collections where the existing collection has not been capitalised.

1.48 The cost of capital charge on the fixed asset investments in the Trading Funds is calculated at a specific rate applicable to those entities, and is based on their underlying net assets.

Foreign Exchange

1.49 Transactions that are denominated in a foreign currency are translated into Sterling using the General Accounting Rate ruling at the date of each transaction. US$ and Euros are purchased forward from the Bank of England. Monetary assets and liabilities are translated at the spot rate applicable at the Balance Sheet date and the exchange differences are reported in the Operating Cost Statement.

1.50 Overseas non-monetary assets and liabilities are subject to annual revaluation and are translated at the spot rate applicable at the Balance Sheet date. The exchange differences are taken to the Revaluation Reserve for owned assets, or the Donated Asset Reserve for donated assets.

2. Analysis of Net Resource Outturn

Request for Resources 1: Provision of Defence Capability	2006-07						2005-06
	Other Current Expenditure	Grants	Operating Appropriation in Aid	Total Net Resource Outturn	Total Net Resource Estimate	Total Net Outturn Compared With Estimate	Restated Total Net Resource Outturn
	£000	£000	£000	£000	£000	£000	£000
TLB HOLDER							
Commander-in-Chief Fleet	2,192,016	3,040	(47,178)	**2,147,878**	2,143,658	(4,220)	2,184,168
General Officer Commanding (Northern Ireland)	391,298	-	(1,953)	**389,345**	410,242	20,897	478,933
Commander-in-Chief Land Command	4,426,743	128	(104,751)	**4,322,120**	4,310,881	(11,239)	4,254,179
Commanding-in-Chief RAF Strike Command	1,972,123	-	(47,895)	**1,924,228**	1,909,667	(14,561)	2,125,506
Chief of Joint Operations	427,663	-	(27,203)	**400,460**	366,411	(34,049)	382,295
Chief of Defence Logistics	13,183,008	1,432	(358,275)	**12,826,165**	13,374,460	548,295	13,067,529
Adjutant General's Command	1,596,989	15,834	(27,782)	**1,585,041**	1,571,725	(13,316)	1,745,550
Commander-in-Chief Personnel & Training Command	852,110	6,975	(97,173)	**761,912**	812,178	50,266	793,222
Central	2,371,221	171,587	(385,867)	**2,156,941**	2,214,473	57,532	2,303,380
Defence Estates	3,053,756	-	(358,479)	**2,695,277**	2,572,717	(122,560)	2,205,839
Defence Procurement Agency	1,806,149	-	(21,161)	**1,784,988**	2,135,391	350,403	2,695,495
SIT (Science, Innovation, Technology)	520,719	3,892	(464)	**524,147**	527,399	3,252	501,595
Total (RFR 1)	**32,793,795**	**202,888**	**(1,478,181)**	**31,518,502**	**32,349,202**	**830,700**	32,737,691

From 1 April 2006, Commander-in-Chief Fleet and 2nd Sea Lord/Commander-in-Chief Naval Home Command TLBs have merged into one Naval TLB.
From 1 April 2006, Chief of Defence Logistics, the Defence Procurement Agency TLB and Defence Estates TLB became Single Balance Owners (SBSOs). All assets and associated OCS costs were transferred from TLBs to the SBSOs. Prior year figures have been restated to reflect these transfers.

Request for Resources 2: Conflict Prevention	2006-07						2005-06
	Other Current Expenditure	Grants	Operating Appropriation in Aid	Total Net Resource Outturn	Total Net Resource Estimate	Total Net Outturn Compared With Estimate	Restated Total Net Resource Outturn
	£000	£000	£000	£000	£000	£000	£000
Programme Expenditure: Sub-Saharan Africa*	29,538	-	-	**29,538**	31,486	1,948	30,355
Programme Expenditure: Rest of the World*	77,985	-	(9,914)	**68,071**	73,040	4,969	79,616
Peace Keeping: Rest of the World	1,356,454	-	(5,643)	**1,350,811**	1,323,000	(27,811)	945,877
Total (RFR 2)	**1,463,977**	**-**	**(15,557)**	**1,448,420**	**1,427,526**	**(20,894)**	1,055,848

* prior year outturn figures restated to reflect correct attribution to geographical areas

Request for Resources 3: War Pension Benefits	Other Current Expenditure	Grants	Operating Appropriation in Aid	2006-07 Total Net Resource Outturn	Total Net Resource Estimate	Total Net Outturn Compared With Estimate	2005-06 Total Net Resource Outturn
	£000	£000	£000	£000	£000	£000	£000
War Pensions Benefits Programme costs	-	1,036,803	-	1,036,803	1,046,661	9,858	1,064,862
War Pensions Benefits Programme costs – Far Eastern Prisoners of War	-	1,270	-	1,270	1,000	(270)	3,730
War Pensions Benefits Programme costs – British Limbless ex-Servicemen's Association	-	-	-	-	-	-	3
Total (RFR 3)	**-**	**1,038,073**	**-**	**1,038,073**	**1,047,661**	**9,588**	**1,068,595**

	Other Current Expenditure	Grants	Operating Appropriation in Aid	2006-07 Total Net Resource Outturn	Total Net Resource Estimate	Total Net Outturn Compared With Estimate	2005-06 Total Net Resource Outturn
	£000	£000	£000	£000	£000	£000	£000
Total Net Resource Outturn	**34,257,772**	**1,240,961**	**(1,493,738)**	**34,004,995**	**34,824,389**	**819,394**	**34,862,134**

Provision of Defence Capability (RfR1)

2.1 The net outturn is £31,518,502,000 against an Estimate of £32,349,202,000; an underspend of £830,700,000.

The principal explanations for the underspend in RfR1 relate to capital spares and a reduction in Annually Managed Expenditure (£666,526,000) following a review of the value of nuclear provisions prior to the quinquennial review by the Nuclear Installation Inspectorate during 2007-08, which resulted in a significant release to the Operating Cost Statement. A detailed explanation of the variances against the Departmental Expenditure Limit is shown in paragraphs 285 to 286 within Resources, in the Performance Report.

Conflict Prevention (RfR2)

2.2 The following table shows the conflict prevention net resource outturn and capital expenditure summarised by each of the Operations, and compared against the Estimate (voted funding) for the year.

Operation	Net Resource Outturn £000	Capital Costs £000	2006-07 Total £000	2005-06 Restated Outturn £000
Peace Keeping Expenditure				
Afghanistan	564,096	178,208	742,304	199,348
Iraq	786,715	169,447	956,162	957,598
Programme Expenditure				
Balkans	55,878	543	56,421	62,853
Global pool*	12,193	-	12,193	16,937
African pool*	29,538	-	29,538	30,355
Total RfR2	**1,448,420**	**348,198**	**1,796,618**	**1,267,091**
Total Estimate	1,427,526	449,000	1,876,526	1,431,273
Difference – savings/(excess)	(20,894)	100,802	79,908	164,182

* prior year outturn figures restated to reflect correct attribution to geographical areas

2.3 A breakdown of the net operating and capital costs for the three main Operations is shown in the following table, alongside the Departmental Allocation for the year and the Outturn for 2005-06.

	Iraq			Afghanistan			Balkans		
	Total Departmental Allocation 2006-07 £000	Total Outturn 2006-07 £000	Total Outturn 2005-06 £000	Total Departmental Allocation 2006-07 £000	Total Outturn 2006-07 £000	Total Outturn 2005-06 £000	Total Departmental Allocation 2006-07 £000	Total Outturn 2006-07 £000	Total Outturn 2005-06 £000
Operating Cost (by area)									
Direct costs									
Service manpower	111,000	99,779	80,237	51,000	49,487	7,575	12,000	11,006	11,509
Civilian manpower	15,000	14,733	14,213	3,000	4,340	1,627	5,000	5,310	4,949
Infrastructure costs	89,000	83,136	81,407	99,000	100,928	10,522	12,000	12,853	12,633
Equipment support	214,000	206,065	220,232	122,000	111,739	24,399	6,000	5,557	7,840
Other costs and services	139,000	137,273	111,186	77,000	89,215	37,595	14,000	13,997	11,824
Income	5,000	4,720	10,054	4,000	(2,008)	7,792	(9,000)	(9,573)	2,369
Stock consumption	212,000	218,010	218,920	140,000	164,205	57,171	13,000	15,100	9,332
Indirect costs									
Stock write-off	-	238	51	-	-	(2)	-	-	-
Provisions	2,000	5,547	1,560	-	18	-	-	720	(437)
Depreciation and amortisation (inc Urgent Operational Requirements – UORs)	20,000	14,443	33,611	21,000	39,113	1,255	-	293	2,376
Fixed asset write-off	-	-	21,848	-	-	-	-	-	-
Cost of capital	-	2,771	4,441	(1,000)	2,500	183	-	147	284
Total Operating Costs	**807,000**	**786,715**	**797,760**	**516,000**	**559,537**	**148,117**	**53,000**	**55,390**	**62,679**

	Iraq			Afghanistan			Balkans		
	Total Departmental Allocation 2006-07	Total Outturn 2006-07	Total Outturn 2005-06	Total Departmental Allocation 2006-07	Total Outturn 2006-07	Total Outturn 2005-06	Total Departmental Allocation 2006-07	Total Outturn 2006-07	Total Outturn 2005-06
	£000	£000	£000	£000	£000	£000	£000	£000	£000
Capital Cost (by area)									
Capital addition (including UORs and Recuperation)	195,000	169,447	159,838	254,000	178,208	51,231	-	543	174
Net Book Value of fixed asset disposals	-	-	-	-	-	-	-	-	-
Total Capital	195,000	169,447	159,838	254,000	178,208	51,231	-	543	174
Total by Operation	1,002,000	956,162	957,598	770,000	737,745	199,348	53,000	55,933	62,853

The Net Operating Costs and Total by Operation in Table 2.3 include all income attributable to each Operation. The Net Resource Outturn by Operation in Table 2.2 excludes the excess Appropriations in Aid attributable to RFR2 and paid to the Consolidated Fund (see Note 5 – Analysis of income payable to the Consolidated Fund).

2.4 In accordance with the accounting principles agreed with HM Treasury, the Department has identified the costs of operations on the basis of net additional costs. Expenditure such as wages and salaries for permanently employed personnel are not included as these costs would have been incurred in the normal course of business. Costs of activities such as training and exercises which would have been incurred, but which have been cancelled due to operational commitments, have been deducted.

Negative numbers are shown in brackets. However, when comparing outturn against Estimate, excesses are shown in brackets.

The "positive income" figures in the operational costs represent income foregone (loss of receipts) as a result of those operations. The "negative income" figures represent income generated on operations (e.g. support to other nations in respect of catering and medical services).

Major Changes in Operational Costs

2.5 Explanation for the major movements in operational costs are:

Between 2005-06 and 2006-07:

The increase in service manpower costs in 2006-07 is the result of the new operational allowance paid to service personnel on operations with effect from 1 April 2006.

The overall increase in costs of operations in Afghanistan in 2006-07, particularly Urgent Operational Requirement (UOR) expenditure, is the direct result of the increased tempo of the operation in the Helmand Province in the south of the country.

Between 2006-07 Outturn and Estimate:

The excess in non-cash costs, such as depreciation charges for military equipment and the firing of guided weapons, missiles and bombs in Afghanistan were higher than forecasted at the time the Estimates were prepared. This is the direct result of the increased tempo of the operation in the Helmand Province in the south of the country.

When the capital estimate was prepared, it was based on UORs that had been financially approved. Not all UORs were subsequently delivered prior to the end of the financial year resulting in an underspend against capital costs.

War Pensions Benefits – Programme Costs (RfR3)

2.6 The Chief Executive of the Veterans Agency is not a Top Level Budget Holder, but exercises all the responsibilities for the programme costs.

3. Reconciliation of Net Resource Outturn to Net Operating Cost

	Outturn	Supply Estimate	2006-07 Outturn compared with Estimate	2005-06 Outturn
	£000	£000	£000	£000
Net Resource Outturn (Statement of Parliamentary Supply)	34,004,995	34,824,389	819,394	34,862,134
– Less income scored as Consolidated Fund Extra Receipts and included in operating income and interest (inc. excess operating Appropriation in Aid) (Note 5)	(56,326)		56,326	(468,599)
Net Operating Cost	**33,948,669**	**34,824,389**	**875,720**	34,393,535

Net Resource Outturn is the total of those elements of expenditure and income that are subject to Parliamentary approval and included in the Department's Supply Estimate. Net operating cost is the total of expenditure and income appearing in the Operating Cost Statement. The Outturn against the Estimate is shown in the Statement of Parliamentary Supply.

4. Reconciliation of Resources to Cash Requirement

	Note	Estimate	Outturn	Savings / (Excess)
		£000	£000	£000
Resource Outturn	2	34,824,389	**34,004,995**	819,394
Capital:				
Purchase of fixed assets:				
– RfR 1	13/14	7,547,068	**7,214,767**	332,301
– RfR 2	13/14	449,000	**348,198**	100,802
– RfR 1 Capitalised provisions	13/14		**12,843**	(12,843)
– Investments	15		**4,400**	(4,400)
Non operating cost A in A:				
Proceeds on sale of fixed assets	10/13/14	(541,829)	**(489,808)**	(52,021)
Repayment of loans made to the Trading Funds	15	(14,323)	**(8,479)**	(5,844)
Accruals adjustments:				
Non-cash transactions-				
Included in operating costs	23.1	(7,708,802)	**(6,430,478)**	(1,278,324)
Included in net interest payable	12	(85,219)	**(126,414)**	41,195
Capitalised provisions shown above			**(12,843)**	12,843
		(7,794,021)	**(6,569,735)**	(1,224,286)
Cost of capital charge	23.1	(2,807,894)	**(3,241,907)**	434,013
Changes in working capital other than cash, excluding movements on creditors falling due after one year		1,499,047	**(264,834)**	1,763,881
Increase in creditors falling due after one year			**82,454**	(82,454)
Use of provisions for liabilities and charges	20	584,814	**413,347**	171,467
Adjustment for movements on cash balances in respect of collaborative projects	23.5		**(51,949)**	51,949
Net cash requirement	23.5	**33,746,251**	**31,454,292**	**2,291,959**

5. Analysis of income payable to the Consolidated Fund

In addition to Appropriations in Aid, the following income relates to the Department and is payable to the Consolidated Fund (cash receipts being shown in italics).

	2006-07 Forecast		2006-07 Outturn	
	Income	Receipts	Income	Receipt
	£000	£000	£000	£000 s
Operating income and receipts – excess A in A Request for Resources 1	-	-	34,608	34,608
Operating income and receipts – excess A in A Request for Resources 2	-	-	5,047	5,047
Other operating income and receipts not classified as A in A	-	-	16,671	16,671
Subtotal operating income and receipts payable to the Consolidated Fund	-	-	56,326	56,326
Other amounts collectable on behalf of the Consolidated Fund	-	-	-	-
Total income payable to the Consolidated Fund	-	-	56,326	56,326

6. Reconciliation of income recorded within the Operating Cost Statement to operating income payable to the Consolidated Fund

	Note	2006-07 £000	2005-06 £000
Operating Income	11	1,429,392	1,390,997
Income included within other operating costs			
– Refunds of formula based VAT recovery		51,250	31,669
– Foreign exchange gains		39,230	9,711
– Other		(71)	(11)
Interest Receivable		30,263	26,821
Gross Income		1,550,064	1,459,187
Income authorised to be appropriated in aid		(1,493,738)	(1,346,570)
Operating Income payable to the Consolidated Fund	5	56,326	112,617

7. Non-Operating income – Excess A in A

	2006-07 £000	2005-06 £000
Principal repayments of voted loans	8,479	53,237
Proceeds on disposal of fixed assets	489,808	321,083
Non-operating income – excess A in A	-	-

8. Non-Operating income not classified as A in A

	Income £000	Receipts £000
The Department has no non-operating income not classified as A in A	-	-

241

9. Staff Numbers and Costs

9.1 The average number of full-time equivalent persons employed during the year was: Service 198,090[P] (2005-06: 203,290) and Civilian 90,650 (2005-06: 95,750). Source: Defence Analytical Services Agency.

	Permanent Staff	Temporary Staff	Armed Forces	Ministers	2006-07 Total	2005-06 Total
Analysis of Staff Numbers	89,576	1,070	198,090	4	288,740	299,040

In order to align with the total pay costs incurred during the year, shown below, the calculation of the average number of staff uses monthly statistics to identify an average number employed for the year. The staff numbers quoted reflect the number of personnel employed in organisations within the Departmental Boundary for the Annual Accounts (see page 193) and therefore exclude those within the Trading Funds. The numbers reported within the Performance Report include employees in the MoD Trading Funds. More information on the Department's staff numbers, and the statistical calculations used, is available on the website: http://www.dasa.mod.uk.

9.2 The aggregate staff costs, including grants and allowances paid, were as follows:

	2006-07 £000	2005-06 £000
Salaries and wages	8,728,349	8,603,882
Social security costs	641,539	644,726
Pension costs	1,761,944	1,751,740
Redundancy and severance payments	72,430	254,503
	11,204,262	11,254,851
Made up of:		
Service	8,422,935	8,262,776
Civilian	2,781,326	2,992,075
	11,204,262	11,254,851

Principal Civil Service Pension Scheme

9.3 The Principal Civil Service Pension Scheme (PCSPS) is an unfunded multi-employer defined benefit scheme. The Ministry of Defence is unable to identify its share of the underlying assets and liabilities. The Scheme Actuary (Hewitt Bacon Woodrow) valued the scheme as at 31 March 2003. Details can be found in the resource accounts of the Cabinet Office at: www.civilservice-pensions.gov.uk.

For 2006-07, total pension contributions of £340,578,000 were payable in respect of the various schemes in which MoD civilian staff were members. Contributions to the PCSPS in the year were £323,481,000 (2005-06: £309,639,000) at four rates in the range of 17.1 to 25.5 percent of pensionable pay, based on salary bands (the rates in 2005-06 were between 16.2% and 24.6%)[6]. The scheme's Actuary reviews employer contributions every four years following a full scheme valuation. From 2007-08, the salary bands will be revised but the rates will remain the same. The contribution rates are set to meet the cost of the benefits accruing, to be paid when the member retires, not the benefits paid during the period to existing pensioners.

Employees can opt to open a partnership pension account, a stakeholder pension with an employer contribution. Employer contributions are age-related and range from 3% to 12.5% of pensionable pay. Employers also match employee contributions up to 3% of pensionable pay. In addition, employer contributions of 0.8% of pensionable pay were payable to the PCSPS to cover the cost of the future provision of lump sum benefits on death in service and ill health retirement of these employees.

P Denotes provisional. Due to Joint Personnel Administration being introduced to the RN and RAF during 2006, manpower numbers for the RN from November 2006, and the RAF from February 2007, are provisional and subject to review.

6 The 2005-06 Annual Accounts quoted a rate of 25.6% which is only applicable to Prison Officers with Service prior to 1987; reference to this rate has been removed from the 2006-07 Accounts.

Armed Forces Pension Scheme

9.4 The Armed Forces Pension Scheme (known as AFPS 05) is an unfunded, non-contributory, defined benefit, salary-related, contracted out, occupational pension scheme. A formal valuation of the AFPS was carried out as at 31 March 2005 by the scheme's actuary, the Government Actuary's Department. Scheme members are entitled to a taxable pension for life and a tax-free pension lump sum if they leave the Regular Armed Forces at or beyond normal retirement age; those who have at least two years service who leave before age 55 will have their pensions preserved until age 65. Pensions may be payable to the spouse, civil partner, partner or to eligible children. Death-in-service lump sums are payable subject to nomination. AFPS 05 offers ill-health benefits if a career is cut short by injury or illness, irrespective of cause. Additionally, if the injury or illness is mainly attributable to service, compensation for conditions caused on or after 6 April 2005 will be considered under the Armed Forces Compensation Scheme (AFCS).

AFPS 05 members who leave before the age of 55 may be entitled to an Early Departure Payment, providing they have at least 18 years service and are at least 40 years of age. The Early Departure Payment Scheme pays a tax-free lump sum and income of between 50% and 75% of preserved pension between the date of the individual's departure from the Armed Forces and age 55. The income rises to 75% of preserved pension at age 55 and is index linked. At age 65, the Early Departure Payment stops and the preserved pension and preserved pension lump sum are paid.

For 2006-07, total employers' pension contributions payable were £1,421,366,000. This figure includes £1,419,529,000 payable to the AFPS, (2005-06 £1,404,451,000) based on rates determined by the Government Actuary. For 2006-07, the rates were 34.3% of total pay or 36.3%[7] of pensionable pay (34.3% and 36.3% for 2005-06) for officers. The 2006-07 rates for other ranks were 21.3% of total pay or 21.8% of pensionable pay (21.3% and 21.8% for 2005-06). The contribution rates reflect benefits as they are accrued, not costs actually incurred in the period, and reflect past experience of the scheme. Further information on the Armed Forces Pension Scheme and the Armed Forces Compensation Scheme can be found at the website: www.mod.uk/DefenceInternet/AboutDefence/WhatWeDo/Personnel/Pensions/ArmedForcesPensions/.

Other Pension Schemes

9.5 The Armed Forces Pension Scheme incorporates the following schemes: the Non-Regular Permanent Staff Pension Scheme, the Gurkha Pension Scheme and the Reserve Forces Pension Scheme. The membership of these schemes is approximately 3.68% of the AFPS total membership and the employers' contributions to the schemes are included in the figure payable to the AFPS, at paragraph 9.4.

Certain other employees are covered by schemes such as the National Health Service Pension Scheme and the Teachers' Pension Scheme. The figure for total employers' pension contributions at paragraph 9.3 includes contributions in respect of these schemes.

7 Joint Personnel Administration was introduced for the RAF and RN during 2006 and calculates SCAPE as a percentage of pensionable pay (this change will be effective for the Army in 2007). Note 9 includes all the percentage rates (including the previously unpublished pensionable pay rates for 2005-06) used to calculate the 2006-07 contributions.

10. Other Operating Costs

	2006-07	2005-06 Restated
	£000	£000
Operating expenditure:		
— Fuel	415,637	369,463
— Stock consumption	1,140,287	1,038,865
— Surplus arising on disposal of stock (net)	4,078	(16,372)
— Provisions to reduce stocks to net realisable value	90,771	(165,851)
— Stocks written off (net)	94,903	758,698
— Movements: includes personnel travelling, subsistence/relocation costs and movement of stores and equipment	774,031	728,875
— Utilities	319,591	291,347
— Property management *	1,257,963	1,366,781
— Hospitality and entertainment	4,337	5,364
— Accommodation charges *	465,946	443,917
— Equipment support costs	3,793,183	3,542,240
— Increase/(Decrease) in nuclear and other decommissioning provisions	(438,617)	(94,964)
— IT and telecommunications	718,780	642,546
— Professional fees	482,706	552,917
— Other expenditure	1,749,867	1,507,545
— Research expenditure and expensed development expenditure	987,649	994,480
— PFI service charges **		
IT and Telecommunications	424,930	307,269
Property Management	348,863	243,342
Transport	193,806	182,601
Equipment Support	121,454	123,619
Plant and Machinery	58,607	12,681
Depreciation and amortisation:		
— Intangible assets (Note 13)	1,152,633	1,314,570
— Tangible owned fixed assets (Note 14)	4,545,251	5,236,589
— Donated assets depreciation – release of reserve	(53,984)	(57,991)
— Tangible fixed assets held under finance leases (Note 14)	219	4,685
Impairment on fixed assets (Notes 13 & 14):		
— Arising on Quinquennial valuation	302,843	254,156
— Arising on Other items	4,682	182,344
Impairment – release of reserve	(131,820)	(23,696)
(Surplus) arising on disposal of tangible and intangible fixed assets		
— Tangible and Intangible fixed assets	(123,135)	(458,384)
— Donated assets – release of reserve	-	(20,975)
Fixed assets written off – net	730,325	(301,805)
Investment write down on share values	-	4,774
Capital project expenditure write off/(write on)	58,830	(22,145)
Bad debts written off	26,557	8,398
Increase/(decrease) in bad debts provision	4,298	1,439
Rentals paid under operating leases		
— Plant and Machinery	11,604	18,975
— Other	126,521	52,938
Auditors' remuneration – audit work only ***	3,600	3,500
Grants-in-Aid	61,319	61,087
Exchange differences on foreign currencies: net deficit/(surplus)	(2,293)	8,207
War Pensions Benefits	1,038,574	1,069,133
Total Other Operating Costs	**20,764,796**	**20,171,162**

* The prior year figure for Property Management has been restated by a reduction of £136,779,000, and Accommodation charges has been increased by £136,779,000 to reflect a more accurate disclosure of expenditure.

** PFI service charges have been separately disclosed. Prior year figures for Property Management (£243,734,000), IT and telecommunications (£112,703,000), Equipment Support (£72,202,000), Movements (£91,815,000), Other expenditure (£228,483,000) and Rentals paid under operating leases (£120,575,000) have been restated to reflect the PFI service charges previously disclosed within these headings and now disclosed separately.

*** Auditors' remuneration: No charge is made for non-audit work carried out by the auditors.

11. Income

	RfR 1	RfR2	2006-07 £000 Total	2005-06 £000 Total
Income Source				
External Customers				
Rental income – property	28,752		28,752	49,444
Receipts – personnel	62,077		62,077	55,171
Receipts – sale of fuel	105,592		105,592	56,559
Receipts – personnel related	152,332		152,332	175,369
Receipts – supplies and services	186,410		186,410	176,466
Receipts – provision of service accommodation	214,744		214,744	180,779
Receipts – NATO/UN/US Forces/Foreign Governments	294,139	20,604	314,743	316,403
Other	154,703		154,703	193,634
Other Government Departments, Trading Funds and QinetiQ				
Rental income – property	618		618	440
Receipts – personnel related	-		-	3,281
Reverse tasking*	29,275		29,275	26,384
Dividends from Investments (Note 15.4)	49,617		49,617	39,387
Income from provision of goods and services	130,072		130,072	113,218
Other	457		457	4,462
	1,408,788	**20,604**	**1,429,392**	**1,390,997**

*Receipts for invoiced good and or services supplied to the Trading Funds and QintiQ Group plc by MoD.

The introduction of Joint Personnel Administration has resulted in single and family accommodation receipts being attributed to Receipts – provision of service accommodation. The 2005-06 income was attributable to Rental Income – property, Receipts – personnel related and Receipts – provision of service accommodation.

Fees and Charges

11.1 Where the Department has spare capacity, it provides a range of services to external organisations. The majority of these services are in the form of military support to foreign governments and other government departments. Where appropriate, costs are recovered in accordance with HM Treasury's Fees and Charges Guide. On a smaller scale, the Department provides services to support charities, local community initiatives as well as commercial companies where there is a defence interest.

12. Net Interest Payable

	2006-07 £000	2005-06 £000
Interest receivable:*		
— Bank interest	(25,705)	(21,553)
— Loans to Trading Funds	(4,556)	(4,664)
— Loan to a Self Financing Public Corporation – QinetiQ**	-	(603)
— Other interest receivable	(2)	(1)
	(30,263)	(26,821)
Interest payable:		
— Bank interest	148	18
— Loan interest	3,237	3,348
— Unwinding of discount on provision for liabilities and charges (Note 20)	126,414	1,211,110
— Finance leases and PFI contracts	67,551	64,480
— Late payment of Commercial debts	9	15
	197,359	1,278,971
Net interest payable	167,096	1,252,150

*Interest receivable of which £831,000 is payable to the Consolidated Fund (£765,000 in 2005-06).

**prior to flotation in February 2006

13. Intangible Assets

Intangible assets include development expenditure in respect of fixed assets in use and assets under construction where the first delivery into operational use of the asset type has taken place.

	Single Use Military Equipment £000	Others £000	Total £000
Cost or Valuation*			
At 1 April 2006	28,407,033	1,010,541	29,417,574
Additions**	1,658,196	86,170	1,744,366
Impairment	(27,978)	(6,529)	(34,507)
Revaluations	773,533	21,357	794,890
Other movements***	(459,265)	(590,317)	(1,049,582)
At 31 March 2007	30,351,519	521,222	30,872,741
Amortisation			
At 1 April 2006	(6,377,543)	(57,336)	(6,434,879)
Charged in Year	(1,020,335)	(132,298)	(1,152,633)
Impairment	5,065	2,327	7,392
Revaluations	(185,057)	(7,756)	(192,813)
Other movements***	1,042,948	19,866	1,062,814
At 31 March 2007	(6,534,922)	(175,197)	(6,710,119)
Net Book Value:			
At 31 March 2007	23,816,597	346,025	24,162,622
At 1 April 2006	22,029,490	953,205	22,982,695

* Intangible asset valuations are based on the actual costs incurred over time where available, or derived by applying a ratio to the tangible fixed asset valuations based on the historical relationship between development and production costs. The intangible asset valuations were indexed using the appropriate Gross Domestic Product (GDP) deflator to determine the opening balance sheet valuation.

** Additions on intangible and tangible fixed assets (Note 14) include accruals amounting in total to £2,666,839,000 (2005-06: £2,514,869,000).

*** Other movements comprise reclassifications to tangible fixed assets and transfers to operating costs.

14. Tangible Fixed Assets

	Dwellings	Other Land and Buildings	Single Use Military Equipment (SUME)	Plant and Machinery	Transport	IT and Comms Equipment	Assets under Construction (SUME)	Assets under Construction (Others)	Total
	£000	£000	£000	£000	£000	£000	£000	£000	£000
Cost or Valuation									
At 1 April 2006	3,389,738	17,507,699	60,567,231	5,879,095	8,211,044	1,467,688	12,594,334	1,063,132	110,679,961
Additions*	2,786	41,798	404,400	31,605	32,523	206,391	4,471,464	627,632	5,818,599
Capitalised provisions**	-	6,647	6,196	-	-	-	-	-	12,843
Donations	-	-	-	80	-	-	-	-	80
Impairment	(31,648)	(402,709)	275,448	(30,518)	2,011	(33,482)	(744)	(1,216)	(222,858)
Disposals	62	(327,696)	(233,848)	(115,998)	(496)	-	-	-	(677,976)
Revaluations	170,044	1,314,033	1,529,615	348,294	236,415	27,504	343,099	43,529	4,012,533
Other movements***	85,269	808,004	3,162,544	(1,213,675)	1,231,589	140,464	(5,041,939)	(306,410)	(1,134,154)
At 31 March 2007	3,616,251	18,947,776	65,711,586	4,898,883	9,713,086	1,808,565	12,366,214	1,426,667	**118,489,028**
Depreciation									
At 1 April 2006	(477,042)	(1,964,232)	(29,077,813)	(2,604,972)	(4,299,142)	(481,802)	-	-	(38,905,003)
Charged in year	(116,965)	(598,417)	(2,850,548)	(257,420)	(503,908)	(218,212)	-	-	(4,545,470)
Impairment	746	12,625	(119,894)	5,620	(1,854)	45,205	-	-	(57,552)
Disposals	-	-	232,394	78,655	254	-	-	-	311,303
Revaluations	(38,358)	(397,885)	(558,690)	(199,318)	(114,378)	(14,807)	-	-	(1,323,436)
Other movements**	(14,231)	(536,848)	906,769	728,043	(446,642)	(5,423)	-	-	631,668
At 31 March 2007	(645,850)	(3,484,757)	(31,467,782)	(2,249,392)	(5,365,670)	(675,039)	-	-	**(43,888,490)**
Net Book Value: At 31 March 2007	**2,970,401**	**15,463,019**	**34,243,804**	**2,649,491**	**4,347,416**	**1,133,526**	**12,366,214**	**1,426,667**	**74,600,538**
At 1 April 2006	2,912,696	15,543,467	31,489,418	3,274,123	3,911,902	985,886	12,594,334	1,063,132	71,774,958
Asset Financing									
Owned	2,458,134	13,263,800	34,243,804	2,516,766	4,290,412	1,090,951	12,366,214	1,426,667	71,656,748
Donated****	308,126	1,665,021	-	40,320	123	-	-	-	2,013,590
Long Lease	176,099	102,179	-	-	-	-	-	-	278,278
Short Lease	621	58,193	-	-	-	-	-	-	58,814
Operating Lease	-	8,489	-	-	-	-	-	-	8,489
Finance Lease	-	-	-	-	420	-	-	-	420
On-Balance Sheet PFI	27,421	343,147	-	92,405	56,461	42,575	-	-	562,009
PFI residual interest	-	22,190	-	-	-	-	-	-	22,190
Net Book Value: At 31 March 2007	**2,970,401**	**15,463,019**	**34,243,804**	**2,649,491**	**4,347,416**	**1,133,526**	**12,366,214**	**1,426,667**	**74,600,538**

* Additions on intangible assets (Note 13) and tangible fixed assets include accruals amounting in total to £2,666,839,000 (2005-06: £2,514,869,000).

** Fixed Assets as at 31 March 2007 include capitalised provisions at cost of £110,777,000 (2005-2006: £195,698,000).

*** Other movements comprise reclassifications between tangible fixed asset categories, intangible assets, assets under construction, stock and transfers to operating costs.

**** Assets have been valued on the same basis as all other properties used by the Department.

2006-07 Quinquennial Revaluation

14.1 All Land and Buildings with the exception of Assets Under Construction, are subject to a quinquennial revaluation, which is being conducted on a rolling programme. During 2006-07, 25% of Land and Buildings were re-valued by two external organisations: the Valuation Office Agency, who dealt with the UK estate, and GVA Grimley, who were responsible for the overseas estate. These valuations were undertaken in accordance with the Royal Institute of Chartered Surveyors Appraisal and Valuation Manual and were on the basis of the existing use value to the Department. Due to the specialised nature of the Departmental estate, the majority of assets were valued using the Depreciated Replacement Cost method.

As a result of the valuations undertaken in 2006-07, the net increase to Land and Buildings assets was £137,555,000. Impairments charged to the Operating Cost Statement were £414,575,000. Impairments incurred as a result of previous quinquennial reviews have been reversed through the Operating Cost Statement in 2006-07 to the sum of £146,653,000. Net asset write-ons credited to the Operating Cost Statement were £38,897,000.

14.2 Data from the 2005-06 quinquennial review (Land and Buildings) was included within the 2005-06 Annual Accounts, although not processed within the Fixed Asset Register. As a result of processing the data, there has been an increase in the net book values of Buildings (£44,623,000), and a reversal of impairments through the Operating Cost Statement in 2006-07 of £26,108,000. The net increase to Land assets was £25,236,000 and impairments charged to the Operating Cost Statement were £40,032,000. The reversal of previously impaired land assets was credited to the Operating Costs Statement in 2006-07 to the sum of £1,033,000. Release of reserve charges for the quinquennial revaluation of donated assets totalled £126,405,000.

14.3 The 2007-08 Financial Reporting Manual permits entities to use the most appropriate valuation methodology available, including applying appropriate indices, to uplift non-property fixed assets to current values. This approach has been adopted by the Department for the 2006-07 accounts. However, a small proportion of Plant and Machinery had been professionally re-valued by the Valuation Office Agency prior to the decision to adopt the use of indices for non land and buildings assets, and these valuations have been included within the 2006-07 accounts.

The net book value decrease of the valuations for plant and machinery was £7,541,000. Impairments charged to the Operating Cost Statement were £26,954,000, and impairments incurred as a result of previous quinquennial reviews have been reversed through the Operating Cost Statement in 2006-07 to the sum of £4,924,000.

15. Investments

| | Trading Funds | | Other Investments | QinetiQ Group plc | Total |
| | Public Dividend Capital | Loans | | | |
	£000	£000	£000	£000	£000
Balance at 1 April 2006	184,254	86,039	1	243,838	514,132
Additions:					
Met Office		4,400			4,400
Loan Repayments:					
UK Hydrographic Office		(388)			(388)
Met Office		(1,097)			(1,097)
Defence Aviation Repair Agency		(4,840)			(4,840)
ABRO		(2,154)			(2,154)
Revaluations				(9,991)	(9,991)
Balance at 31 March 2007	**184,254**	**81,960**	**1**	**233,847**	**500,062**
Balance at 1 April 2006	184,254	86,039	1	243,838	514,132

Public Dividend Capital and Loans at 31 March 2007 were held in the following Trading Funds:

	Public Dividend Capital	Loans	Interest Rates % p.a.
	£000	£000	
Defence Science Technology Laboratory	50,412	-	
UK Hydrographic Office	13,267	10,605	8.375
Met Office	58,867	9,303	4.45 – 5.65
Defence Aviation Repair Agency	42,303	40,510	4.20 – 5.00
ABRO	19,405	21,542	5.625
Balance at 31 March 2007	**184,254**	**81,960**	

Analysis of loans repayable by instalments:

	Due within one year	Due after one year	Total
	£000	£000	£000
UK Hydrographic Office	421	10,184	10,605
Met Office	2,534	6,769	9,303
Defence Aviation Repair Agency	4,840	35,670	40,510
ABRO	2,154	19,388	21,542
Balance at 31 March 2007	**9,949**	**72,011**	**81,960**

During the year two new loans totalling £4,400,000 were made, both to the Met Office, at an interest rate of 5.65% per annum. The loans are repayable over three years, with the final instalments due in January 2010.

A Civil Network Loan of £2,400,000 was made to fund the cost of restructuring the regional infrastructure. Civil forecasting services were centralised onto two sites, Exeter and Aberdeen, delivering substantial efficiencies. The loan was required to fund staff exit and transfer costs and investment in new infrastructure and IT.

A Commercial Loan of £2,000,000 was made in support of the commercial strategy. It was used to enhance the Met Office's commercial capability by increasing the staff skill base, improving basic internal commercial processes and rationalising product and service offerings.

Investment in QinetiQ Group plc

15.1 On 1 April 2006, the Department's shareholding in QinetiQ Group plc, 124,885,445 (19.3%) Ordinary Shares (nominal value 1p each), were valued at 195.25p per share; a total value of £243,838,831.36. The market price of the shares had fallen to 187.25p per share on 31 March 2007; a reduction in the total market value of £9,990,835.60 to £233,847,995.76.

Holders of Ordinary Shares in QinetiQ Group plc are entitled to receive notice of, attend, speak and vote at general and extraordinary meetings of the company and have one vote for every share owned.

The Department also holds one Special Share in QinetiQ Group plc, and one Special Share in each of two of its subsidiary companies, QinetiQ Holdings Limited and QinetiQ Limited. The Special Shares can only be held by the Crown and give the Government the right to: implement and operate the Compliance System, prohibit or restrict QinetiQ from undertaking activities, which may lead to an unmanageable conflict of interest that would be damaging to the defence or security interests of the United Kingdom, and to veto any transaction, which may lead to unacceptable ownership of the company. The Special Shareholder must receive notice of, and may attend and speak at, general and extraordinary meetings. The Special Shares carry no voting rights, except to enforce certain aspects of the compliance regime. The shareholder has no right to share in the capital or profits of the company other than – in the event of liquidation – to be repaid the capital paid up in respect of the shares before other shareholders receive any payment.

Other Investments

15.2 As at 31 March 2007, investments, including Special Shares, were held in the following:

	7.5% Non-cumulative Irredeemable Preference Shares at £1 each
Chamber of Shipping Limited	688 Shares
British Shipping Federation Limited	55,040 Shares

249

	Preferential Special Shares at £1 each
Devonport Royal Dockyard Limited	1 Share
Rosyth Royal Dockyard Limited	1 Share
AWE plc	1 Share
AWE Pension Trustees Limited	1 Share
QinetiQ Group plc	1 Share
QinetiQ Holdings Limited	1 Share
QinetiQ Limited	1 Share
BAE Systems Marine (Holdings) Limited	1 Share

	Non Preferential Shares of £1 each
International Military Services Limited	19,999,999 Shares

The Department has a 100% interest in the non-preferential shares of International Military Services Limited, a company registered in England. International Military Services Limited ceased trading on 31 July 1991. Following settlement of outstanding contracts, the company will be liquidated. The Department has written down the value of the investment to nil.

The 7.5% Non-cumulative Irredeemable Preference Shares in Chamber of Shipping Limited and British Shipping Federation Limited are valued at 1p each reflecting the value at which shares would be recovered by the two companies should membership by the Department be ceded, as laid down in the Articles of Association of the respective companies.

Special Shares confer on the Secretary of State for Defence special rights regarding ownership, influence and control, including voting rights in certain circumstances, under the individual Articles of Association of the relevant companies in which the shares are held. Further detailed information can be obtained from the companies' individual annual reports and accounts, which can be obtained from:

Company	Registration Number
Devonport Royal Dockyard Limited, Devonport Royal Dockyard, Devonport, Plymouth PL1 4SG	02077752
Rosyth Royal Dockyard Limited, c/o Babcock BES, Rosyth Business Park, Rosyth, Dunfermline, Fife KY11 2YD	SC101959
AWE plc, AWE Aldermaston, Reading, Berkshire RG7 4PR	02763902
AWE Pension Trustees Limited, AWE Aldermaston, Reading, Berkshire RG7 4PR	02784144
QinetiQ Group plc, 85 Buckingham Gate, London SW1E 6PD	04586941
QinetiQ Holdings Limited, 85 Buckingham Gate, London SW1E 6PD	04154556
QinetiQ Limited, 85 Buckingham Gate, London SW1E 6PD	3796233
BAE Systems Marine (Holdings) Limited, Warwick House, PO Box 87, Farnborough Aerospace Centre, Farnborough, Hants, GU14 6YU	01957765

Net Assets of Trading Funds

15.3 The reported net assets, after deducting loans due to MoD, of the investments held in Trading Funds at 31 March 2007 and 31 March 2006 were:

	31 March 2007	31 March 2006
	£000	£000
Defence Science and Technology Laboratory	242,600	218,000
UK Hydrographic Office	51,315	46,907*
Met Office	198,700	182,293*
Defence Aviation Repair Agency	89,085	82,904
ABRO	49,953	47,598
Total	**631,653**	**577,702**

* Balance restated.

250

Dividends from Investments

15.4 The following dividends, shown as income in Note 11.

	31 March 2007 £000	31 March 2006 £000
QinetiQ	4,309	6,091
Defence Science and Technology Laboratory	6,000	3,000
UK Hydrographic Office	9,171	6,296
Met Office *	18,937	Nil
Defence Aviation Repair Agency	6,000	12,000
ABRO	5,200	12,000
Total	**49,617**	**39,387**

* Dividends in respect of financial years 2004-05, 2005-06 and 2006-07.

16. Stocks and Work in Progress

	31 March 2007 £000	31 March 2006 £000
Work in progress	11,670	34,244
Raw materials and consumables	5,309,724	6,015,687
Assets declared for disposal*	-	2,296
	5,321,394	**6,052,227**

* Assets have been declared for displosal as part of the DSDA Rationalisation Programme, however the Net Book Value of these assets cannot easily be identified.

17. Debtors

17.1 Analysis by type

	31 March 2007 £000	31 March 2006 £000
Amounts falling due within one year		
Trade debtors	233,860	177,539
Deposits and advances	28,207	54,355
Value Added Tax	317,118	320,544
Other debtors	213,501	275,363
Staff loans and advances*	46,072	41,921
Prepayments and accrued income	633,614	506,324
Current part of PFI prepayment	41,647	156,716
	1,514,019	**1,532,762**
Amounts falling due after one year		
Trade debtors	286,160	28,000
Other debtors	3,165	2,457
Staff loans and advances*	51,843	50,371
Prepayments and accrued income**	1,382,232	1,307,565
	1,723,400	**1,388,393**
Total Debtors	**3,237,419**	**2,921,155**

* Staff loans and advances includes loans for house purchase. The number of staff with house purchase loans was 12,167 (2005-06:11,712).

** Prepayments falling due after one year include an amount of £407,000,000 in respect of an adjudication decision where an appeal is pending: the amount represents an amount paid into an Escrow Account in the financial year 2002-03 and interest earned on it since that date.

17.2 Intra-Government Balances

	Amounts falling due within one year		Amounts falling due after more than one year	
		£000		£000
	2006-07	2005-06	2006-07	2005-06
Balances with other central government bodies	374,454	366,301	14,873	30,143
Balances with local authorities	949	1,433	-	-
Balances with NHS Trusts	5,770	12,864	787	-
Balances with public corporations and trading funds	24,040	7,576	-	-
Subtotal: intra-government balances	405,213	388,174	15,660	30,143
Balances with bodies external to government	1,108,806	1,144,588	1,707,740	1,358,250
Total Debtors at 31 March	**1,514,019**	**1,532,762**	**1,723,400**	**1,388,393**

The table above provides an analysis of the balances in Table 17.1 by customer type.

18. Cash at Bank and in Hand

	2006-07	2005-06
	£000	£000
Balance at 1 April	1,018,245	438,411
Net Cash Inflow/(Outflow):		
Received from Consolidated Fund	31,025,000	31,262,178
Utilised	(31,569,569)	(30,682,344)
Increase/(decrease) during year	(544,569)	579,834
Balance at 31 March	**473,676**	**1,018,245**
The following balances at 31 March were held at:		
Office of HM Paymaster General	157,237	684,585
Commercial Banks and Cash in Hand	316,439	333,660
Balance at 31 March	**473,676**	**1,018,245**

The cash at bank balance includes £204,434,000 (2005-06: £256,381,000) of sums advanced by foreign governments to the Department on various collaborative projects where the United Kingdom is the host nation. Advances made by foreign governments for the procurement of defence equipment on their behalf are also included in this amount. The corresponding liability for these advances is shown under creditors due within one year.

19. Creditors

19.1 Analysis by type

	31 March 2007 £000	31 March 2006 £000
Amounts falling due within one year		
VAT	47,131	36,320
Other taxation and social security	234,373	240,255
Trade creditors	880,088	546,569
Other creditors*	266,872	351,519
Payments received on account	14,940	25,920
Accruals and deferred income	5,003,057	4,465,599
Current part of finance leases	2,595	4,378
Current part of imputed finance lease element of on-balance sheet PFI contracts	18,391	15,168
Current part of NLF loans**	1,904	1,797
Amounts issued from the Consolidated Fund for supply but not spent ***	229,588	658,881
Consolidated Fund extra receipts due to be paid to the Consolidated Fund – Received	39,655	102,983
	6,738,594	**6,449,389**
Amounts falling due after more than one year		
Other creditors	12,186	101,618
Accruals	190,579	176,686
Finance leases	43	2,639
Imputed finance lease element of on-balance sheet PFI contracts	640,107	642,523
NLF loans**	46,431	48,335
Loans – other	85,800	85,800
	975,146	**1,057,601**

* Other creditors includes amounts advanced by foreign governments to the Department in respect of various collaborative projects where the United Kingdom is the host nation and for the procurement of defence equipment on their behalf of £204,434,000 (2005-06 – £256,381,000).

** Loans are from the National Loans Fund in respect of the Armed Forces Housing Loans. These are fully repayable between years 2012 and 2028, with the last instalment due on 20 February 2028. Interest on the loans is payable at rates ranging from 4% to 7% per annum.

*** The amount comprises amounts drawn down and deemed drawn down from the Consolidated Fund for 2006-07 less the Net Cash Requirement for 2006-07.

19.2 Intra-Government Balances

	Amounts falling due within one year £000		Amounts falling due after more than one year £000	
	2006-07	2005-06	2006-07	2005-06
Balances with other central government bodies	481,008	806,936	132,231	134,135
Balances with local authorities	448	781	-	-
Balances with NHS Trusts	10,782	2,938	-	-
Balances with public corporations and trading funds	104,919	66,884	-	3,874
Subtotal: intra-government balances	597,157	877,539	132,231	138,009
Balances with bodies external to government	6,141,437	5,571,850	842,915	919,592
Total Creditors at 31 March	**6,738,594**	**6,449,389**	**975,146**	**1,057,601**

The table above provides an analysis of the balances in Table 19.1 by contractor type.

20. Provisions for Liabilities and Charges

	Nuclear Decommissioning	Other Decommissioning And Restoration Costs	Early Retirement Commitments	Other	Total
	£000	£000	£000	£000	£000
At 1 April 2006	4,299,488	117,571	526,511	1,331,374	6,274,944
Increase in Provision	273,595	13,943	102,251	174,554	564,343
Unwinding of discounting	90,840	1,956	9,422	74,795	177,013
Amounts released	(712,207)	(23,969)	(18,404)	(89,335)	(843,915)
Reclassifications	(798)	11,438	(58,588)	47,948	-
Amounts capitalised	12,843	-	-	-	12,843
Utilised in year	(53,118)	(12,948)	(116,357)	(230,924)	(413,347)
At 31 March 2007	3,910,643	107,991	444,835	1,308,412	5,771,881

Analysis of amount charged / (credited) to Operating Cost Statement

	2006-07	2005-06
	£000	£000
Charged/(credited) to:		
Property management	(8,724)	10,334
Staff costs	68,826	274,509
Nuclear and Other Decommissioning provisions	(438,612)	(95,111)
War Pensions Benefits	1,000	2,200
Other costs	97,938	21,632
Net interest (receivable)/payable	126,414	1,211,110
	(153,158)	1,424,674
Made up of:		
Increase	564,343	610,274
Release	(843,915)	(396,710)
	(279,572)	213,564
Unwinding of discount	126,414	1,211,110
Net increase in provisions	(153,158)	1,424,674

The unwinding of the discount charge for Other Liabilities includes the change in discount rate from 2.8% to 1.8% applied to the Locally Engaged Civilian Pension Schemes. The charge arising from the change in rate has been taken to the General Fund (Note 21).

Nuclear Decommissioning

20.1 Nuclear decommissioning provisions relate principally to the cost of facility decommissioning and the treatment and storage of nuclear waste arising from operations at MoD sites, operations of Royal Navy submarines and for the Departmental share of planning and constructing a national repository for the eventual disposal of that waste. MoD is also responsible for the Atomic Weapons Establishment (AWE).

MoD liabilities relating to civil nuclear sites and the associated value of provisions and funding for decommissioning costs at 1 April 2005 (£4,320,528,000) were transferred to the newly formed Nuclear Decommissioning Authority sponsored by the Department of Trade and Industry.

The liabilities include the costs associated with decommissioning and care and maintenance of redundant facilities (the conditioning, retrieval and storage of contaminated materials), research and development and the procurement of capital facilities to handle the various waste streams.

Calculation of the provision to cover the liabilities is based on schedules of information received by the MoD from major decommissioning contractors. These schedules are based on technical assessments of the processes and methods likely to be used in the future to carry out the work. Estimates are based on the latest technical knowledge and commercial information available, taking into account current legislation, regulations and Government policy. The amount and timing of each obligation are therefore sensitive to these factors. These sensitivities and their likely effect on the calculation and amount of the liabilities are reviewed on an annual basis.

The latest estimate of the undiscounted cost of dealing with the MoD's nuclear liabilities is £8,385,008,000 (2005-2006: £9,753,827,000).

The estimate of £3,910,643,000 (2005-06: £4,299,488,000) at 31 March 2007 represents the liabilities discounted at 2.2% to the balance sheet date and expressed in 2006-07 money values.

The estimated timescale over which the costs will need to be incurred is as follows:

	31 March 2007
	£000
Up to 3 years	319,790
From 4 – 10 years	819,435
Beyond 10 years	2,771,418
Total	**3,910,643**

During 2006-07, schedule and cost estimates have been reviewed and updated in preparation for the quinquennial review that is to take place with the Nuclear Installations Inspectorate during 2007-08. The resulting estimates incorporate risk and uncertainty appropriate to each type of expenditure and take into account progress made to date since the original estimates made in 2000. The provision has been reduced as a result of this review.

Other Decommissioning and Restoration

20.2 Other decommissioning and restoration provisions relate primarily to contaminated sites where the Department has a constructive or a legal obligation to restore the sites for normal use. The estimated payments are discounted by the Treasury discount rate of 2.2% in real terms. During 2006-07 provisions have been created for Land Quality Assessments in respect of chemical weapon agent contamination (£5,807,000) and for the removal of asbestos (£3,914,000). Provisions for decommissioning work at RRH Portreath (£15,022,000) and at vacated London sites (£4,853,000) have been released to the Operating Cost Statement following a review of the requirement.

Early Retirement Pensions

20.3 The Department meets the additional costs of benefits beyond the normal civil service pension scheme benefits in respect of employees who retire early by paying the required amounts annually to the pension schemes over the period between early departure and normal retirement date. The Department provides for this in full when the early retirement programme becomes binding by establishing a provision for the estimated payments discounted by the Treasury discount rate of 2.2% in real terms. During 2006-07, provisions were created to increase the early departure scheme for civilian employees in Northern Ireland as a result of "normalisation", announced in 2005-06 (£24,682,000), within RAF Strike Command (£6,750,000) for redundancies within the DLO (£13,783,000) and within Central TLB (£18,264,000) to extend the Departmental scheme announced in 2004-05. Provisions were released to the Operating Cost Statement for specific redundancies no longer required (£4,819,000) and following the review of a specific early retirement scheme (£6,742,000).

Other

20.4 Other provisions include costs arising from the disposal of fixed assets; redundancy and relocation costs associated with reorganisation and restructuring and amounts payable under guarantees, litigation and contractual arrangements. During 2006-07, provisions have been created for an increase in legal claims (£70,980,000), and the pension provision for locally employed personnel overseas has been increased by £6,630,000 on advice from the Government Actuary's Department and by £50,600,000 as a result of the change in the Treasury discount rate from 2.8% to 1.8% for pensions. A further increase in provisions has been created for potential claims by contractors (£21,043,000). Following a review of the requirement, provision of £51,604,000 have been released to the Operating Cost Statement in respect of Army and RAF restructuing programmes, and of £25,453,000 in respect of Trading Fund restructuring. Existing provisions include those concerning an adjudication decision where an appeal is pending (£376,860,000).

21. General Fund

The General Fund represents the total assets less liabilities of each of the entities within the accounting boundary, to the extent that the total is not represented by other reserves and financing items.

	2006-07 £000	2005-06 £000
Balance at 1 April	72,490,177	69,254,944
Net Parliamentary Funding		
– Drawn Down	31,025,000	31,262,178
– Deemed	658,881	-
Year end adjustment		
– Supply (Creditor)/Debtor – current year	(229,588)	(658,881)
Net Transfer from Operating Activities		
– Net Operating Costs	(33,948,669)	(34,393,535)
– CFERs paid and repayable to Consolidated Fund	(56,326)	(470,388)
Non-cash charges:		
– Cost of Capital (OCS)	3,241,907	3,106,369
– Auditors' Remuneration (Note 10)	3,600	3,500
– Change in the Discount Rate-Pension Provision (Note 20)	(50,600)	-
Transfer from/(to) Revaluation Reserve (Note 22)	2,321,586	4,450,319
Transfer from/(to) Donated Asset Reserve (Note 22)	(21,785)	(64,329)
Balance at 31 March	**75,434,183**	**72,490,177**

22. Reserves

	Revaluation Reserve £000	Donated Asset Reserve £000	Investment Reserve £000
At 1 April 2006	16,635,683	2,113,028	242,590
Arising on revaluation during the year (net)	2,846,996	59,153	(9,991)
Additions during the year	-	80	-
Transfers and reclassifications	(31,324)	5,297	-
Transferred (to) / from Operating Cost Statement	-	(185,804)	-
Transferred (to) / from General Fund	(2,321,586)	21,785	-
At 31 March 2007	**17,129,769**	**2,013,539**	**232,599**

23. Notes to the Cash Flow Statement

23.1 Reconciliation of operating cost to operating cash flows

	Note	2006-07 £000	2005-06 £000
Net operating cost	OCS	33,948,669	34,393,535
Non-cash transactions:			
– Depreciation and amortisation charges	10	(5,644,119)	(6,497,853)
– Impairment in value of fixed assets	10	(175,705)	(412,804)
– Provisions to reduce value of stock to its net realisable value	10	(90,771)	165,851
– Stocks written off – net	10	(94,903)	(758,698)
– Auditors' remuneration	10	(3,600)	(3,500)
– Surplus/(deficit) arising on disposal of stock	10	(4,078)	16,372
– Surplus/(deficit) arising on disposal of tangible fixed assets	10	123,135	123,377
– Surplus/(deficit) arising on disposal of investments (QinetiQ)	10	-	355,982
– Fixed Assets written on/(off) – net	10	(730,325)	301,805
– Capital project expenditure written on/(off)	10	(58,830)	22,145
– Amounts written off investments	10	-	(4,774)
– Bad debts written off	10	(26,557)	(8,398)
– Bad debts provision	10	(4,298)	(1,439)
– Movement in provisions for liabilities and charges (excluding capitalised provisions)	20	279,573	(212,014)
– Unwinding of discount on provisions for liabilities and charges	20	(126,414)	(1,211,110)
– Cost of capital	21	(3,241,907)	(3,106,369)
		(9,798,799)	(11,231,427)
Increase/(decrease) in stocks/WIP		169,875	239,473
Increase/(decrease) in debtors		347,119	81,614
(Increase)/decrease in creditors		(206,751)	(696,215)
Less movements in creditors relating to items not passing through the OCS		*(76,237)*	*600,926*
Use of provisions		287,357	477,154
Net cash outflow from operating activities		**24,671,233**	**23,865,060**

23.2 Analysis of capital expenditure and financial investment

	Note	2006-07 £000	2005-06 £000
Intangible fixed asset additions	13	1,744,366	1,549,968
Tangible fixed asset additions	14	5,818,599	5,568,181
Less movement on fixed asset accruals & creditors		(301,213)	(169,781)
Proceeds on disposal of tangible fixed assets		(489,808)	(299,316)
Proceeds of redemption of Redeemable Preference Shares in QinetiQ		-	(21,766)
Proceeds of Shares in QinetiQ		-	(357,771)
Loans made to Trading Funds	15	4,400	6,000
Repayment of loans made to the Trading Funds and QinetiQ	15	(8,479)	(53,237)
Net cash outflow from investing activities		**6,767,865**	**6,222,278**

23.3 Analysis of capital expenditure and financial investment by Request for Resources

	Capital expenditure £000	Loans etc £000	A in A £000	Net Total £000
Request for Resources 1	6,913,554	(4,079)	(489,808)	6,419,667
Request for Resources 2	348,198			348,198
Request for Resources 3				
Net movements in debtors/creditors	301,213			301,213
Total 2006-07	**7,562,965**	**(4,079)**	**(489,808)**	**7,069,078**
Total 2005-06	7,118,149	(47,237)	(678,853)	6,392,059

23.4 Analysis of financing

	Note	2006-07 £000	2005-06 £000
From the Consolidated Fund (Supply) – current year	21	31,025,000	31,262,178
From the Consolidated Fund (Supply) – prior year	21	-	127,275
Advances from the Contingencies Fund		-	1,839,814
Repayments to the Contingencies Fund		-	(1,839,814)
Repayment of loans from the National Loans Fund		(1,797)	(1,695)
Capital elements of payments in respect of finance leases and on-balance sheet PFI contracts		(9,020)	(10,385)
Loans – Other		-	26,300
Net financing		**31,014,183**	**31,403,673**

23.5 Reconciliation of Net Cash Requirement to increase/(decrease) in cash

	Note	2006-07 £000	2005-06 £000
Net cash requirement		(31,454,292)	(30,603,297)
From the Consolidated Fund (Supply) – current year	23.4	31,025,000	31,262,178
From the Consolidated Fund Supply – prior year	23.4	-	127,275
Amounts due to the Consolidated Fund received and not paid	19	39,655	102,983
Amounts due to the Consolidated Fund received in the prior year and paid over		(102,983)	(369,096)
Movement on Collaborative balances		(51,949)	59,791
Increase/(decrease) in cash		**(544,569)**	**579,834**

24. Notes to the Statement of Operating Costs by Departmental Aim and Objectives

The net costs of the Departmental Objectives are determined as follows:

Objective 1: Achieving success in the tasks we undertake

This objective comprises the following:

	2006-07			2005-06		
	Gross	Income	Net	Gross	Income	Net
	£000	£000	£000	£000	£000	£000
Operations	1,463,977	(20,604)	1,443,373	1,055,848	(16,062)	1,039,786
Other military tasks	1,611,502	(86,229)	1,525,273	1,751,704	(53,287)	1,698,417
Contributing to the community	421,920	(25,357)	396,563	566,648	(72,362)	494,286
Helping to build a safer world	516,874	(171,085)	345,789	610,690	(279,090)	331,600
Total	**4,014,273**	**(303,275)**	**3,710,998**	3,984,890	(420,801)	3,564,089

Costs are identified as follows:

- **Operations** comprises the additional costs incurred deploying the Armed Forces in military operations, e.g. in Iraq and Afghanistan, over and above the costs of maintaining the units involved at their normal states of readiness.

- **Other military tasks** include ongoing military commitments, e.g. to security in Northern Ireland and Overseas Commands, and the costs of identifying and countering the threat of terrorist attack on the UK mainland, and of maintaining the integrity of UK waters and airspace.

- **Contributing to the community** includes ongoing support activities, e.g. search and rescue, administration of cadet forces. In addition, it includes the costs of assistance to other Government Departments and agencies, e.g. in counter drugs operations.

- **Helping to build a safer world** includes the costs of Defence diplomacy undertaken to build confidence and security with our allies. It also includes the Department's support of wider British interests.

Objective 2: Being ready to respond to the tasks that might arise

The costs of delivering the military capability to meet this objective are analysed among force elements of the front line commands, including joint force units where these have been established, and a small number of centrally managed military support activities.

In addition to the direct operating costs of the front line units, they include the attributed costs of logistical and personnel support, identified by reference to the output costs of supplier Management Groupings.

In common with all objectives, these also contain a share of the costs of advising Ministers and accountability to Parliament, and apportioned overheads for head office functions and centrally provided services.

With effect from April 2006, intangible and tangible fixed assets were transferred from TLBs to Single Balance Sheet Owners (SBSOs) The related operating costs (e.g. depreciation and cost of capital charge) have been apportioned to outputs by the SBSOs using the percentage of costs attributed to the Management Grouping in 2005-06 as a basis for the apportionment. Where Front Line TLBs had peviously allocated some asset costs directly to final outputs, the methodology used in 2006-07 has resulted in some variances in costs attributed to final outputs from those reported in 2005-06. Restructuring within RAF Strike Command resulted in a more accurate alignment of costs to outputs.

The complexity of the cost apportionment model used to calculate costs by Departmental Objective, prevents the prior year figures being restated using the 2006-07 methodology.

The total comprises the full costs, including support services, of force elements grouped under the following headings:

	2006-07			2005-06		
	Gross	Income	Net	Gross	Income	Net
	£000	£000	£000	£000	£000	£000
Royal Navy						
Aircraft carriers	348,985	(10,050)	338,935	363,720	(9,392)	354,328
Frigates and Destroyers	1,667,001	(58,421)	1,618,580	1,385,909	(30,940)	1,354,969
Smaller warships	403,709	(13,386)	390,323	424,510	(11,840)	412,670
Amphibious ships	349,766	(10,823)	338,943	296,158	(5,935)	290,223
Strategic sealift	46,738	(684)	46,054	43,742	(2,675)	41,067
Fleet support ships	375,291	(8,996)	366,295	347,915	(3,473)	344,442
Survey and other vessels	97,893	(3,759)	94,134	74,755	(2,389)	72,366
Naval aircraft	1,117,280	(34,106)	1,083,174	1,170,120	(31,482)	1,138,638
Submarines	2,286,998	(82,943)	2,204,055	3,441,777	(48,510)	3,393,267
Royal Marines	577,469	(20,530)	556,939	550,066	(10,153)	539,913
	7,281,130	(243,698)	7,037,432	8,098,672	(156,789)	7,941,883
Army						
Field units	9,143,183	(311,830)	8,822,353	8,696,394	(204,079)	8,492,315
Other units	1,993,020	(109,495)	1,883,525	2,204,945	(218,263)	1,986,682
	11,127,203	(421,325)	10,705,878	10,901,339	(422,342)	10,478,997
Royal Air Force						
Strike/attack and offensive support aircraft	2,156,574	(89,446)	2,067,128	1,832,257	(54,774)	1,777,483
Defensive and surveillance aircraft	1,691,662	(67,060)	1,624,602	2,409,986	(61,914)	2,348,072
Reconnaissance and maritime patrol aircraft	635,269	(22,436)	612,833	620,778	(15,043)	605,735
Tankers, transport and communications aircraft	1,262,576	(51,779)	1,210,797	1,304,193	(56,750)	1,247,443
Future capability	45,837	(1,566)	44,271	20,370	(372)	19,998
Other aircraft and RAF units	1,489,798	(62,572)	1,427,226	886,603	(36,854)	849,749
	7,281,716	(294,859)	6,986,857	7,074,187	(225,707)	6,848,480

	2006-07			2005-06		
	Gross	Income	Net	Gross	Income	Net
	£000	£000	£000	£000	£000	£000
Centre Grouping						
Joint and multinational operations	448,581	(23,744)	424,837	495,378	(21,187)	474,191
Centrally managed military support	447,486	(80,637)	366,849	491,589	(92,020)	399,569
Maintenance of war reserve stocks	787,274	(16,868)	770,406	465,421	(7,225)	458,196
	1,683,341	(121,249)	1,562,092	1,452,388	(120,432)	1,331,956
Total Objective 2	27,373,390	(1,081,131)	26,292,259	27,526,586	(925,270)	26,601,316

Most groupings are self explanatory. The following, however, should be noted.

- **Smaller warships** includes mine hunting and offshore patrol vessels.

- **Amphibious ships** includes assault ships providing platforms for landing craft and helicopters, and Royal Fleet Auxiliary landing support ships.

- **Strategic sealift** is the Roll-On Roll-Off ferry facility supporting the Joint Rapid Reaction Force.

- **Fleet support ships** includes Royal Fleet Auxiliary ships providing tanker and replenishment support to warships.

- **Survey and other vessels** includes ocean and coastal survey and ice patrol ships.

- **Naval aircraft** include Sea King, Lynx and Merlin helicopters deployed in anti-submarine, airborne early warning, Royal Marine support, and reconnaissance and attack roles.

- **Submarines** includes the operating costs of submarines, nuclear weapons systems and logistical support of nuclear propulsion, including nuclear decommissioning. The costs attributed to submarines in 2005-06 include the increased cost (£1,085,000,000) incurred following the change in the discount rate, from 3.5% to 2.2%, applied to the Department's provisions for nuclear decommissioning.

- **Army – Field units** includes 1 (UK) Armoured Division, 3 (UK) Division, Joint Helicopter Command and Theatre troops.

- **Army – Other units** includes Regional Divisions and Land support and training.

- **Strike/attack and offensive support aircraft** includes Tornado GR4, Joint Force Harrier and Jaguar aircraft deployed in strike/attack and offensive support roles.

- **Defensive and surveillance aircraft** includes Typhoon, Tornado F3 and Sentry AEW1 aircraft deployed in UK air defence, and NATO and UN peacekeeping commitments. The improved alignment of costs in 2006-07 including the allocation of the RAF Logistics Hub and Air Traffic Services to Other aircraft and RAF units has resulted in the major year on year variance.

- **Reconnaissance and maritime patrol aircraft** includes Canberra and Nimrod R1 aircraft deployed on reconnaissance, and Nimrod MR2 aircraft on maritime patrol. (Tornado GR4 included in **strike/attack and offensive support aircraft** also undertake reconnaissance roles).

- **Tankers, transport and communications aircraft** includes C-17, Hercules, Tristar and VC10 aircraft providing air transport and air to air refuelling, and smaller transport aircraft (BAe 125/146 and Squirrel/Augusta 109 helicopters) used in a rapid communications role.

- **Future capability** includes the Joint Test and Evaluation Group (for 2006-07) and the development and use of geographic information.

- **Other aircraft and RAF units** includes ground forces (e.g. the RAF Regiment) and miscellaneous aircraft not included elsewhere and for 2006-07, the RAF Logistics Hub and Air Traffic Services.

- **Joint and multinational operations** includes Chief of Joint Operations HQ and the costs less receipts of UK participation in NATO.

- **Centrally managed military support** includes intelligence operational support and Special Forces.

- **Maintenance of war reserve stocks** includes the holding costs and charges of munitions and other stocks, above the levels required for planned consumption. Costs for 2006-07 include the accelerated write-off of dumb munitions (£112,000,000).

Objective 3: Building for the future

This objective comprises the following elements:

	2006-07			2005-06		
	Gross	Income	Net	Gross	Income	Net
	£000	£000	£000	£000	£000	£000
Research	1,026,433	(104)	1,026,329	1,041,105	(159)	1,040,946
Equipment programme	1,925,892	(44,882)	1,881,010	2,163,356	(44,767)	2,118,589
Total	2,952,325	(44,986)	2,907,339	3,204,461	(44,926)	3,159,535

- **Research** comprises the costs, including capital charges, of the Science, Innovation, Technology TLB, and research expenditure incurred by other TLBs.

- **Equipment Programme** refers to the administration and programme costs, primarily of the Defence Procurement Agency, associated with specifying requirements for and procurement of fighting equipment and other assets. The values of fixed asset additions are shown in Notes 13 and 14.

Attribution to Objectives

Gross expenditure of £30,442,213,000 (86.0%) (2005-06 – 78.1%) and Operating Income of £1,059,149,000 (74.1%) (2005-06 – 63.5%) were allocated to tasks, force elements or activities directly supporting the Objectives. The rest was apportioned in one of two ways:

- by means of cost attributions to "customer" Management Groupings, using local output costing systems to identify the full local costs of services provided. Cost attributions from suppliers are analysed onward to final outputs on advice from the recipients. If specific advice is not given, attributed costs are assumed to follow the same pattern as locally incurred expenditure;

- as an element of central overhead, shared among objectives in proportion to all other attributions. The force elements etc. described above receive a share of the expenditure and income components of these overheads, on the basis of their net costs.

The central overheads comprised:

	2006-07			2005-06		
	Gross	Income	Net	Gross	Income	Net
	£000	£000	£000	£000	£000	£000
Support for Ministers and Parliament	15,062	(19)	15,043	19,155	(87)	19,068
Departmental corporate services	1,170,115	(309,963)	860,152	825,530	(280,807)	544,723
Strategic Management	240,183	(1,822)	238,361	303,154	(7,208)	295,946

- **Support for Ministers and Parliament** includes provision of advice to Ministers and the costs, wherever incurred in the Department, of dealing with Parliamentary business.

- **Departmental corporate services** comprises internal support functions, e.g. payment of bills, payroll administration and medical care for Service personnel, and costs of Departmental restructuring. Costs attributed to corporate services in 2005-06 included the surplus on the sale of shares in QinetiQ Group plc (£355,982,000).

- **Strategic management** includes policy-making functions in strategic, personnel, scientific and medical matters.

Capital employed

The deployment of the Department's capital in support of its objectives does not follow the pattern of operating costs. Net assets totalling £76,629,869,000 (80.8%) support the military capability required to meet Objective 2. The remainder comprises assets wholly attributable to tasks within Objective 1 (£2,207,816,000 – 2.3%), and intangible assets, fighting equipment and other assets under construction, and assets related to equipment procurement within Objective 3 (£15,987,751,000 – 16.9%), and payment of War Pensions Benefits (-£15,346,000).

25. Capital Commitments

Capital commitments, for which no provision has been made in these financial statements, were as follows:

	31 March 2007 £000	31 March 2006 £000
Contracted but not provided for	17,849,412	18,906,646

26. Financial Commitments

26.1 Commitments under operating leases:

Commitments under operating leases to pay rentals during the year following the year of these accounts are given in the table below, analysed according to the period in which the lease expires.

	Land and Buildings		Other	
	31 March 2007 £000	31 March 2006 £000	31 March 2007 £000	31 March 2006 £000
The Department was committed to making the following payments during the next year in respect of operating leases expiring:				
Within one year	8,984	11,458	84,439	9,860
Between two and five years	11,298	14,811	104,359	167,785
After five years	156,482	155,575	688,573	755,075
	176,764	181,844	877,371	932,720

26.2 Obligations under finance leases:

Obligations under finance leases are as follows.

	31 March 2007 £000	31 March 2006 £000
Rentals due within 1 year	2,595	4,378
Rentals due after 1 year but within 5 years	43	2,639
Rentals due thereafter	-	-
	2,638	7,017

27. Private Finance Initiative (PFI) Commitments

Charge to the Operating Cost Statement and future commitments

27.1 The total amount charged in the Operating Cost Statement in respect of off-balance sheet PFI transactions and the service element of on-balance sheet PFI transactions was £1,147,660,000 (2005-06: £869,512,000); and the payments to which the Department is committed during 2007-08, analysed by the period during which the commitment expires, is as follows.

	31 March 2007 £000	31 March 2006 £000
Expiry within 1 year	11,028	1,875
Expiry within 2 to 5 years	172,654	81,912
Expiry within 6 to 10 years	178,205	236,188
Expiry within 11 to 15 years	335,233	213,235
Expiry within 16 to 20 years	67,317	54,519
Expiry within 21 to 25 years	219,874	240,046
Expiry within 26 to 30 years	21,213	11,600
Expiry within 31 to 35 years	171,964	120,350

Off Balance Sheet

27.2 The following information is provided for those schemes assessed as off Balance Sheet:

Project Description	Capital Value* £000	Prepayment 31 March 2007 £000	Contract Start **	Contract End
Training, Administration and Financial Management Information System: Provision of training administration and financial management information systems to the Army Recruiting and Training Division	36,000	-	Aug 1996	Nov 2009
Hazardous Stores Information System: Provision of an information management service for hazardous stores safety datasheets with 2,000 users	1,000	-	Oct 1997	Oct 2007
Defence Fixed Telecommunications System: Integration of 50 fixed telecommunications networks used by the Armed Forces and MoD, including the delivery of voice, data, LAN interconnect and other WAN services	70,000	-	Jul 1997	Jul 2012
Medium Support Helicopter Aircrew Training Facility: Provision of 6 flight simulator training facilities, covering three different types of helicopter, at RAF Benson	114,000	-	Oct 1997	Oct 2037
Hawk Synthetic Training Facility: Provision of replacement simulator training facilities at RAF Valley	19,000	-	Dec 1997	Dec 2015
Joint Services Command and Staff College (JSCSC): Design and delivery of a new tri-service Command and Staff Training College infrastructure and supporting services, including single residential accommodation and married quarters. (Of the total amount, £64 million relates to on-balance sheet)	92,800	-	Jun 1998	Aug 2028
Attack Helicopter Training Service: Provision of full mission simulator, 3 field deployable simulators, ground crew, maintenance and armament training	165,000	-	Jul 1998	Sep 2027
Family Quarters Yeovilton: Provision of married quarters accommodation for 88 Service families at RNAS Yeovilton	8,200	-	Jul 1998	Jul 2028
RAF Lyneham Sewage Treatment: Refurbishment of existing sewage treatment facilities, serving a population of 7,000, to meet regulatory standards at RAF Lyneham	3,800	-	Aug 1998	Aug 2023
Thames Water (formally known as Tidworth Water and Sewage): Pathfinder project providing water, sewerage and surface water drainage, serving a population of 12,000 military and dependants at Tidworth	5,000	-	Feb 1998	Aug 2018
RAF Mail: Provision of informal messaging services for the RAF	12,000	-	Nov 1998	Nov 2008
Fire Fighting Training Units: Provision of fire fighting training for the Royal Navy	22,500	-	Apr 1999	Jan 2021
Light Aircraft Flying Training: Provision of flying training and support services for Air Experience Flying and University Air Squadron Flying Training	20,000	-	Apr 1999	Mar 2009
Tornado GR4 Synthetic Training Service: Provision of aircraft training service at RAF Marham and RAF Lossiemouth	61,700	-	Jun 1999	Jun 2031

Project Description	Capital Value* £000	Prepayment 31 March 2007 £000	Contract Start **	Contract End
Army Foundation College: Provision of teaching and training facilities for the further vocational education and military training of high-quality school leavers	73,400	44	Feb 2000	Dec 2029
RAF Cosford/RAF Shawbury Family Quarters: Provision of married quarters accommodation for 145 Service families at RAF Cosford and RAF Shawbury	15,100	-	Mar 1999	Jun 2025
Central Scotland Family Quarters: Provision of married quarters accommodation for 164 Service Families in Central Scotland	24,700	-	Aug 1999	Jan 2021
Tri-Service Material Handling Equipment: Provision of tri-service materials handling capability	35,000	-	Jun 2000	Jun 2010
Commercial Satellite Communication Service (INMARSAT): Provision of world-wide commercial satellite communication system for Royal Navy Ships.	2,600	-	Mar 2001	Mar 2008
E3D Sentry Aircrew Training Service: E3D Sentry simulators instructors and maintainers at RAF Waddington	6,900	-	Jul 2000	Dec 2030
Lynx MK 7 and 9 Aircrew Training Service: Provision for simulator training facility for Lynx MK 7 and 9 helicopter aircrew	15,400	-	Jul 2000	Jul 2025
Tri-Service White Fleet: Provision, management and maintenance of support vehicles in the UK	40,000	-	Jan 2001	Jan 2011
Family quarters at Wattisham: Provision of married quarters accommodation for 250 Service families	34,200	-	May 2001	Mar 2028
Family quarters at Bristol/Bath/Portsmouth: Provision for married quarters accommodation for 317 Service families	78,000	-	Nov 2001	Sep 2028
Defence Housing Information Systems: Provision of a management information system for Defence Housing	11,600	-	Oct 2001	Sep 2010
Marine Support to Range and Aircrew Training: Provision of management, manning, operation and maintenance of Air Support Craft and Range Safety Craft	11,800	-	Dec 2001	Dec 2012
Astute Class Training: Provision of a training environment for crewmen and maintainers to support Astute Class submarines for 30 years	79,600	-	Sep 2001	Jan 2037
Strategic Sealift (RoRo): Provision of strategic sealift services based on six RoRo ferries in support of Joint Rapid Reaction Force deployments	173,150	-	Jun 2002	Dec 2024
Material Handling Equipment: Provision of tri-service material handling equipment for Army, Navy and RAF storage depots	7,820	-	Aug 2002	Jul 2010
Aquatrine Project A: Provision of water and waste water services	154,000	89,840	Apr 2003	Nov 2028
Aquatrine Project B: Provision of water and waste water services	86,400	30,802	Sep 2004	Mar 2030
Aquatrine Project C: Provision of water and waste water services	363,600	64,248	Oct 2004	Mar 2030
Hayes Records and Storage: Pan-Government Records Management and Archive Services	11,100	-	Sep 2003	Sep 2028
Defence Sixth Form College: Development of a sixth form college to help meet the future recruitment requirements in the Armed Forces and MoD Civil Service	20,000	-	Jun 2003	Aug 2033
Colchester Garrison: Redevelopment, rebuilding and refurbishment to provide accommodation and associated services (messing, education, storage, workshops)	539,000	150,567	Feb 2004	Feb 2039
Skynet 5: Range of satellite services, including management of existing Skynet 4 satellites	1,360,930	112,117	Oct 2003	Feb 2020
C Vehicles: Provision of Earthmoving and Specialist plant, Engineer Construction Plant and Material Handling Equipment and support services	703,000	37,187	Jun 2005	Jun 2021
Portsmouth 2 Housing: Provision of 148 Family Quarters in Portsmouth	27,092	7,981	Oct 2005	Oct 2030

* The capital value is based on private sector partners' capital investment, where known, or otherwise the capital value of the public sector comparator.

** The date when the contracts were signed.

On Balance Sheet

27.3 The following PFI projects are treated as on balance sheet. The service payment commitments for the year 2007-08 are included in the table shown at 27.1.

Project Description	Capital Value* £000	Net Book Value 31 March 2007 £000	Contract Start **	Contract End
Defence Helicopter Flying School: Provision of helicopter flying training services	93,027	26,866	Apr 1997	Mar 2012
RAF Lossiemouth Family Quarters: Redevelopment and re-provision of 279 family quarters	24,745	27,421	Jun 1998	Aug 2020
Joint Services Command and Staff College: Command and Staff College for military and civilian personnel (also see JSCSC – Off Balance Sheet)	64,000	72,983	Jun 1998	Aug 2028
RAF Fylingdales: Provision of guaranteed power supply	7,486	3,839	Dec 1998	Dec 2023
Main Building Refurbishment: Redevelopment and management services for MoD Main Building	347,914	233,772	May 2000	May 2030
Naval Communications: Submarine fleet communications service	58,491	44,676	Jun 2000	Dec 2030
Defence Electronic Commerce Service: Strategic partnership to deliver e-business environment to share information between MoD and trading partners	11,410	1,200	Jul 2000	Jul 2010
Defence Animal Centre: Redevelopment of new office and residential accommodation, animal husbandry and training support	10,047	14,430	Aug 2000	Nov 2026
Heavy Equipment Transporters: Provision of vehicles to replace existing fleet and meet future requirements	58,000	50,744	Dec 2001	Jul 2024
Field Electrical Power Supplies: Provision of generator sets to support operational electrical requirements in the field	73,410	67,949	Jun 2002	Jun 2022
Devonport Armada Single Living Accommodation: Provision of Support Services and Fleet Accommodation Centre services at Devonport Naval Base	44,513	18,129	Jul 2004	Mar 2029
Project Allenby/Connaught: Rebuild, refurbishment, management and operation of facilities for Service accommodation at Aldershot, Tidworth, Bulford, Warminster, Larkhill and Perham Down	1,117,332	-	Mar 2006	Apr 2041
Northwood: Rebuild, refurbishment, management and operation of facilities for the Permanent Joint Headquarters	161,500	-	Jul 2006	Oct 2031

* The capital value is based on private sector partners' capital investment, where known, or otherwise the capital value of the public sector comparator.

** The date when the contracts were signed.

No specific contingent liabilities have been identified in respect of the PFI contracts listed above.

	31 March 2007 £000	31 March 2006 £000
Imputed finance lease obligations under on-balance sheet PFI contracts comprises:		
Rentals due within 1 year	18,391	15,167
Rentals due after 1 year but within 5 years	90,521	82,448
Rentals due thereafter	549,585	560,075
	658,497	657,690
Less interest element	7,366	14,013
	651,131	643,677

28. Financial Instruments

28.1 FRS 13, Derivatives and Other Financial Instruments, requires disclosure of the role which financial instruments have had during the period in creating or changing the risks an entity faces in undertaking its activities. Because of the largely non-trading nature of its activities and the way in which government Departments are financed, the Department is not exposed to the degree of financial risk faced by business entities. Moreover, financial instruments play a much more limited role in creating or changing risk than would be typical of the listed companies to which FRS 13 mainly applies. Financial assets and liabilities are generated by day-to-day operational activities and are not held to change the risks facing the Department in undertaking its activities.

Liquidity risk

28.2 The Department's revenue and capital resource requirements are voted annually by Parliament and are, therefore, not exposed to significant liquidity risks.

Interest rate risk

28.3 A significant proportion of the Department's financial assets and liabilities carry nil or fixed rates of interest. The exposure to interest risk is, therefore, not significant.

Foreign currency risk

28.4 The Department enters into forward purchase contracts with the Bank of England to cover the majority of its foreign exchange requirements. The Department has changed its policy for the Forward Purchase contracts to extend the purchase period up to five years thereby benefiting from the increased certainty of longer term future rates. The details of the outstanding foreign currency contracts are as follows:

Currency	Foreign currency	Weighted average exchange rate	31 March 2007 Sterling	31 March 2006 Sterling
	US$/Euro 000	(=£1)	£000	£000
			2007/2008 delivery	2006/2007 delivery
US Dollar	2,258,250	1.79	1,263,836	1,077,839
Euro	1,957,000	1.43	1,365,429	1,093,972
			2008/2009 delivery	2007/2008 delivery
US Dollar	2,073,000	1.81	1,145,771	1,032,949
Euro	2,126,000	1.42	1,498,720	1,085,456
			2009/2010 delivery	
US Dollar	1,328,000	1.84	721,119	-
Euro	1,634,000	1.40	1,169,141	-
			2010/2011 delivery	
US Dollar	919,000	1.88	487,944	-
Euro	1,087,000	1.39	784,205	-
			2011/2012 delivery	
US Dollar	445,000	1.90	234,187	-
Euro	540,000	1.38	391,219	-
Total			**9,061,571**	4,290,216

The 31 March 2007 mid-market closing rates for US Dollar and Euro were £/$ 1.9614 and £/Euro 1.4735 respectively.

267

Fair values

Financial assets

28.5 The Department's financial assets include investments in, and loans made to, MoD Trading Funds and QinetiQ Group plc. The net assets of these bodies (excluding MoD loans), the interest rates applicable to these loans and the market value of the shareholding in QinetiQ are shown in Note 15. Other financial assets' fair values approximate to their book values.

Financial liabilities

28.6 The Department's liabilities include loans from the National Loans Fund, obligations under finance leases and PFI contracts and a loan from the Atomic Weapons Establishment amounting in total to £795,271,000 (2005-06: £800,640,000). The fair values of these liabilities will be different from their book values but since these represent only 5.9% of the gross liabilities and provisions, the impact on the Department's net assets will not be material. The fair values of provisions for liabilities and charges are not materially different to their book values, which are stated after discounting at the Treasury rate of 2.2%. Other liabilities' fair values approximate to their book values.

29. Contingent Liabilities and Contingent Assets Disclosed under FRS 12

Contingent Liabilities

29.1 Contingent liabilities estimated at some £1,474,972,000 (2005-06: £1,575,055,000) have been identified. The balance primarily comprises of site restoration liabilities of some £400,000,000 (2005-06: £400,000,000) relating to the British Army Training Units in Canada and indemnities, that are quantifiable, of £886,800,000 (2005-06: £979,500,000) granted to contractors and suppliers.

The Department holds a number of sites where it may be necessary to carry out remediation work in respect of contamination. It is not cost effective or practicable to identify all levels of contamination at individual sites nor to assess the likely cost of any remediation work necessary. As any liability cannot, therefore, be quantified it is not appropriate to include a provision in accordance with FRS 12.

Contingent Assets

29.2 A US salvage company, Odyssey Marine Exploration, has found what is believed to be the wreck of HMS Sussex, which sank in the Western Mediterranean in 1694 carrying gold and silver coins estimated to be valued at the time at £1 million. If confirmed as HMS Sussex, the wreck and its contents are legally the property of Her Majesty's Government.

A licensing agreement was signed on 27 September 2002 between the Disposal Services Agency of the Ministry of Defence, on behalf of Her Majesty's Government, and Odyssey for further archaeological exploration of the wreck of HMS Sussex and recovery of artefacts et cetera. Full responsibility for the project, including the sale of the artefacts has been transferred to the Department. Proceeds from the sale of any artefacts will be surrendered to HM Treasury.

The Department will be responsible for the preservation of any part of the wreck brought up as part of the salvage effort.

30. Contingent Liabilities not required to be disclosed under FRS 12 but included for Parliamentary Reporting and Accountability

Quantifiable (Unrestricted)

30.1 The MoD has entered into the following quantifiable contingent liabilities by offering guarantees, indemnities or by giving letters of comfort. None of these is a contingent liability within the meaning of FRS12 since the likelihood of a transfer of economic benefit in settlement is too remote.

UNRESTRICTED –Indemnities	1 April 2006 £000	Increase in year £000	Liabilities crystallised in year £000	Obligation expired in year £000	31 March 2007 £000	Amount reported to Parliament by Departmental Minute £000
Residual liability for the remediation of unidentified contamination in parts of the former Rosyth Naval Base which has been sold to Rosyth 2000 plc.	Up to 1,000				Up to 1,000	
Liabilities arising from insurance risk of exhibits on loan to the Army, Navy and RAF Museums.	2,726		(191)		2,535	

Quantifiable (Restricted)

30.2 Details of restricted indemnities are not given because they are sensitive due to commercial confidentiality and/or national security.

Unquantifiable (Unrestricted)

30.3 The MoD has entered into the following unquantifiable contingent liabilities by offering guarantees, indemnities or by giving letters of comfort. None of these is a contingent liability within the meaning of FRS12 since the possibility of a transfer of economic benefit in settlement is too remote.[8]

- Indemnity given in relation to the disposal of Gruinard Island in the event of claims arising from the outbreak of specific strains of anthrax on the Island.

- Indemnity to Devonport Royal Dockyards Ltd (DRDL) in respect of nuclear risks under the Nuclear Installations Act 1965.

- Indemnity to the Babcock Group in respect of nuclear risks under the Nuclear Installations Act 1965.

- Indemnities to DRDL and the Babcock Group in respect of non-nuclear risks resulting from claims for damage to property or death and personal injury to a third party.

- Indemnity to Rolls Royce Power for the non insurance of the Rolls Royce Core Factory and the Neptune Test Reactor facility for death and personal injury to a third party.

- Indeminity for residual commercial contracts claims liabilities arising from the disbanding of DERA as a MoD Trading Fund and the formation of QinetiQ on 1 July 2001.

- Indemnity for residual employee disease liability arising from the disbanding of DERA as a MoD Trading Fund and the formation of QinetiQ on 1 July 2001.

- Indemnity for public liability arising from the disbanding of DERA as a MoD Trading Fund and the formation of QinetiQ on 1 July 2001.

Unquantifiable (Restricted)

- Details on restricted liabilities are not given because they are sensitive due to commercial confidentiality and national security.

These liabilities are unquantifiable due to the nature of the liability and the uncertainties surrounding them.

8 A contract was signed in May 2007 for Service Life Insurance which will enable Service personnel to access life insurance cover throughout their service career. Reported to Parliament, this is an unquantifiable liabilty for the MoD.

31. Losses and Special Payments

CLOSED CASES: these comprise losses and special payments which have been formally signed off to date subsequent to a satisfactory completion of all the case work relating to the loss or special payment. Closed cases, therefore, include some cases which in the previous year were shown under Advance Notifications.	Arising in 2006-07	Reported in 2005-06 as Advance Notifications
	£000	£000
Total (excluding gifts, special payments and War Pensions Benefits) under £250,000 each: 11,212 cases	14,935	
Total (excluding gifts, special payments and War Pensions Benefits) over £250,000 each: 26 cases (detailed below)	94,384	281,120
Losses of pay, allowances and superannuation benefits		
An administrative error arising from the introduction of the Army Pay system in December 2000 led to the overpayment of £2.9M of public money to 428 soldiers during the period February to December 2006. (Central)	2,900	
Bookkeeping losses and adjustments		
Bookkeeping Losses: £37M relates to the write-off of legacy project balances and £4.0M of this relates to the write off of residual balances post migration to the Single Balance Sheet Owners. This loss represents four cases. (DPA)	44,933	
The write-off of unsupported asset balances within TLBs following the migration of assets to the single Balance Sheet Owners. This loss represents three cases. (DLO, STC and CJO)	41,169	
In preparation for the implementation of the Order to Cash system, a reconciliation was undertaken of debtor balances. This highlighted a number of problems where prepaid amounts were duplicated against income and debtor balances. The balances have now been reconciled to the current Defence Bills Debtor balance, and the adjustment written off as a bookkeeping loss. This loss represents three cases. (Central)		6,175
A detailed reconciliation of the Fixed Asset Register with the General Ledger for the Central Top Level Budget was undertaken prior to the transfer of assets and balances to the Single Balance Sheet Owners. The write-off is in respect of the final un-reconciled balance which had arisen over a period of several years. (Central)		4,515
A bookkeeping adjustment within the General Ledger to reconcile with the fully supported cash and bank Control Accounts. There has been no physical loss of cash. (Central)	2,329	
Losses arising from failure to make adequate charges		
The costs of maintenance work incurred on hirings for the Rhine and European Group Support Unit in Naples which should have been charged to individual landlords during the period 1999 to March 2005. (Central)	2,037	
Claims waived or abandoned		
A commercial compensation package agreed as a result of slippage in the delivery dates by the Contractor and the unavailability of components for the Counter-Battery Radar programme has resulted in a write-off. (DPA)		540
Metropole Building re-wire project. The loss arising from a legal dispute between MoD and a former contractor. (Central)		1,400
Following an annual review of the Service Level Agreement, a claim for Service Level Failure Charges against EDS waived (Armed Forces Personnel Administration Agency – AFPAA). (Central)		1,096
Stores and other losses		
Item of aircraft spares transferred from the Westlands Managed store in RNAS Culdrose to HMS WESTMINSTER at Rosyth Naval Base: whilst there is a clear audit trail confirming receipt by Ship's staff in Rosyth, the item had not been brought to Ship's charge and cannot be located. (FLEET)		630
Constructive Losses		
Delays in Phase 1 projects at the Defence Academy resulted in a constructive loss. (Central)	532	
The cancellation of Civil Pallet Conversion Kits within the A400M aircraft procurement programme. (DPA)	484	
This constructive loss arose from the UK Government decision not to proceed into production for the long range anti-tank guided weapons system. (DPA)		194,820
The extended range ordnance modular charge system (ERO/MCS) was cancelled due to technical difficulties with the MCS that could not be resolved. This produced an estimated constructive loss. The MoD was able to recover £10.3M through a negotiated settlement package. (DPA)		37,047
A loss arose as the result of the UK Government decision to reduce the number of Nimrod MRA4 procured from 18 to 12. (DPA)		32,550
A constructive loss arose as a result of a settlement between the Department and a manufacturer for the provision of Manportable Remote Control Vehicles. (DPA)		1,354
An agreement was breached with a Contractor that required contracts for nuclear cores to be placed within a certain timeframe rendering MoD liable to pay default costs. (DPA)		562
A constructive loss arose in respect of the Voice Monitoring and Analysis Facility due to several factors including a limited capability and a change in policy placing the onus on contractors to provide their own capability testing. Changes in procurement policy should ensure that losses of a similar nature do not occur again. (DLO)		431

CLOSED CASES: (continued)	Arising in 2006-07	Reported in 2005-06 as Advance Notifications
	£000	£000
Gifts		
Total under £250,000 each: 35 cases	316	
Total over £250,000 each: 7 cases (detailed below)	23,694	
3 Infrastructure Projects and Equipment to the Iraqi Government. Details of the transfer were notified to the House of Commons in a Departmental Minute dated 18 April 2006. (CJO)	20,363	
110 Landrovers to the Lebanese Armed Forces. Details of the transfer were notified to the House of Commons in a Departmental Minute dated 9 October 2006. (Central)	1,000	
Non-lethal military equipment to the Government of Nepal. Details of the transfer were notified in a Departmental Minute dated 12 February 2007. (Central)	850	
Cash gift to the Afghan Government to equip Afghan Territorial Force in Helmand Province. Details of the transfer were notified to the House of Commons in a Departmental Minute dated 30 October 2006. (CJO)	500	
Non-lethal military equipment for the Palestinian Presidential Guard. Details of the transfer were notified in a Departmental Minute dated 8 February 2007. (Central)	376	
Camp Smitty and Camp Driftwood Infrastructure to the Government of Iraq. Details of the transfer were notified to the House of Commons in a Departmental Minute dated 21 June 2006. (CJO)	314	
Camp Abu Naji (Maysan) Infrastructure to the Government of Iraq. Details of the transfer were notified to the House of Commons in a Departmental Minute dated 28 June 2006. (CJO)	291	
International Courtesy Rules		
Supplies and services provided on a reciprocal basis to Commonwealth and Foreign Navy vessels during visits to British Ports at Clyde, Portsmouth, Devonport and Gibraltar. (Central)	1,027	
Special Payments		
Total under £250,000 each: 136 cases	274	
Total over £250,000 each: 8 cases (detailed below)	68,912	9,449
The contract for the Landing Ship Dock (Auxiliary) incurred additional expenditure of £32M for 2006-07. The second ship built at Swan Hunter, RFA Lyme Bay, is nearing completion by BAE Systems. (DPA)	32,000	
Ex-gratia element of Northern Ireland Royal Irish Regiment redundancy payment relating to Normalisation arrangements in the Province. This represents 1,531 payments made during 2006-07. A provision has been made for further payments during 2007-08, which is disclosed as an Advance Notification. (AG)	26,894	
In November 2001 proceedings were brought against the MoD by a contractor for non-compliance with certain terms of their commercial Marketing Agreement. A number of preliminary issues were determined by the Arbitrator at an interim Arbitration hearing in July 2002. The Arbitrator declared in favour of the MoD on some issues and in favour of the contractor on others. A final settlement was agreed in 2006. (DLO)	5,508	
Ex-gratia element of the Northern Ireland civilian redundancy payment relating to Normalisation arrangements in the Province. This represents 215 payments made during 2006-07. A provision has been made for future payments which is disclosed as an Advance Notification. (GOCNI and Central)	3,010	
Payment to the Armed Forces Memorial Trust, for the memorial to be erected at the National Memorial Arboretum in Staffordshire, to commemorate all members of the Armed Forces who have lost their lives on duty since the end of the Second World War. (Central)	1,500	
An extra contractual payment resulting from the late supply of Government Furnished Equipment to the TITAN & TROJAN project. (DPA)		4,465
An ex-gratia payment in full and final settlement of the Armoured Vehicle Training Service cancelled PFI programme. (DPA)		2,900
Following the closure of the last RAF base in Germany (RAF Brüggen), it was decided that the UK would withdraw from the Central European Pipeline System (CEPS). This resulted in payments of £2.1M during FY 2005-06, to ensure that the UK has no further involvement or liability in respect of the CEPS. (DLO)		2,084

CLOSED CASES: (continued)	Arising in 2006-07	Reported in 2005-06 as Advance Notifications
	£000	£000

War Pensions Benefits (WPB):

Claims Abandoned-WPB

Irrecoverable overpayments of war pensions relating to 2,623 cases amounting to £631,177 (2005-06: 2,785 cases amounting to £506,421) were written off. These represent overpayments of pensions which occur for a number of reasons outside of the MoD's control; this represented 0.04% of the total war pension payments budget of £1.037 billion. All overpayments are recorded as amounts outstanding and action is taken to recover these amounts. In financial year 2006-07, over £1.9M of overpayments were recovered. Where the overpayment was found to be irrecoverable, the decision was taken to waive the amount owed.	631	

Special Payments-WPB

Total number of payments made during the year were 885 (2005-06: 943) and amounted to £5,215,885 (2005-06: £5,815,084). These payments were for War Disability Pensions, and were made under the authority of Treasury Dispensing Instruments but outside the scope of the Service Pension order. These relate to the following payments:

(a) Far Eastern Prisoners of War Ex-gratia payments

In the 2000 pre Budget speech, the Chancellor of the Exchequer announced that ex-gratia awards of £10,000 would be paid to surviving members of British groups held prisoner by the Japanese during the Second World War or their surviving spouses. Although the majority of cases have been paid in previous financial years, 186 claims were processed and paid in financial year 2006-07. The total payment amounted to £1,860,000.	1,860	
Following a Judicial Review announced in November 2003, the scheme was expanded to allow payments to qualifying Gurkhas in Nepal. Within financial year 2006-07, 63 successful claims were processed. The total payment amounted to £630,000. A further £1,000,000 was charged to the Operating Cost Statement by way of a provision to reflect the likely payments in financial year 2007-08.	1,630	

(b) Empire Air Training Scheme Pensions

These Payments relate to members of the Royal Australian Air Force who were trained under the Empire Air Training Scheme and were subsequently selected for service in the RAF. The British Government agreed in June 1942 that it would contribute towards pensions in respect of disablement or death due to the service with the RAF.

In 2006-07 the total number of cases were 306 (2005-06: 335 cases) and the cost amounted to £1,110,189 (2005-06: £1,466,066).	1,110	

(c) Noise Induced Sensorineural Hearing Loss

During financial year 2006-07, 217 cases (2005-06: 219 cases) were paid under the Dispensing Instruments and the total amount payable was £538,337 (2005-06: £523,676).	538	

(d) Crown Agents Supplementation payments

Crown Agents Financial Services make payments to ex-members of the colonial forces who are resident in the UK and who have been awarded a disablement pension by the colonial government. The payment is a supplementation amount that increases the disablement pension to the rate equivalent to a UK war pension.

The Veterans Agency re-imburses Crown Agents Financial Services for these payments. During financial year 2006-07, the total number of cases was 13 (2005-06: 16 cases) and the amount payable was £77,358 (2005-06: £95,340).	77	

	Arising in 2006-07 £000	Reported and arising in prior years £000
ADVANCE NOTIFICATIONS: these comprise losses and special payments, which arose during 2006-07 and prior years, but where the cases have not yet been formally signed off to date. A formal sign off cannot take place until all the work necessary to establish the validity of the loss or special payment, and the exact amount thereof, has been satisfactorily concluded. The amounts shown below are, therefore, only the best estimates, and are reflected in these accounts where appropriate. It is likely that, in many instances, the final value of these losses and special payments will differ from the estimates below when they are reported as closed in future years. Should the final value be less than £250,000, they will not be separately identified.		
Notified in prior years		
The value of 8 Chinook Mk3 helicopters has been written down by £205M under prudent accounting practices while the MoD establishes a way forward for the programme. The write down has arisen because, although the terms of the contract had been met, the helicopters do not currently meet the operational requirement and could not acquire Military Aircraft Release. The MoD intends to convert the MK3 airframes to a modified MK2 standard as a way forward, with a revaluation exercise of the 8 aircraft at the point of asset delivery. (DPA)		205,000
Slippage in the construction programme for two Landing Ship Dock (Auxiliary) caused delay in supplying design information and equipment to a contractor. This resulted in a claim on the MoD relating to the associated delay and dislocation costs. Following review, the potential loss has been reduced. (DPA)		53,836
A potential claim against a contractor on the Airborne Stand-Off Radar programme has been abandoned resulting in a loss, but other benefits have been secured in compensation. (DPA)		28,000
Cancellation of the Alternative Launcher Drive System programme has resulted in a potential write-off. (DPA)		4,000
A contractor is claiming extra costs resulting from the late delivery of unusable Global Positioning System chips in respect of the Storm Shadow missile programme, purchased via Foreign Military Sales. However, the MoD is attempting to re-claim from the supplier of the Government Furnished Equipment, via the US Courts. A related write-off of £1.8M for Variation of Price was recorded in the 2004-05 accounts. (DPA)		4,000
Uncleared balances in respect of Income Tax and National Insurance balances to be written off in AFPAA's books. (Central)		1,479
A food component was withdrawn from Operational Ration Packs following discovery in tests that deterioration of the product's packaging could over time compromise the safety of the contents. The Contractor accepted liability in principle for this defect and agreed to supply a replacement product utilising an alternative packaging arrangement, at no cost to MoD, subject to being able to develop a replacement product that could be warranted fully fit for purpose. This development work is continuing and, if successful, will substantially mitigate the overall loss to the MoD brought about by a combination of loss of use of the original product and the cost of its removal/destruction. (DLO)		1,400
Notified during the year		
Cash Loss		
A potential loss has been identified in respect of an overpayment made to an MoD contractor. Whilst repayment is being actively pursued, there is no assurance that the overpayment can be recovered owing to the statute of limitation restrictions. (Central)	372	
Losses arising from failure to make adequate charges		
The Payment of staff from public finds within a non-public organisation covering the period April 1999 to March 2007 – The British Möhnessee Sailing Club. (Land)	1,264	
The Payment of staff from public funds within a non-public organisation covering the period April 1999 to March 2007 – The British Dömmersee Yacht Club. (Land)	1,225	
Mill Hill Garrison Pre-School Playgroup, a private enterprise, was allowed to trade from MoD property for the period April 1995 to March 2005 without due rent being raised. (Land)	267	
Bookkeeping losses and adjustments		
A bookkeeping loss arising from the write-off of unsupported asset balances as a result of the 2006-07 asset verification exercise. (DE and DLO)	21,135	
A bookeeping loss has arise in respect of the write-off of an unsubstantiated debtor balance. The write-off has been accounted for during 2006-07. (DLO)	12,893	
A bookkeeping loss has arisen in respect of the write-off of a number of unsubstantiated Control Account Balances. The loss has been accounted for during 2006-07 and comprises erroneous balances on five Control Accounts that are believed to have been caused by system errors, spread over a period of four years. There has been no physical loss of cash. (DLO)	7,180	
Claims waived or abandoned		
Service Level Failure Charges against EDS waived in respect of 2006-07 – (AFPAA). (Central)	3,456	
Stores Losses		
The Cadet Hut, Kings School Winchester was destroyed by fire. (Land)	252	

ADVANCE NOTIFICATIONS: (continued)	Arising in 2006-07	Reported and arising in prior years
	£000	£000
Constructive Loss		
As a result of the UK's interpretation of the Oslo Declaration on dumb cluster munitions, the Multiple Launch Range System containing the M26 bomblet was declared as out of service by the secretary of State for Defence on 20 March 2007. The announcement also resulted in the withdrawal of the BL755 Air to Ground unguided Cluster Bomb. Although plans were in place to dispose of the munitions, the revised out of service date has resulted in a write-off of £112m (£101m for M26 and £11m for BL755). (DLO)	112,000	
A contract for an Integrated Biological Detection System was not progressed as a result of production delays and a strategic decision to reduce the numbers of systems required. (DPA)	25,916	
The Nuclear, Biological and Chemical Battlefield System Application Project, was cancelled by mutual agreement with the Contractor. Technical difficulties in pre-existing software introduced significant risks into the project which threatened its future success. (DPA)	14,165	
A MoD funded project to be conducted by the US Government, will now not go ahead as it relied on the finalisation of another US project which has been cancelled. This decision was outside of the management control of the MoD. The disclosure is for the full loss although there remains a possibility that some of the loss may be mitigated through an alternative use of the facilities raised in preparation for the original trial. (SIT)	794	
A loss arising from the decision to close a 5 year old Sullage Treatment Plant as result of a lack of a technical solution to suppress gas emissions, the need to replace corroded sullage vessels and a re-appraisal of the overall operational and financial effectiveness of the plant in light of changed circumstances. Construction costs of £1.3m have been offset by a recovery from the construction company who accepted liability of £0.6m in respect of the corroded sullage vessels. (DLO)	700	
During the deployment of UK forces to Iraq, arrangements were made by several seagoing units to hire and load shipping containers. The hire and lease should have been agreed through the Defence Container Management Service. On completion of the hire agreement the containers were not returned directly to the sub-contractor. All containers were taken off hire in August 2005. Partial write off action was taken in October 2006 (£0.2M). Work is continuing to progress additional write off action for approximately £0.2M. (FLEET)	420	
During 2005, the MoD entered into a contract for the lease of 1,410 Airwave Radios, with the requirement for 210 being deferred until 2006-07. The final 210 radios were not required and contract termination costs have been incurred. (Central)	348	
Fruitless Payments		
The estimated repair costs to the Type 45 Long Range Radar Antenna which was damaged during installation. (DPA)	700	
On 11 September 2006 4 Sea King Gnome 1T engines were transported from Rolls Royce East Kilbride to HMS Sultan using the Defence Storage and Distribution Agency. On arrival at HMS Sultan they were found to have been transported in the incorrect orientation, additionally one had suffered impact damage. All 4 engines had to be returned to the workshop for a full strip and overhaul at a total cost of £0.5M.		
Special Payments		
Ex-gratia element of Northern Ireland Royal Irish Regiment redundancy payment relating to Normalisation arrangements in the Province. This represents payments due to be made during 2007-08. Payments made during 2006-07 are disclosed as a Closed Case. (AG)	41,020	
Ex-gratia element of the Northern Ireland civilian redundancy payments relating to Normalisation arrangements in the Province. This represents payments due to be made in the period 2007-2010. Payments made during 2006-07 are disclosed as a Closed Case. (GOCNI and DE)	14,112	

32. Related Party Transactions

32.1 The Defence Science and Technology Laboratory, the UK Hydrographic Office, the Met Office, the Defence Aviation Repair Agency and ABRO operate as Executive Defence Agencies financed by Trading Fund.

The Initial Public Offering for QinetiQ Group plc completed the transformation of the MoD's in-house research and development organisation into an international defence technology and security company. MoD retains a 19.3% shareholding in the company and also holds a Special Share; further details can be found at Note 15 – Investments, to these accounts. The MoD also appoints a Non-Executive Director to QinetiQ's Board; the appointment is currently held by Mr Colin Balmer.

The Navy Army Air Force Institutes (NAAFI), the Oil and Pipelines Agency and, following reclassification, the Fleet Air Arm Museum, are Public Corporations. The Trading Funds, QinetiQ Group plc, the Oil and Pipelines Agency, NAAFI and the Fleet Air Arm Museum are regarded as related parties outside the Departmental Boundary with which the Department has had material transactions. All transactions are carried out on terms which are contracted on an arms length basis, and are subject to internal and external audit.

Oil and Pipelines Agency (Public Corporation)

Agency Fees (excluding VAT): £1,730,000 (2005-2006: £1,747,000)

Director Defence Fuels Group is a member of the Board of Directors.

Fleet Air Arm Museum (Public Corporation)

Grant-in-Aid: £593,724 (2005-2006: £579,036)

Assistant Chief of Staff Aviation, CinCFleet, Whale Island; Assistant Director Joint Manoeuvre, MoD, London; Director Operations, DG Helicopters, DE&S; Commanding Officer RNAS Culdrose and Commanding Officer RNAS Yeovilton are members of the Board of Trustees.

Executive Non Departmental Public Bodies (NDPBs)

32.2 The following are Executive NDPBs of the MoD. They are designated NDPBs under the National Heritage Act 1983 and produce their own annual accounts, in accordance with the Charities (Accounts and Reports) Regulations 1995, on an accruals basis, and are regarded as related parties. During the year, each Executive NDPB had a material transaction with the Department, as listed below:

National Army Museum

Grant-in-Aid: £5,292,879 (2005-2006: £4,871,546)

The Department is not represented on the Board.

Royal Air Force Museum

Grant-in-Aid: £6,774,110 (2005-2006: £7,104,192)

The Department is not represented on the Board.

Royal Marines Museum

Grant-in-Aid: £740,788 (2005-2006: £783,252)

Director Royal Marines and Regimental Sergeant Major, Royal Marines Corps are members of the Board of Trustees.

Royal Naval Museum

Grant-in-Aid: £895,502 (2005-2006: £1,025,044)

Naval Base Commander Portsmouth and the Naval Secretary, CinCFleet, Whale Island were members of the Board of Trustees during the financial year.

Royal Navy Submarine Museum

Grant-in-Aid: £561,997 (2005-2006: £548,317)

Rear Admiral Submarines is a member of the Board of Trustees.

Other

32.3 Sir Ian Andrews, Second Permanent Under Secretary of State, is a trustee of the Imperial War Museum. Mr Charles Miller Smith, a Non-Executive Director on the Defence Management Board, is also the Chairman of Scottish Power. The Imperial War Museum and Scottish Power are therefore regarded as related parties of the Ministry of Defence and transactions between the organisations during the year were:

		£000
Imperial War Museum	Various transactions-Payments	164
	Various transactions-Receipts	2
Scottish Power	Various transactions-Payments	1,283

During the year various works of art and other items were transferred to and from the Imperial War Museum. No value was attributed to these items.

The Department also pays a number of grants to other bodies outside the Departmental Boundary. These include Grants-in-Aid to the Royal Hospital Chelsea, Skill Force and the Commonwealth War Graves Commission.

In addition, the MoD has had a number of transactions with other government departments and central government bodies. Most of the transactions have been with: the Foreign & Commonwealth Office, the Cabinet Office, HM Revenue & Customs, the Department for International Development, the Home Office, the Treasury Solicitor, the Office of Communications, the National School of Government and the Department for Work and Pensions.

Joint Ventures

32.4 Within the Departmental accounting boundary, see page 193 for further information, the Department does not have any Joint Ventures. Some of the Trading Funds have set up Joint Ventures and the Department is involved in collaborative projects with various foreign countries for the development and production of single use military equipment.

33. Events After the Balance Sheet Date

The financial statements included in the Annual Report and Accounts were authorised for issue (defined as the date of dispatch to HM Treasury) by the Accounting Officer on 23 July 2007.

34. Non-Operational Heritage Assets

34.1 The Department owns a range of non-operational heritage assets from historically significant defence equipment, through archive information, to museum and art collections. In accordance with HM Treasury's Financial Reporting Manual (FReM), non-operational heritage assets are valued except where the cost of obtaining a valuation for the asset is not warranted in terms of the benefits it would deliver or where it is not possible to establish a sufficiently reliable valuation.

On the above basis, no non-operational heritage assets, except land, were valued at the year-end.

34.2 The scope and diversity of the holdings of non-operational heritage assets which are not valued are illustrated by the examples detailed in the table below:

Item	Location	Description
HMS Victory	Portsmouth	HMS Victory is the world's oldest commissioned warship and is most famous for her role as Lord Nelson's Flagship at the Battle of Trafalgar. HMS Victory is open to the public, details are available at: www.hms-victory.com
Army Historic Aircraft Flight	Middle Wallop	Formed in 1977, the flight consists of seven aircraft and makes public appearances between May and September. Further information can be found at: www.deltaweb.co.uk/haf/index.htm
Battle of Britain Memorial Flight	RAF Coningsby	The Memorial Flight operates 11 mainly World War II aircraft that appear at several hundred public events each year and can also be viewed at their hangar at RAF Coningsby. Further information is available at: www.bbmf.co.uk/index.html
Pickling Pond	HMNB Portsmouth	Pickling or mast ponds enabled long lengths of timber to be soaked before being used to build ships; well seasoned planks would not split or shrink in the water.
Enigma Machine	RAF Cosford	Cryptographic equipment captured during WW2 and used at Bletchley Park to assist in the breaking of German signal traffic.
MoD Art Collection	Various locations	The MoD Art Collection comprises approximately 800 works of fine art and 250 antiques such as clocks and furniture. Many other miscellaneous items, such as photographs and manuscripts are contained in the archive. At the core of the collection are works commissioned by (and bequeathed to) the Admiralty during the 19th century, and those given to the Admiralty and to the War Office by the War Artists Commission at the end of the Second World War. Items from the MoD art collections are displayed in conference rooms and senior officers' accommodation throughout the Defence estate. The most important items are on permanent public display in the National Maritime Museum and on temporary loan to many other public museums and galleries.
Records and artworks	London, Gosport, Stanmore	The Admiralty and Institute of Naval Medicine Libraries and the Air Historical Branch (RAF) comprise text and records of historical and research items. Although not open to the public, access is available on application.
Artefacts, records and artworks	Various locations	Over one hundred Regimental and Corps Museums and collections exist across the country. Ownership of the buildings and contents of the museums varies between the MoD, local authorities and regimental associations. The museums, which are open to the public, trace the history of the regiments and comprise displays of uniforms, weapons, medals and records. Further information is available at: www.army.mod.uk/museums/index.htm.

35. Entities within the Departmental Boundary

The entities within the boundary during 2006-07 were as follows:

Executive Agencies
Armed Forces Personnel Administration Agency
British Forces Post Office
Defence Analytical Services Agency
Defence Bills Agency
Defence Communication Services Agency
Defence Estates
Defence Medical Education Training Agency
Defence Procurement Agency
Defence Storage and Distribution Agency
Defence Transport and Movements Agency
Defence Vetting Agency
Disposal Services Agency
Duke of York's Royal Military School
Ministry of Defence Police and Guarding Agency
People, Pay and Pensions Agency
Service Children's Education
Veterans Agency

Advisory Non-Departmental Public Bodies
Advisory Committee on Conscientious Objectors
Advisory Group on Medical Countermeasures
Animal Welfare Advisory Committee
Armed Forces Pay Review Body
Central Advisory Committee on War Pensions
Defence Nuclear Safety Committee
Defence Scientific Advisory Council
National Employer Advisory Board
Nuclear Research Advisory Council
Review Board for Government Contracts
War Pensions Committees

Stakeholder Advisory Group – Op Telic Health Research Programme Review Board

Independent Monitoring Board – Independent Board of Visitors for Military Corrective Training Centre

36. Votes A Statement – Statement of Approved Maximum Armed Forces Numbers

36.1 Votes A provide the formal mechanism by which Parliament sets limits for and monitors the maximum numbers of personnel retained for service in the Armed Forces. They are presented to the House shortly before the start of each financial year (late February), and form part of the Parliamentary Supply process.

36.2 Votes A numbers represent uppermost limits for Service manpower; they neither predict actual strengths nor act as a control over numbers in the Services. The Vote includes a contingency margin to cover unforeseen circumstances. Manpower levels are monitored routinely, and if it is anticipated that the numbers could be breached, then a Supplementary Estimate may be required to increase the limit.

36.3 The tables included below compare, for each service, the numbers voted by the House of Commons with the maximum numbers maintained and the date at which this peak occurred. The aggregate maximum numbers maintained may not equal the sum of Officers plus Men and Women as these categories peak at different times of the year. The 'Men and Women' categories represent the Service's Ratings and Other Ranks

36.4 Maximum numbers of personnel to be maintained for service with the Armed Forces:

		Numbers voted by the House of Commons	Maximum numbers maintained	Peak Dates
Naval Service	Officers	8,280	7,670	May 2006
	Men and Women	33,770	31,730	April 2006
	Aggregate	42,050	39,390	April 2006
Army Service	Officers	16,425	15,190	June 2006
	Men and Women	110,520	99,750	April 2006
	Aggregate	126,945	114,835	April 2006
Air Force Service	Officers	11,180	10,313	April 2006
	Men and Women	40,930	38,416	April 2006
	Aggregate	52,110	48,729	April 2006

36.5 Maximum numbers of personnel to be maintained for service with the Reserve Forces:

		Numbers voted by the House of Commons	Maximum numbers maintained	Peak Dates
Naval Service	Officers	8,280	7,327	April 2006
	Men and Women	8,420	6,871	November 2006
	Aggregate	16,700	14,191	May 2006
Army Service	Officers	18,500	15,270	January 2007
	Men and Women	65,500	55,850	January 2007
	Aggregate	84,000	71,120	January 2007
Air Force Service	Officers	5,400	4,135	July 2006
	Men and Women	17,650	9,954	June 2006
	Aggregate	23,050	14,053	July 2006

36.6 Maximum numbers of personnel to be maintained for service as special members with the Reserve Forces:

		Numbers voted by the House of Commons	Maximum numbers maintained	Peak Dates
Naval Service	Officers	720	111	March 2007
	Men and Women	1,300	104	March 2007
	Aggregate	2,020	215	March 2007
Army Service	Officers	1,000	-	-
	Men and Women	5,000	106	October 2006
	Aggregate	6,000	106	October 2006
Air Force Service	Officers	150	52	March 2007
	Men and Women	400	45	March 2007
	Aggregate	550	97	March 2007

Due to a new personnel administration system (Joint Personnel Administration) being introduced to the Royal Navy and Royal Air Force during 2006-07, the numbers maintained for the Royal Navy from November 2006 and the Royal Air Force from February 2007 are provisional and subject to review.

intentionally left blank

intentionally left blank

Annexes

Annex A

Accountability to Parliament

Ministers have accounted to Parliament during 2006-07 on all aspects of the Department's business. 4,831 Parliamentary Questions were tabled, Defence Ministers participated in 17 debates on defence issues in the main chamber of the House of Commons and nine in the House of Lords, responded to twelve Adjournment Debates in Westminster Hall; and one urgent question in the House of Commons, and made eight oral statements to the House of Commons and six to the House of Lords. They also made 114 written statements to the House of Commons and the House of Lords. Details are published in Hansard.

Evidence to House of Commons Defence Committee

Since 1 April 2006 the Ministry of Defence has also given evidence to the House of Commons Defence Committee on a number of occasions covering a wide range of issues, and the Government has responded to a number of the Committee's reports. All Committee publications, including published evidence given to the Committee, are available at www.parliament.uk/parliamentary_committees/defence_committee.cfm.

Session 2005/06

Reports (Government Responses are listed in brackets after the report they relate to)		
Seventh Report HC 824 and HC 1137 (HC 1488)	The Defence Industrial Strategy	published 10 May 2006
Eighth Report HC 986 (HC 1558)	The Future of the UK's Strategic Nuclear Deterrent: the Strategic Context	published 30 June 2006
Ninth Report HC 1366 (HC 1601)	Ministry of Defence Main Estimates 2006-07	published 29 June 2006
Tenth Report HC 823 (HC 1602)	The Work of the Met Office	published 26 July 2006
Eleventh Report HC 1054 (HC 58)	Educating Service Children	published 6 September 2006
Twelfth Report/First Joint Report of session 2005-06 HC 873 (Cm 6954)	Strategic Export Controls: Annual Report for 2004, Quarterly Reports for 2005, Licensing Policy and Parliamentary Scrutiny	published 3 August 2006
Thirteenth Report HC 1241 (HC 1603)	UK Operations in Iraq	published 10 August 2006
Fourteenth Report HC 1711 (HC 180)	Armed Forces Bill: proposal for a Service Complaints Commissioner	published 8 November 2006

Session 2006/07

Reports (Government Responses are listed in brackets after the report they relate to)		
First Report HC 56 HC 318)	Defence Procurement 2006	published 8 December 2006
Second Report HC 57 (HC 376)	Ministry of Defence Annual Report and Accounts 2005-06	published 13 December 2006
Third Report HC 129 (HC 317)	Costs of operations in Iraq and Afghanistan: Winter Supplementary Estimate 2006-07	published 7 December 2006
Fourth Report HC 59 (HC 304)	The Future of the UK's Strategic Nuclear Deterrent: the Manufacturing and Skills Base	published 19 December 2006
Fifth Report HC 233 (HC 344)	The work of the Committee in 2005 and 2006	published 22 January 2007
Sixth Report HC 177 (HC 481)	The Defence Industrial Strategy: update	published 15 February 2007
Seventh Report HC 159 (HC511)	The Army's requirement for armoured vehicles: the FRES programme	published 21 February 2007
Eighth Report HC 84 (HC 512)	The Work of the Defence Science and Technology Laboratory and the funding of defence research	published 1 March 2007
Ninth Report HC 225 – I and II (HC 551)	The Future of the UK's Strategic Nuclear Deterrent: the White Paper	published 7 March 2007
Tenth Report HC 379 (HC 558)	Cost of Military Operations: Spring Supplementary Estimates 2006-07	published 12 March 2007
Eleventh Report HC 462	Strategic Lift	published 5 July 2007

The Defence Committee also undertook a number of visits to military establishments both in the UK and overseas as part of its inquiries, as shown in the table below.

Defence Committee visits to military establishments

Date of Visit	Establishment	Related Inquiry
24 Apr 06	Colchester Garrison	Educating Service Children
11 May 06	Met Office	The Work of the Met Office
4-9 Jun 06	Iraq	UK Operations in Iraq
2-7 Jul 06	Pakistan and Afghanistan	The UK Deployment in Afghanistan
15 Sep 06	Faslane and Coulport,	The Future of the UK's Strategy Nuclear Deterrent: the manufacturing and skills base
26 Sep 06	AWE Aldermaston	The Future of the UK's Strategy Nuclear Deterrent: the manufacturing and skills base
27 Sep 06	Devonport	The Future of the UK's Strategy Nuclear Deterrent: the manufacturing and skills base
28 Sep 06	Flag Officer Sea Training "Thursday War", Plymouth	Familiarisation visit
30 Oct – 2 Nov 06	British Forces Cyprus	Familiarisation visit/various inquiries

Evidence to Select Committees of the House of Commons and House of Lords

Since 1 April 2006 the Ministry of Defence has also given written and oral evidence on various issues to the following Select Committees of the House of Commons and House of Lords: All Committee publications, including published evidence given to the Committee, are available at: http://www.parliament.uk

Session 2005/06

Reports (Government Responses are listed in brackets after the report)		
Select Committee on the Armed Forces Bill HC 828 – I and II	Armed Forces Bill	published 9 May 2006
Joint Committee on Human Rights HC 701 – I and II	The UN Convention against Torture	published 26 May 2006
HoL EU Committee HL 209	Current Developments in European Defence Policy	published 17 July 2006
Welsh Affairs Committee HC 1129 (HC 1657)	The Future of RAF St Athan	published 25 July 2006
Constitution Committee HC 236 – I and II	Waging War: Parliament's role and responsibility	published 27 July 2006

Session 2006/07

HoL EU Committee HL 17	Current Developments in EU Defence Policy	published 12 Jan 2007

Evidence to Public Accounts Committee and Reports

We have also given evidence to the Public Acconts Committee, as shown in the tables below.

Sessions 2005/06

Reports (Government Responses are listed in brackets after the report)		
Fiftieth Report	Major Projects Report 2005	HC 889 (Cm 6908)

Session 2006/07

Reports (Government Responses are listed in brackets after the report)		
Fourteenth Report	Delivering Digital Tactical Communications Through the Bowman CIP Programme	HC 358 (CM 7077)
Thirteenth Report	Smarter Food Procurement in the Public Sector	HC 357 (CM 7077)
Thirty-Fourth Report	Recruitment and Retention in the Armed Forces	HC 43
Thirty-Sixth Report	Reserve Forces	HC 729
MoD Evidence Major Projects Report 2006	Oral Evidence given by Sir Peter Spencer KCB Chief of Defence Procurement and Lieutenant General Sir Andrew Figgures CBE, Deputy Chief of Defence Staff (Equipment Capability), Ministry of Defence.	HC 295-i
Recruitment and Retention In the Armed Forces	Oral evidence given by Mr Bill Jeffrey, CB, Permanent Under Secretary of State Mr Chris Baker, OBE, Director General, Service Personnel Policy and Brigadier Stephen Andrews CBE, Deputy Chief of Defence Staff Personnel, Ministry of Defence.	HC 43-i

Public Accounts Committee Recommendations

Fiftieth Report (2005/06) Major Projects Report 2005

PAC Recommendations	Response Reported in the Treasury Minute
PAC conclusion (i): The Department has reduced the forecast costs of its top 19 projects by some £700 million. These reductions in forecast costs were not the result of better project management but were cuts needed to bring the Defence Equipment Plan under control. The Department achieved these reductions by cutting the numbers or capability of equipment, and has yet to demonstrate that it can consistently manage individual projects to deliver the planned operational benefits to the Armed Forces to cost and time.	The Department noted the Committee's comments. However, the Committee's conclusion simplifies a complex and dynamic process. Good project and programme management requires trading among all the variables of cost, time, and performance, as was re-emphasised by Smart Acquisition. Many factors influence the MoD's Equipment Plan, including changes to priorities, developments in technology, the impact of operations and project cost pressures. In responding to these factors, the Department must work within the constraints of its overall resource allocation. Where such factors result in additional costs, changes must be made elsewhere in the Plan to maintain overall balance. The Department has a robust planning mechanism in place to ensure that these adjustments are made in such a way that it delivers a balanced and coherent set of equipment capabilities to the front line within the resources available.
PAC conclusion (ii): Some of the latest capability cuts are short-term expediencies which may result in an erosion of core defence capability or in higher costs throughout the life of individual projects. When deciding how to live within its overstretched budget, the Department should not make short-term cuts without first spelling out the longer-term negative impacts in terms of core capability or poor value for money.	The Department notes the Committee's recommendation. The Department has a robust planning process that ensures before any decisions are taken in respect of major projects, comprehensive Impact Statements are generated which set out the consequences of the proposed action. These are prepared in consultation with all stakeholders including Front Line Commands. This process ensures that when decisions are taken, it is with full visibility of the impact on capability, risk, value for money and other key factors. The changes to the Department s processes and structure being introduced following the Defence Industrial Strategy under the Enabling Acquisition Change initiative will encourage greater consideration of the long term impact of initial acquisition decisions.
PAC conclusion (iii): The Department's defined levels of capability do not include the quantity of equipment bought. So they can allow quantities to be cut to offset cost overruns, without affecting measured capacity. In defining threshold levels (minimum acceptable capability) and objective levels (full capability desired) for equipment capability on projects coming forward for approval, the Department should reflect quantities as well as performance characteristics.	The Department does not accept this recommendation. The July 2004 White Paper *Delivering Security in a Changing World: Future Capabilities* explicitly emphasised the Department s focus on effects based warfare – focusing on the impact our Armed Forces can deliver, rather than the number of platforms that we use. In the process of balancing defence capability within the Department s resource allocation, it is possible that platform numbers will change. Nevertheless, the fact remains that it is the capability delivered rather than the platform numbers on which we are focussed. Where the required capability can be delivered from fewer platforms, it is appropriate that resources are allocated to other priorities within the Programme.

PAC Recommendations	Response Reported in the Treasury Minute
PAC conclusion (iv): Despite previous assurances that it had restructured many of its older projects, at considerable cost, to address past failures, the Department still attributes much of its historic poor performance to so called "toxic legacy" projects which continue to accumulate considerable time and cost overruns. The Department cannot indefinitely hide behind past deficiencies, while claiming to be taking a proactive approach to addressing the problems. It is time that these projects were put on a firm footing with realistic performance, time and cost estimates against which the Department and industry can be judged.	The Department agrees that the older legacy projects need to be put on a firm footing with realistic estimates of time, cost and performance but the Department rejects the assertion that it is hiding behind past deficiencies. The Department has been open about the problems involved with older and larger projects, which remain in the MPR population for several years because of their very long-term nature. Substantial improvements to equipment acquisition practice have been, and continue to be made and have resulted in improvements, and we are determined to build on these; but the fact remains that it is impossible to alter retrospectively the terms of approvals which did not fully reflect current best practice for projects where approvals were given and contracts were let many years ago, to reflect the standard which would now apply. The Department can evidence a proactive approach to the problems. In July of this year the Department signed a production contract with BAE Systems for twelve Nimrod MRA4 aircraft, one of the older and most problematic projects. On the Astute programme the Department is currently working with BAE Systems and other critical suppliers in pursuit of the DIS to achieve an affordable and sustainable submarine programme. In support of this MoD has ordered four packages of long lead items with BAE Systems, Rolls Royce and their suppliers, which will ensure the long-term viability of the supply chain and the maritime industrial base.
PAC conclusion (v): The Department has improved its practice in setting meaningful in-service dates, but still not all future in-service dates represent the delivery of useable capability to the frontline. In defining these dates it needs to incorporate areas such as logistic support and training to enable the Armed Forces to use the equipment effectively.	The Department agrees with the Committee's recommendation. It plans to deliver effective military capability to the Front Line Commands, which requires the eight Lines of Development (LoD) – Training, Equipment, Personnel, Infrastructure, Logistics, Concepts and Doctrine, Organisation – associated with each project to be in a mature enough state to support and maintain the equipment that delivers the capability effect. LoD are intended to apply coherence to the evolution of defence capability. The choice of In Service Date (ISD) is therefore now made with this requirement in mind and after wide consultation with stakeholders. It is already part of the routine project management process within the Department to monitor and deliver the equipment, with its associated LoD, at ISD.

PAC Recommendations	Response Reported in the Treasury Minute
PAC conclusion (vi): In co-operating with the United States on defence projects, the United Kingdom is the junior partner, which reduces our influence over the project's direction. Conversely, a lack of focused leadership has stymied progress on many European collaborative projects. The Department should routinely analyse co-operative projects to see how far the expected benefits are delivered, so that it can make better-informed decisions before committing to future co-operative acquisitions.	The Department notes the Committee's conclusions about cooperation with the US and within Europe. While the US's far larger defence budget and requirements inevitably constrain the influence we can exert, we are able to ensure our operational capability requirements are met. For European collaborative programmes, Organisation Conjointe de Cooperation en matiere d'Armement (OCCAR) was established in 1996 to improve project management and build a centre of expertise using best procurement practice; greater empowerment by nations and the abandonment of "juste retour" are two of the many improvements over previous arrangements. The Department agrees with the Committee's recommendation that routine analysis of co-operative projects should help inform future acquisition decisions. The Department requires all projects to be subject to evaluation as set out in *Joint Services Publication (JSP) 507: MoD guide to Investment Appraisal and Evaluation*.
PAC conclusion (vii): The Department has introduced key supplier management to assess the performance of its 18 largest suppliers, but much of the innovation which will drive better acquisition performance comes from the second and third tiers of the supply chain. The Department considers that these arrangements have already had a beneficial impact by focusing suppliers on areas for improvement, but to maximise the benefits the Department should progressively extend the principles of key supplier management through its supply chain	The Department agrees with this conclusion and recommendation, which echoes one of the themes of the DIS (referred to specifically at paragraph C1.16 of the white paper). The Department is examining with industry ways to improve the process of bringing innovation to bear. We are also looking to extend the principles of key supplier management. We are encouraged by evidence that industry is responding to the challenge of developing and improving supply chains. The Department will consider with industry further ways to improve relationships and performance across the supply chain to ensure that we capture and promote best practice.
PAC conclusion (viii): The DIS aims to promote a sustainable and globally competitive defence manufacturing sector but the Department has not traditionally quantified or measured these wider benefits. The Department should more accurately quantify what these wider beneficial outcomes might be at the time defence acquisition decisions are made, and should monitor their achievement throughout the life of the project. .	The Department agrees with this recommendation. The creation of a sustainable and globally competitive defence manufacturing sector will benefit defence acquisition by ensuring that the capability requirements of the Armed Forces can be met, now and in the future, and that we retain in the UK those industrial capabilities needed to ensure appropriate sovereignty and/or contribute to collaborative efforts. The DIS emphasises the need for a Through Life Capability Management approach to acquisition, taking account of all available factors at the key decision points and monitoring performance throughout the life cycle of the individual equipment or service contract. Wider factors will continue to be considered in acquisition decisions where appropriate. The Department acknowledges that further work on quantifying those wider benefits could be advantageous and work currently in hand in MoD on the Defence supply chain, together with wider discussions between MoD and the Defence Industries Council may offer scope to develop quantification of the kind that the committee advocates.

Thirteenth Report (2006-07): Smarter Food Procurement in the public Sector

PAC Recommendations	Response Reported in the Treasury Minute
PAC conclusion (v): For many children and adults, publicly provided meals form a key element in their daily diet, but not all public bodies make the most of the opportunity to promote healthier eating. They and their contractors should assess regularly the dietary requirements of all their existing and potential customers, including the elderly and those from ethnic and religious minority communities, canvassing customer views as part of regular quality audits of catering services. Frontline organisations should work with contract caterers to introduce healthier food combined with educational events that encourage healthy eating, and introduce 'traffic light' systems to highlight the nutritional value of each menu option.	The MoD accepts this conclusion. The MoD's nutritional policy is set by the Expert Panel on Armed Forces Feeding (EPAFF), whose overarching aim is to educate Service personnel about nutrition and healthy eating. Under the direction of EPAFF, a series of nutritional guides for commanders, caterers and individuals has been developed and issued. In addition, a nutritional DVD has also been made available to all Service units with a supporting presentation to reinforce the message being sent to recruit training units. The MoD also established a web-based service for personnel to seek nutritional advice from their consultant dieticians and nutritionists.
PAC conclusion (vi): There are wide disparities in the prices paid by public bodies for the same food items, ranging from between 32 pence and £1.10 for a standard 800g loaf of wholemeal bread, and between 17 and 44 pence for a pint of milk. Following the example of the Ministry of Defence, Departments should conduct regular benchmarking surveys or draw upon publicly available or commercially generated pricing information, and secure explanations from frontline organisations where significant price variations exist. They should also encourage greater use of e-procurement methods to stimulate increased competition and greater transparency of prices through, for example, e-auctions.	The MoD accepts this conclusion. The use of e-auctions contributed to the savings achieved within food procurement as part of the Supply Chain Excellence Programme. The MoD continues to conduct regular benchmarking surveys and e-auctions.
PAC conclusion (vii): A lack of commercial skills and knowledge about the specialist food and catering market undermines the ability of frontline procurers to strike good deals with the major national wholesale food or multi-national contract catering companies. The three Departments (the Department for Education and Skills, the Ministry of Defence and the NHS Purchasing and Supply Agency) and the Prison Service, working with the Office of Government Commerce, should use their collective purchasing power to negotiate with the major food and catering firms for a larger share of the £95M earned annually by contract catering firms from their suppliers by way of volume discounts and rebates.	The MoD does not accept that there is a lack of commercial skills/market knowledge within its organisation, which prevents it from placing competitive sourcing arrangements. The MoD has a dedicated commercial team and employs within the Defence Food Services Integrated Project Team, staff with specialist food and catering knowledge, who continue to refresh their knowledge of the market through training, development and research. The MoD has also invested in developing a Category Management Team that supports the activities of the commercial and catering staff and shares information with other Government Departments via the OGC's Food Procurement Group.
PAC conclusion (xi): The Committee expects to see measurable progress within two years (by 2008-09) towards savings of some £20 million promised by the Ministry of Defence over the five year life of its new main food contract.	The conclusion is accepted by the MoD, in so far as their contract will realise the quoted savings over the life of the contract.

Thirteenth Report (2006-07): Smarter Food Procurement in the public Sector

PAC Recommendations	Response Reported in the Treasury Minute
PAC conclusion (xii): The National Audit Office has demonstrated that it is possible for public bodies to increase the proportion of food purchased competitively from local or regional producers while complying with EU requirements. Following the lead of the Ministry of Defence in working with the UK meat industry, the three departments together with the Department of Environment, Food and Rural Affairs, should explore with UK food producers ways to increase the amount of UK produce purchased by the public sector. Public bodies should also be able to demonstrate that the animal welfare and food production practices of their suppliers adhere to the standards under which UK producers operate and satisfy themselves that enough independent spot checks and inspections are taking place.	The conclusion is accepted, in part, by MoD as it reflects the present working practices within the Department, particularly in the context of the department's working relationship with the UK meat industry. The MoD does, however, need to ensure the year round availability of its 'Core List' commodities, which supply our worldwide operational commitments. This cannot be achieved, cost effectively, with a policy of local or regional buying alone.
PAC conclusion (xiv): Public sector procurers should seek to increase the proportion of food purchased from 'Fair Trade' sources that offer the same standard at a competitive price. In some cases fair trade products will be more expensive but departments should work with the supply chain to improve competitiveness while still securing a fair price for producers.	This conclusion is accepted by MoD, It is the intention of the MoD to test, through its Food Selection Panel, a wider range of fair trade products in the future for inclusion on the 'Core List'.

Fourteenth Report (2006-07): Delivering Digital Tactical Communications through the Bowman CIP Programme

PAC Recommendations	Response Reported in the Treasury Minute
PAC conclusion (i): There is no individual within the Department with full responsibility for ensuring that the Bowman CIP project meets its objectives. In 2006, the Department belatedly appointed a senior officer to act as Senior Responsible Owner. But he lacks the authority and time to effectively discharge this onerous responsibility and is only supported by a small staff. In applying the Senior Responsible Owner concept, the Department should equip those appointed to such challenging positions with the funding, authority and trust to fully discharge their responsibilities in line with the guidance issued by the Office of Government Commerce.	The Department notes the Committee's views and agrees that in its earlier stages the Bowman and CIP projects would have benefited from stronger high-level governance arrangements. The Department believes that the governance arrangements, which were developed in the light of the OGC guidance in 2003 and as the programme evolved provide a robust framework for delivering the Bowman CIP programme. The senior officer now responsible for the delivery of networks such as Bowman CIP that underpin Network Enabled Capability (NEC) has the authority, position within the Department and support to ensure that obstacles to delivery are addressed and overcome while maintaining coherence with other projects supporting the wider NEC capability. It is the Department's policy that large and complex projects or groups of projects will have a senior responsible owner appointed on behalf of and accountable to the Defence Management Board. In addition, under the Department's Defence Acquisition Change Programme, the Directors of Equipment Capability will fulfil the senior responsible owner role for each of their projects that are not covered by specific SRO appointments. Although the senior responsible owner may not have full financial or command/line management authority over all those delivering the projects, he or she will be empowered, have a good knowledge of the requirement, be competent to resolve conflicting priorities and be able to exert influence outside traditional management or command chains. This is consistent with the OGC guidance.

Fourteenth Report (2006-07): Delivering Digital Tactical Communications through the Bowman CIP Programme

PAC Recommendations	Response Reported in the Treasury Minute
PAC conclusion (ii): The Department took nine months to approve the revised deal struck with General Dynamics UK in October 2005. Time is money for the Department and its contractors, and delaying delivery of a much-needed capability could also cost lives. The Department intends to action the relevant recommendations from its Enabling Acquisition Change review to improve its in-house approvals processes. The Department should also engage the Treasury and other relevant government departments in developing a leaner, more responsive approval process so that decisions can be made in a more-timely manner.	The Department agrees that responsiveness is an important attribute of the investment approvals process, alongside the need to ensure that proposals are soundly based and provide good value for money. Implementation of the recommendations of the Enabling Acquisition Change report is being taken forward through the Defence Acquisition Change Programme. A number of changes to the approvals process have already been made. These include: • the involvement of the Defence Management Board in the most significant investment decisions; • the addition of the Defence Commercial Director to membership of the Department's Investment Approvals Board; and • the delegation of the approval of the lower value lower risk equipment and support projects to the new Defence Equipment and Support organisation. Other changes that will be introduced shortly include: • a more streamlined scrutiny process which aims to ensure that project teams have, at an early stage, a clearer picture of the information required at the main decision points and simplifies the production of business cases; • for larger projects, the inclusion of support costs in Main Gate equipment approvals; • independent cost estimates; and • the requirement to carry out commercial due diligence before contract signature. The Department is engaged with HM Treasury to develop a more responsive procurement approvals process. Although engagement with other Government Departments does take place in the context of the approvals process, this does not impact on approval timelines.

Fourteenth Report (2006-07): Delivering Digital Tactical Communications through the Bowman CIP Programme

PAC Recommendations	Response Reported in the Treasury Minute
PAC conclusion (iii): The Bowman CIP project timescale was clearly unrealistic, and the inherent complexity and technological challenges were under-estimated. The Department should re-design its scrutiny processes and better align these and its assurance processes so that they are fit to deal with the challenges of modern defence acquisitions and to take into account the culture of over-optimism endemic in much defence procurement.	The Department accepts the general thrust of the Committee's views. The Department recognises that the timescales set for the Bowman and CIP projects were challenging and was aware of the potential technical and complexity challenges, but on balance believed that the risks were worth taking in order to achieve coherence between the two projects and the earliest possible delivery of this important new capability. The deployment on operations of a militarily useful Bowman CIP from April 2005 was an important step forward. The Department recognises, as a general issue, the need for greater realism in the planning of defence capability and agility in the acquisition system. Changes being introduced through the Defence Acquisition Change Programme, including the streamlining of process, better cost estimating and greater use of incremental acquisition are aimed at improving the acquisition system to provide better delivery of capability to the front line, and improved value for money for the taxpayer.
PAC conclusion (iv): The vehicle conversion challenge posed by the unexpected variation in the land vehicle fleet could have been predicted if the fleet had been properly surveyed before contracts were placed. The problem was compounded by the absence of good data on vehicle configurations, and the practice, particularly in the army, of modifying vehicles without managing and tracking the modifications. Until the Department obtains adequate standing information on vehicle condition and configuration, it should re-emphasise to Users the importance of maintaining standard configurations wherever possible and should survey representative samples of vehicles before commencing modification work.	The Department accepts that there is an issue with capturing and tracking information about modifications to vehicles. The UK armed forces' vehicle fleet consists of many types, which in some cases are themselves sub-divided into many variants according to role and parent unit. This fleet is, in some cases, up to 40 years old and over time and for good reasons has been subject to extensive modifications to meet the evolving operational or safety environment. Given the general knowledge the Department had about the age and condition of the vehicle fleet, it was recognised that configuration control was an issue at the outset of Bowman conversion. A platform presentation programme was put in place that brought some commonality to the fleets but could not allow for platform-to platform variations. The Department accepts in retrospect that more detailed survey and preparation work would have enabled the true scale of the variations present in the vehicle fleets to be better understood and the conversion programme to have proceeded more smoothly. As a result in part of experience with the Bowman CIP conversion programme the Department is working hard to address vehicle configuration control issues and believes significant improvements will flow as more capable electronic engineering and configuration management systems enter service. Until then, the better use of existing data alongside revised processes within the Army will deliver worthwhile improvements.

Fourteenth Report (2006-07): Delivering Digital Tactical Communications through the Bowman CIP Programme

PAC Recommendations	Response Reported in the Treasury Minute
PAC conclusion (v): Complex new systems such as Bowman CIP are more expensive to support and will require more on-going training than their simpler predecessors. To encourage more serious consideration of Through Life Management issues and better inform future investment decisions, the Department should validate the quality of the key data underpinning decisions on the delivery of through life management capability including measures of financial maturity, and clarity about the capability needed.	The Department agrees that clarity on requirements and the quality of data are key factors in the successful delivery of through life capability management. The Defence Acquisition Change Programme is addressing these issues. For example, the Department's capability planning process has been reformed to support through life capability management and now follows a multi-stage process to establish capability requirements, identifying risk and pressures relating to such areas as the industrial capacity, funding and maintaining the effectiveness of current capability. Implementation of this process is expected to mature towards the end of 2007. Much of the data that underpins this work is generated by the newly formed Defence Equipment and Support (DE&S) organisation through its equipment Through Life Management Plans (TLMPs). The DE&S has initiated a programme of work to simplify and improve the design of TLMPs and complete a 100 per cent refresh of the data they contain by the end of the current financial year.
PAC conclusion (vi): Bowman CIP was accepted in service in March 2004 with 27 major provisos that reflect the limited operational capability of the initial system. The Department should only accept that General Dynamics UK has cleared the provisos on the basis of robust trials-based evidence and should not pay any outstanding amounts until it is satisfied that the Armed Services are getting the capability they asked for.	The Department agrees with the Committee on the importance of robust testing and trialing as a basis for accepting equipment into service. Acceptance of the next increment of Bowman CIP (Bowman CIP 5) will be based on the evidence gathered through extensive trialing activity in 2006 and 2007. These trials will graduate from highly demanding technical field trials to operational field trialing in the hands of the user. This trialing methodology will ensure that the capability delivered by General Dynamics UK is fully verified and validated before it is deployed on operations. Included in this process is the clearance of outstanding provisos against full systems acceptance. In order to ensure the delivery of the required capability a number of significant outstanding payments to General Dynamics UK remain and will be held pending the delivery of the contracted requirement.

Fourteenth Report (2006-07): Delivering Digital Tactical Communications through the Bowman CIP Programme

PAC Recommendations	Response Reported in the Treasury Minute
PAC conclusion (vii): The Department has removed several important capabilities from the existing Bowman CIP programme. The Department has developed plans which it is confident will now deliver the most vital aspects of capability without further delay. The capabilities being delayed, such as the ability to communicate with allies, remain important, not least to reduce the risk of further friendly fire deaths. The Department is confident that, to date, no lives have been lost due to this deferral. It should, within the next year, develop a realistic forward plan to ensure the Armed Forces do not have to forego these capabilities for longer than is absolutely necessary.	The Department remains confident that the revised Bowman CIP programme approved in 2006 will deliver the coherent and stable austere Bowman CIP capability necessary to provide the basis for Network Enabled Capability in the land environment. The Department notes that this level of capability, Bowman CIP 5, will improve on the ability of the current version to communicate with allies by secure voice by also providing an ability to transfer standard formatted messages or e-mail with allies, as explained in the supplementary memorandum of evidence submitted in response to Question 155. Bowman CIP will therefore increasingly contribute to our Combat Identification capability and the minimisation of the risk of fratricide.

The Department continues to believe that the deferral of technically risky capability from the current Bowman CIP programme was prudent. The Department confirms that it is working to define plans for future capability releases beyond Bowman CIP 5 and expects to consider these plans as part of its routine planning process. Among the factors that will shape these plans are the ability of the front line to absorb further large-scale changes and the constraints imposed by operational tempo.

The Department envisages a periodic capability release programme providing both capability enhancements and maintenance that will be informed by the current validation work on the delivery of deferred capability. |
| **PAC conclusion (viii): In addition to the timescale slippage, the Department has agreed to pay a further £121M to General Dynamics UK to deliver Bowman CIP, despite a much reduced number of platforms to be converted, and some aspects of the requirement being shuffled to another project. Securing value for money in the long-term will require the Department and General Dynamics UK to work together collaboratively to cost-effectively deliver and sustain the capability required by the Armed Forces. To support this objective, the Department and General Dynamics should regularly assess the strength of their relationship.** | The Department agrees with the Committee on the importance of working in partnership with industry to secure long-term value for money. The Department's Key Supplier Management process employs a range of tools aimed at improving and maintaining the relationship with our key suppliers, and measuring and driving performance improvement in both the supplier and the Department.

The Integrated Project Team (IPT) dealing with Bowman CIP and General Dynamics UK have been actively engaged in that process. Looking ahead, the IPT is also working to measure and improve the strength of its partnering with General Dynamics UK and other companies involved in this work. This should yield benefit within the remainder of the current contract as well as informing any potential longer-term partnering arrangements. |

Annex B

Organisation and Mangement of Defence

Secretary of State and Ministers

The Secretary of State is responsible for the formulation and conduct of defence policy, and for providing the means by which it is conducted. He is supported by a Minister of State for the Armed Forces, a Minister of State for Defence Equipment & Support and a Parliamentary Under-Secretary of State and Minister for Veterans. The Secretary of State and his three Ministerial colleagues are accountable to Parliament – which votes public money to the MoD for defence purposes.

Principal Advisers

Ministers are supported by the senior management of the MoD, headed jointly by the (military) Chief of the Defence Staff and the (civilian) Permanent Under Secretary. They share equal responsibility for much of the Department's business and their roles reflect the importance of both military and civilian advice on operational, political, financial and administrative matters. The Permanent Under Secretary is the Government's principal civilian adviser on defence and has primary responsibility for defence policy, finance and the administration of the Department. The Chief of the Defence Staff (CDS) is the professional head of the Armed Forces and the principal military adviser to the Secretary of State and the Government.

The Defence Council

The Defence Council is the senior Departmental committee. It is chaired by the Secretary of State, and comprises the other Ministers, the Permanent Under Secretary, the Chief of the Defence Staff and senior military officers and officials at the head of the Armed Services and the Department's major corporate functions. It provides the formal legal basis for the conduct of defence in the UK through a range of powers vested in it by statute and Letters Patent.

The Defence Management Board

The Defence Management Board is the highest non-ministerial committee in the MoD. Chaired by the Permanent Under Secretary, it is the main corporate board of the MoD, providing senior level leadership and strategic management of defence. Its role is to deliver the Defence Aim set out in the Public Service Agreement and it owns the Defence Vision. The Board is made up of the non-ministerial members of the Defence Council, and three external, independent non-executive members.

Capability Review

The Cabinet Office published its Capability Review of the MoD on 27 March 2007. One of the key recommendations was to clarify and simplify the MoD's operating model. As a result, the Department is undertaking a review of Head Office to define a leaner and more strategically focussed structure. Therefore, the top level structure of the Department may be subject to alteration over 2007-08. See *Business Management* paragraphs 274-276 and the Essay on *The Capability Review (page 147)* for further information.

Top Level Budgets

The delivery of defence outputs falls to Top Level Budget holders – Service Commanders-in-Chief and the heads of other major delivery organisations. Top Level Budget holders are responsible for the delivery of specific outputs – typically elements of military capability or supporting services to other Top Level Budgets. At the conclusion of each planning round, the outputs and the related resources for each Top Level Budget are set out in Service Delivery Agreements between the Permanent Under Secretary and the Chief of the Defence Staff on the one hand and the Top Level Budget holder, or Service Chief where appropriate, on the other hand.

Figure 9 Top Level Budget structure of the Ministry of Defence[1]

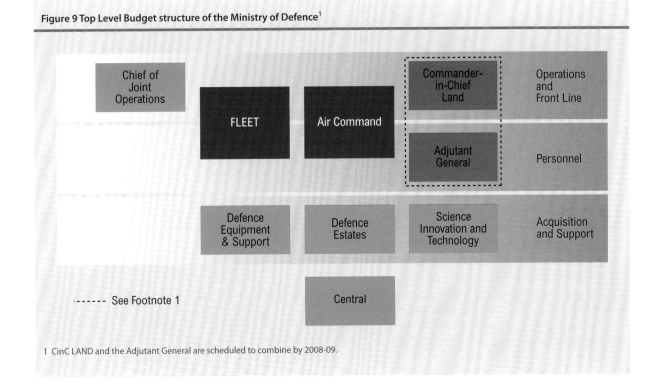

1 CinC LAND and the Adjutant General are scheduled to combine by 2008-09.

Top Level Budget Roles

Central TLB

The role of the Central TLB is to provide the framework to enable MoD to act as both a Department of State and as the Strategic Headquarters of the Armed Forces. It provides three key functions: Head Office – strategy and policy, allocation of resources against objectives and targets, monitoring performance, and setting standards; Military Capability – providing centrally managed force elements at defined readiness states (including Special Forces, medical and intelligence services); and Corporate Services – delivering cost-effective and efficient centralized Corporate Services to the wider Department e.g. finance and personnel services.

Chief of Joint Operations (CJO)

With a few exceptions, CJO is responsible for running all military operations from the Permanent Joint Headquarters in Northwood. Military assets are assigned to CJO for the duration of the operation only. In addition to these operational responsibilities, CJO is responsible for the Sovereign Base Areas and British Forces in Cyprus, Gibraltar, the South Atlantic Islands and Diego Garcia.

Fleet

The single Fleet TLB was formed on 1 April 2006 by merging the old TLBs of Commander in Chief Fleet (CINCFLEET) and the Second Sea Lord/Commander in Chief Naval Home Command TLBs. Headed by Commander in Chief Fleet, the TLB is responsible for providing warships and trained crews and Royal Marines to CJO at agreed readiness states. CINCFLEET maintains an operational command and control capability, in particular for the nuclear deterrent force. This TLB is also responsible for the provision of personnel: recruitment, individual and collective training and career management.

Air Command

Air Command was formed on 1 April 2007 as a result of the merger of the RAF's Personnel and Training Command and Strike Command. The creation of a single Command, with a single fully integrated Headquarters, will better equip the RAF to provide a coherent and coordinated single Air focus to the other services, MoD Head office, the Permanent Joint Headquarters and the rest of MoD. Air Command is responsible for providing aircraft, trained aircrews and other force elements to CJO at agreed readiness states. In order to do this it undertakes a wide range of functions including providing the recruitment and training of RAF personnel. It undertakes the basic flying training for all three services. In addition, it maintains aircraft and aircrew for Quick Reaction Alert to defend UK airspace and conduct Search and Rescue Operations.

Land Command[1]

LAND is responsible for providing the land component military capability (Army formations and equipment) to CJO at agreed readiness states through collective training and the generation of military capability of units, brigades and divisions.

Defence Equipment and Support (DE&S)

DE&S is a new Top Level Budget established through merger of the Defence Procurement Agency and the Defence Logistics Organisation. It was formed on 1 April 2007 as a result of the Defence Acquisition Change Programme to become an integrated procurement and support organisation. The role of this TLB is therefore to equip and support the UK's Armed Forces for current and future operations. It acquires and supports through-life, including disposal, equipment and services ranging from ships, aircraft, vehicles and weapons, to electronic systems and information systems.

Science | Innovation | Technology

The prime output of this TLB ensures the Department has access to sound technical advice and technology to support military operations and future strategic capabilities, including nuclear and missile defence issues and policy, provision of technical support, and adaptation of equipment for defence requirements.

Defence Estate (DE)

DE is responsible for managing and developing the Defence Estate in a sustainable manner, in line with acknowledged best practice and Government policy.

Additional information on the Organisation and Management of Defence is available from the following sources:

- MoD Framework Document available at www.mod.uk;

- Corporate Governance Returns available at www.mod.uk.

1 CINC Land and the Adjutant General are scheduled to combine by 2008-09.

Annex C

PSA Target 2: Detailed Assessment Against Performance Indicators

A. Afghanistan: Broadly on course – minor slippage

By end 2007-08: Accountable and democratic structures for Afghanistan's governing institutions and Armed Forces, representing Afghanistan's ethnic diversity, and operating with respect for human rights.

- Despite significant challenges resulting form the difficult security situation, there has been further good progress. To build the capacity of the Afghan National Police and the broader justice sector, HMG has funded the deployment of five police mentors and a senior police advisor to help senior Afghan police officers with the reorganisation of the Afghan National Police in Helmand. A governance advisor was also deployed to promote the development of transparent provincial governance.

- The tri-departmental Helmand quick-impact projects fund has increased its activity. HMG is also funding a UN High Commission for Refugees Afghan refugee registration programme, a donation to a new Pashtun BBC radio programme, and sending Afghan military personnel on a regional disaster management course.

B. Balkans: Broadly on course – minor slippage

By end 2007-08: Western Balkan states at peace within and between themselves and continuing on the path to closer integration with the EU and NATO.

- The Western Balkan states remain at peace within and between themselves, but inter-ethnic tensions persist. Serbia was awarded NATO Partnership for Peace (PfP) status, but lack of cooperation with the International Criminal Tribunal of the Former Yugoslavia continues to stall their Stabilisation and Association Agreement. Bosnia and Montenegro were also invited to join PfP.

- HMG has provided considerable support both multilaterally (through the EU and NATO) and bilaterally, to help establish the conditions that will help the process of integration, with particular diplomatic focus on Kosovo's final status process. Conflict prevention programmes are helping states and ethnic communities to address the underlying causes of instability in the Balkans; helping to remove the barriers to further EU and NATO integration.

C. Democratic Republic of Congo (DRC): Broadly on course – minor slippage

By end 2007-08: Reduced cross border interference in Eastern DRC, a stable government in Kinshasa overseeing accountable security services and a reduction in militia operating outside such democratic government control. (This target will focus on DRC but will necessarily take account of wider Great Lakes conflict dynamics).

- HMG made a significant contribution to the success of presidential, parliamentary and provincial assembly elections in DRC in the second half of 2006; declared credible and transparent by all observers. New government now appointed but still more likely to turn to military rather than political means to impose its will. Insufficient accommodation of opposition views. HMG supported local election monitoring (by DFID, FCO and UK parliamentarians) through funding of the Independent Electoral Commission.

- Steady improvement in regional relations has reduced the threat of border interference in Eastern Congo. Armed groups still operating but reductions in activity in Ituri, Kivus and Katanga. Internally displaced person (IDP) numbers thought likely to have reduced.

- Post election, priority HMG programmes include a focus on reform of DRC's security services to counter ongoing abuses by the army and police.

D.   Iraq: Not on course – major slippage

By end 2007-08: A stable, united and law abiding state, within its present borders, cooperating with the international community, no longer posing a threat to its neighbours or to international security, abiding by all its international obligations and providing effective, representative and inclusive government for all its people.

- Progress towards Iraqi self-reliance continues, but sectarian violence, particularly in Baghdad, remains a significant problem. However, Prime Minister Maliki's determination to implement an effective Baghdad Security Plan is encouraging.

- Najaf province was handed over to Provincial Iraqi Control in December. The UK's transition plans continue, but Basra remains a significant challenge, with police corruption and infiltration by militias the main impediment. The HMG-funded policing project is making some progress, in particular the establishment of a Department of Internal Affairs to tackle corrupt and criminal elements of the Iraqi Police Service. Operation Sinbad continues to make progress, with the Iraqi Army leading the latter stages of the operation in Basra.

E.   Middle East Peace Process (MEPP): Not on course – major slippage

By end 2007-08: Maximising the opportunity of Israeli withdrawal from Gaza and parts of the West Bank, significant progress towards a negotiated settlement resulting in the emergence of an independent, democratic, and viable Palestinian state with a reformed security sector, living side by side in peace and security with Israel.

- The security situation has deteriorated, with emerging intra-Palestinian violence. However, there have been some positive developments, and the Israeli-Palestinian Gaza cease-fire agreed on 25 November is holding. Talks between Hama and Fatah on a National Unity government continued.

- HMG continues to drive forward an initiative to build Palestinian Capacity, engaging international partners, especially the EU. HMG is providing technical support to the Office of the President to enable long-term reform, and planning for the economic regeneration of the Occupied Territories once the political situation allows. We have also helped maintain some areas of the Palestinian Authority Security Forces, and are encouraging their further development through engagement with the United States Security Coordinator's team.

F.   Nepal: Broadly on course – minor slippage

By end 2007-08: A stable Nepal with a durable ceasefire in place with the Maoists, democratic institutions restored with respect for human rights and significant progress towards a constitutional settlement.

- Substantial progress made towards the restoration of democracy. Peace talks between the Government of Nepal and Maoists resulted in the signing of a Comprehensive Peace Accord and the adoption of an interim constitution and formation of an interim parliament, including Maoist MPs. There are however, potential difficulties following riots in the Terai, a lack of political agreement on the election system to be used and questions over Maoist commitment to the weapons management process.

- The UK has played a significant part in the peace process, through our support for the UN and engaging closely with EU partners, India and the US. We have continued to support democracy building and inclusion through engagement and funding of influential NGOs and civil society, and reducing human rights violations through co-operation with the Office of the UN High Commissioner for Human Rights.

G.   Nigeria: Broadly on course – minor slippage

By end 2007-08: Local and central government effectively managing and resolving conflict and a reduction in the number of people affected by conflict.

- Tensions and politically motivated crime are increasing due to the election campaign; including the murder of some potential candidates for governor and a rise in hostage taking in the Niger Delta. The political situation is likely to worsen in the run-up to the presidential elections in April 2007.

- HMG is supporting the work of a coalition of NGOs working on a large-scale information campaign against violence during the elections. Through radio, television and other channels of information, this campaign is reaching millions of Nigerians, spreading messages about political tolerance and peaceful elections. The campaign is targeting disenfranchised youth easily manipulated for political reasons.

H. Sierra Leone: Broadly on course – minor slippage

By end 2007-08: Ongoing stable and democratic government overseeing accountable security services and a reduction in regional militia.

- Government remains stable ahead of the mid-2007 Presidential and Legislative elections. Approaching elections have caused a general slowdown in government; including progress on Anti-Corruption Commission prosecutions. Allegations of manipulation in electoral preparations have been made against all parties, suggesting an increased risk that elections will not be free and/or credible (hence the move from an assessment of 'ahead', in the FCO 2006 Autumn Performance Report, to 'broadly on course').

- HMG's substantial assistance is credited for the professionalism and accountability of the security services. HMG continues to provide a large amount of technical assistance to help increase the sustain-ability of the security sector. Ex-combatants within the region are not currently posing a direct threat to Sierra Leone.

I. Sudan Broadly on course – minor slippage[2].

By end 2007-08: A fully implemented comprehensive peace agreement between the Government of Sudan and the Sudan People's Liberation Movement (SPLM), progress towards a stable and democratic government, a reduction in militia operating outside democratic control, and a reduction in the number of deaths through violent conflict.

- HMG continues to press for full implementation of the Comprehensive Peace Agreement (CPA) and provides technical assistance on disarmament, demobilisation and reintegration planning in support of the CPA. HMG funds support to the Sudanese People's Liberation Army to transform it from a guerrilla fighting force to a disciplined armed force developing civil control and operating with respect for human rights and the rule of law.

- On Darfur, progress has been slow and erratic. HMG continues to push for progress on the military and political tracks agreed by the international community in November 2006 and press the non-signatory groups to eschew violence and adopt the Darfur Peace Agreement. HMG also continues to push the Government of Sudan to consent to transition to a hybrid UN/African Union (AU) mission in Darfur and has provided significant resources to the existing AU mission. But the humanitarian situation is precarious owing to the difficult security situation and the climate of fear affecting humanitarian organisations following a series of attacks.

J. UN Peacekeeping: Broadly on course – minor slippage

By end 2007- 08: All potential UN peacekeeping missions should follow the principles of integrated and comprehensive planning set out in the Brahimi Report of 2000, incorporating these from the onset of the planning process and carrying them forward into mission deployment with appropriate training of personnel and systematic processes for learning lessons and applying best practice.

- All new mandates take account of the multi-dimensional nature of UN missions based on Brahimi principles. A recent example is UN Security Council Resolution 1706 on Sudan, adopted in August 2006. This resolution called for an integrated strategy for the disarmament, resettlement and repatriation of foreign combatants in Sudan, incorporating military, political, social and justice-related aspects. Integrated planning for this mission took place under a high level UN Secretary General directive, however it has not yet deployed due to Sudanese objections. The Integrated Missions Planning Process has still to be firmly embedded in pan-UN culture.

2 This Performance Indicator was drawn up before the beginning of the conflict in Darfur, and the judgment of progress therefore does not cover the situation in Darfur. If there were a Performance indicator for Darfur, it would be judged as *Not on course – major slippage.*

K. UN Peacekeeping: Met

By end 2007- 08: A 5% increase in the number of states contributing effective peacekeepers to regional and international Peace Support Operations (PSOs) under a UN mandate, with adjustment where necessary for changes in the demand for peacekeepers.

- HMG supports work to improve the quantity and quality of peacekeepers. There are now 60 percent more military and police deployed on UN Peace Support Operations (PSOs) than there were in 2004. HMG continues to support the development of the UN's best practice, including the development of standard training modules for peacekeepers and Disarmament Demobilisation Reintegration (DDR) standards. HMG works with a range of current and potential troop contributing countries to improve their capacity for peacekeeping. Recent examples include China and Mongolia: since 2004 China have increased their contribution to UN PSO by 62%, and Mongolia has increased its contribution 50 fold.

L. African Peacekeeping: Broadly on course – minor slippage

By end 2007-08: Increased capacity in the African Union (AU) and sub-regional security organisations to manage peacekeeping missions.

- HMG support remains instrumental in helping the African Union (AU) develop the African Standby Force (ASF). Key conceptual ASF documentation was agreed in October 2006.

- Progress towards the AU's target of five regional brigades remains uneven. HMG top priorities are the West (ECOWAS – the Economic Community of West African States) which is making good progress, and the East (EASBRIG – the East African Standby Brigade) which in January took an important step forward by creating a new political umbrella body. Short-term crisis response on Darfur and Somalia is necessarily affecting AU prioritisation, diverting resources from long-term ASF development.

- HMG continues to make major contributions to expanding the pool of trained African peacekeeping personnel (some 11,000 African personnel since 2004).

Annex D

Performance Management

Since 2000, the strategic management of the MoD has been underpinned and facilitated by the Defence Balanced Scorecard. At the highest conceptual level, the Defence Balanced Scorecard is a framework that helps the Defence Management Board (DMB) translate strategy into operational objectives that drive both behaviour and performance. This is articulated in the Departmental Plan that sets out the Department's top level strategic objectives, including its Public Service Agreement (PSA) targets. The Defence Balanced Scorecard tells the Board how well the Department is doing in terms of the objectives that underpin the Plan and thus provides insight into its ability to achieve the Defence Vision.

The first Balanced Scorecards were devised for private sector bodies. As a public sector organisation, with outputs not expressed in financial terms, the Department has adapted the model to reflect better the nature of defence. Accordingly, the four perspectives of the Defence Balanced Scorecard (Purpose, Resources, Enabling Processes and Future Capabilities) summarise the breadth of defence activity and cover the MoD's main areas of business;. This Balanced Scorecard for 2006-07 is at Figure 10 below.

Figure 10 Defence Balanced Scorecard 2006/07

Purpose

Are we fit for today's challenges and ready for tomorrow's tasks?

Current Operations: To succeed in Operations and Military Tasks today.
Future Operations: Be ready for the tasks of tomorrow.
Policy: Work with allies, other Governments and multilateral institutions to provide a security framework that matches new threats and instabilities.
Wider Government: Contribute to the Government's wider domestic reform agenda, and achieve our PSA and PPA targets

Resources

Are we using our resources to best effect?

Finance: Maximise our outputs within allocated financial resources.
Manpower: Ensure we have the people we need.
Estate: Maintain an estate of the right size and quality, managed in a sustainable manner to achieve defence objectives.
Reputation: Enhance our reputation amongst our own people and externally.

Defending the United Kingdom and its interests: acting as a force for good in the world

Enabling Processes

Are we a high performing organisation?

Personnel: Manage and invest in our people to give of their best.
Health and Safety: A safe environment for our staff, contractors and visitors.
Logistics: Support and sustain our Armed Forces.
Business Management: Deliver improved ways of working.

Future Capabilities

Are we building for future success?

Future Force Effects: More flexible Armed Forces to deliver greater effect.
Efficiency and Change: More flexible and efficient organisations and processes to support the Armed Forces.
Future Capabilities and Infrastructure: Progress future equipment and capital infrastructure projects to time, quality and cost estimates.
Future Personnel Plans: Develop the skills and professional expertise we need for tomorrow.
Science Innovation and Technology: Exploit new technologies.

There are a number of strategic objectives in each perspective – and 17 in total. Performance against each of the objectives is assessed on a quarterly basis. Against each objective, targets setting out required levels of performance are agreed and those in the Department who are responsible for achieving the objectives – for delivery. Detailed performance indicators and metrics are also agreed. The Performance Indicators are a mixture of lag indicators (which inform the Board about actual achievements) and lead indicators (which are used to encourage difference behaviours). Assessments may be quantitative or qualitative, and will either be provided by objective sources or subjected to lower level scrutiny and audit – by Front Line Commands or the Resources and Plans Directorates, for example. Agreeing the objectives, targets, performance indicators and metrics is an annual exercise, conducted prior to the publication of the Departmental Plan.

The DMB receives a detailed performance report four times a year. For each objective in the Departmental Plan, the report will include an assessment of actual performance from the previous and current quarter, and a forecast of performance at the end of the next three to four financial years. Analysis of the issues highlighted by the performance assessments included in the report, together with an assessment of the key risks that could jeopardise the achievement of objectives. In addition to the new Strategic Risk process established by the Defence Management Board during 2006-07 (see paragraphs 271-272 under *Business Management*) a 'bottom up' risk picture is presented associating individual risks with particular objectives from the Departmental Plan. This is drawn from the Risk Register consolidated from those maintained by TLBs and Process Owners. The information, and assessments, that the DMB receive are used to inform board discussion and decision – they may, for example, support decisions to adjust strategic direction and priorities, or the reallocation of resources. And as the Department's performance against PSA targets is assessed in the Defence Balanced Scorecard, the assessments are also used to inform reports to Parliament, No 10, HM Treasury and the Cabinet Office.

The Department's approach, and the data systems underpinning it, have been subject to continuing review, in 2002 by the Department's internal auditors, and in 2003-04 and 2006-07 by the National Audit Office for the 2002 and 2004 Spending Review PSA data systems respectively. The December 2006 *Third Validation Compendium Report* on the quality of data systems underpinning the 2004 Spending Review Public Service Agreements was generally positive about the Department's data systems, none of which were assessed as 'not fit for purpose'. And it found no weaknesses in the quality of disclosure in the Department's public performance reports.

In addition, in June 2005 the NAO published a report on the Department's arrangements for assessing and reporting military readiness following an extensive review which concluded that the Department had a good and continuously improving system for reporting readiness; and in October 2005 the NAO published a report on Joint Targets, including the Joint Target for Conflict Prevention shared by MoD, FCO and DfID.

More specifically:

- On **Operations** (PSA target 1) the Department provides a periodic and formal overall assessment through its Public Service Agreement and Annual Performance Reports. These assessments are underpinned by an appropriate and robust system for judging performance on operations and military tasks against the objectives established by Ministers. Further details are set out in the Department's supplementary memorandum to the House of Commons Defence Committee, published in its report on the MoD Annual Report and Accounts 2005-06 (HC57 dated 28 November 2006). In the *Third Validation Compendium Report* the NAO concluded that the data system is fit for the purpose of measuring and reporting performance" against this target;

- on **Conflict Prevention** (PSA target 2, joint with FCO and DfID) the NAO concluded in the *Third Validation Compendium Report* that the data system addressed the majority of risks to data quality, but needed strengthening to ensure that remaining risks were adequately concerned. In particular, the processes for assessing performance needed to be documented more clearly. The report noted that procedures had been put in place to address this. The results were reflected in the relevant Departmental Spring Performance Reports;

- on **Readiness** (PSA target 3) the National Audit Office found in its 2005 report on *Assessing and Reporting Military Readiness* that the Department has a good system for defining, measuring and reporting the readiness of the Armed Forces which compares well with those used by other countries. It noted that the readiness reporting system is continuously evolving to incorporate further improvements. In the *Third Validation Compendium Report* it concluded that while broadly fit for purpose the PSA readiness reporting system should be further strengthened, primarily to establish a system to report performance against the ability to deploy, sustain and recover the Armed Forces. This work has now concluded and the results are set out at paragraph 49 and table 5 in the Annual Report and Accounts;

- on **European Security** (PSA target 4, joint with FCO) the NAO concluded in the *Third Validation Compendium Report* that, as with conflict prevention, the compilation and assessment process needed to be documented more thoroughly to ensure consistency of judgment over time. Further work has since been done to address this point;

- on **Manning Balance** (PSA target 5) the NAO concluded in the *Third Validation Compendium Report* that the data system was fit for the purpose of measuring and reporting performance; and

- on **Equipment Procurement** (PSA target 6), the NAO's annual *Major Projects Report* covers cost, time and performance data for a sample of large projects. The Comptroller and Auditor General also validated performance against the Defence Procurement Agency's key targets, which include the PSA data set. The NAO concluded in the *Third Validation Compendium Report* that the data system was fit for the purpose of measuring and reporting performance.

Additionally, the financial data underpinning assessment of the 2004 efficiency target ultimately derives from the Departmental Resource Accounts, which are Audited by the NAO. Defence Internal Audit validates logistics efficiency data every year, and in 2006-07 also reviewed the efficiencies achieved by the People Programme. These reports are visible to the NAO. The NAO itself conducted a wider review of the Government's efficiency programme during the year (*The Efficiency Programme: A Second Review of Progress*). This included reporting on a number of the programmes within the defence efficiency programme, and specifically cited as an example of good practice the comprehensive auditing framework established to assess efficiencies arising from the Defence Logistics Transformation Programme (which comprises some 40% of the Department's efficiency programme by value).

The Department's approach to strategic management and performance continues to attract interest from wider audiences, including other Government Departments, local authorities, and other nations' Ministries or Departments of Defence. In addition, MoD performance managers are regularly invited to address and take part in international strategic and performance management symposia. This interaction provides the opportunity to share ideas and pick up examples of good practice from others than can help improve the strategic management of the Department.

Annex E

Defence Agency Performance

Name	Overall performance Number and % of targets achieved			Year on year performance – number and % of targets met which were directly comparable with the previous year		Relative performance against comparable targets in 05/06 (better/same/worse)
	06/07	05/06	04/05	06/07	05/06	
Armed Forces Personnel Administration Agency	8/9 89%	9/10 90%	8/8 100%	5/6 83%	7/8 88%	1/3/2
British Forces Post Office[2]	4/6 66%	6/6 100%	6/7 86%	4/6 50%	5/5 100%	1/3/2
Defence Analytical Services Agency	10/12 83%	8/10 80%	8/8 100%	8/9 89%	4/5 80%	3/6/0
Defence Bills Agency[2]	7/7 100%	6/6 100%	6/6 100%	3/3 100%	6/6 100%	2/0/1
Defence Communication Services Agency[2]	5/5 100%	5/5 100%	6/7 86%	5/5 100%	4/4 100%	3/0/2
Defence Estates[2]	15/22 68%	15/22 68%	10/15 67%	10/11 91%	4/6 67%	9/1/1
Defence Medical Education and Training Agency	4/6 67%80%	3/6 50%	5/7 71%	4/6 67%80%	3/5 60%	2/2/2
Defence Procurement Agency[2]	7/7 100%	7/7 100%	7/8 88%	7/7 100%	7/7 100%	6/0/1
Defence Storage and Distribution Agency	6/6 100%	6/6 100%	6/6 100%	6/6 100%	6/6 100%	1/0/5
Defence Transport and Movements Agency[2]	6/6 100%	5/6 83%	5/6 83%	6/6 100%	5/6 83%	2/3/1
Defence Vetting Agency	8/9 89%	11/16 69%	6/12 50%	7/8 88%	9/13 69%	5/0/3
Disposal Services Agency[2]	6/6 100%	5/6 83%	5/6[12] 83%	4/4 100%	2/2 100%	3/0/1
Duke of York's Royal Military School[2]	5/6 83%	4/6 67%	5/8 63%	4/5 78%	2/4 50%	1/1/3
MoD Police and Guarding Agency	4/10 40%	3/8 38%	4/9[22] 44%	1/3 33%	0/4 0%	2/1/1
People, Pay and Pensions Agency	8/9 89%	8/8 100%	9/9[32] 100%	5/6 83%	3/3 100%	3/0/3
Service Children's Education	25/30[3] 83%	27/34 79%	18/34 53%	25/30 83%	25/32 78%	12/3/15
Veterans Agency	8/8 100%	7/7 100%	7/7 100%	6/6 100%	6/6 100%	4/0/2

[1] Where there are multiple elements to a target, these have been counted separately.
[2] Agency status removed 1 April 07
[3] Performance against one key target cannot be measured since the Department for Children, Schools and Families have not issued Key Stage 3 ICT Performance figures due to data collection problems.

Organisational changes

The Armed Forces Personnel Administration Agency (AFPAA) merged with the Veterans Agency on 1 April 2007 to form the Service Personnel and Veterans Agency. On the same date agency status was removed from eight defence Agencies. The majority of these changes were a consequence of the creation of the Defence Equipment and Support organisation.

Armed Forces Pay and Administration Agency

The roll out of Joint Personnel Administration (JPA) has been a significant milestone in the history of AFPAA and Service Personnel Management. For the first time individual service men and women across the Armed Forces have direct access to personnel administration services and an enquiry centre through improved processes and new technology. The Armed Forces' morale and hence operational effectiveness depends in part on the Agency's continued ability to deliver a quality service that relieves individuals of administrative worries and distractions.

The JPA project, coupled with the decision to merge the agency with the Veterans Agency on 1 April 2007, resulted in an intense level of activity and a significant strain on its resources. These two major activities did not prevent AFPAA continuing successfully to deliver a wide range of customer services to a high standard.

The agency met all but one of its key targets and sub-elements, narrowly missing the target relating to JPA target costs, mainly because of the need to adjust the programme to match the realigned Defence Information Infrastructure programme upon which JPA depends.

British Forces Post Office

The Agency has focussed its efforts towards both maintaining and enhancing the effective and efficient distribution of mail to deployed personnel. Stringent performance targets challenged BFPO during a period of increased deployment of personnel to Afghanistan and little reduction to commitments in Iraq. The Agency missed Key Target (KT) three, related to delivery of Official mail in the UK due to manpower shortages. This perversely caused BFPO to narrowly fail against KT four, relating to transit times for the delivery and collection at Defence Mail Centres. Notwithstanding these KT failures, BFPO's customers continue to be fully satisfied with the quality of service provided by the Agency.

The impending relocation of the agency has also been a high priority. Greater automation and new working practices will allow BFPO to maximise the potential of the new building and to further improve the service provided to the defence community.

Defence Analytical Services Agency

Overall performance has been high with excellent performance against Service Level Agreements, Project Agreements, the production of National Statistics and in the Customer Satisfaction Survey. However the Agency missed one element of a Key Target on timeliness in answering PQs which was beyond the Agency's control and one element of another target that related to the provision of consultancy service.

There have also been difficulties in the provision of Service manpower data and some outputs have had to be suspended. The Agency is continuing to work towards resolving the JPA manpower data problems, so that the full advantages of the system in terms of improved information can be realised.

DASA's Information Strategy was approved by its Owners Advisory Board in October 2006, setting the framework for DASA to move coherently towards its goal of being the information provider of choice within the Department.

Defence Bills Agency

This was the last year of operation for the DBA prior to the removal of Agency status, which was precipitated by the advent of MoD's new Financial Management Shared Service Centre (FM SSC), of which the DBA will form a part. Throughout the period overall performance was strong with the Agency meeting all of its key targets. The Order to Cash accounts receivable processes continue to develop with stronger links forged with the Top Level Budget organisations. In addition the DBA has continued to contribute to the Purchase to Pay project, an involvement which will ensure that the systems and processes, when delivered, will be a better fit for the new FM SSC business.

Defence Communication Services Agency

This was the last year of the DCSA and saw the Agency meet and exceed all its key targets whilst continuing the development of a number of important projects that enables the defence community to meet the Defence Vision. Support to the Armed Forces military and peacekeeping operations is a key Agency output and this high level of performance has been maintained within the context of continuing increased demand for the essential information services provided by the Agency. This activity is worldwide and involves the deployment of complex military and commercial solutions in response to the operational tempo of supporting operations. The Agency remained at the hub of all defence-wide programmes operating in a time of challenging Defence Budgets and it was the Agency's top priority to deliver continuing performance improvement

Defence Estates

Details relating to Defence Estates can be found at paragraphs 315-339.

Defence Medical Education and Training Agency

DMETA continued to train and prepare secondary care personnel to meet the Commanders' in Chief requirements to support deployed operations and exercises. Adjustments were made to manage both the increased operational tempo and the numbers of casualties being repatriated to the UK. This has required expansion of clinical and supporting activities in Selly Oak Hospital, Birmingham, a new task, accomplished by reorganisation and enhancement of the Royal Centre for Defence Medicine and the Defence Medical Rehabilitation Centre at Headley Court.

Despite uncertainty over the application process for medical training, DMETA secured training places for all medical officers selected for entry into specialist training. All Nurse and Allied Health Professionals' training has now relocated to the Defence School of Secondary Health Care in Birmingham, where uniformed graduates achieve consistently higher numbers of distinctions than their civilian peers. However the agency missed two Key Targets, relating to individual military continuation training and customer satisfaction after the targets had been increased from previous year.

Defence Storage and Distribution Agency

2006-07 was an extremely busy year for the Agency. It had to deliver the savings stipulated by the Future Defence Supply Chain Initiative whilst maintaining service levels and working towards a routine seven day supply chain for Issue of Materiel by October 2007. It delivered successfully against its extremely tough Key Targets, whilst reducing the manpower, budgetary and location footprints. Against a manpower target of 4729 posts, there were 4562 filled posts as at 1 March 2007, an overachievement of 167.

The Agency has maintained the very high customer service levels in its Explosive Business Area whilst delivering a tenfold increase in the volume of munitions delivered to operational theatres. For the Non Explosive Business Area (NEBA) the Agency successfully achieved routine delivery within twelve days with an ever-reducing resource and is on course to achieve the seven day target by October 2007. In the NEBA receipt activity was 4% more than forecast by customers. Whilst Issue activity was 6.8% less than forecast, the number of high priority demands requiring far quicker processing increased significantly from July 2006.

Defence Transport and Movements Agency

The past year has again followed the very high operational tempo of the previous four and has been exceptionally busy and demanding. Support to operations has remained DTMA's focus, with sustainment and roulement of forces deployed to Iraq and Afghanistan continuing at high levels and requiring significant planning and management. The extensive overseas exercise programme and support to overseas garrisons, has increased the demands placed on the Agency and its staff.

DTMA has also been actively engaged in a number of key projects: firstly replacement of existing processes for aircraft tasking with a new system (Boeing Operational Control System), which spans the complete airlift process for inputting airlift bids. Secondly, the implementation of the Defence Travel project, which aims to improve the way the MoD books travel through the introduction of an on-line self-booking facility. Initial Operating Capability was achieved for the Defence Travel Modernisation Organisation, who will be responsible for the implementation of the Defence Travel project, in December 06. All DTMA Key Targets have been met with transactions and services successfully provided within agreed Time, Quality, Quantity and Cost.

Defence Vetting Agency

The Agency delivered successfully against its Key Targets, exceeding against eight targets or sub-targets and narrowly missing the ninth (relating to completion of developed vetting cases) by 1%. Another notable achievement was the award of Charter Mark accreditation in recognition of the level of customer service it provides. The DVA's reputation for providing a quality vetting product continued to attract new repayment business from other Government Departments, which increased by some 30% over the previous year. Working closely with the Cabinet Office, the Agency is also moving forward on its strategy to become a Shared Services provider for national security vetting and be recognised as the lead authority across government on security vetting process and risk based assessment of cases.

Disposal Services Agency

This was another successful year in which the DSA achieved all its Key Targets and secured £84M in gross sales income. Two ex-Royal Navy Type 23 frigates were handed over to the Chilean Navy with very positive media impact. The DESO/DSA Joint Venture Agreement formula proved very successful in addressing key support issues for Type 23 frigates and future export opportunities. Regeneration work on HMS Sandown was overseen by the Agency prior to handover to Estonia. A UK Submarine Rescue System agreement was signed with James Fisher Defence Ltd and a Memorandum of Agreement with BAES.

DSA was increasingly involved in disposals activities in ten overseas locations including Iraq and Afghanistan. Overall Customer Satisfaction remains high at 94% and the Agency successfully launched its new online auction functionality. The website experienced a period of intense activity and at its peak was processing 500 new users every hour. The use of credit card payments (another first for the DSA) will be built upon during the coming year.

Duke of York's Royal Military School

The school ceased to be an Agency on 1 April 2007. During the year it sustained its good performance both academically and financially. Although failed to meet one sub-target relating to the generation of income, that was due to factors beyond its control. There was continuing high performance at GCSE, an increased performance at A level and an increased percentage of high grades achieved. The school continues to provide extremely good value for money and a dynamic high quality education for service children, with results well above national averages.

Ministry of Defence Police and Guarding Agency

This has been a challenging year for the Agency to continue to deliver an effective policing and guarding service to the MoD estate in a climate of increased budget restrictions and where a major gap in Agency finances had been identified. Work is on going to close this with assistance from customers and stakeholders. The Agency continues to deliver a professional policing and guarding service to the defence estate in support of the Defence Mission and wider MoD objectives. It met four of its targets and sub-elements in full and another relating to efficiency in part. The

crime detection rate increased substantially from 39% to 72%, whilst customer satisfaction also increased markedly, although falling short of the target. The agency also missed its targets on the delivery of agreed customer tasking and recruitment from ethnic communities. Increasing the diversity of MDP officers will continue to be a priority.

People, Pay and Pensions Agency

This was the first full year of operation for the PPPA which was launched in April 2006, building on the previous Pay and Personnel Agency. The Agency met all its targets and sub-elements, other than one related to average timeliness for salary payments, expenses payments and pensions awards. It has continued to deliver already established services such as salary and expenses payments and pensions awards while introducing new shared HR services. These services included internal recruitment, welfare, early retirement, redundancy, and the MoD outplacement scheme. Other successes have included the successful delivery of the Band B and Band D Assessment Centres. Customer satisfaction for pay and pensions services have continued to rise and the Agency is now in the top quartile of similar businesses providing services to internal customers. Satisfaction in new services is much lower, but this is not unexpected at this stage of a radical shared services programme. Further improvements have been made to hardware platforms, software and power supply with significant improvements in performance and resilience.

Service Children's Education

The Agency performed particularly well against its Key Targets. Key Target one, which compares the performance of SCE students against the English National Average, saw eleven of the twelve sub-elements across Key Stages 1-3 met or exceeded, the target for GCSE results narrowly missed and 97% of A-Level entries exceeding the level required. SCE continued to compare extremely favourably with Local Education Authorities in the UK (Key Target two), being notionally placed at 15th, 15th and 8th (of 150) in Key Stages 1-3 respectively. The Agency again improved its performance in supporting students at the higher level of attainment (Key Target three), meeting or exceeding the national performance level in nine of the twelve sub-targets. Although performance against Key Target four improved from 2005-06, it narrowly failed (by less than two points) to match the level of improvement in the UK. However the small SCE cohort produces a disproportionate impact on overall Agency performance at this level. The final Key Target confirmed that parental satisfaction with SCE at its schools remains exceptionally high at 90% of respondents.

Veterans Agency

The Veterans Agency achieved all its Key Targets. Notable achievements included further reducing appeals clearance time from 217 days in 2005-06 to 207 days in conjunction with the Department of Constitutional Affairs Court Services, and reducing the average time for claims to war pension by a further 5.8% to 49 working days. The Agency also worked in partnership with AFPAA in preparation for their merger on 1 April 2007, ensuring a smooth transition to a single Agency and some improvements to services.

Trading Funds

Table 32 Defence Trading Fund Performance

Name	Overall Performance Number and % of targets achieved			Year on Year Performance – number and % of targets met which were directly comparable with the previous year		Relative performance against comparable targets in 05/06 (better/ same/worse)
	06/07	05/06	04/05	06/07	05/06	
ABRO	4/5 80%	4/5 80%	3/5 60%	4/5 80%	3/4 75%	4/1/0
Defence Aviation Repair Agency (DARA)	4/4 100%	3/4 75%	5/5 100%	3/3 100%	1/2 50%	1/1/1
Defence Science and Technology Laboratory (DSTL)	5/6 83%	8/10 80%	7/7 100%	4/5 80%	4/5 80%	2/3/0
Met Office	4/4 100%	5/5 100%	3/6[1] 50%	2/2 100%	1/1 100%	2/0/0
UK Hydrographic Office (UKHP)	3/6 50%	3/6 50%	4/6 67%	3/5 60%	2/4 50%	2/0/2

Notes:
1. Previously reported as 4/7 because two sub-elements had been counted independently

ABRO

ABRO is the defence engineering business that provides repair, re-manufacture and engineering of land based equipment in support of the UK Armed Forces.

2006-07 has been a challenging year for ABRO both by responding to the challenges created by current operations as well as reacting to changes in the defence industry driven by the modernisation of logistics support to the front line.

An extensive programme for the in-depth repair and upgrade of the FV430 fleet was announced by the MoD in March 2006, resulting in substantial additional work for ABRO's armoured vehicle repair centre at Bovington. ABRO's other armoured vehicle centre at Donnington, successfully met customer demands for support to the Warrior and Combat Vehicle Reconnaissance (Tracked) fleets. The one-stop shop service that ABRO provides the Armed Forces continued to meet customer demands for repair and maintenance across the full range of land based equipments both from its own (ABRO's) current workshops and an increasing number of in-barracks support locations.

ABRO has performed well this year, achieving revenues of £137.2M (2005-06: £137M) and delivered four of its five Key Targets. Net profit achieved was £4M and the Return on Capital Employed was 7.1%.

ABRO continues in its role within the MoD/BAES Land System Partnering Agreement and is developing wider partnerships with other key defence Original Equipment Manufactures both in the UK and overseas.

Looking to the future, ABRO must position itself securely in the wider maintenance, repair and overhaul market while improving effectiveness and efficiency so that value for money performance against tight deadlines is best in class.

Defence Aviation Repair Agency

DARA provides deep level maintenance, repair and overhaul services for military aircraft, systems and components. As a Trading Fund, it also has freedom to compete for other commercial work. The MoD defence-related work accounts for the vast majority of DARA's revenue, either directly with the MoD or as a sub-contractor to defence Original Equipment Manufacturers. A key objective of DARA is to provide a responsive, flexible and highly competitive service to the UK Armed Forces.

Following the Ministerial announcement in February 2006 about the future of DARA's six businesses, DARA has closed the Fast Jet business at St Athan and the Engines business at Fleetlands on time and to budget. This was due, in some significant part, to the constructive relationship DARA has with its various Trades Unions. Working closely with them, DARA was able to keep compulsory redundancies to a minimum and meet the needs and aspirations of as many employees as possible through voluntary means. Many employees took up opportunities to retrain for posts in other areas of DARA while others were able to secure positions in the wider MoD and in other Government Departments.

Work continues to determine whether sale of DARA's Rotary and Components businesses will offer MoD best value for defence and better long-term prospects for the business and their employees.

The merger of DARA's remaining business (Electronic and Large Aircraft (VC10)) was announced in a Ministerial statement on 22 May 2007 and work is underway to develop a unified support group. Formal TUs consultations commenced on 24 May 2007 and are due to end 6 July 2007.

Notwithstanding the backdrop of closure and uncertainty, DARA has achieved all its Key Targets for the period and has turned in a solid business performance. This is attributable and testament to the professionalism and pride of the DARA workforce who continue to play an important role supporting the front line.

Defence Science and Technology Laboratory

DSTL's core role is to provide independent, objective, high quality, scientific, analytical, technological and engineering advice and services to the MoD and UK Armed Forces. It carries out only work which must be done in Government. Its mission is to create the winning edge for the UK Forces and Government through the best use of science and technology, by delivering timely advice and solutions to the Government's most important defence and national security related problems in the most efficient and effective manner.

Although turnover rose from £353M during 2006-07 to £367M, this was entirely due to one large contract handled on behalf of the US DoD. Excluding Ploughshare, net profit for DSTL increased slightly from £22.6M in 2006-07 to £22.8M and ROCE fell from 9.1% to 7.9% over the same period, both remained ahead of expectations following the cut in DSTL's margin on ascertained cost contracts; this was mainly due to delays in the iLab programme where costs have slipped into the next year coupled to ongoing internal efficiencies. Manpower change rates continued to be held below the target for the sixth consecutive year, indicating a reduction in real terms of the cost to customers.

As well as achieving the ROCE target, DSTL achieved all but one of its other five Key Targets. The targets on delivering high quality outputs and achieving a high score for scientific and technical capability in technical benchmarking were comfortably achieved, as were the in-year milestones aimed at bringing DSTL onto three sites by 2009, and at ensuring DSTL has an integrated corporate business environment in place by the end of 2008-09. The customer satisfaction target was not achieved; however, 29% of customers surveyed reported that DSTL's level of service had increased and only 7% felt that it had decreased. Priority areas for improvement have been identified and are reflected both in action plans and in an additional Key Target for the coming year.

DSTL's wholly owned technology management company, Ploughshare Innovations Ltd, successfully completed its second full year of operations. Nine new licence agreements have been signed since Ploughshare was formed and a further 20 agreements are under negotiation. Income from licence agreements has more than doubled in two years. The first sale of a spin-out company (Acolyte Biomedia Ltd to the £M Corporation) has taken place.

Looking to the future, DSTL will be seeking to develop its partnerships with the new Defence Equipment and Support organisation, other customers, industry and science and technology providers, in the context of the Defence Industrial Strategy and the Defence Technology Strategy, while continuing to invest in DSTL's future capabilities. The strategic integrated laboratory improvement programme 'i lab' remains a key enabler to this, with the most significant issues over the next three years being (a) to rationalise the DSTL estate to three core sites in order to maximise synergy and coherence of delivery to customers, and to reduce unnecessary duplication in laboratories, facilities and support functions, and (b) to ensure DSTL has in place an integrated corporate business environment by the end of 2008-09. These themes are reflected in DSTL's new Key Targets.

Met Office

2006-07 was another very successful year at the Met Office in which it met all of its Key Performance Targets (KPT) for the second year running. It has also been an important year for clarifying its vision and strategic direction. In 2006-07 it published a new vision, 'making our forecasts essential to everyone, every day' and outlined its strategic direction in 'Shaping our Future' which accompanies an updated Corporate Plan 2007–2011.

The role and future direction of the Met Office were scrutinised in-year by the House of Commons Defence Committee which underlined the importance of its public task, including its work in support of defence and the wider priorities of Government. It also drew attention to the Met Office's international reputation for scientific excellence in weather forecasting and climate research and the importance of its commercial performance.

The Met Office continued to play a major role in informing Governments, businesses and individuals of the range of possible outcomes of climate change, underpinned by climate research and prediction studies carried out at the Met Office Hadley Centre. The world leading reputation of the Hadley Centre was confirmed in an independent review commissioned by Defra and MoD which concluded, amongst other things, that: "It is beyond dispute that the Met Office Hadley Centre occupies a position at the pinnacle of world climate science and in translating that science into policy advice'. The major contribution made by the Met Office Hadley Centre both to the Stern Review and the Intergovernmental Panel on Climate Change Fourth Assessment Report, are two examples of just how vital and high-profile its climate prediction work now is.

There were also notable advances in Numerical Weather Prediction (NWP). The Met Office ensemble forecasting system was developed to provide uncertainty estimates for short-range forecasts. The Met Office also introduced a new NWP model for the North Atlantic and Europe that has helped improve the accuracy of weather forecasts for the UK, as reflected in the achievement of the challenging KPT for forecast accuracy.

Turnover in 2006-07 was £171.0M compared to £170.4M in 2005-6. Whilst the Met Office had a good trading year with operating profit improvements and a reduction in interest charges, exceptional costs increased leading to a slight decrease in profit before dividend from £9.5M in 2005-06 to £8.8M. Profit from commercial activities rose significantly from £2.8M in 2006-07 to £3.9M in 2006-07. ROCE decreased from 5.3% in 2005-06 to 4.0%, but remained Return on Capital Employed above the 3.5% target.

The future for the Met Office is one of responsibility, opportunity and challenge. Ongoing responsibility to provide essential day-to-day weather forecasts; exploiting new opportunities by packaging its weather and climate change science in a way that is meaningful to customers; and responding to the challenge of staying ahead in a growing marketplace by continuing to offer world-class science, customer focus and service excellence.

UK Hydrographic Office

The UKHO has four Top Level Objectives:

- Operational Support to defence

- Support to the UK's 'Safety of Life at Sea' treaty Obligations

- Developing profitable business streams

- Organisational Excellence

UKHO's vision is "to remain the world leader in the supply of marine navigational information and services". The navigational and other products and services provided to the defence customer, primarily the Royal Navy, are crucial to the conduct of operations globally. The UKHO also plays a central role, in support of the Maritime and Coastguard Agency, in discharging the UK's obligations under the UN Safety of Life at Sea convention – such as by providing charting of UK waters. It has built up a significant commercial business; supplying navigational charts, publications and other services with world-wide coverage to mariners.

The UKHO has had another very successful year's trading and continues to provide excellent support to the Defence Customer. Net profit of £7.5M (£9.9M 2005-06) and ROCE of 12.2% (17.2% 2005-06) were ahead of target. Return on Commercial sales were strong, with income growth in both paper and digital.

Mike Robinson took over as Chief Executive in July 2006. He has refocused the Agency's commercial strategy on its core market, the Merchant Marine, and in particular on positioning for the transition from paper to digital navigation. The role of Chief Executive had previously been combined with that of National Hydrographer. On his appointment, the roles were split. Rear Admiral Ian Moncrieff has been appointed National Hydrographer and takes the lead on developing the relationships with the UKHO's international partners, on whom it is largely dependant for data supply to support the world-wide series. The UKHO's top priorities remain support for defence and discharging SOLAS obligations.

Further information

Further details on Trading Funds can be found in individual Trading Fund annual reports and accounts at:

- ABRO – www.abrodev.co.uk;
- DARA – www.daranet.co.uk;
- DSTL – www.dstl.gov.uk;
- Met Office – www.met-office.gov.uk;
- UKHO – www.ukho.gov.uk

Annex F

Government Standards

Fraud

The MoD emphasis on the deterrence and detection of irregularity, including fraud, theft and corruption was augmented during the year by the introduction of the Defence Irregularity Reporting Cell. This cell, jointly supported by the MoD Police Fraud Squad, the Defence Fraud Analysis Unit (DFAU) and the Defence Estates Fraud Prevention Unit, now acts as the central point for the reporting and recording of all suspicions and the allocation of these to the appropriate investigative authorities including line management. It also monitors to conclusion the progress of investigations, including those separately identified and handled by Service Police authorities under Service reporting procedures. This simplification of reporting procedures, which provides for whistleblowing disclosure, will become fully effective during 2007-08. It is thought, however, to have already contributed during the year to the identification of a record number of 421 suspicions with an estimated value of £0.68M compared to 382 cases valued at £1.65M in the previous year. Full publicity was given to the new process and incorporated in a pan-MoD programme of 68 presentations to an aggregate audience of 4793 staff conducted by the DFAU. The recorded increase in suspicions includes significant rises in the volume of cases involving travel and subsistence claims and in personnel management cases such as abuse of flexi-time or leave and sick related incidents. Following earlier endorsement by PUS and CDS of the Departmental policy of zero tolerance regarding irregularity, including fraud, theft and corruption, a revised and updated Departmental policy statement has been prepared for issue in May 2007.

Bill Payment

This was the last year of operation for the Defence Bills Agency (DBA) prior to the removal of Agency status which was precipitated by the advent of MoD's new Financial Management Shared Service Centre (FM SSC), of which the DBA will form a part. Throughout the period overall performance was strong with the Agency meeting all of its Key Targets. The Order to Cash accounts receivable processes continue to develop with stronger links forged with the Top Level Budget organisations. In addition, DBA has continued to contribute to the Purchase to Pay project, an involvement which will ensure that the systems and processes, when delivered, will be a better fit for the new FM SSC business.

Table 33 Bill Paying Performance – Proportion of Bills Settled within Thirty Calendar Days

	2006-07		2005-06	
	Target	Achieved	Target	Achieved
Defence Bills Agency	99.9% (within 11 days)	99.9% 5,268,462 invoices representing £20.79B	99.9% (within 11 days)	99.9% 5,621,028 invoices representing £20.18B
ABRO	100%	95% 74,237 invoices representing £80.6M	100%	96% 70,959 invoices representing £74.2M
Defence Aviation Repair Agency	100%	96% 14,305 invoices representing £146.4M	100%	96.38% 14,922 invoices representing £165.4M
Defence Science and Technology laboratory	98%	98.23% 32,893 invoices representing £204.13M	98%	98.4% 36,742 invoices representing £238.5M
Met Office	99%	99.55% 12,722 invoices representing £68.774M	99%	99.48% 12,689 invoices representing £57.909M
UK Hydrographic Office	100%	98.4% 14,382 invoices representing £46.9M	100%	98.8% 12,998 invoices representing £48.6M

Open Government

Freedom of Information

During 2006-07, the MoD continued to attract more requests for information than any other Central Government Department. The operating procedures designed for the introduction of the FOI Act in January 2005 were reviewed and strengthened as necessary in the light of the first full year's experience. The internal guidance available to MoD staff was revised and developed to reflect the evolving guidance issued by the Information Commissioner and the Ministry of Justice (then the Department of Constitutional Affairs). The Access to Information Toolkit, which provides a facility to monitor and manage FOI requests to some 1000 users across the MoD, was upgraded and improved. The Department's formal training programme has also been revised and updated in response to policy and procedural changes, and to users' requirements.

The MoD website has been developed to make it easier to submit FOI requests for information to the Department electronically. The Publication Scheme has been extended with new Classes of Information added. The MoD actively participated in the Information Commissioner's workshops on further development of the Publication Scheme.

Table 34 Requests for information under the Freedom of Information Act in Financial Year 2006/2007

Category	MoD Performance	Total for Government Departments
Number of requests received	3185	17754
Of these:		
% of requests answered within 20 working days	83%	80%
% of requests answered 'in time' (1)	88%	90%
% of requests that were late	12%	10%
Total of 'resolvable' requests (2)	2658	13282
Of these:		
% of resolvable requests where information was granted in full	70%	60%
% of resolvable requests where information was withheld in full	11%	19%

Notes:
(1) 'In time' means that the timescale for response has been extended under the terms of section 10 of the FOI Act 2005.
(2) 'Resolvable requests' are those were it is possible to provide a substantive response. They exclude requests which are lapsed or on hold, where information was not held, and where it was necessary to provide advice and assistance since in each of these cases it would not have been possible to resolve the request in the form it was asked.

Asbestos Contaminated Files

Work to re-establish access to the information contained in records affected by asbestos contamination in the Old War Office Building continued in 2006-2007. The full scale project to reconstitute the records, which commenced in December 2005, was extended by six months when it became apparent that the affected records contained more pages than expected; work is now due to be completed in early 2008. Following successful scanning, the original files are being destroyed in accordance with both security and health and safety regulations. FOI requests that have been frustrated because of the asbestos contamination are being answered in date-of-receipt order as reconstituted records become available.

Transfer of Files to The National Archives

The routine review and transfer of records to The National Archives (TNA) has continued. In 2006-2007 over 8,200 files were reviewed and released to general access. In addition, MoD has continued to support TNA in dealing with FOI requests for files that are held by TNA but not available to the public.

Ministerial Correspondence

Ministry of Defence Ministers and Agency Chief Executives' Performance in Replying to correspondence from Members of Parliament, Members of Devolved Legislatures, Members of the European Parliament, and Peers.

Table 35: Requests for Information under the Freedom of Information Act between 1 April 2006 and 31 March 2007

	Target set for despatch (working days)	Number of letters received for answer	Percentage of replies within target
Ministry of Defence (excluding Defence Agencies)	15	6,797	50
Defence Agencies/Trading Funds			
ABRO	15	2	100
Armed Forces Personnel Administration Agency[1]	15	145	97
British Forces Post Office[2]	15	-	-
Defence Analytical Services Agency	15	-	-
Defence Aviation Repair Agency	15	3	100
Defence Bills Agency[2]	10	-	-
Defence Communication Services Agency[3]	15	-	-
Defence Estates	15	2	100
Defence Medical Education and Training Agency	15	-	-
Defence Procurement Agency	15	-	-
Dstl	15	1	100
Defence Storage and Distribution Agency	15	-	-
Defence Transport and Movements Agency[4]	15	-	-
Defence Vetting Agency[5]	7	2	100
Disposal Services Agency	15	-	-
Duke of York's Royal Military School	15	-	-
Ministry of Defence Police	15	2	0
People, Pay and Pensions Agency	10	3	100
Service Children's Education	15	-	-
The Met Office	15	12	92
UK Hydrographic Office	15	-	-
Veterans Agency[1]	15	1,054	100

1 On 1 April 2007, AFPAA and the VA merged to become the Service personnel and Veterans Agency.
2 With effect from 1 April 2007, both PFPO and DBA lost their Agency status.
3 With effect from 2 April 2007, DCSA lost its Agency status and is now part of DE&S as Information and Systems and Services.
4 With effect from 1 April 2007, DTMA lost its Agency status and became Defence Supply Chain Operations and Movements.
5 With effect from 31 March 2007, DSA lost its Agency status.

Sponsorship

Table 36 satisfies the Cabinet Office requirement to publish details of individual commercial sponsorship deals that are valued in excess of £5,000, VAT exclusive, and where they supplement Government funding of any Departmental core business.

Table 36: Sponsorship between 1 April 2006 and 31 March 2007

Activity	TLB	Individual Sponsors	Company Contribution £ VAT EX
HMS Albion loan of vehicles	Fleet	Land Rover UK	63,000
HMS Bulwark loan of vehicles		Land Rover UK	35,000
HMS Illustrious loan of vehicles		Land Rover UK	30,000
HMS Ocean loan of vehicles		Land Rover UK	27,000
Royal Navy Presentation Team		Jaguar Cars Ltd	34,495
RNAS Culdrose Air Day 2006		Lockheed Martin Ltd	21,277
RNAS Yeovilton		Jaguar	53,000
HMS Ark Royal Re-Dedication Ceremony		Babcock Engineering Service	8,510
		Serco Denholm Ltd	6,383
		Land Rover/Jaguar	63,000
		Agusta Westland	4,255
		Lockheed martin	4,255
		Rolls-Royce Marine	4,255
		BAE Systems	8,510
RAF Aerobatic Display Team	PTC	Serco	10,000
		BAE Systems	10,000
		BAE Systems	25,000
		Breitling	12,500
RAF Hercules Display Team	STC	Land Rover UK	11,668
Battle of Britain Memorial Flight		Autologic	20,000
		Land Rover	12,000
		LDV	16,000
DESO Symposium 2007	Centre	Defense News (U.S. publication)	10,582
DESO Symposium 2007 Evening Reception		Finmeccanica UK	17,021
Blue Eagles Display Team	AG	Breitling UK	12,000
		Special Event Services	30,000
		GM UK (SAAB)	15,000
		EDS	25,000
The Rheindahlen and Elmpt Bulletin	Land	Mitsubishi Motors Bruggen	19,700
Royal Regiment of Wales		Brains Brewery	15,000
Formation Parade, Regimental Ski Team		Scottish and Southern Energy	8,000
and Corps of Drums		Taylor Woodrow	9,900
Colchester Military Festival		Sir Robert McAlpine	9,900
		RMPA, Sodexho, Atkins	9,900
		Lagan Keltbray	9,900
Total			**672,011**

Advertising

Spending by the Royal Navy on advertising and public relations expenditure was £10.3M. This includes the costs of national and regional advertising, recruitment activities, publications, the website, and various other promotional activities. This expenditure supports recruiting, raises public awareness of the Naval Service and helps to spread a positive image of the Royal Navy and Royal Marines. The Army's Recruiting Group national marketing spend in 2006-07 for both the Regular and Territorial Army, Officer and Soldier, was £23.3M. This encompassed television, press, radio and internet advertising, the production of DVDs and print media such as brochures and pamphlets, response handling and fulfilment, the Camouflage youth information scheme, the ArmyJobs website, marketing research and tracking as well as overarching production and design work In 2006-07, spending by the Inspectorate of Recruiting (RAF) on recruitment advertising and marketing totalled £10.4M. This comprised expenditure on a wide range of marketing activities for both the RAF and RAuxAF including all media and production for advertising campaigns, response handling, the RAF Careers and Youth websites, literature, films, exhibitions, events, sports sponsorships, educational programmes, customer relationship marketing, promotional items and all marketing research.

Better Regulation

The Armed Forces Act received Royal Assent in November 2006. The MoD is not currently sponsoring any primary legislation. No Regulatory Impact Assessments were completed in 2006-07, although a number are in progress and will be published at www.mod.uk once they are finalised.

Civilian Recruitment

The MoD has a legal obligation to the Civil Service Commissioners to publish summary information about our recruitment processes and the use of permitted exceptions to the principles of fair and open competition and selection on merit. The information published in Table 37 also meets these requirements. The Department's recruitment figures for 2006-07 are at paragraph 311 of this report and include figures for permanent and temporary (casual) recruitment. The following information on the use of permitted exceptions has been collated separately and does not include figures for temporary (casual) recruitment. Table 37 contains information about the MoD's recruitment exceptions in the last twelve months; it includes details of the number of individuals who were appointed and their appointment circumstances.

Use of temporary staff continues to be required in order to manage reductions and unit closures or to meet specialist skills shortages. Secondments are recognised as a beneficial development opportunity but have been more focussed on the business needs during this turbulent period.

The transformation of the Civilian Human Resource as part of the People Programme will bring significant change to the recruitment flexibility offered to meet Government initiatives for the long term unemployed and those who require supported employment.

Table 37: Civilian Recruitment

	2006/07		2005/06		2004/05	
	Non-Industrial	Industrial	Non-Industrial	Industrial	Non-Industrial	Industrial
Total number of staff recruited [1] [2]	2,860	1,070	3,510	1,130	5,480	1,700
Number and percentage of women recruited [2]	1,250 (43.7%)	250 (23.7%)	1,510 (43.1%)	290 (25.6%)	2,440 (44.6%)	470 (27.4%)
Number and percentage of ethnic minorities recruited [3] [2]	120 (6.5%)	30 (4.2%)	170 (7.2%)	20 (3.00%)	130 (4.2%)	20 (1.2%)
Number and percentage of people with disabilities recruited [3] [2]	10 (0.4%)	0	10 (0.3%)	TBC	40 (0.7%)	20 (1.2%)
Appointments of less than 12 months in respect of those posts specified in Annex A of the CSCRC.	4	0	0	0	0	0
Extensions up to a maximum of 24 months, of appointments originally made for a period of less than 12 months (with reasons). [4]	14	0	28	2	28	3
Recurrent short term appointments.	2	30	2	27	31	60
Short term appointments where highly specialised skills are required. [5]	2	0	10	0	16	0
Appointments under Government programmes to assist the long term unemployed. [6]	0	0	0	0	1	0
Secondments. [7]	0	0	6	0	4	0
Extensions to secondments (with reasons). [8]	0	0	3	0	4	0
Re-appointments of former civil servants.	45	17	35	4	95	28
Transfers of staff with their work (not under TUPE).	9	2	2	3	20	1
Transfers of staff from other public services without work (excluding public bodies staffed exclusively by civil servants). [9]	5	0	2	0	78	0
Appointments of surplus acceptable candidates to shortage posts.	0	0	3	0	3	0
Appointments of disabled candidates under modified selection arrangements.	1	0	3	1	11	2
Supported employment appointments.	0	0	0	0	3	0
Number of exceptions reserved for the Commissioners' use.	0	0	0	0	0	1
Any appointments exceptionally approved by the Commissioners under the Orders in Council, outside the terms of the Code.	0	0	0	0	0	0

Notes:

[2] No diversity information for the Defence Procurement Agency (DPA) is known and not included in these figures for 2004/05.

[3] Figures are compiled from questionnaires returned by individual recruits.

[4] The majority of these extensions were to meet short-term requirements to whilst permanent replacements were sought. Fair and open competition has been used wherever possible.

[5] This shows the number of staff recruited where the requirement was short term and required specialist skills and where holding an open competition would not have identified any further candidates.

[6] An exception approved by the Commissioners following the launch of the Governments Welfare to Work – New Deal Programme. Figures exclude those New Deal candidates recruited through normal open and fair competition.

[7] Excludes other Government departments, but includes for example, local authorities, hospitals, etc.

[8] Extension due to a requirement to utilise one individual's knowledge of PPP/PFI.

[9] Figures for 2004/5 include 74 Police Officers transferred from Home Office Police Forces.

Annex G

Defence Equipment Programme and Collaborative Procurement

Major Projects are defined as the twenty largest equipment projects that have passed their main investment decision point (Main Gate), and the ten largest equipment projects that have passed their initial investment decision (Initial Gate), by value of forecast spend remaining. The List of Major Projects was set at 1 April 2006, and the list below includes information for the end of the financial year, 31 March 2007. The following tables show key performance information of Major Projects that have passed Main Gate approval, broken down by capability area. The precise definition of In Service Date (ISD) varies with different equipment, although, in general terms, it can be taken to refer to the date on which the equipment is expected to be available and supportable

in service in sufficient quantity to provide a useable operational capability. The dates quoted for ships and submarines are based on the acceptance date from the contractor of the First of Class, not the date by which the equipment (or a specified number of pieces of equipment) will contribute to the operational capability of the Royal Navy.

Battlespace Manoeuvre

The Battlespace Manoeuvre area incorporates capabilities designed to provide direct battlefield engagement: theatre airspace; tactical mobility; expeditionary logistic support; nuclear, biological and chemical defence; battlefield engineering; special projects; and combat service support. While most of the equipment will be utilised by the Army, it also covers significant capabilities used by other services

Table 38 Capability Manager Battlespace Manoeuvre Equipment Programme

Post Main Gate Projects

Equipment	Description	Current Forecast Cost (£millions)	Current Forecast ISD	Quantity Required Current
Ground Manoeuvre				
Ground Manoeuvre C Vehicle Capability PFI	Commercial Provision of 'C' Class vehicles	702	2006	n/a
Terrier	Armoured earthmoving vehicle	296	2008	65
Next Generation Light Anti-armour Weapon	Short range anti-armour weapon	314	2008	14,002
Expeditionary Logistics & Support				
A400M	Heavy transport aircraft	2,616	2011	25
Support Vehicle (Cargo and Recovery)	Cargo and recovery vehicles and trailers	1,338	2008	4852 Cargo; 288 Recovery; 69 Trailers
Theatre Airspace				
Meteor/BVRAAM	Air-to-Air missile	1,204	2013	Note 1
Typhoon	Fighter Aircraft	Note 2	2003	232

Notes:
(1) Weapon Numbers are classified
(2) Current forecast cost for Typhoon is classified due to commercial sensitivities

and joint organisations; for example, the RAF's Typhoon and assets that will belong to the Joint Helicopter Command.

Precision Attack

The Precision Attack area covers the above-water and under-water battlespaces, and deep target attack. It contains programmes ranging from nuclear submarines and surface warships to sonars, torpedoes air-launched weapons and artillery systems, for delivery to all three services. The table below does not reflect major equipment programmes where orders have not yet been placed, such as the future aircraft carriers.

Information Superiority

This capability area covers intelligence, surveillance, target acquisition and reconnaissance, and command, control and information infrastructure. Most projects are inherently tri-service in nature.

Table 39 Capability Manager Precision Attack Equipment Programme

Post Main Gate Projects

Equipment	Description	Current Forecast Cost (£millions)	Current Forecast ISD	Quantity Required Current
Above-Water Effect				
Type 45 Destroyer	Anti-air warfare destroyer	6,110	2009	6
Under-Water Effect				
Astute Class Submarine	Attack submarine	3,656	2009	3
Nimrod Maritime and Reconnaissance Attack Mk4	Reconnaissance and attack patrol aircraft	3,516	2010	12
Sting Ray	Life extension and capability enhancement	592	2006	Note 1
Deep Target Attack				
Brimstone	Advanced Air-Launched anti-armour Weapon	911	2005	Note 1
Guided Missile-Launch Rocket System (GMLRS)	Rocket weapon system	263	2007	4080
Joint Combat Aircraft (JCA)	Attack aircraft	1,913	Note 2	Note 2

Notes:

(1) Weapon numbers are classified

(2) Joint Combat Aircraft Main Gate Business Case was tailored for development only to match the US procurement cycle. Approval for ISD and quantities required approval will be sought as part of Main Gate Production Business Case.

Table 40 Capability Manager Information Superiority Equipment Programme

Post Main Gate Projects

Equipment	Description	Current Forecast Cost (£millions)	Current Forecast ISD	Quantity Required Current
Bowman	Tactical voice and data communications	2,014	2004	43,000 radios
CIP	Three interreiated projects (combat DBL infrastructure, PBISA)	338	2005	n/a

Collaborative Procurement

A list of collaborative programmes is published on the MoD website. We made progress on a number of collaborative procurement issues.

European Defence

The European Defence Agency entered its second year with work gathering pace on a wide range of projects and initiatives in the areas of armaments and industry/ markets. The UK's pivotal role in the development of the Code of Conduct on Defence Procurement came to fruition when 22 members of the then 24 participating Member States signed up to the voluntary Code which entered into force on 1 July 2006. By 28 February 2007, 130 contract opportunities had been posted on the Electronic Bulletin Board at an estimated value of €6.5bn. The scope of the EBB was widened on 29 March 2007 to include sub-contract opportunities. European Commission work on opening up the European Defence Equipment Market led to an Interpretative Communication (IC) on the use of Article 296 of the Treaty of Rome (issued 6 December 2006) in which the UK played a key role in its development. Following issue of the IC, the Commission turned its attention to preparing the way for a possible Defence Directive. The MoD initiated a number of consultations in response to inform the way forward.

OCCAR (Organisation for Joint Armaments Co-operation)

OCCAR has now reached a reasonable state of maturity, and attention is turning to sustainment of its future. This work centred on the establishment of a formal working relationship with the European Defence Agency (building on the complementary nature of their roles) and was the subject of a well-attended seminar held in September 2006. Work also continued on deepening OCCAR's competences, with particular focus on in-service support. On OCCAR managed programmes, the A400M Wing Assembly Building was opened in Filton, Bristol; final deliveries of the COBRA (Counter Battery Radar) system were made to the British Army; and two further firings were successfully undertaken on the Principal Anti-Air Missile System programme.

Typhoon Future Protocols

The agreement and signature of a Strategic Cooperative Arrangement for Typhoon in April 2007 was a logical evolution of the Typhoon Future protocols signed last year. It demonstrated that, at board level, there is a willingness to change behaviours and move forward to improve the programme efficiency for production and development as well as through-life support. Significant progress on achieving greater through-life efficiencies has already been made over the last six months.

A set of metrics has been developed jointly by EF GmbH (Eurofighter company based in Munich) and NETMA (NATO Eurofighter and Tornado Management Agency) and is under trial usage, leading to functional implementation from June 2007 onwards. The performance metrics should have clear benefit for all in the future analysis of the strategic management of the programme.

Letter of Intent (LoI) Framework Agreement

As part of the six nations LoI focus on recognising

European industry's efforts to restructure, we continued to work closely with partners to pursue measures aimed at removing barriers to industrial and equipment co-operation. During 2006-07 the six nations started to consider future activities of the LoI and its relationship with the European Defence Agency, with a view to ensuring that a transparent relationship with EDA is maintained and appropriate LoI outputs are assimilated into the EDA to the benefit of the wider membership.

United States of America

Through a number of fora, including the Bilateral Defence Acquisition Committee, we continued to work closely with the US Departments of Defense and State to press for improved information and technology exchange on a number of programmes, including the Joint Strike Fighter.

Annex H

Non Departmental Public Bodies

The Department sponsors five executive and eleven advisory Non-Departmental Public Bodies (NDPBs), two Public Corporations, a Stakeholder Advisory Board and an Independent Monitoring Board. Discussion is ongoing regarding the classification of a number of other bodies with links to the Department. A brief description of the Executive NDPBs and Public Corporations is set out below. Details of their funding from the Defence Budget and total gross expenditure can be found at paragraph 32.2 to the Departmental Resource Accounts on page 275. More detailed information on these and the other bodies sponsored by the Department can be found at the MoD website at www.mod.uk.

Executive NDPBs

The Principal Service Museums are the repositories of world-class collections of objects and artefacts relating to the heritage of the Armed Forces. In addition to raising public awareness of the history, traditions and achievements of the Armed Services and encouraging scholarship and research into their history, the museums directly support the strategic aims and policies of the Armed Forces and play an important role in service recruitment and education.

The National Army Museum's visitor numbers rose by 86.5% from 107,576 to 200,675. 4,746 digital images of objects in the Collection were created and the Museum's website was redesigned, attracting 653,550 electronic visitors. Special Exhibitions during the year included 'The Somme', 'Painting the Troubles: An Artist in Northern Ireland' and 'Captive' – a look at the lives of British Prisoners of War over the centuries. The Museum's core collection of heritage military vehicles moved to new purpose-built premises in Stevenage. Important items added to the National Collection, included 17th century oil paintings of Colonel John Hutchinson, Parliamentarian Governor of Nottingham during the Civil War and his famous wife and biographer, Lucy; and papers of Major Allen Holford-Walker describing the first British tank attack at the Battle of Flers Courcelette in September 1916.

The RAF Museum contains the world's only exhibition relating to the history of the Cold War, which was opened at Cosford in February 2007 by HRH Princess Royal, with Baroness Thatcher. Since opening, the new exhibition has welcomed a record number of visitors and has set a new standard in the display and interpretation of historic artefacts and material. The Museum's Access & Learning Development Division is introducing a range of interactive history and science classroom experiences where students and teachers may download the sessions and teaching materials for use within their own environment.

The Royal Marines Museum's total visitor numbers increased by 6% due to the success of the Museum's Heritage Centre in Devon. A new exhibition titled "End of Empire" was installed in the Museum's permanent galleries and there was successful fundraising for the refurbishment of the Museum's Medal Room, with the Heritage Lottery Fund awarding a grant of £50,000. Full accreditation was achieved from the Museums, Libraries and Archives Council (MLA) and the Museum received recognition as an Investor in People under the new standard.

The Royal Naval Museum mounted a very successful special exhibition 'Dreadnoughts' to mark the 100th anniversary of the launch of HMS Dreadnought, receiving over 60,000 visitors. A series of popular workshops were developed to make the Museum's collections accessible to school children, together with a family programme for schools holidays, which brought in nearly 10,000 new visitors – mostly children – in their first year of operation. Overall visitor numbers held up well at around 200,000. The Museum, assisted by the Heritage Lottery Fund, began work on its ambitious three year 'Sea Your History' Project, the aim of which is to improve public access to the collections of the four Naval Museums by digitising over 15,000 objects from their holdings, and placing them on a special new website at www.seayourhistory.co.uk. The first section of the new site went 'live' in December 2006 and other sections will follow in 2007/08.

The Royal Navy Submarine Museum's visitor numbers increased by 9%, and the results of a Heritage Lottery Fund survey conducted during 2006 indicated a very high level of public satisfaction both with the new John Fieldhouse Building and the Museum as a whole. The Museum operated a 'transport-paid' scheme for local schools that gave thousands of children the opportunity for extra-curricular activities which otherwise would have been denied them because of budgetary constraints. The Museum was gifted the fifth scale builders model of HMS Vanguard. This impressive artefact, the last of its type ever to be used by the Admiralty, is an important addition to the Museum's collection. A major achievement was the granting of Accreditation by MLA.

Public Corporations

The Fleet Air Arm Museum was reclassified as a Public Corporation by the Office of National Statistics. VisitBritain renewed the Museum's Quality Assured Visitor Attraction Status, and the MLA awarded Accredited Museum status. School visits increased to over 10,000 pupils of all ages, and the Museum continued to host "Flying Start Challenge" in co-operation with the aerospace and engineering companies in the region, in which students are required to design and build a "device" which meets the competition criteria set for the day. The three years of painstaking work on the Museum's Corsair WW2 fighter continued to draw attention for its groundbreaking approach and received two awards from conservation and historical organisations.

Oil and Pipeline Agency: The strategic importance of the Government Pipeline and Storage System (GPSS) was clearly demonstrated following the Buncefield incident. There has been record throughput of aviation fuel through the system helping to alleviate fuel supply problems at some of the major airports. New pump stations contributed to this success. In the southern sector of the GPSS, key pipelines and tankage were the subject of major maintenance works that were implemented successfully to programme and budget. Buncefield also raised many regulatory issues and the activities of the OPA were subject to intense scrutiny, resulting in a statement of satisfaction by the regulatory authorities with the performance of the Agency in managing the operation and maintenance of the GPSS.

Annual Public Appointment Plan

The Committee on Standards in Public Life recommended in its Tenth Report that departments produce annual plans setting out policy and practice relating to public appointments. The MoD's Annual Public Appointment Plan includes diversity figures and targets that were previously included in the now discontinued Cabinet Office publication *Delivering Diversity in Public Appointments*.

Policy

The MoD is committed to following the Code of Practice of the Commissioner for Public Appointments. All MoD Non-Departmental Public Bodies, Public Corporations and Independent Monitoring Boards are encouraged to follow the Code of Practice whether or not an appointment is Ministerial and therefore formally within the remit. In practice the majority of MoD public appointments are Ministerial. The Department is fully committed to improving diversity throughout its workforce and this is reflected in our approach to filling public appointments. Paragraph 313 set out the initiatives and actions we have taken to improve diversity. MoD public appointments are made entirely on merit. Remuneration is based on the sum needed to attract suitably qualified candidates and to reflect the time commitment and regularity of work involved in the position.

Report on Achievement of Objectives

The diversity targets for public appointments to MoD Non-Departmental Public Bodies, Public Corporation and Independent Monitoring Board to achieve during the period of this Annual Report and the actual figures achieved by our public appointees to Non-Departmental Public Bodies are shown in Table 41. We are currently considering whether to move to a unified recruitment centre serving the whole Department. This could benefit our public appointments by widening the field of potential candidates, and particularly by identifying the best ways to communicate with minority groups.

Within the overriding principle of selection based on merit, we aim to improve the representation of women, people from minority ethnic backgrounds and people with disabilities within our public appointments to MoD NDPBs, Public Corporation and Independent Monitoring Boards. Our policy is in line with the Government's long-term objectives of equal representation of men and women, pro-rata representation of people from minority ethnic backgrounds and the increased participation of people with disabilities. We also promote the benefits of diversity within their membership.

Table 41: Diversity targets for public appointment to MoD Non-Departmental Public Bodies, Public Corporation and Independent Monitoring Board

		2006-07	2008	2009
Women	Target	33%	35%	35%
	Achieved	19%		
Ethnic minorities	Target	3.5%	4%	4.5%
	Achieved	0.5%		
Disabled People	Target	5.5%	5.5%	6%
	Achieved	9%		

Glossary

1SL/CNS. First Sea Lord and Chief of the Naval Staff: Professional head of the Navy. Member of the Defence Management Board, the Admiralty Board and the Chiefs of Staff Committee and the Chair of the Navy Board. Currently held by an officer of the rank of Admiral.

2nd PUS. 2nd Permanent Under Secretary. The Deputy to the Permanent Under Secretary. Member of the Defence Council and Defence Management Board, the Admiralty, Army and Air Force boards and their executive committees, the Acquisition Policy Board, the Investment Approvals Board, official chair of the Defence Environment and Safety Board, and joint head, with the Vice Chief of the Defence Staff, of the Central Top Level Budget organisation.

2SL/CNH. Second Sea Lord and Commander-in-Chief Naval Home Command. The Royal Navy's Principal Personnel Officer of the rank of Vice Admiral, and a member of the Admiralty and Navy Boards. Also known as the Chief of Naval Personnel. He has responsibility for maintaining operational capability by providing correctly trained manpower through recruitment into the Royal Navy and Royal Marines and individual training.

ABRO. A Trading Fund Agency of the MoD formally known as Army Base Repair Organisation. ABRO provides engineering support (including complex repair and servicing, re-manufacture and assembly) and fleet management services to the MoD, the defence industry and other commercial businesses for land based equipment ranging from radios to battle tanks.

ACPP: Africa Conflict Prevention Pool. The arrangements run jointly by the MoD, FCO and DfID to deliver the Government's conflict prevention objectives in Africa. The ACPP has an annual budget of £31M.

Activity Levels. The proportion of regular military personnel deployed on operations and other military tasks.

Admiralty Board. The Admiralty Board is chaired by the Secretary of State for Defence and is delegated by the Defence Council to administer the activities and personnel of the Royal Navy.

AFB: Air Force board. The Air Force Board is chaired by the Secretary of State for Defence and is delegated by the Defence Council to administer the activities and personnel of the Royal Air Force.

AFBSC Air Force Board Standing Committee. The AFBSC conducts the day-to-day business of managing the Royal Air Force on behalf of the Air Force board. It brings together, under the Chief of the Air Staff (CAS), the RAF operational and personnel commanders, and supports the CAS in his executive role, his management and operational advisory roles, and as the professional head of the RAF.

AFCS: Armed Forces Compensation Scheme. A scheme, introduced from 6 April 2005, for members and ex-members of the Regular Armed Forces (including Gurkhas) and Reserve Forces, to pay compensation for injuries, illnesses or deaths which are caused by service on or after 6 April 2005. In the event of a Service person's death caused by service, benefits are payable to eligible dependants.

AFPS: Armed Forces Pension Scheme. The non-contributory defined benefits pension scheme covering all members of the Armed Forces.

AG: Adjutant General.
a) The Army's Principal Personnel Officer, of the rank of Lieutenant General, and a member of the Army Board and the Executive Committee of the Army Board. He has responsibility for providing trained army officers and other ranks through recruitment into the Army and individual training. He also provides education services to children of all members of the Services on long-term foreign postings.

b) The Top Level Budget (TLB) organisation managed by the Adjutant General.

ALI: Adult Learning Inspectorate. The ALI is a statutory non-departmental public body that inspects and reports on the quality of education and training for adults and young people funded by public money.

AME: Annually Managed Expenditure. Spending included in Total Managed Expenditure that does not fall within Departmental Expenditure Limits (DELs), such as nuclear provisions and War Pension Benefits. Expenditure in AME is generally less predictable and/or controllable than expenditure within DELs.

AMP: Air Member for Personnel. The RAF's Principal Personnel Officer, of the rank of Air Marshall, a member of the Air Force Board and Air Force Standing Committee. He is responsible for providing trained RAF officers and other ranks through recruitment into the RAF, individual training and subsequent management.

Anti-surface weapons. Weapons designed to attack targets on the surface of the land or sea.

AFPAA: Armed Forces Personnel Administration Agency. Responsible for provision of personnel services, including administration of pay and pensions, for the Armed Forces. Merged with the Veterans Agency from April 2007 to form the Service Personnel and Veterans Agency.

APB: Acquisition Policy Board. The MoD's top level board, chaired by the Minister for Defence Procurement or, in his absence, the PUS. It overseas the development of defence acquisition policy and processes and defence industrial policy, and reviewing and monitoring the coherence of acquisition performance targets.

Apprentices. New entrants to the Armed Forces undertaking training in particular skilled trades.

Appropriations-in-aid (A-in-A). Receipts used to offset expenditure. They generally arise from the provision of repayment services, the sale of surplus goods or of equipment purchased on behalf of the Defence Sales Organisation. Excess A-in-A are subject to Consolidated Fund Extra Receipt (CFER).

Army Board. The Army Board is chaired by the Secretary of State for Defence and is delegated by the Defence Council to administer the activities and personnel of the Army.

Army Reserve See **Regular Reserves.**

Assessment Centre. The formal process used by the MoD to assess suitability of civil servants for promotion into junior management (Band D) and middle management (Band B) grades.

Assets. Can be either financial or non-financial. Financial assets include monetary gold, bank deposits, IMF Special Drawing Rights, loans granted bonds, shares, accounts receivable, and the value of the government's stake in public corporations. Non-financial assets consist of fixed capital (such as buildings and vehicles); stock, land and valuables.

ASTA: Aircrew Synthetic Training Aids. A Full Mission simulator that replicates all aspects of a real flying mission, allowing pilots to match the aircraft and its weapons against interactive attacks, whilst experiencing the pressures and demands of high speed jet flight. A cockpit trainer, a lower level device, is primarily used to introduce the pilot to the cockpit environment and procedures.

ASTOR: Airborne Stand Off Radar. A new capability which will provide a long range all weather theatre surveillance and target acquisition system capable of detecting moving, fixed and static targets.

AWE: Atomic Weapons Establishment. One of the largest high technology research, design development and production facilities in the UK. Its primary task is to produce and maintain the warheads for the UK's independent nuclear deterrent.

BAES: An international company engaged in the development, delivery and support of advanced defence and aerospace systems in the air, on land, at sea and in space. It designs, manufactures and supports military aircraft, surface ships, submarines, fighting vehicles, radar, avionics, communications and guided weapons systems.

Balance Sheet. A financial statement showing the assets, liabilities, and net worth of a business on a specified date.

Band B. A grade in the civilian rank structure immediately below the Senior Civil Service. Previously know as Unified Grades 6 and 7.

Battalion. An Army fighting unit, usually comprising between 400 – 800 personnel, commanded by a Lieutenant Colonel. See **Regiment.**

Berlin Plus Arrangements. Arrangements negotiated between the European Union and NATO to allow for the EU to have access to NATO's assets and capabilities so that NATO can support the EU, so that there's full transparency between the two organisations and so that we cooperate with the most efficient, the most effective mechanisms possible so that resources are used in the most efficient way.

BOWMAN. A tri-Service tactical communications and information system.

BNFL: British Nuclear Fuel plc. An international nuclear energy business, involved in fuel manufacture, reactor design and services, as well as decommissioning and environmental services; cleaning up the legacy of the Cold War.

Brigade. An Army Brigade is a collection of units that have been formally grouped together for a specific purpose, commanded by a Brigadier. A fighting Brigade will contain a mix of infantry, Reconnaissance, Armoured, Engineer, Artillery and Logistic units together with supporting specialist capabilities. The composition of a Brigade will differ depending on its responsibility but usually contains about 5,000 soldiers.

BTEC. Business and Technology Education Council. Vocational qualifications to prepare students for employment or for progression to higher education, often taken as an alternative to A-levels.

BVRAAM: Beyond Visual Range Air-to-Air Missile. The next generation air-to-air weapon, also known as Meteor, which will provide Typhoon with the capacity to combat projected air-to-air threats throughout the life of the aircraft and contribute to the superiority requirements of UK and NATO operations.

Capability Reviews. A Cabinet Office initiative, launched in early 2006, aimed at improving the capability of the Civil Service to meet today's delivery challenges and be ready for tomorrow's. The reviews will help departments to identify where they need to improve and what support they need to do so. The reports on these reviews will be published, with clear assessments of current performance and key actions to be taken to improve. Capability Reviews supersede Performance partnership Agreements.

CAS: Chief of the Air Staff. Professional head of the Royal Air Force, member of the Defence Council and Defence Management Board, the Air Force Board and the Chiefs of Staff Committee, and Chair of the Air Force Board Standing Committee. Currently held by an officer of the rank of Air Chief Marshal.

CBRN: Chemical, Biological, Radiological and Nuclear materials. Unconventional materials potentially capable of use in weapons of wide area impact, often collectively known as Weapons of Mass Destruction.

CBW: Chemical and Biological Warfare. The use of chemical and biological weapons in conflict. Possession and use of Chemical and biological Warfare is illegal under the Chemical Weapons Convention and the Biological and Toxin Weapons Convention.

CDL: Chief of Defence Logistics. Head of the Defence Logistics Organisation TLB. Member of the Defence Council and Defence Management Board, Acquisition Policy Board and Investment Approvals Board. The post was disestablished on creation of the DE&S organisation headed by the CDM on 2 April 2007.

CDP: Chief of Defence Procurement. Head of the Defence Procurement Agency TLB and member of the Defence Council and Defence Management Board, Acquisition Policy Board and Investment Approvals Board. The post was disestablished on creation of the DE&S organisation headed by the CDM on 2 April 2007.

CDM: Chief of Defence Materiel. The head of Defence Equipment and Support, launched on 2 April 2007 as a result of merging the Defence Procurement Agency and Defence Logistics Organisation. Member of the Defence Council and Defence Management Board, Investment Approvals Board and Acquisition Policy Board.

CDS: Chief of Defence Staff. The professional head of the UK Armed Forces and principal military adviser to the Secretary of State for Defence and the Government. Member of the Defence Council and Defence Management Board, and Chairman of the Chiefs of Staff Committee.

CFE: Treaty on Conventional Armed Forces in Europe. A treaty which established comprehensive limits on conventional military equipment in Europe (from the Atlantic to the Urals) mandated the destruction of excess weaponry and provided for verification and inspection.

CFER: Consolidated Fund Extra Receipt. Receipts realised in excess of amounts authorised as Appropriations in Aid of the supply Estimates, or of kinds which HM Treasury does not allow Departments to use in aid of expenditure. Such receipts are surrendered to the Consolidated Fund as Extra Receipts.

CGS: Chief of the General Staff. Professional head of the Army, member of the Defence Council and Defence Management Board, the Army Board and Chiefs of Staff Committee, and the Chair of the Executive Committee of the Army Board. Currently held by an officer of the rank of General.

CJO: Chief of joint Operations.

a) the senior joint military operational commander, of the rank of Vice Admiral, Lieutenant General or Air Marshall, responsible for running all military operations other than those so large that a more senior officer is required, or those undertaken predominantly by one Service such that it makes sense for the operation to be commanded by the operational TLB led by that Service (CINCFLEET, Land Command, or Strike Command). Military assets are assigned to CJO only for the duration of the operation.

b) The Top Level Budget organisation managed by CJO, including the Permanent joint Headquarters, the Sovereign Base Areas in Cyprus and British forces in Gibraltar and the Falkland Islands.

CINCFLEET: Commander-in-Chief Fleet. The Royal Navy's principal operational commander, of the rank of Admiral, and a member of the Admiralty and Navy Boards.

CINCLAND: Commander-in-Chief Land.

a) The Army's principal operational commander, of the rank of General, and a member of the Army Board and Executive Committee of the Army Board.

b) Top Level budget organisation managed by CINCLAND responsible for the delivery of trained expeditionary armed forced to CJO at agreed readiness rates.

CINCAIR: Commander-in-Chief Air Command.

a) The Royal Air Force's principal operational commander, of the rank of Air Chief Marshall, and a member of the Air Force Board and Air Force Board Standing Committee.

b) Top Level Budget organisation managed by Air Command responsible for the deliver of trained expeditionary air power to CJO at agreed readiness levels.

CIS: Communication and Information systems.

Civil Contingencies Act. The Act, and accompanying non-legislative measures, will deliver a single framework for civil protection in the United Kingdom capable of meeting the challenges of the twenty-first century. The Act is separated into two substantive parts: local arrangements for civil protection and emergency powers. It Received Royal Assent in November 2004.

CMS: Common Military Skills. Core military skills in which recruits are trained in the first stages of their training.

COBRA: Counter-Battery Radar. A 3-D phased radar system designed to locate enemy artillery at very long ranges.

Combat I.D.: The process of combining situational awareness, target identification and specific tactics, techniques and procedures to increase operational effectiveness of weapons systems and reduce the incidence of casualties caused by friendly fire.

Commission. The legal authority of an Officer's appointment to the Armed Forces. Precise terms vary according to Service and specialisation within each Service.

Conflict Prevention. Early warning, crisis management, conflict resolution, peacemaking, peacekeeping, and peace-building activity and an associated strengthening of international and regional systems and capacity.

Corps:
a) An organised collection of Regiments or groupings of soldiers that share a common area of specialist expertise to ensure common practice and that common interests can be catered for efficiently.

b) An Army fighting unit comprising two or more divisions with associated specialist supporting units, commanded by a Lieutenant General.

COS: Chiefs of Staff Committee. The Chiefs of Staff Committee is chaired by the Chief of the Defence Staff. It is the main forum in which the collective military advice of the Chiefs of Staff is obtained on operational issues. The PUS attends the COS Committee.

Cost of Capital Charge. An annual non-cash charge applied to each department's budget. It is 3.5% of the net assets of the department and is used to make departments aware of the full cost of holding assets.

CSA:
a) **Chief Scientific Adviser.** The MoD's senior expert scientific advisor, recruited externally, Head of Science Innovation and Technology TLB, member of the Defence Council and Defence Management Board and Chair of the Investment Approvals Board.

b) **Customer Supplier Agreement.** An agreement, usually between TLBs, detailing in terms of quality, quantity and timeliness the outputs required from the supplier to enable the customer to meet its defence outputs.

CSPS: Civil Service Pension Scheme.

CTLB: Central TLB. The Central Top Level Budget organisation has responsibility for the MoD Head Office, covering Defence policy as well as Departmental policy on the equipment programme, resources, finance, personnel and security, as well as a range of non-Head Office functions. The Central TLB provides a diverse range of corporate services for the MoD as a whole. These include pay, bill payment, consultancy services, accountancy, some training, statistical analysis, central IT systems, public relations, defence exports and policing. The Central TLBs remit also encompasses provision of medical services.

CTP: Career Transition Partnership. A partnering arrangement between Right Management Consultants and the MoD to deliver improved resettlement services to all ranks from the Armed Forces.

Current expenditure on goods and services is the sum of expenditure on pay, and related staff costs, plus spending on goods and services. It is net of receipts from sales. It excludes capital expenditure, but includes expenditure on equipment that can only be used for military purposed since that is counted as current expenditure. It differs from final consumption in that capital consumption is not included.

Current prices. Prices prevailing at the time.

CVR(T): Combat Vehicle Reconnaissance (Tracked). A light tank used for reconnaissance.

DAC: Defence Audit Committee. The Defence Audit Committee is a subcommittee of the Defence Management Board, chaired by an independent non-executive member of the DMB. It reviews and constructively challenges the adequacy of internal controls, risk management and assurance processes within the MoD. In particular it reviews the Department's assurance arrangements and Statement on Internal Control contained within the Departmental Resource Accounts (the DRAc) annually and reports on these to the Accounting Officer.

DACP: Defence Acquisition Change Programme. The Defence Acquisition Change Programme is a single coherent acquisition reform programme that has been initiated to deliver aspects of the cultural, behavioural, procedural and organisational change identified in the Defence Industrial Strategy and the recommendations from the Enabling Acquisition Change report.

DARA: Defence Aviation Repair Agency. In 1999, DARA brought together the RAF maintenance Group Defence Agency (MGDA) and the Naval Aircraft Repair Organisation (NARO). It is the largest Government owned aerospace repair facility within Europe, delivering one-stop-shop aerospace support to the MoD, overseas governments and Industry. DARA became a Trading Agency of the MoD in April 2001. Following changes in provision of aviation support, the Government announced in May 2007 that DARA's residual functions will be merged with ABRO from April 2008.

DASA: Defence Analytical Services Agency. DASA was created in July 1992 and provides National Statistics on Defence and other corporate information, forecasting and planning and consultancy, advice and research services to the MoD.

DBA: Defence Bills Agency. Primarily responsible for paying bills submitted to the MoD by defence contractors.

DCSA: Defence Communication Services Agency. Provided telecommunications and related services to the MoD and was part of the DLO. Disestablished from 1 April 2007 on creation of DE&S.

DE: Defence Estates. The Top Level Budget organisation that manages and maintains the defence estate. DE ceased to be an Agency in April 2007.

DE&S: Defence Equipment & Support. DE&S is the single organisation (formed on 2 April 2007) from merging the Defence Procurement Agency and Defence Logistics Organisation) responsible for the procurement and support of equipment used by the Armed Forces.

Defence Aim. The Defence Aim is set out in the MoD's Public Service Agreement. It is to deliver security for the people of the UK and Overseas territories by defending them, including against terrorism, and act as a force for good by strengthening international peace and security.

Defence Balanced Scorecard. The Defence Balanced Scorecard is a framework that helps the DMB to translate strategy into operational objectives that drive both behaviour and performance. This strategy is articulated in the Departmental Plan, which sets out the department's top level strategic objectives, including our Public Service Agreement (PSA) targets. The Defence Balanced Scorecard tells the DMB how well Defence is doing in terms of the objectives that underpin the plan. Ultimately this assessment tells the DMB whether Defence is 'succeeding' and gives them an insight into the department's ability to achieve the Defence vision.

Defence Budget. Under Cash Accounting, the amount of money planned to be spent during a financial year. Under Resource Accounting and Budgeting (RAB), the sum of resources planned to be consumed during a financial year. See Resource budgeting.

Defence Council. The Defence Council is chaired by the Secretary of State for Defence and provides the formal legal basis for the command and administration of the Armed Forces under a range of powers vested in it by statute and Letters Patent.

Defence Estate. The built facilities and rural land required to deliver defence output.

Defence Mission. The objectives of the Ministry of Defence are to provide the capabilities needed: to ensure the security and defence of the United Kingdom and Overseas Territories, including against terrorism; to support the Government's foreign policy objectives particularly in promoting international peace and security.

DTC: Defence Technology Centre. Centres of excellence for conducting innovative, cutting edge research for enhanced UK Defence capability. They are exemplars for research collaboration between Government, UK Defence, Small-Medium Sized Enterprises, and Universities.

Defence Vision. The Defence Vision set out by the Defence Management Board, is: *Defending the UK and its interests; Strengthening international peace and stability; A Force for good in the world. We achieve this aim by working together on our core task to produce battle-winning people and equipment that are: Fit for the challenge of today; Ready for the tasks of tomorrow; Capable of building for the future.*

DEFRA: Department for Environment, Food and Rural Affairs. DEFRA is the Government Department responsible for all aspects of the environment, rural matters, farming and food production.

DEL: Departmental Expenditure Limit. DELs are firm plans for three years for a specific part of a department's expenditure. In general the DEL will cover all running costs and all programme expenditure except, in certain cases, spending is included in departmental AME because it cannot be reasonably be subject to close control over a three year period. DELs are divided into current and capital budgets.

Depreciation. Also termed capital consumption. The measure of the wearing out, consumption or other loss of value of a fixed asset whether arising from use, passage of time or obsolescence through technological and market changes.

DERA: Defence Evaluation and Research Agency. On 2 July 2001 DERA was split into two parts: QinetiQ, and the Defence Science and Technology Laboratory (Dstl).

DESB: Defence Environment and Safety Board. Chaired by the Under Secretary of State or, in his absence, the 2nd PUS, provides direction, sets objectives, monitors, reviews and reports on performance with regard to the environment and safety in defence.

Devolved Administrations. The devolved administrations of Scotland, Wales and Northern Ireland have responsibility for certain defined areas of domestic Government in their parts of the UK.

DFAU: Defence Fraud Analysis Unit. A dedicated unit within the Defence Internal Audit organisation to evaluate suspected irregularities, support police authorities, promote risk awareness, record reported fraud and theft, liaise with the Treasury and provide advice on procedures and policy.

DfES: Department for Education and Skills. Government Department responsible for setting education and skills policy in England. Now the Department for children, schools and families – and the Department for Innovation, Universities and Skills on 28 June 2007.

DfID: Department for International Development. Government Department responsible for the UK's development aid and work to get rid of extreme poverty.

DH: Department of Health. Government Department responsible for setting health and social care policy in England, and sets standards and drives Modernisation across all areas of the NHS, social care and public health.

DIA: Defence Internal Audit. The MoD's principal Internal Auditing body, whose primary role is the provision of independent and objective advice on the economy, efficiency and effectiveness of systems and controls at all levels of the Department. It reports directly to the Defence Audit Committee.

DII: Defence Information Infrastructure. A fully networked and managed information system being acquired to support Defence worldwide, underpinning much of the defence Change Programme.

Direct Entry Officers. Army officers (previously called Mainstream officers) who either come direct from civilian life or from the ranks of the Army, commissioned on completion of the 11 month Royal Military Academy Sandhurst (RMAS) Commissioning Course. They will normally be under the age of 29 on entry to RMAS.

DIS:
a) **Defence Industrial Strategy.** Announced on 15 December 2005, the Defence Industrial Strategy is aimed at ensuring that our Armed Forces are provided with the equipment that they require, on time, and at best value for money. It aims to identify the sustainable industrial base required to retain within the UK those industrial capabilities (including infrastructure, skills, intellectual property and capacity).

b) **Defence Intelligence Staff.** Organisation that provides timely, all-source intelligence assessments to: guide Departmental decision making on the formulation of Defence policy and the commitment and employment of the UK's military forces; inform decisions on the generation and maintenance of operational military capability, including through the Equipment Programme; and contribute to wider national intelligence collection and assessment.

Division. An Army Division made up of two or more Brigades depending on the specific role it is to undertake and is configured in a similar fashion to a Brigade but on a larger scale, commanded by a Major General. 1 (UK) Division and 3 (UK) Division are fighting Divisions. 2, 4 and 5 Division are responsible for administrative support of specific geographical areas within the UK.

DLO: Defence Logistics Organisation. The Top Level Budget organisation formed on 1 April 1999 to bring together the logistics support organisations in the Royal Navy, Army and Royal Air Force and Centre staff. It contains a number of specialist Defence Agencies. With effect from 2nd April 2007, Defence Logistic and Defence Procurement Agency have merged to form the new Defence Equipment & Support TLB.

DLTP: Defence Logistics Transformation Programme. A single coherent programme of work incorporating all logistic transformation activities across Defence to achieve improved operational effectiveness, efficiency and flexibility.

DMB: Defence Management Board. The Defence Management Board (DMB) is the highest, non-ministerial committee in the MoD. Chaired by PUS, it is essentially the main corporate board of the MoD, providing senior level leadership and strategic management of Defence. Its role is to deliver the Defence Aim set out in the Public Service Agreement. It comprises the non-ministerial members of the Defence Council and a number of non-executive members. It is responsible for the role of Defence, providing strategic direction, vision and values; for Objectives and targets, establishing the key priorities and defence capabilities necessary to deliver the MoD's Departmental objectives; for Resource allocation and strategic balance of investment to match Defence priorities and objectives; and for Performance management, managing and driving corporate performance.

DMS: Defence Medical Services. Comprises the Defence Medical Services Department and the three single Service medical directorates.

DOC: Directorate of Operational Capability. DOC provides an independent source of evaluation and audit within the Armed Forces on a range of issues, including operational lessons learnt studies and appraising the care and welfare of Armed Forces initial training establishments.

DPA: Defence Procurement Agency. The DPA was the Top Level Budget Organisation responsible for the procurement of equipment to meet new requirements. It is also a Defence Agency. It is located mainly at Abbey Wood, Bristol. With effect from 2nd April 2007, Defence Logistic and Defence Procurement Agency have merged to form the new Defence Equipment & Support TLB.

DRDL: Devonport Royal Dockyards Ltd. A company which runs and owns the Devonport Royal Dockyards in Plymouth.

DSDA: Defence Storage and Distribution Agency. The Defence Agency that provides the Armed Forces with storage and distribution services.

DSL: Debut Services Ltd. A joint venture between Bovis Lend lease Ltd and Babcock Infrastructure Services to provide property maintenance and capital works projects across Defence.

DSTL: Defence Science and Technology Laboratory. An agency and trading fund of the MoD created from part of DERA on 2 July 2001. It provides specialist scientific and technical support to the MoD.

DTC: Defence Technology Centre. A formal collaborative arrangement between industry and academic experts in a particular technology, funded jointly by participants and the MoD, who work together to generate and enhance the technology vital to the delivery of future UK Defence capabilities.

DU: Depleted Uranium. Uranium is a natural element found in soil, water and mineral deposits. It is a heavy metal, nearly twice as dense as lead, is radioactive and chemically toxic. DU is a waste product, (what is left after the removal of some of the more radioactive parts of natural uranium for use in the nuclear industry) and being a very dense and hard metal is an ideal core for tank shells designed to pierce armoured vehicles.

DUOB: Depleted Uranium Oversight Board. An independent panel of scientists and veterans' representatives appointed to oversee the MoD's depleted uranium (DU) screening programme.

DWR: Deep Waste Repository. A facility for the storage of nuclear waste deep underground.

EAC: Enabling Acquisition Change. An internal study established to examine the MoD's ability to conduct Through Life Capability Management. The study team report was published on 3 July 2006.

ECAB: Executive Committee of the Army Board. ECAB conducts the day-to-day business of managing the Army on behalf of the Army Board. It brings together, under the Chief of the General Staff, the Army operational and personnel commanders, and supports the CGS in his executive role, his management and operational advisory roles, and as the professional head of the Army.

Environment Agency. The environmental regulator for England and Wales.

ERW: Explosive Remnants of War. Unexploded ordnance (such as bombs, missiles and artillery shells), which may be primed, fused, armed or prepared for use, and may have been abandoned.

ESDP: European Security and Defence Policy. The European Union has agreed on the establishment of a European Security and Defence Policy to ensure it has the tools to undertake crisis management operations, where NATO as a whole is not engaged, in support of its Common Foreign and Security Policy.

Ethnic Minority. A group within a community which differs ethnically from the main population.

EU: European Union. The framework for economic and political co-operation between 25 European countries. It began as a post-war initiative between six countries pooling control over coal and steel to guarantee a more peaceful
future for Europe. It now manages co-operation on issues as wide-ranging as the environment, transport and employment, and has increasing influence in defence and foreign policy.

EUFOR. The EU-led peacekeeping force responsible for security in Bosnia-Herzegovina.

FCO: Foreign and Commonwealth Office. The Government department responsible for UK foreign and security policy.

Finance Director. The MoD's senior finance officer, responsible for all aspects of the Department's financial performance and a member of the Defence Management Board.

Fleet. The Top Level Budget (TLB) organisation managed by Commander-in-Chief Fleet which was formed on 1 April 2006 from the CINC Fleet TLB and Chief of Naval Personnel TLB.

FOI: Freedom of Information. An Act giving a right of public access to recorded information held by public authorities subject to certain defined exemptions.

FRES: Future Rapid Effects System. A project to enhance the deployability of UK Land Forces by delivering a family of medium weight, network capable armoured vehicles, such as armoured personnel carriers, reconnaissance, command and control, and or ambulance vehicles. The project is currently in the Assessment Phase.

FE: Force Element. An Armed Force grouping used for the measurement of readiness. This may be an armoured brigade in the Army, an individual ship in the Royal Navy or an individual aircraft or squadron of aircraft in the Royal Air Force.

Full-Time Equivalent. A measure of the size of the workforce that takes account of the fact that some people work part-time.

Full-Time Reserve Service. Individuals on FTRS fill Service posts on a full-time basis while being a member of one of the reserve services, either as an ex-regular or as a volunteer. In the case of the Army and the Naval Service, these will be posts that would ordinarily have been filled by regular service personnel, in the case of the RAF, FTRS personnel also fill posts designated solely for them.

GDP: Gross Domestic Product. The sum of all output (or income or expenditure) in the economy, excluding net property income from abroad.

GOCNI: General Officer Commanding Northern Ireland.
a) The senior military officer in command of the Armed Forces in Northern Ireland, of the rank of Lieutenant General. He is responsible for military aid to the civil power and counter terrorist operations in Northern Ireland;

b) The joint-Service Top Level Budget organisation managed by GOCNI. With effect from April 2007, The General Officer Commanding Northern Ireland has been incorporated into Command-in-Chief Land Command TLB.

Global Conflict Prevention Pool . Global Pool Conflict Prevention Pool (GCPP) consists of geographical and thematic strategies focused on conflict prevention, conflict resolution and / or post-conflict reestablishment throughout the world.

Gurkhas. Citizens of Nepal recruited and employed in the Army under the terms of the 1947 Tri-Partite Agreement. They remain Nepalese citizens but in all other respects are full members of HM Forces.

GWMB: Guided Weapons, Missiles and Bombs. Explodable munitions which incorporate guidance mechanisms.

HCDC: House of Commons Defence Select Committee. The Defence Committee is appointed to examine on behalf of the House of Commons the expenditure, administration and policy of the Ministry of Defence and any associated public bodies.

Headline Goal 2010. The aim, adopted by the European Union at the Helsinki European Council in December 1999, to be able to deploying 50-60,000 troops, capable of conducting the full range of crisis management tasks, within 60 days, sustainable for up to a year, with air and naval support as necessary, before the end of 2003.

Heavy Equipment Transporter. A 120 tonne tractor and trailer unit tank transporter, capable of carrying battle tanks and fighting vehicles straight to the front line at speeds of up to 50 mph on road or off road over harsh terrain.

HMG: Her Majesty's Government.

HNBS: Harrier Night Bombing System.

HOME: Head Office Modern Environment. The HOME programme was a comprehensive Modernisation package using the redevelopment of MoD's Main Building as a catalyst for organisational and cultural change to make the MoD Head Office a better, more streamlined, organisation in which to work and enable it to provide more effective support and leadership for UK Defence capability.

HQ: Headquarters.

HR: Human Resources. Civilian personnel management, organisation and arrangements.

HSE: Health and Safety Executive. The Health and Safety Executive is responsible for regulation of risks to health and safety arising from work activity in Britain.

Hydrographic Office. See **UK Hydrographic Office.**

IAB: Investment Approvals Board. The Investment Approvals Board (IAB) is responsible for central scrutiny of equipment requirements, major capital works and Information Technology projects. It makes recommendations to Ministers on the procurement of major defence equipment. The IAB is chaired by the Chief Scientific Adviser and includes the Vice Chief of the Defence Staff, the 2nd Permanent Under Secretary, the Chief of Defence Materiel, and the Defence Commercial Director.

ICT: Information and Communications Technology.

ICT FS: Information and Communications Technology Fundamental Skills.

Industrial staff. Civilian staff in certain pay bands often performing manual work.

Insensitive munitions. Munitions incorporating design features to reduce the risk of inadvertent reaction to specified stimuli, such as heat, shock and impact.

In-Service Date. The date on which equipment being procured is expected to be available and supportable in service in sufficient quantity to provide a valuable operational capability.

ISAF: International Security Assistance Force. The NATO controlled peacekeeping force providing security in Kabul since the fall of the Taliban in 2001. More than 30 countries contribute troops.

IS: Information Systems.

ISO 9001: is the internationally recognised standard for an organisation's internal Quality Management. The term 'quality' refers to all those features of a product or service which are required by the customer.

Intake. Those entering the Armed Forces or Civilian workforce.

IT: Information Technology.

JPA: Joint Personnel Administration. A modern commercial information system enabling provision of pay, pensions and administration services for military personnel, JPA was introduced to the RAF from April 2006, the RN in December 2006 and the Army in April 2007.

JRRF: Joint Rapid Reaction Forces. A substantial pool of capabilities, composed of all readily available forces, from which tailored force packages of up to Brigade level or equivalent for operations on land, sea and air can be assembled and deployed quickly.

KFOR: NATO Kosovo Force. The International NATO led peacekeeping force whose main role is maintaining a secure civilian environment.

LAN: Local Area Network. Two or more connected computers in a room or building.

Land Command. See CINCLAND.

Locally Entered/Engaged Personnel. Civilian personnel working for one of the Armed Forces or directly for the Ministry of Defence who are recruited at overseas MoD locations normally for work at those locations. Also includes Gurkhas.

LS: Large Scale. Operational deployments of division size or equivalent for warfighting or other operations.

Main Gate. The main investment point for a procurement project, comprising In-depth review timed to coincide with the most critical point of the project – the point at which the "Assessment" phase ends and user requirements, system requirements, time and cost can be set with confidence.

MAMBA weapon locating radar. Mobile Artillery Monitoring Battlefield Radar, a radar system that can instantly track incoming mortars, shells and rockets and will help troops pinpoint the enemy's position for rapid counter attacks.

MANPADS: Man Portable Air Defence Systems. Systems designed for military air defence use, and are surface to air missiles, usually shoulder launched and fired by an individual or more than one individual acting as crew.

MDP: Ministry of Defence Police. The non-regional, national police force headed by a Chief Constable, responsible for providing effective policing of the Defence Estate.

Memorandum of Understanding. A formal signed agreement between partners setting out how they will work together in a process to achieve agreed goals.

MIDIT: Means of Identifying and Developing Internal Talent. The MoD's internal corporate development scheme for civilian personnel.

Military Aid to the Civil Authorities: MACA. The provision of military assistance: in time of emergency such as natural disasters and major emergencies; to provide more routine assistance for special projects or events of significant social value to the civil community in the creation and development of local community projects; of individual assistance by full-time attachment to social service or similar organisations; or for the maintenance of law, order and public safety using specialist capabilities or equipment, in situations beyond the capability of the Civil Power.

Military Tasks. The framework on which the MoD bases its detailed planning for the size, shape and capabilities of the Armed Forces, reflecting the broad types of tasks and operations in which they are likely to be involved.

MoD: Ministry of Defence.

MS: Medium Scale. Operational deployments of brigade size or equivalent for warfighting or other operations.

MND(SE): Multi National Division (South East). The UK led element of the Multinational Forces in Iraq responsible for the four southern provinces of Al Basrah, Al Muthanna, Dhi Qar, and Maysan.

NAAFI: Navy, Army and Air Force Institutes. Official trading organisation of HM Forces, providing retail and leisure services to the Services and their families.

NAO: National Audit Office. The independent organisation responsible for scrutinising public spending on behalf of Parliament, reporting to the Public Accounts Committee. It audits the accounts of all government departments and agencies as well as a wide range of other public bodies, and reports on the economy, efficiency and effectiveness with which government bodies have used public money.

NATO: North Atlantic Treaty Organisation. A regional defence alliance formed in 1949 under the Washington Treaty. Its general aim is to "safeguard the freedom, common heritage and civilisation" of its members by promoting "stability and well-being in the North Atlantic area". Members agree that an armed attack against one shall be considered an attack against them all, and that they will come to the aid of each other. Currently there are 26 member countries with the headquarters in Brussels.

Naval Manning Agency. Created on 1 July 1996 and dissolved as an agency 1 April 2004. Its mission was: to ensure that sufficient manpower is available on the trained strength and deployed effectively in peace, transition to war or war.

Naval Service. The Royal Navy (including QARNNS) and the Royal Marines together.

Navy Board. The Navy Board conducts the day-to-day business of managing the Royal Navy on behalf of the Admiralty Board. It brings together, under the Chief of the Naval Staff, the Royal Navy's operational and personnel commanders, and supports the CNS in his executive role, his management and operational advisory roles, and as the professional head of the Royal Navy.

NCO: Non-commissioned officer. Ratings of Leading Hand and above in the Royal Navy, other ranks of lance corporal and above in the Army and other ranks of corporal and above in the Royal Marines and Royal Air Force.

NDA: Nuclear Decommissioning Authority. The body sponsored by the DTI responsible for nuclear clean-up issues.

NDPB: Non-Departmental Public Bodies. Public bodies carry out a wide range of functions on behalf of government. As part of the commitment to transparency and accountability, the Cabinet Office collects and publishes annually information about public bodies as a whole, to supplement information about individual bodies already contained in departmental annual reports.

Near Cash. Direct Resource Defence Expenditure, including accurals.

NEC: Network Enabled Capability. A programme to enhance military capability through the exploitation of information. Implemented through the coherent and progressive development of Defence equipment, software, processes, structures and individual and collective training, NEC will enable the MoD to operate more effectively in the future strategic environment by more efficient sharing and exploitation of information within the UK Armed Forces and with our coalition partners.

NED: Non Executive Director. Non Executive Directors serve on various boards and audit committees within the Ministry of Defence, providing independent scrutiny and advice on defence business from their experience in Industry.

Net Cash Requirement. The amount of actual money that MoD requires from the government in order to fund its activities. The NCR takes account of the movements in working capital levels (debtors, creditors and stocks) but not non-cash costs.

NHS: National Health Service. Set up on 5th July 1948, the NHS provides healthcare for all citizens, based on need, not the ability to pay, and is funded by the tax payer and managed by the Department of Health, which has the responsibility to provide healthcare to the general public through the NHS.

Non-cash items. Non cash items include various notional transactions such as depreciation, impairments and cost of capital that appear in the operating cost statement under RAB.

Non-industrial staff. All Civil servants who are not Industrial staff.

NPT: Treaty on the Non-Proliferation of Nuclear Weapons. An international treaty to limit the spread of nuclear weapons and the foundation of the international nuclear disarmament and non-proliferation system.

NRA: Net Recoverable Amount.

NRF: NATO Response Force. Giving NATO a significant crisis response capability, the NRF is a powerful multi national military force with land, air, maritime and command elements, designed to stand alone for up to 30 days. It is not a permanent or standing force.

NRV: Net Realisable Value. The estimated disposal sale value of an item of materiel not expected to be used or sold in the ordinary course of business. The estimated disposal sale value may be nil or scrap in appropriate circumstances, and will be net of any costs incidental to the sale, e.g. agent's fees, to the extent that these are identifiable to individual items or sales contracts and are deducted from the sales proceeds on a net receipt basis.

Nursing Services. Queen Alexandra's Royal Naval Nursing Service, Queen Alexandra's Royal Army Nursing Corps, and Princess Mary's Royal Air Force Nursing Service.

OCCAR: Organisation Conjoint de Cooperation en matièrs d'ARmement. An Administrative Arrangement established on 12th November 1996 by the Defence Ministers of France, Germany, Italy and the UK. Its aim is to provide more effective and efficient arrangements for the management of certain existing and future collaborative armament programmes.

OECD: Organisation for Economic Co-operation and Development. The OECD comprises 30 countries sharing a commitment to democratic government and the market economy. Its work covers economic and social issues from macroeconomics, to trade, education, development and science and innovation.

Officer. A member of the Armed Forces holding the Queen's Commission. Includes ranks from Sub-Lt/2nd Lt/Pilot Officer up to Admiral of the Fleet/Field Marshal/Marshal of the Royal Air Force. Excludes NCO's.

Officer cadet. An entrant from civil life to the officer corps of the Armed Forces.

OGC: Office of Government Commerce. An independent Office of the Treasury which aims to work with the public sector as a catalyst to achieve efficiency, value for money in commercial activities and improved success in the delivery of programmes and projects.

Operating Cost Statement. The statement in departmental resource accounts that shows the current income and expenditure on an accrual basis. It is similar to the profit and loss statement on commercial accounts. This is the Public Sector's equivalent of a commercial organisation's Profit and Loss Account.

Operational TLBs. The TLBs directly responsible for the planning and management of military operations and the delivery of front-line capability. Operational personnel are those working in these TLBs plus some other small groups.

OPG: Office of HM Paymaster General. The Office of HM Paymaster General is part of HM Treasury. It is responsible for holding the working balances of Government Departments and other public bodies in accounts at the Bank of England and making them available to the National Loans Fund overnight to reduce the government's borrowing costs, and provides cash flow information to the Treasury.

OSCE: Organisation for Security and Co-operation in Europe. With 55 States drawn from Europe, Central Asia and America, the OSCE is the world's largest regional security organisation, bringing comprehensive and cooperative security to a region that stretches from Vancouver to Vladivostok. It offers a forum for political negotiations and decision-making in the fields of early warning, conflict prevention, crisis management and post-conflict rehabilitation, and puts the political will of the participating States into practice through its unique network of field missions.

Other Ranks. Members of the Royal Marines, Army and Royal Air Force who are not officers. The equivalent group in the Royal Navy is known as "Ratings".

Outflow Those leaving the Armed Forces or Civil Service for any reason. Those who rejoin and then leave again will be counted twice if the time period includes both exit dates.

Outturn and **estimated outturn** describe expenditure actually incurred, or estimated on the basis of actual expenditure to date.

Part-time. Civil servants working fewer than 37 hours a week (36 hours in London), excluding meal breaks.

PCPF: Parliamentary Contributory Pension Fund. The fund of the parliamentary pension scheme.

People Programme: A programme to enable MoD civilians to make the best contribution to the Defence capability. This will be achieved by: maximising our pool of talent and skills; matching people and their skills to the jobs that need to be done, now and in the future; and by raising our collective performance by improving management, training and development throughout the Department.

PPPA: People, Pay & Pensions Agency. The organisation providing civilian pay and personnel services, including the administration of pensions, the payment of salaries of MoD civilian staff and the payment of fees. Launched on 7 April 2006.

PCRU: Post Conflict Reconstruction Unit. An organisation set up to enhance the Government's ability to plan, develop and deliver effective and co-ordinated post conflict stabilisation activity. The organisation is interdepartmental.

PFI: Private Finance Initiative. A system for providing capital assets for the provision of public services. Typically, the private sector designs, builds and maintains infrastructure and other capital assets and then operates those assets to sell services to the public sector. In most cases, the capital assets are accounted for on the balance sheet of the private sector operator.

PPP: Public Private Partnership. An initiative through which the private sector is involved in the delivery of public services by providing management and service delivery expertise and sometimes the provision of assets. Improved value for money is the essential prerequisite, with better quality of service provision a highly desirable addition. It is delivered through several mechanisms including Private Finance Initiative, Partnering, Wider Markets Initiative and Contractor Logistic Support.

PSA: Public Service Agreement. An agreement between HM Treasury and each Government Department setting out each department's aim, objectives and key outcome-based targets. They form an integral part of the spending plans set out in Spending Reviews. Progress against the PSA targets is assessed and reported via the Defence Balanced Scorecard.

PSI: Proliferation Security Initiative. The Proliferation Security Initiative is a global effort that aims to stop shipments of weapons of mass destruction, their delivery systems, and related materials worldwide. It was announced by President Bush on May 31, 2003.

PSG: Professional Skills for Government. Professional Skills for Government is a key part of the Government's Delivery and Reform agenda. It is a major, long-term change programme designed to ensure that civil servants, wherever they work, have the right mix of skills and expertise to enable their Departments or agencies to deliver effective services.

PTC: RAF Personnel and Training Command. The Top Level Budget organisation managed by the RAF's Principal; Personnel Officer, the Air Member for Personnel. PTC provides trained personnel to Strike Command and other TLBs. PTC merged with STC from April 2007 to form Air Command.

PUS: Permanent Under Secretary. PUS is the Government's principal Civilian advisor on Defence and has the primary responsibility for Policy, Finance, Management and Administration in the department. He is the MoD Accounting Officer reflecting his responsibility to the Secretary of State for the overall organisation, management and staffing of the department and financial procedures and other matters. He is personally accountable to Parliament for the expenditure of all public money voted for defence purposes, chairs the Defence Management Board and is Secretary of the Defence Council.

PVR: Premature Voluntary Release. Those who leave the Armed Forces voluntarily before the end of their agreed engagement or commission period. Now known as voluntary outflow.

PRT: Provincial Reconstruction Team. A combination of international military and civilian personnel based in one of Afghanistan's provinces with the aim of extending the authority of the Afghan central government and helping to facilitate development and reconstruction by contributing to an improved security environment. PRTs also aim to support the reform of the Afghan security sector – disarmament and demobilisation of militias; building an accountable national army and national police force under government control; stamping out the drugs trade; and helping build a legal system.

QARNNS: Queen Alexandra's Royal Naval Nursing Service. The Royal Navy's internal nursing service.

QinetiQ Group plc. A defence technology and security company, formerly part of DERA, partially owned by the MoD. QinetiQ was floated in March 2006 to become QinetiQ Group plc, but still retains a shareholding.

Quick Impact Projects. Programmes aimed at kick-starting local economies and creating employment opportunities in immediate post-conflict environments. Projects are identified and implemented by local groups with international assistance. Examples include the reconstruction and refurbishment of schools in Iraq.

RAB. Resource Accounting and Budgeting.

RAF: The Royal Air Force.

Rank. Grade within the Military structure.

Ratings. Junior military personnel in the Royal Navy.

Real terms figures are amounts adjusted for the effect of general price inflation relative to a base year, as measured by the GDP market price deflator.

Regiment. A formed unit of personnel sharing a common identity and area of expertise, carrying the spirit of the people who have gone before.

Regular Reserves. Former members of the UK regular forces who have a liability for service with the Reserve forces. Includes the Royal Fleet Reserve, Army Reserve and Royal Air Force Reserve as well as other individuals liable to recall.

RES: Race Equality Scheme. The MoD Race Equality Scheme sets out how the Department is fulfilling its obligations under the Race Relations (Amendment) Act 2000.

Resource Accounting. The accounting methodology used to record expenditure in the departmental accounts which replaced cash accounting. It applies UK generally accepted accounting practice (UK GAAP) used in private industry and other Government Departments to departmental transactions. Spending is measured on an accruals basis.

Resource Budget. The sum of a department's resource Departmental Expenditure Limit and resource Annually Managed Expenditure. It is the budget for current expenditure on an accruals basis.

Resource budgeting. The budgeting regime adopted for the spending plans set in the 2000 Spending Review. It is derived from resource accounting rules, but there are several differences in treatment between resource accounts and resource budgets.

RFA: Royal Fleet Auxiliary Service. The civilian manned fleet, owned by the Ministry of Defence. Its main task is to supply warships of the Royal Navy at sea with fuel, food, stores and ammunition which they need to remain operational while away from base. It also provides aviation support for the Royal Navy, together with amphibious support and secure sea transport for Army units and their equipment. Its employees are full-time civil servants, but who come under the Naval Discipline Act when deployed to sea under naval command.

RfR: Request for Resources. An accruals-based measure of current expenditure which forms part of a Resource Estimate. It represents the basic unit of Parliamentary control.

RM: Royal Marines. Sea-going soldiers who are part of the Naval Service.

RMR: Royal Marines Reserve. The volunteer reserve service of the Royal Marines. See **Volunteer Reserves.**

RN: Royal Navy. The sea-going defence forces of the UK, including ships, submarines, Naval aircraft and their personnel, and Queen Alexandra's Royal Naval Nursing Service, but excluding the Royal Marines and the Royal Fleet Auxiliary Service (RFA).

RNAS: Royal Naval Air Station. An air base operated by the Fleet Air Arm.

RNR: Royal Naval Reserve. The volunteer reserve service of the Royal Navy. See Volunteer Reserves.

RO-RO Shipping. Ships designed to allow cargo, such as vehicles, to be loaded by being rolled instead of lifted, often with a drive-through concept with bow and stern doors. It is commonly used in the in the ferry trades to transport cars and goods vehicles, but also used to transport military vehicles.

RPC: Regional Prime Contracts. Five regionally-based contracts for the provision of construction and maintenance services on the Defence Estate across Great Britain, where stand-alone arrangements are not appropriate. The objective of Regional Prime Contracting is to achieve better long-term value for money through improved Supply Chain Management, incentivised payment mechanisms, continuous improvement, economies of scale, and partnering.

RRUs: Regional Rehabilitation Units. Facilities located around the UK and in Germany containing doctors, physiotherapists and Remedial Instructors providing assessment and rehabilitation for physical injuries sustained by Service personnel.

SALW: Small Arms and Light Weapons. Personal weapons, such as pistols, rifles and light machine guns.

SC: Supply Chain.

SS: Small Scale. Operational deployment of battalion size or equivalent.

SSR: Security Sector Reform. This aims to help developing and transitional countries manage their security functions in a democratically accountable, efficient and effective way by initiating and supporting reform and providing appropriate education and training.

SSRB: Senior Salaries Review Body. The independent body advising the Government on Senior Civil Service pay.

SSSI: Sites of Special Scientific Interest. Protected sites of particular environmental and scientific importance, including wetlands, rivers, heathlands, meadows, beaches, moorland and peat bog. The Defence Estate contains 289 SSSIs.

STC: Strike Command. The RAF's operational Top Level Budget organisation, providing aircraft and trained aircrews to CJO. STC merged with PTC from April 2007 to form Air Command.

SCAPE: Superannuation Contributions Adjusted for Past Experience.

TLB: Top Level Budget. The major organisational grouping of the MoD. There are three types: "Operational", "Military Support" and "HQ and other support".

TLCM: Through Life Capability Management. An approach to the acquisition and in-service management of military capability in which every aspect of new and existing military capability is planned and managed coherently across all Defence Lines of Development from cradle to grave.

TNA: The National Archives is responsible for looking after the records of central government and the courts of law, and making sure everyone can look at them.

Trading Fund. Trading Funds were introduced by the Government under the Trading Funds Act 1973 as a 'means of financing trading operations of a government department which, hitherto, have been carried out on Vote'. They are self-accounting units that have greater freedom, than other government departments, in managing their own financial and management activities. They are also free to negotiate their own terms and conditions with their staff and for this reason their grading structures do not always match that of the rest of the Ministry, and this is reflected in some of the tables. MoD Trading Funds are ABRO, DARA, DSTL, the Met Office, and the UK Hydrographic Office.

UAV: Unmanned Aerial Vehicle. An unmanned aerial vehicle (UAV) is an aircraft with no onboard pilot. UAV can be remote controlled or fly autonomously based on pre-programmed flight plans or more complex dynamic automation systems. UAV are currently used in a number of military operations, including reconnaissance and attack.

UKAEA: United Kingdom Atomic Energy Authority. A non-departmental public body, responsible to the Department of Trade and Industry. Its primary task today is managing the decommissioning of its nuclear reactors and other radioactive facilities used for the UK's nuclear research and development programme in a safe and environmentally responsible manner and to restore its sites for conventional use.

UKHO: UK Hydrographic Office. A trading fund agency of the MoD responsible for surveying the seas around the UK and elsewhere to aid navigation.

UOR: Urgent Operational Requirement. Additional capability requirements for specific operations met using a streamlined version of the Department's normal procurement procedures. This provides speedy and flexible procurement of capabilities.

UNFICYP. The United Nations Force in Cyprus, which polices the line separating the Greek and Turkish Cypriot communities.

VAT: Value Added Tax.

VAW: Veterans Awareness Week. A week to raise the profile of veterans. The first took place in July 2005.

VCDS: Vice Chief of the Defence Staff. The deputy to the Chief of the Defence Staff. Joint head of the Central Top Level Budget organisation with the 2nd PUS, and a member of the Defence Council, Defence Management Board, Chiefs of Staff Committee and Investment Approvals Board.

Veterans Agency. Formerly the War Pensions Agency. Responsible for veterans' affairs, including war and service pensions, service records, military graves, medals and welfare issues. The Veterans Agency merged with the Armed Forces Personnel Administration Agency from April 2007 to become the Service Personnel and Veterans Agency.

VFM: Value for Money. Value for Money (VfM) is HM Treasury's terminology to assess whether or not an organisation has obtained the maximum benefit from the goods and services it acquires and/ or provides, within the resources available to it. It not only measures the cost of goods and services, but also takes account of the mix of quality, cost, resource use, fitness for purpose, timeliness and convenience to judge whether or not, when taken together, they constitute good value.

Voluntary Outflow. Those who leave the Armed Forces voluntarily before the end of their agreed engagement or commission period. Previously known as voluntary release or premature voluntary release (PVR).

Voluntary Release. See **Premature Voluntary Release.**

Volunteer Reserves and Auxiliary Forces. Civilian volunteers who undertake to give a certain amount of their time to train in support of the Regular Forces. Includes the Royal Naval Reserve, the Royal Marines Reserve, Territorial Army and the Royal Auxiliary Air Force. Does not include Royal Fleet Auxiliary Service (RFA). Some Volunteer Reservists undertake (paid) Full-Time Reserve Service.

VOP: Variation of Price. A contractual provision providing for variation in contract prices if inflation over the period of the contract falls outside defined bands.

Vote. An individual Supply Estimate by Parliament. Replaced by Requests for Resources since the introduction of Resource Budgeting in 2001, except for Votes A setting maximum numbers of personnel to be maintained by the Armed Forces.

WAN: Wide Area Network. A computer network covering a large geographic area, such as the internet or a network of bank cash dispensers.

War Pensions Agency. See Veterans Agency.

WEAG: Western European Armaments Group. A group of European countries established in 1993 with the objective of more efficient use of resources through, inter alia, increased harmonization of requirements; the opening up of national defence markets to cross-border competition; to strengthen the European defence technological and industrial base; and cooperation in research and development. The group closed in May 2005 with many of its activities now undertaken by the European Defence Agency.

WPB: War Pensions benefits. A non-contributory financial benefit paid to people who have been disabled as a result of conflict, or to dependants of those killed in conflict.

Index

Printed in the UK by The Stationery Office Limited
on behalf of the Controller of Her Majesty's Stationery Office
ID5582946   07/07   19585
Printed on Paper containing 75% recycled fibre content minimum.